BUDGET GUIDE
ITALY

BY BRONWEN CUNNINGHAM

As well as writing books for children, Bronwen Cunningham has written travel articles for the *Sunday Times* and has collaborated on a cookery book, *Eatability*, with Jocasta Innes. Her interests in cooking, travel and the countryside have combined in a long association with Italy, from her first visits as a child to Rome to a recent one as delegate to the Italian-British Twinning Conference, and months of travel and research all over the country for this book. Her children's books include *The Puffin Joke Book*, which has sold over half a million copies.

PUBLISHED BY THE AUTOMOBILE ASSOCIATION
FANUM HOUSE, BASINGSTOKE, HAMPSHIRE RG21 2EA

WRITTEN BY BRONWEN CUNNINGHAM

EDITED, DESIGNED AND PRODUCED BY THE PUBLISHING DIVISION OF THE AUTOMOBILE ASSOCIATION.

MAPS © THE AUTOMOBILE ASSOCIATION 1992

ILLUSTRATIONS: ALAN ROE

ILLUSTRATION PAGE 6 AND 7: NAOMI DAVIS

COVER DESIGN: THE PAUL HAMPSON PARTNERSHIP

EVERY EFFORT IS MADE TO ENSURE ACCURACY, BUT THE PUBLISHERS DO NOT HOLD THEMSELVES RESPONSIBLE FOR ANY CONSEQUENCES THAT MAY ARISE FROM ERRORS OR OMISSIONS. WHILST THE CONTENTS ARE BELIEVED CORRECT AT THE TIME OF RESEARCH, CHANGES MAY HAVE OCCURRED SINCE THAT TIME OR WILL OCCUR DURING THE CURRENCY OF THIS BOOK.

TYPESET BY: SERVIS TYPESETTING LTD, MANCHESTER

PRINTED AND BOUND IN GREAT BRITAIN BY: BENHAM AND CO LTD, COLCHESTER

A CIP CATALOGUE RECORD FOR THIS BOOK IS AVAILABLE FROM THE BRITISH LIBRARY.

PUBLISHED BY THE AUTOMOBILE ASSOCIATION, FANUM HOUSE, BASINGSTOKE, HAMPSHIRE RG21 2EA

ISBN 0 7495 02940

CONTENTS

HOW TO USE THE GUIDE

ATION
BINO

ederico 35.

10pm. Sunday 3-9pm.
Telephone code 722.

ACCOMMODATION
Urbino is only a small town
and doesn't have many
hotels in the centre, so try
and book in advance..

EATING
Il Gi
Fran
Raffa
pasta,
the ba
and
chicke

Our budget guide aims to help you enjoy your visit to Italy without spending your money either wastefully or unsuspectingly.

First read the *Introduction* thoroughly because the information given there is essential to your budgeting success, from travel and accommodation to shopping and moneysavers.

Each of the eight chapters that follow gives major centres for the region and a variety of outings both to well known architectural and tourist attractions and also to relatively undiscovered places. The chapters contain moneysaving tips appropriate to the region and comprehensive *Orientation* sections with tourist offices, accommodation addresses, places to eat, banks, etc.

Two *Budget for a day* charts for the regions covered give you an idea of the cost of a day's outing. As a rough guide to converting lire to sterling take off the lire noughts and divide by two. In addition, each chapter has a map of the region and several outings maps.

Prices given in the book were correct at the time of research. Changes may have occurred since then, but you will still have an idea of what you can expect to pay.

Italian place names in the text are given their appropriate accents which will help you with pronunciation – where you see an accent over a letter you accentuate the sound. If an Italian name differs considerably from the English version it will be bracketed in the text, ie Florence (Firenze). But in the maps all place names are in Italian as it is these you will see on road signs and local maps.

Finally, we look forward to receiving your recommendations and discoveries and you will find a reader's report form to complete at the end of the book.

eysaver
are not obliged to have breakfast in
r hotel unless you agreed to the terms
forehand. It is usually cheaper to have
coffee and croissant at a bar – either in
he hotel bar or down the road.

Local Flavour
La Grappa is a fiery spirit made by distilling the pulp left after the grapes have been pressed. Made in several regions, the best known comes from Bassano del Grappa, 35km (21¾ miles) north east of Vicenza.

BUDGET FOR A DAY
Cable car return ticket
STRESA LIDO to MONTE MOTTARONE
Picnic lunch -
rolls, local salami, cheese and a drink
Boat trip, return ticket
BAVENO to ISOLA BELLA
....ssion to Palace and gardens

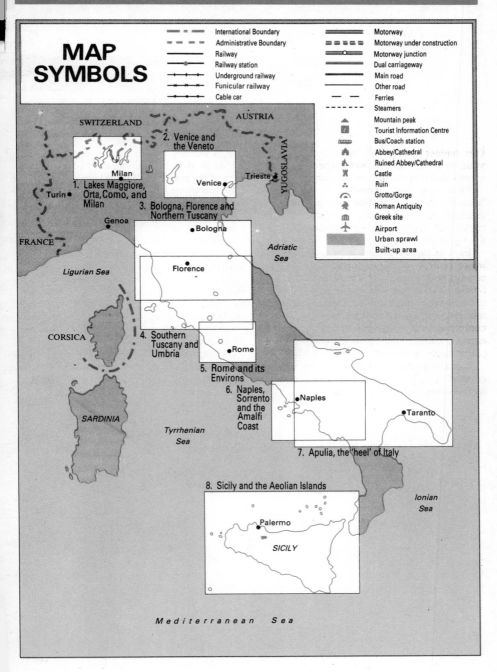

MAP SYMBOLS

— ·· —	International Boundary
— — —	Administrative Boundary
———	Railway
——•—	Railway station
++++	Underground railway
×–×–×	Funicular railway
•–•–•	Cable car

	Motorway
	Motorway under construction
	Motorway junction
	Dual carriageway
	Main road
	Other road
— —	Ferries
- - - - -	Steamers
	Mountain peak
	Tourist Information Centre
	Bus/Coach station
	Abbey/Cathedral
	Ruined Abbey/Cathedral
	Castle
	Ruin
	Grotto/Gorge
	Roman Antiquity
	Greek site
✈	Airport
	Urban sprawl
	Built-up area

SWITZERLAND
AUSTRIA
FRANCE
Turin
Milan
Genoa

2. Venice and the Veneto
1. Lakes Maggiore, Orta, Como, and Milan
Venice
Trieste
YUGOSLAVIA

3. Bologna, Florence and Northern Tuscany
Bologna
Florence

Ligurian Sea
Adriatic Sea

CORSICA
4. Southern Tuscany and Umbria
Rome
5. Rome and its Environs
6. Naples, Sorrento and the Amalfi Coast
Naples
Taranto

SARDINIA
Tyrrhenian Sea

7. Apulia, the 'heel' of Italy

8. Sicily and the Aeolian Islands
Palermo
SICILY

Ionian Sea

Mediterranean Sea

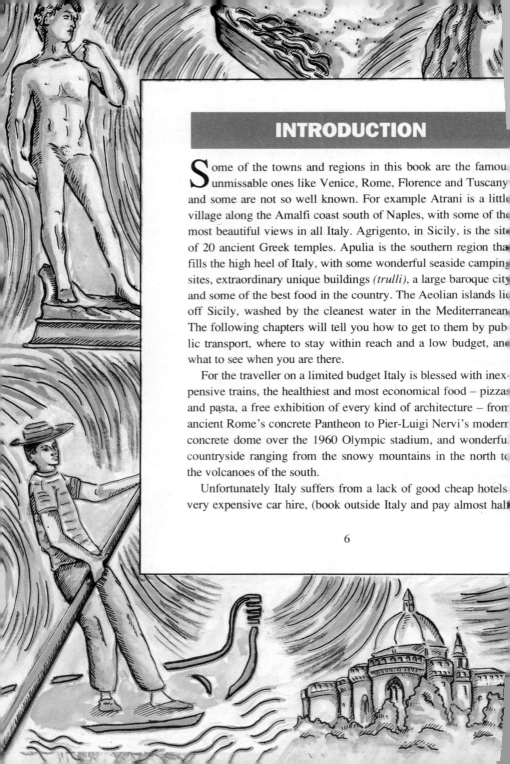

INTRODUCTION

Some of the towns and regions in this book are the famous unmissable ones like Venice, Rome, Florence and Tuscany and some are not so well known. For example Atrani is a little village along the Amalfi coast south of Naples, with some of the most beautiful views in all Italy. Agrigento, in Sicily, is the site of 20 ancient Greek temples. Apulia is the southern region that fills the high heel of Italy, with some wonderful seaside camping sites, extraordinary unique buildings *(trulli)*, a large baroque city and some of the best food in the country. The Aeolian islands lie off Sicily, washed by the cleanest water in the Mediterranean. The following chapters will tell you how to get to them by public transport, where to stay within reach and a low budget, and what to see when you are there.

For the traveller on a limited budget Italy is blessed with inexpensive trains, the healthiest and most economical food – pizzas and pasta, a free exhibition of every kind of architecture – from ancient Rome's concrete Pantheon to Pier-Luigi Nervi's modern concrete dome over the 1960 Olympic stadium, and wonderful countryside ranging from the snowy mountains in the north to the volcanoes of the south.

Unfortunately Italy suffers from a lack of good cheap hotels, very expensive car hire, (book outside Italy and pay almost half

6

he price) and is cursed with expert purse and bag-snatchers in ome of the big cities.

Plan in advance, if you can: book hotels, hire cars and buy ain tickets in advance. Remember that, except for a brief period hen Britain alters the clocks, Italy is one hour ahead of Green- ich Mean Time. Be prepared for shabby buildings, crumbling one, primitive plumbing, breakfasts that are one gulp of coffee nd a roll and huge midday meals that will weigh you down arough the long hot siesta.

First rule in the book – travel light; never take more luggage aan you can carry for at least 90 metres (100yds). Two smaller ags are better than one large one, it gives you better balance nd is easier to stow in luggage racks. This gives you freedom to ispense with porters and taxis, and reach the less expensive ho- ls. It also helps to arrive about 2kg (5lbs) underweight to allow or the good meals to come.

The biggest moneysaver is knowing a little bit of the lan- uage. Bone up on the 'cheap' words – *meno costoso* = cheap, *no sconto* = discount. Also see the list of useful phrases, page). Italy is not the inexpensive country it used to be. (Note: there no single word for cheap in Italy, only 'less expensive'.)

Italy is also rich in art, buildings, sculpture, scenery, delicious od and friendly people, with hot days and warm nights. This ook will show you how to find and enjoy some of the best parts this beautiful country.

GETTING TO ITALY

BY TRAIN

Rail tickets and couchettes can be booked and paid for by credit card directly over the telephone to British Rail International at London's Victoria train station. Telephone 071-834 2345, allowing 48 hours' notice before travelling. For enquiries telephone 071-828 0892. Both offices are open 8am-6pm Monday to Saturday, 9am-5pm Sunday. You can buy tickets in advance in person at Victoria, the office is near platform two, open 7.25am-10pm.

Wasteel Travel, 121 Wilton Road, London SW1, telephone 071-834 7066 also sell tickets for travel to and within Italy (eg Pisa to Florence £3.75; more expensive than in Italy, but convenient).

Discount travel is available for over 60s, but citizens of any country must first buy a British Rail senior citizen's card for £16 to qualify to buy a Rail Europe card for £5, which gives a 30 per cent reduction on Italian travel (50 per cent reduction in France). A sample return Victoria–Milan, costing £150, costs £102 for senior citizens. Also enquire about the new InterRail Plus 26 passes, and routes to major Italian destinations.

Coming from Britain there are through coaches crossing Paris in the summer, but out of season you may have to change train stations. For example coming from Calais or Boulogne and arriving at Paris Nord, you might depart from Paris Lyons. If you need a meal, the big brassy mirrored brasserie, L'Européen across the road from the Gare de Lyons does good seafood. Otherwise there is a *hamburger à cheval* in the station bar. Leave luggage in lockers on floor below; a large locker, sufficient for three people, costs 25 francs. Also, out of season there may be no breakfast on the overnight Milan train, so be prepared. A couchette in a six-bunk compartment costs about £8.

All persons under 26 qualify for Inter Rail passes, giving up to 50 per cent reductions.

Students need an ISIC card (£5), available at student unions, or a YIEE card (£4) for non-students, issued by the Federation of International Youth Travel Organisations (FIYTO). Children four to 11 go for half price, 12 and 13 for two-thirds price, under four, free travel.

The address of International Rail Centre (for correspondence) is Victoria Station, London SW1V 1JY. For any correspondence query, telephone 071-630 8544.

The United States office of British Rail is 1500 Broadway, 10th Floor, New York, NY 10036, telephone 212 382 3737.

For CIT's (Citalia's) rail department at Croydon telephone 081-686 0677.

BY COACH

Contact National Express and Eurolines for information on coaches (long-distance buses) from Victoria coach station, Buckingham Palace Road, London SW1. Telephone 071-730 0202.

If you are a student, contact London Student Travel, 52 Grosvenor Gardens, London SW1W 0AU, telephone 071-730 3402.

Coach prices are not significantly less than air charter flights or discount rail fares.

BY AIR

Alitalia and British Airways fly regular schedules direct from Manchester and Birmingham as well as Heathrow and Gatwick. There are frequent flights (scheduled or charter) to all the Italian airports mentioned in later chapters where travel to and from the airport is described, except for Bari, which is not well served out of season.

Italy Sky Shuttle runs a reliable charter service to many Italian destinations from Gatwick and Luton mainly, but also some flights from Manchester, Glasgow and from *handwritten: TEL: 071 700 2922   LUTON £197 on SAT*

Bristol. Thomson's *Air Fares* catalogue lists cheaper charter flights only, as does Citalia's *Italy for a Song*. They also offer good value car hire, booked with the air ticket and paid for outside of Italy.

Alitalia 27 Piccadilly, London W1. Telephone 071-745 8200.

Italy Sky Shuttle 227 Shepherds Bush Road, Hammersmith, London W6 7AS. For reservations telephone 081-748 1333.

Citalia Marco Polo House, 3-5 Lansdowne Road, Croydon CR9 1LL. For reservations telephone 081-686 5533.

If you are travelling from the USA it may pay you to fly with a budget fare to London, Paris, Frankfurt or Amsterdam and fly or go on by rail from there.

Charter flights can offer the best value, and are less likely to be subject to delays if you travel out of season. June can be a bargain month. Prices do not rise regularly from March to October, but rise and fall according to bank holidays, Easter and school holidays, so check the schedules carefully.

Discounts for children under two include: 10 per cent of the adult fare on British Airways; £20 charge on Alitalia; free if sitting on parent's lap on Italy Sky Shuttle. For children from two to 12 there is 25 per cent discount on British Airways, and 20 per cent discount on Alitalia and Italy Sky Shuttle. Students aged 12 to 25 with proof of age and school attendance get 25 per cent discount on British Airways and 20 per cent discount on Alitalia.

Other discounts include:

PEX or APEX flights Payment on reservation. Fixed arrival and departure dates, including one Saturday night. From North America the stay must be not less than one week, not more than 90 days.

SUPERPEX Cheapest scheduled flight. Must be bought at least 14 days in advance.

Eurobudget Pay for ticket at time of reservation, with return date left open.

Italy Sky Shuttle 20 per cent discount on scheduled flights.

Italy Sky Shuttle can book you a one-way charter and return scheduled flight.

GETTING TO LONDON AIRPORTS FROM LONDON

Gatwick Trains go every 15 minutes during the day from Victoria, once an hour between midnight and 6am. The journey takes about 30 minutes and costs £6.30. For British Rail at Gatwick airport telephone (0293) 200000.

National Express coaches leave from Victoria coach station every hour, taking 70 minutes; £5.80. Telephone 071-730 0202. Green Line coaches operate from Victoria, telephone 071-668 7261. British Airways and Caledonian Airways go from North Terminal, other flights from South Terminal at Gatwick.

If you are travelling by car from the M23 motorway take exit nine and follow signposts. Open-air car parking is £3.30 per day; covered parking is £8.20 per day for first five days, then £3.30 per day. Pay before you pick up your car.

Heathrow By underground go to Heathrow Central station on the Piccadilly Line. The trip takes 50 minutes, with trains every six minutes; £2.10. London Transport telephone 071-222 1234.

By bus, London Airbus-Express operates from Victoria and Euston, every 20 minutes, 6am-8.30pm. Journey 1 hour; £5. On the Woking-Heathrow railair link, coaches run daily from Woking railway station, Monday to Saturday 7.30am, 8am, 8.45, then hourly till 9.45pm; Sunday, 7.45, 8.20, then hourly till 9.20pm. Journey time is 50 minutes; single fare £3.50. Coaches go to all four terminals. Return services operate Monday to Saturday, 7.30am and hourly to 9.30pm, Sunday 8.20am and hourly till 9.20pm. Telephone 071-928 5100 (24 hours). You can buy a through rail ticket to Heathrow.

By car get to Heathrow on the M4 motorway – exit 4 for terminals 1, 2 and 3; and M25 motorway – exit 14 for terminal 4. The covered long-stay car park costs £6.30 per day for the first seven days, then £4 per day.

Luton Trains leave from St Pancras and Kings Cross every half hour, with a coach link from Luton train station to the airport. The journey costs £6.90 and takes 45 minutes.

Green Line coach 757 goes from Eccleston Bridge near Victoria train station half-hourly (hourly on Sundays); £5. The journey takes 75 minutes. Telephone 071-668 7261.

By car, Luton airport is south east of Luton, two miles from M1 junction 10. Open-air parking, £2.50 daily; covered, £3.

WEATHER, AND WHEN TO GO

January is the coldest month everywhere, though from Rome south there will be twice as much sunshine as in London, and warmer temperatures. The north, however, which has a continental climate, will be colder in January and February and not at all pleasant with fog, ice and rain. Venice, however, on the coast, has clearer skies in the winter than inland cities, and the carnival month of February is often bright and dry.

March to May in the south and Sicily can be very changeable, with some weeks hot and sunny, then cool again. Don't expect certain hot weather for seaside holidays in those months. But because of this varied weather and occasional rain, the south is at its most flower-decked and green in these pre-spring and summer months.

In the north, from Florence upwards, temperatures rise quite quickly through April and May, until, like Rome and Naples, it reaches its peak of hot and humid weather from June to August. These are months of sudden and dramatic thunderstorms. When it rains, it buckets, so go prepared.

From September to October, the weather

The summer sun warms these houses which are part of the Agriturist scheme

is usually cooler, gentler, and a pleasant time to be in towns as well as the countryside all over Italy. But of course days for sightseeing are shorter. And from about 20 October there is a regular drop in pressure, and cold fronts and rain sweep across the Mediterranean.

November is Venice's wettest month, Florence cools and Tuscan hills become cloud-shrouded. But the south will still be warm, and Sicily in November could offer fine autumnal weather for a touring visit.

GETTING ABOUT

BY TRAIN

The state railway, FS (Ferrovia dello Stato) is efficient, ubiquitous, often crowded and less expensive than bus travel.

There are several different kinds of train. Beginning with the slowest, they are:

Locale or *accelerato* – stops at every station – very slow.

Diretto – a bit quicker.

Espresso – quicker again – these stop at principal stations.

Rapido, EC and IC – a fast train between big cities. Some are only first class and on some you have to reserve a seat. You must pay a 30 per cent supplement.

Super-Rapido Italiano or TEE (Trans-Europe Express) trains are only first class and require a higher supplement.

Children under four (not occupying a seat) are free; for children from four to 12 there is a discount of 50 per cent; men over 65 and women over 60, on purchase of a senior citizen's card (price £5) get 30 per cent reduction if they have a British Railcard (price £16).

You can buy your train ticket in advance at travel agents. Tickets are good for three days, or you can buy an open ticket and write in the date of your journey on the back which saves queueing at stations. But be sure to ask if you need a supplement; there's a fine of L10,000 if you haven't got one.

BY CAR

There are tolls on most motorways and petrol is expensive, and driving inside Italy is both more expensive and more hair-raising than in most countries. The rule of the road is to cede to traffic on the right, unless you are approaching a main road in the countryside. Speed limits are 50kph (30mph) in built-up areas, 90kph (56mph) on country roads, and 110kph (68mph) on motorways at weekends, 130kph (80mph) on weekdays. Your toll ticket is time-stamped on the motorways, so any speeding will be immediately detected, and you may be fined heavily on the spot. The road police are a separate entity, called the Polizia Stradale. Lorries are banned from driving on Sundays, clearing the roads in one respect, but it's a popular day for private drivers.

To give some idea of motorway tolls, the rate for the route from Rome to Florence, 255km (158miles) is L16,000. A Viacard, costing L50,000 or L90,000, saves queueing at toll stations.

In towns, be aware that traffic lights are often suspended above the road. And watch out for *divieto di sosta* (no parking) signs on doors and in streets, offending cars may be towed away. Wearing seat belts in the front seats is now compulsory in Italy.

Petrol stations tend to close midday for the siesta (except on motorways) and finish for the night about 7.30pm, but you may find self-service pumps open 24 hours, taking L10,000 notes. Very few garages take credit cards.

When taking secondary roads rather than motorways or the old, straight main roads, (such as the Cassia from Florence to Rome) do some careful map reading, especially in Tuscany and Umbria, because the roads may be extremely winding and hilly, taking much more time than the distance shows.

Be sure to carry your driving licence, written permission from the owner if you have been lent a car, and the car documents whenever you drive – you may be asked for them. If the Polizia Stradale stop you (often for no good reason), it is expedient to be extremely polite.

If you break down, dial 116 at the nearest telephone box. Tell the operator where you are, the registration number and type of car, and help will be sent from the nearest ACI (the Italian motoring organisation office.) If your car takes more than 12 hours to repair, show the fuel card you got when you bought petrol coupons (these can be purchased in Britain from the Automobile Association), and you will be given a free car to drive for up to 10 days. (This does not apply to motorcycles.) The ACI has a special 24-hour number that can be dialled for help: Rome 06/4212.

Car hire is best booked before coming to Italy. You will probably have to pay a deposit when picking up your car, even if you have paid for the hire in the UK (up to about L70,000). This is supposed to cover a full tank of petrol, but check that it is full, and when you return the car, make sure it is full again, or they will charge you the difference (in their favour) plus 19 per cent VAT. Most firms ask you to pay the cost of hire as a deposit, and then you have to pay VAT of 19 per cent when you return the car. If you hire a car in Italy from a small local firm, check the tyres carefully before driving away. Some firms only hire to people over 21.

You can arrange for a car to meet you after a train journey – from car hire company Maggiore, contact Avis, Eurotrains and Hertz. A railway station will send a telegram to the nearest branch for you.

Mopeds can be hired in the towns from about L15,000 per day; helmets are compulsory. These are not advised for novice drivers.

Notes for drivers The British Driving Licence is valid but (unless you have a UK pink licence) should be accompanied by a translation – available from the AA and RAC in Britain. Drivers must always carry the log-book with them. Speed limits, unless otherwise signposted are: 50kph (30mph) in built-up areas; 90kph (56mph) outside built up areas; 130kph (80mph) on motorways, for vehicles over 1100cc.

Petrol in Italy is considerably more expensive than in the UK or US, so be sure to get your petrol coupons before you go from CIT telephone 081-686 0677, and from the AA and RAC. You can buy them at Italian frontier points from ACI, but you must not pay in Italian currency.

Motorway tolls are also a considerable expense. Consult motoring organisations for the cheapest routes.

All cars must carry a warning triangle, which can be hired from ACI offices at the frontier for a deposit of L1,500. Keep the receipt, and L1,200 will be refunded when you leave.

Petrol concessions are available in the following packages:

1 For tourists visiting northern Italy, £67.30 provides 12 petrol coupons worth L15,000 each and five motorway vouchers worth L2,000 each.

2 For tourists visiting central and southern Italy, £108 provides 12 petrol coupons worth L15,000 each, eight motorway vouchers worth L2,000 each, and one petrol voucher worth L120,000, which must be exchanged for six petrol coupons (worth L20,000 each) at an ENIT or ACI office in the following regions: Abruzzo, Basilicata, Calabria, Campania, Lazio, Molise, Puglia, Sardinia and Sicily (the regions which stretch from Rome south).

3 For tourists visiting southern Italy, £148.70 provides 12 petrol coupons worth L15,000 each, 10 motorway vouchers worth L2,000 each and one petrol voucher worth L240,000 to be exchanged in: Basilicata, Calabria, Campania, Molise, Púglia, Sardinia and Sicily.

4 This packet costs £189.40, and the vouchers can only be redeemed in Basilicata, Calabria, Sardinia and Sicily.

These offers give you a 15 per cent discount on current prices; any unused coupons will be refunded by the office where you bought them. You need to show your passport and log-book personally when you go to buy coupons.

You will then be issued with a fuel card (*carta carburante*) which you must keep and show for the free breakdown service provided by the ACI. When you exchange your vouchers, you will be given eight extra motorway vouchers.

BY BUS

Although bus travel is more expensive than rail, it is often quicker and more convenient. There are many local country buses radiating from provincial centres, owned by a bewildering number of local bus companies.

Standard fare in towns is L700, whatever the distance. Tickets must usually be bought at tobacconists or newsstands, bus offices or kiosks before boarding. For coaches and buses going outside the cities, the same rule for buying your ticket first often applies, but it is not always the case. Get on at the back of the bus and leave by the middle door, stamping your ticket when you get on. The front door is usually for season ticket holders. In towns you will usually find special offers on tickets, books of 10 at a discount, or special half-fare offers.

There will generally be a flurry of buses early in the morning from about 6-9am, then none or the occasional one or two mid morning, with another cluster at midday taking workers home to their meal, and more transport once more in the evening. It's easy to miss seeing some museum or sight which is only open in the morning.

TAXIS

Taxis do not usually cruise for hire, but must be picked up at taxi ranks or be called by telephone. Watch the meter: the fixed starting charge is from L2,300 to L4,000, the cost per kilometre (five-eighths of a mile) is L1,000. There are extra charges for luggage, night rides, Sundays, public holidays and journeys to airports.

ACCOMMODATION

'Budget' accommodation in this book means L100,000 (£50) and under for a double room.

Your bed for the night will be the biggest single outlay on holiday, so study all the options. Several agencies provide farmhouse or country houses, all over the country, but especially in Tuscany and Umbria, often with a flight deal attached. Some have pools, and if you are travelling with children this may be a great attraction. But they will probably not work out cheaper than individually booked charter flights and cheap hotels, and since most are in the country, this means bringing your car or the expense of hiring one. You gain peace and quiet and children are spared endless sightseeing.

The Italian tourist offices' free traveller's handbook lists tour operators, self-catering and special interest holidays, with addresses, as well as a sample letter for hotel booking. Look at advertisements in Sunday papers for self-catering and villa holidays especially.

CAMPING

Camping is a good family option, and Italy has many camp sites. They fill in August, but you should find space at other months. The Italian tourist office publishes an abridged free list, or write to Federcampeggio, via Emanuele 11, Casella Postale 23, Calenzano, 50041 Firenze. To book a camp site, write to Centro Internazionale Prenotazioni Campeggio, Casella Postale 23, 50041 Firenze, asking for a list and booking form (telephone 055/882391, telex 570397). The Touring Club Italiano (TCI) publishes a full directory of over 1,600 sites and holiday villages and bungalows, *Campeggi e Villaggi Turistici in*

Italia, L25,000. Write to TCI, Corso Italiano, 10 Milano (telephone 02/82561). The AA publishes *Camping and Caravanning Europe*, £6.99. In the USA the National Campers and Hikers Association, 4804 Transit Road, Building No 2. Depew, New York 14043 telephone 716 668-6242, issues camping guides.

Before you go, get an International Camping Carnet from a camping association. Or write, sending passport photos, to the Federazione Italiana del Campeggio, Casella Postale 649, 50100 Firenze.

Average camp site costs are from L3,500 to L5,000 per person per day; about L4,000 per car and tent; and up to L7,000 for a caravan and tent. There is no charge for children under three. Some camp sites (mentioned in the relevant chapters) are in wonderful situations: near Taormina, Sicily, and on Lake Corbara in Umbria, for example. Many inland sites have their own small swimming pools.

AGRITURISM

This is a scheme whereby you can stay cheaply in a farm or in a cottage on the estate. The idea is that you can possibly help in the work, or at least learn something of agricultural life. Minimum stay is usually three to seven nights; provision and lodging varies, sometimes with inexpensive half-board terms. In the following chapters you will find some Agriturist or Vacanze Verdi (a similar scheme) rooms mentioned – places where English is spoken, where they provide pension terms or have some special skill to offer. There are plenty more all over Italy. For a full list write to Agriturist, Corso V Emanuele 101 Roma, telephone 06/6512342, who publish a detailed list with some illustrations; otherwise contact the provincial offices. The addresses are given in the following chapters.

For non-English speaking hosts (the majority) you will need some Italian. All places mentioned here are accessible by public transport.

A slight problem affecting the organisation and comprehensive listing of all 'green' holidays is that several government (central and local) agencies are involved. (An incredibly willing tourist office person in Alberobello, Apulia, spent ages trying to track down a responsible official for a visitor, and finally found one in Bari).

Another agency to contact is Turismo Verde, 20 via Mariano Fortuny, 00196 Rome, for a catalogue (in Italian). For farms in Tuscany try Turismo Verde, piazza Indepenza 10, Firenze, and the same agency in Umbria at 28b via Campo di Marte, 06100 Perugia.

RELIGIOUS INSTITUTIONS

Monasteries and convents have traditionally offered hospitality and shelter to weary travellers; now they need the money as well. Except for those few in towns such as Rome and Florence, they tend to be remote and hard to reach without a car. Among those providing basic rooms are the Monastero di San Antonio in Norcia, Umbria; the Monastery of Praglia near Padua; Eremo delle Carceri at Assisi; Vallombrosa monastery near Florence; Camaldoli, near Arezzo; and Monte Oliveto Maggiore, south of Siena. They will accept men or women, but no couples. Ask at local tourist offices for addresses.

For information about religious institutions contact the Associazione Cattolica Internazionale al Servizio della Giovane, an agency also referred to as Protezione della Giovane (PDG) which has offices in many towns and railway stations, and hostels and pensioni all over Italy for females only. Their head office is at Comitato Italiano di Roma, via Urbana 158, 00184 Roma, telephone 06/

4751989. Also try Domus Pacis, via Torre Rossa 94, 00165 Roma, telephone 06/620163.

HOTELS

Almost all the regions have now standardised their hotel grades starting with the luxury five-star, going down to one-star. There is no longer a separate *pensione* or *locanda* class, which used to mean guest and boarding houses, but these are now classified as one or two-star hotels.

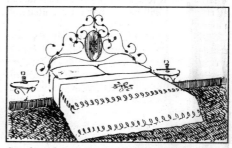

Simple and attractive bed in a Venetian budget hotel

Here is an indication of what you might expect in the star categories in this book:

One-star hotels   These are also known as *pensione* or *locanda*. A few rooms may have private bath, but usually there is only a basin and a bidet with a bathroom or shower along the passage. There may be a very small public room, or none at all. Some do not provide even a cup of coffee, but most give some kind of breakfast. They will be clean. They might have huge rooms and be housed in ancient *palazzos* full of atmosphere, but short of plumbing and needing a lick of paint. For example the Orchidea in Florence, once a *locanda*, now a one-star hotel with only seven rooms, is housed in a 12th-century *palazzo*, birthplace of Dante's wife Gemma Donati.

Each city or region fixes its own price limits on the various grades. So there will be little price variation within the different star categories in the same city, but for the price of a two-star hotel in Venice or Rome (the two most expensive cities), you could stay at a three-star hotel in Umbria. We try on the whole to keep our hotel prices to a maximum of L100,000 for two persons' bed and breakfast, which means three-star or below, and in the big towns and most popular and expensive tourist areas, generally two-star and below. Do be aware that a way hoteliers get round the price limit is by charging a great deal for breakfast. (Again Venice is a culprit there, many hotels quoting only a bed and breakfast price.) But usually you may take the expensive hotel breakfast or not, as you wish. Some hotels don't provide breakfast at all, but most will have a bar for a coffee and brioche (about L2,000).

Not many hotels in these categories have restaurants. Newly built hotels (extremely rare in the cities) will naturally have modern facilities, and will be usually beyond our price range. Most Italian hotels are in old buildings, and it is often impractical and costly for them to install en suite bathrooms and lifts, so they remain one-star. Others somehow fit showers into odd corners or carve up old rooms, spoiling the atmosphere but providing services and gaining a higher star rating and price band. Most two-star and even three-star establishments will have some rooms without private shower.

The phrase *con bagno* may mean shower, basin, bidet and lavatory, or more rarely a bath tub (*vasca*), or sometimes a shower and bidet *without* a private lavatory. If you want to make sure you have both shower and lavatory, ask for *doccia* (shower) and WC (pronounced 'voo chee').

The price of the room will be marked on the back of the door; check it and see that the date is current. Some less scrupulous hoteliers, if challenged on price, might claim that it was last year's price. But the price on the door is what you pay.

Two-star hotels   More rooms here will have en suite showers, there will be a sitting or breakfast room and some hotels will have gardens and parking space. Decoration will be simple, not luxurious.

Note that hotels **are allowed** to put up their prices between 5 and 10 per cent every March, so prices may be higher than those shown here.

HOUSE EXCHANGES

A way to cut costs is to exchange houses. Here are some organisations who coordinate arrangements:

Home Exchange International piazza Mirabello 1, 20121 Milano. Telephone 02/651753.
Intervac via Oreglia 18, 40047 Riola (BO). Telephone 051/910818.
Casa-Vacanze via San Francesco 170, 35121 Padova. Telephone 049/48664.

MONEYSAVERS

Check out good off-season package deals and three or four-night short holidays in the big cities.

Travelling to Italy by air, besides the charter flight reductions, you may get a cheap flight to Rome by Quantas and other air companies which stop there before flying beyond Italy. If you're travelling down by car, make sure you get the discount petrol and motorway coupons from the AA or RAC before you go (these concessions are not available for cars hired in Italy). You may also buy them at the Italian frontier post, from ACI, but you cannot pay in Italian currency (see page 12 for full details).

Italian railways are good value, usually considerably cheaper than buses, and they offer various discount tickets as well. It's worth giving careful thought to how much travelling you are really going to do before buying these tickets, with trains so inexpensive. On the other hand, for long distances you would have to pay extra for supplements on the EC and IC trains.

Travel-at-will ticket (BTLC – *Biglietto Turistico di Libera Circolazione*) Allows unlimited travel on any Italian train, including Rapido, without payment of supplement, available at Milan, Florence, Venice, Rome and Naples railway stations. Prices for second class travel: eight days – £65, 15 days – £79, 21 days – £92, 30 days – £112. There is a 50 per cent reduction for children under 12.

Italy Flexi Railcard IFR allows free travel on certain days. Four days free travel within nine days – £48, eight days free travel within 21 days – £66, 12 days free travel within 30 days – £86.

These tickets allow the traveller free seat reservations, use of Inter-City and Euro City trains without supplement, free deck passage on FS ferries to Sicily and Sardinia, 30 per cent reduction on ferries between Italy and Greece operated by Adriatica di Navigazione and HML shipping companies.

All these tickets can be obtained in Britain before you leave from CIT, Marco Polo House, 3–5 Lansdowne Road, Croydon CR9 1LL, telephone 081-686 0677 (£3 booking fee).

Family cards costing £5 are available at British Rail centres by up to eight people living at the same address, all of whom must be named on the card. At least three, of which one must be an adult, must travel together throughout the journey to qualify. The first adult pays a full ordinary fare, other adults half fare and children under 12 half the reduced fare.

A *Chilometrico* ticket is valid for 3,000km (1,865 miles), which can be used by up to five people at the same time for a maximum of 20 separate journeys, £60.

Inside Italy, day return tickets for a maximum 50km (30 miles) and three-day return tickets for a maximum 250km (155 miles) both have a 15 per cent discount.

Eurorail passes, for travel covering most European countries, can only be bought outside Europe.

All hotels charge per room and not per person, so travelling with a companion is much cheaper. A single room can be about two-thirds that of a double. A room without private shower and lavatory is a considerable saving – usually about two-thirds the cost of one with private facilities.

Breakfasts in bars rather than hotels, or in hotel bars rather than the dining room, can be both cheaper and better. Although breakfast coffee at hotels can often be a pale shadow (you may prefer it that way) of a bar cup. **Drinks of all kinds at the bar are half the price, or less, of what you pay sitting down at a table.** You will seldom be disappointed if you order the house wine in a carafe in *trattorias* – its usually perfectly drinkable and much less expensive than a bottled named variety. Best value drinks at the bar are espresso coffee, about L800, and a glass of wine for the same price. You can always ask for a glass of tap water (*acqua semplice*) to go with it.

Italian department store chains, such as Rinascente and Coin, have smart clothes and are quite pricey, but even the downmarket Upim and Standa have stylish clothes. Best buys all over Italy are shoes and belts and coloured art reproductions, often obtainable at markets and workshops.

SIGHTSEEING

Prepare to be frustrated; all times listed here are subject to variation. And expect to see the dreaded words *in restauro*, meaning that what you have journeyed especially to see is being restored and cannot be seen. Italy has so many sights and so many old buildings, that it's not surprising that half of them always seem to be behind scaffolding and draped in green plastic netting. However, so

much of the pleasure of sightseeing in Italy is wandering about beautiful old cities or exploring wonderful countryside, that it doesn't matter too much if some things are off the list.

Opening times are very tricky, though, and changeable. In principle, state museums and art galleries are closed on Monday and open weekdays 9am-2pm, closing one hour earlier on Sundays and holidays at 1pm. Most do not reopen later in the day, though some of the most famous and much visited, like the Uffizi in Florence, stay open all day. Occasionally a few open on Monday in the summer. Entrance fees range from L2,000 to L4,000, and nationals of European Community countries over 60 and under 18 go free. Private museums and galleries open at different times, usually with a two-hour lunchtime closing, reopening about 4pm or later.

Sightseeing – wandering about beautiful old cities

It's a good idea to travel on Monday when museums are shut, and stay away from trains on Sunday when they are crowded. The midday siesta, from roughly 1.30pm to 4pm, is a good time to be driving into cities, and also (though of course it can be hot at midday in summer) a good time to wander around normally crowded streets in popular tourist towns. Get to popular museums as early as you can – literally when they open. In Urbino, for instance, the National Museum is almost empty at 9am, and begins filling up about 10am when the buses bring day-trippers to the town. If you want to spend time seriously studying in certain museums, it pays to stay a night in the town to be able to get there early. Most outside places, ancient Roman remains, gardens, and so on, open about 9am and close one hour before sunset. Many museums and galleries will not admit you less than one hour before closing time.

See if your vacation includes one of the major public holidays, such as 1 May and 15 August, the latter called the Ferragosto, when all shops, most restaurants, and even some public transport may not be functioning. Aim to stay put; these are not good days to try and get to airports on time.

Churches usually open early for Mass about 7am, but shut tight about 12 noon and usually reopen about 3pm or 4pm for a couple of hours. Important cathedrals such as St Peter's in Rome and St Mark's in Venice don't close at midday. Take plenty of L100, 200 or 500 coins with you, to put in light machines. Be aware that in Holy Week, before Easter, many religious paintings will be shrouded.

State museums close on 1 January, Easter Day, 25 April, 1 May, and the first Sunday in June, 25 August and 25 December.

SHOPPING

Shops are usually open 9am-1pm and 4-7pm or 8pm, closed Sundays. Some clothing stores shut Monday mornings. Some food shops close Saturday afternoons in summer and Thursday afternoons in winter. Half-day closing varies from town to town. Women's hairdressers close Sunday and Monday; men's barbers Sunday afternoon and Monday.

Photographers should note that chemists (*farmacia*) do not sell photographic supplies, but usually sell only medical items. Films are more expensive to buy and process in Italy, so bring film with you.

Prices in shops are usually fixed (*prezzi fissi*), but if you are buying several items there may be a discount (*uno sconto*), especially if you can pay cash. There are genuine bargains in clothing and shoe lines at January and July sales, otherwise prices in Italy are not cheap. Always look around before you buy, and try to buy the local speciality. You will get a better range of goods and prices in the home town: for example glass, masks, lace and velvet in Venice; tooled leather, decorated paper, straw goods and art reproductions in

Florence; silk scarves and ties in Milan and Como; coral and cameos in Naples; puppets in Palermo; and pinocchios in Pisa.

Avoid tourist stalls at prime sights which sell a mixed selection of second-rate bits and pieces from all over Italy – or so they seem, until you buy and find items made in China and Hong Kong. But do not despise two very useful sources of budget shopping – supermarkets and department chains such as Standa and Upim (which is open through the lunch hour), and the weekly large open-air clothing and household goods markets. Italian styling and quality of material is so high that you can find good silk clothing at Standa shops. And they usually have spot reductions, or special rails, or whole bins of absurdly cheap belts and scarves that are definitely worth a browse.

In the markets you can bargain. But you will find such good value, with all-leather lined shoes (*vero cuoio* = real leather) from L30,000, that you don't need to haggle. Florence and Siena have particularly good, enormous markets. The ordinary small-town local market can be a disappointment for clothes, but good for vegetables. The vegetable markets are always worth a visit to

Open market where you can find almost everything

photograph, even if not to buy, and for a look at local life.

Markets usually start about 7am and are finished and swept up at 1pm. In markets, stallholders are often keen to bundle a couple of apples or peaches on and off the scale and give a round figure – L1,000 or L2,000, say. Note the price per kilo, and watch carefully. Be aware that all fruit and vegetables, including melons, are priced by weight. A heavy melon may turn out to be much more expensive than you thought. Get them to weigh first and ask the price – *quanto costa?*

Bringing home food and drink depends not only on taste but on whether you've got

CLOTHES SIZE CONVERSIONS

LADIES

Shoes

Britain	2	3	4	5	6	7	8	9
France	36	37	38	39	40	41	42	43
Italy	32	34	36	37	38	40	41	42
USA	4	5	6	7	8	8	10	11

Blouses, sweaters

Britain	32	34	36	38	40	42	44	46
France	38	40	42	44	46	48	50	52
Italy	40	42	44	46	48	50	52	54
USA	30	32	34	36	38	40	42	44

Dresses, coats

Britain	8	10	12	14	16	18	20	22
France, Italy	34	36	38	40	42	44	46	48
USA	6	8	10	12	14	16	18	20

MEN

Shoes

Britain	5	6	7	8	9	10	11
France, Italy	40	41	42	43	44	45	46
USA	6½	7½	8½	9½	10½	11½	12½

Shirts

Britain, USA	14	14½ 15	15½ 15¾ 16	16½
France, Italy	36	37 38	39 40 41	42

Suits

Britain, USA	34	36	38	40	42	44	46	48
France, Italy	44	46	48	50	52	54	56	58

CHILDREN

Dresses, coats

Europe	1	2	5	7	9	10	12
USA	2	4	6	8	10	13	15

transport or not. Even one bottle of wine can be very heavy after you have walked with it a while. A better buy could be a half bottle of a local liqueur which you wouldn't find exported; dried mushrooms (*porcini*); salami or other sausage. For British buyers the best buy is actually Scotch whisky – cheap, but not exactly a memento.

If space and weight are no object, then some things to buy are:

Pottery – especially from Deruta in Umbria and Grottaglie in Apulia, but also from Orvieto and Siena. There is attractive local majolica ware all over Italy.

Leather goods – in street markets in Naples, Florence and most big towns they sell copies of famous names, Gucci, Vuitton etc. Not the real thing, but not bad.

Silk ties – very reasonable buys.

Olive oil – some of the best comes from Lucca in Tuscany and Bitonto in Apulia. All over Tuscany and Umbria you can buy really thick dark green hand-pressed oil, thicker and tastier than the *extra vergine* you usually find exported, but expensive.

Wines – the local best are listed in the following chapters. DOC (*Denominazione di Origine Controllata*) means the wine has been made under specified conditions, and indicates quality. DOCG (*Denominazione di Origine Controllata e Garantita*) guarantees the authenticity of elite DOC wines.

Posters and reproductions – the best buy. It's worth buying a tube (a large one costs about L3,000) for safe transit.

And always belts, scarves, shoes, bags.

Music tapes – opera or local songs can be a good buy, cheapest of all in markets.

ENTERTAINMENT

No one wants to be indoors on a hot Italian summer evening, so most of the entertainment is out of doors, mainly sitting at cafés, drinking, watching, walking up and down. Night spots are few and far between as well as expensive. But outdoors there is always something to look at – big cities are partly floodlit, and (clutching your belongings tightly, and going if possible with a companion if you are female) that is the time to catch the mood of the place.

Most towns run open-air cinemas, called *arena*, showing American and British films, but dubbed. There may be open-air theatre or opera, and many small towns have their own summer drama and music festivals. There is always a lot of music going on in Italy – tourist offices will provide lists of local concerts. Then there are jazz festivals (Siena and Perugia); opera festivals at Spoleto, Venice, Verona and all over Italy, some open-air in summer, some running through the winter season from December to April or May; and music festivals in Florence, festivals of Puccini, Rossini and Vivaldi. The invaluable traveller's handbook, issued by the Italian Tourist Office, lists addresses and phone numbers of all the many Italian opera houses.

Above all, there are the local festivals, celebrating something or anything: snails, hunting, saints, mussels, crickets; any excuse for a party, fireworks and especially big meals, often eaten in the streets and at which visitors are welcome.

Every town and city will have its own feast day in honour of its patron saint, and these are mentioned in the relevant chapters. Corpus Domini (Corpus Christi) is celebrated about 60 days after Easter, when many towns spread flowers along their streets for a festival called the *Infiorita*.

Then there are the traditional festivals, contests, regattas of all kinds which are a wonderful free show for the budget traveller. It's well worth noting them so that you will know when the town will be busy, and need to book accommodation in advance. Festivals are so exuberant and colourful, it would be a shame to miss one by careless timing. Here are some of them (by no means a complete list); it is always worth checking at the tourist office wherever you are in case there is some local excitement to see.

CALENDAR OF EVENTS

JANUARY 6 Epiphany celebrations in many towns: Piazza Navona, **Rome**. **Piana deglia Albanesi**, near **Palermo** (Sicily).

January 20 Feast of San Sebastian **Aci Reale** (Sicily).

FEBRUARY 3 Feast of St Agata, **Catánia** (Sicily).

February 4 Olive and *bruschetta* festival in **Spello** (Umbria).

Mid February Pre-Lent carnivals, especially in **Viareggio** and **Venice**.

February 9 Pomigliano d' Arco, **Naples**.

February 16 Palio del Viccio (a turkey) in **Bari** (Apulia).

MARCH 19 Pancake festival, **Greve in Chianti** (Tuscany).

March 19 Feast of San Giuseppe. Fairs and food in the Onda Contrada, and donkey races, **Siena** (Umbria).

Easter Holy Week – celebrations in **Assisi** (Umbria).

Good Friday. Candlelight procession in **Assisi** (Umbria), and **Grassina**, near **Florence** (Tuscany).

The Pope leads a torchlight procession from the Colosseum, **Rome**.

Torchlight processions with crucifixes, coffins, hooded figures, **Amalfi** (Campania) and other towns.

Easter Sunday. Explosion of the cart, fireworks in cathedral square, **Florence** (Tuscany).

Easter Monday. Chapel of San Vito, **Lecce** (Apulia).

First Sunday after Easter. National kite festival, San Miniato, **Florence** (Tuscany).

Second Sunday after Easter. Donkey palio in Querceta, **Lucca** (Tuscany).

APRIL First three weeks – Antiques fair in **Todi** (Umbria).

April 1 Procession of the mysteries, **Prócida**, Naples, and also in **Ragusa** (Sicily).

April 2 Liberty festival, historical parade, **Lucca**.

April 3 La Diavolata. Main square of **Catánia** (Sicily).

MAY 1 Parade of floats, **Terni** (Umbria).

First Saturday and Sunday. Procession of St Nicholas, **Bari** (Apulia).

May 15 Race of the giant candles in **Gúbbio** (Umbria). Medieval jousting in **Foligno** (Umbria).

Ascension Day Fiesta del Grillo, Cascine Park, **Florence** (Tuscany); festival of the crickets. **Venice**, wedding of the sea ceremony.

May 28 Procession of the caparisoned horse, **Bríndisi** (Apulia).

Last Sunday Crossbow competition in **Gúbbio** (Umbria).

Whit Sunday Festa della Palombella in **Orvieto** (Umbria).

Last weekend Vogalonga rowing race, **Venice**. Anyone can pay L5,000 and compete in any boat.

The Palio, Siena

JUNE Corpus Domini. Flower carpets in the streets of **Spello** (Umbria), and **Assisi** (Bolsena). Flower festival in **Genzano** (Rome) with flower-carpeted streets.

First Sunday Garlic toast festival, **Montecatini Terme** (Tuscany).

Three weekends Calcio storico; football in costume in **Florence** (Tuscany).

June 4 Navigli festival by the canal with water sports, **Milan**.

June 13 Feast of Sant' Antonio, **Padua**.

June 16-17 Festa di San Ranieri, regatta and lights along the river, **Pisa** (Tuscany).

June 18 Festa del Barbarossa, parades and archery contest, **San Quírico d'Órcia** (Tuscany).

June 24 Festa, 10pm fireworks, **Florence**. Pantomime and painted boats in **Aci Trezza** (Sicily).

June 26 Feast of the lilies, **Naples**. Game on the Ponte di Mezzo, over the Arno, **Pisa** (Tuscany).
JULY 2 Palio horse race in **Siena** (Tuscany).
July 3 Feast of the Bruna (Black Madonna), **Matera** (Basilicata).
First Sunday Regatta of the ancient maritime republics (**Amalfi, Genoa, Pisa, Venice**. Held in **Pisa** 1991, **Venice** 1992, **Amalfi** 1993.
July 11 Ufustinu. Procession and fireworks in **Palermo** (Sicily).
July 11 and 12 Feast of San Paolino, torch-light parade, and crossbow contest, **Lucca** (Tuscany).
Saturday and Sunday Festa del Redentore, **Venice**; fireworks at 11pm on Saturday.
July 16-24 Festa de Noantri, celebration and revelry, **Rome**.
July 25 Joust of the bear, **Pistoia** (Tuscany).
AUGUST Second Sunday, regatta, **Porto Santo Stefano** (Tuscany). Bruscello, plays and food in Montepulciano (Tuscany).
August 6 San Sisto festival, **Pisa** (Tuscany).
August 14 Crossbow contest, **Gúbbio** (Umbria).
August 15 Big national festival. Beefsteak festival in **Cortona** (Tuscany), procession in **Salerno** (Campania).
August 16 Second Palio in **Siena** (Tuscany).
August 17 Palio Marinaro; boat races in **Livorno** (Tuscany).
Last Sunday Bravio delle Botti, barrel-pushing and processions, **Montepulciano** (Tuscany).
August 26 Jousting, **Arezzo** (Tuscany).
SEPTEMBER First Sunday. Joust of the Saracens in **Arezzo**. Gondola race, **Venice**. Lantern festival, **Florence** (Tuscany).
Second Saturday and Sunday Jousting in **Foligno** (Tuscany) – 600 knights. Crossbow contest in **Sansepolcro** (Umbria). Eating and dancing in **Greve de Chianti** (Tuscany).
Third Sunday Wine festival **Impruneta** (Tuscany). Donkey race at **Carmignano** (Tuscany).
September 14 Fair in Piazza San Michele, **Lucca** (Tuscany).
OCTOBER 4 Feast of St Francis celebrated at **Assisi** (Umbria).
NOVEMBER 1 All Souls' Fair. **Perúgia** (Umbria).
November 21 Festa della Salute, **Venice**.

LOCAL CUSTOMS

Italians are a very polite and courteous nation, always ready to communicate with strangers and wish them a good day *buon giorno*, or good evening, *buona sera*, or 'have a good meal', *buon appetito*, frequently said before one eats. Try a reciprocal *buon giorno* in shops or out walking in the country. People will say good morning, or goodbye, *arrivederci*, to a carriage of complete strangers in the train. And no Italian will look askance if you try to speak their language, but will be pleased and eager to help and understand. If you are travelling in outlying areas, it will be very useful to learn some phrases, because not much English is spoken out of the main tourist areas.

Shake hands a lot – when you meet acquaintances again, or leave a group – coming or going, it's a widespread custom that generates good feeling. It is particularly impolite to be drunk in Italy. They are seldom drunk themselves, taking care to drink a lot of *acqua minerale* with the wine.

Italian sociability and sense of style come together in the *passeggiata*, evening walk about 6pm or 7pm, in a principal street or square of most towns and cities. Everyone comes out, smartly dressed, children all done up, old grandmothers in their best, especially at weekends, to saunter up and down, have an ice cream, buy a little cake, drink coffee, eye the girls, eye the boys, talk, exchange gossip, and window-shop. That's the time to observe people, spend money on a sit-down drink with a view, or study the shops. The whereabouts of this walk in towns is given in the following chapters. It's a great evening fashion class.

Dress Italians are very proper, even a little old-fashioned in their behaviour and dress. Clothes are very much part of their image: Italians dress appropriately and smartly and they like to see óthers doing the same. Teens and 20s wear the international uniform, jeans or short skirts, and anything goes. But you will not often see women over 30 in trousers. If a woman wants to stand out as a foreigner, she should wear a pale track suit and an anorak with a scruffy handbag. Italian men will be conservatively but elegantly dressed, with beautiful shoes, and jackets often worn loose on the shoulders, with a small, leather bag containing wallet. All this is generalisation, of course, but appearance is very important to most Italians of any age. The tendency is to throw out last year's handbag, last season's shoes; which is why Italians are such inventive craftsmen and designers, and why you can buy such good quality stylish clothing and accessories not only in opulent specialist shops but even in the markets. Policewomen's uniforms are designed by Fendi, and their shoes by Gucci. Just one example of *la bella figura* – putting on a good show and

Italians of all ages like to dress smartly

looking smart, the essential Italian virtue.

It will be hot everywhere from June to August, so take light clothing in natural fabrics, with lots of shirt changes. Take comfortable flat shoes or sandals (high heels get caught in cobbles and clack on marble floors), and something against the occasional downpour. In spring and autumn there may be cool days, so some jackets and sweaters are needed. At all times have something beside short shorts and bare arms for visiting churches. Only occasionally will you be vetted – at St Marks in Venice, and the cathedral in Pisa, for instance; also St Peter's and the Vatican in Rome. And only the most revealing gear will be barred, but a bit of decorum is polite.

In winter it will be foggy, cold and wet, so dress accordingly. There is a myth that Italy is the land of perpetual sunshine, but it isn't.

In general wear informal chic, dark colours. Men will only need suit and tie in the smartest (non-budget) restaurants. Evening dress is only worn at first nights at the opera and theatre.

Tipping Italians would probably not tip a taxi driver unless he helped with luggage; if you tip, you will be popular. Neither would they leave anything extra in a restaurant where the service is added to the bill; if it is not, give 10 per cent. In bars leave L100 on the counter (there is often a waiting saucer) for each drink. Give the porter L2,000 if he carries a couple of bags to your room, and the doorman L1,500 if he gets you a taxi. Tip the usherette who shows you to your seat in the theatre or cinema (L500 minimum).

STREETWISE

Certain young Italians are adept purse and bag-snatchers. One will drive a scooter at speed while another snatches. Anything loosely hung over a shoulder, a bag or camera, is at risk. They can also spirit away any luggage at stations and airports, and bags in trains. There are honourable exceptions (Venice, Siena, Taormina, for example), but on the whole, the bigger the city and the port, the

more risk. In the various chapters you will find places mentioned for special vigilance. In general, if you follow simple rules and don't put temptation in people's way, you will be fine.

Don't take valuable jewellery with you in the first place. Leave it at home. Wear shoulder straps across your body or round your neck, hold on tight and carry your bag on the non-street side. A money belt is invaluable for cash (notes) and credit cards. It's a great feeling of security having your money safe and hidden, and several L50,000 notes are not bulky.

Never leave anything on view in parked cars. If you have to leave things, hide them in a locked boot. It is worth paying extra for a guarded parking space or garage in cities such as Naples and Rome. It's not a bad idea to carry a camera, handbag, or purse in a tatty-looking shopping or carrier bag.

Take special care on long distance trains at night. Or if you think you may nod off, have your documents attached to you. If you do have anything stolen, report it immediately to the police (telephone 113), and get a form signed by them for your insurance.

USEFUL INFORMATION

OPENING TIMES

Banks open Monday to Friday from about 8.35am-1.35pm and reopen in the afternoon for an hour, between 3pm and 4.30pm. Afternoon times vary, so it is best to get to the bank about 3.30pm. They are shut all Saturday, Sunday and holidays.

Post Offices Most smaller post offices are open 8.30am-1.50pm, Monday to Friday, closing at 12 on Saturday and the last day of the month. Main post offices stay open all day to 8pm, closing at noon on Saturday. Post offices at airports are open 24 hours, as are registered letter and telegraph windows at main post offices. (You do not need to go to a post office to buy a stamp.)

Chemists usually open 8.30am-1pm and 4.30-7.30pm; there will be a notice indicating which chemist is open at night and on holidays.

Telephone Offices SIP and AAST office times vary and are listed in *Orientation* under each major town.

LAVATORIES

·Public lavatories, except those with an attendant, can be rather unpleasant (always carry toilet paper with you). In small cafés the lavatory may still be a unisex hole in the ground. When in doubt, go to the smartest restaurant, and ask for *il bagno, per favore.* Day hotels, *alberghi diurni*, are very respectable places with attendants which provide, for a charge, lavatories, showers, sometimes hairdressing and other amenities.

DRINKING WATER

Tap water is usually perfectly safe in Italy – if it's not, it will be labelled *non potabile* or with P crossed out. Many people drink bottled water, but it is not necessary.

ELECTRICITY

Italian voltage is generally 220, but still occasionally 125 in old buildings, 50 cycles (not 60 as in the US). Pins are round, two-prong. Electrical appliances from Britain and other parts of the Continent will work in Italy (with appropriate plug adaptors); appliances from the USA and Canada will *not*, and attempts to try them could be explosive.

POST AND TELEGRAMS

Internal rates and rates to the UK are the same price; letters up to 20g (0.7oz) L750, postcards L600. Letters can take a very long time, but can be speeded up by sending them express. Express letters (*espresso*) cost L3,050 on top of normal postage. Registered letters (*raccomandata*) also cost an additional L3,050.

A letter from Rome to Bologna travelled faster during the old Roman Empire than it does today. Allow six days for a letter from Rome to Florence. If you want to find out information urgently, always telephone.

Airmail letters to the USA and Canada cost L1,050; postcards are L850 for only a few words, otherwise they cost full letter rate (*via aerea* = air mail). Stamps (*francobolli*) can be bought at tobacco shops (*tabacchi*) with a large black T sign outside.

For *poste restante*, send letters addressed to c/o Palazzo delle Poste, the town, and add *Fermo Posta*. To collect, you must show a passport and pay about L250. Italians may file your letter under your first name, so check, and when writing, underline the surname.

Telegrams cost L815 per word. You can send a message overnight, costing L370 per word, up to 22 words, to be delivered the next morning. Telephone 186 during office hours.

TELEPHONES

There are three ways of telephoning in Italy.
1 Many bars have the black and yellow telephone signs outside indicating a public telephone. Ask if you need *gettoni*. These are tokens costing L200. Buy them from the cashier or a token machine near the telephone. You may be able to use L100, L200 and L500 coins instead. One *gettone* buys five minutes of local calls. If you put in more than you need, press the button for a refund. *Gettoni* can be used as change. They can also be bought at tobacconists, post offices and some newsstands.
2 A *telefono a scatti* means an operator-run metered telephone. In some bars, the proprietor will put you through, the call will be timed by meter, and you pay him at the end. Otherwise use a SIP phone.
3 Phone cards are used in new *scheda* phones found mostly at airports and railway stations, the cards are bought at SIP offices, or from a machine near the telephone for L5,000 or L10,000. You break the corner off the card and insert it into the phone, removing it after your call to re-use it. A date shows duration of the card.

Local calls (*una telefonata urbana*) If using a *gettone*, put it in, dial the local number, and then push the *gettone* knob. The ringing tone sounds rather like a British engaged tone – one slowly repeated sound. For local directory enquiries dial 12.
Long-distance calls (*una telefonata interurbana*) You should put in five or six *gettoni* to begin with. To dial Rome, say, from Bologna, use the code (*il prefisso*) for Rome 06. From Rome you would dial 51 for Bologna with a 0 in front. The local code is listed in this book under each town.
International calls You can only make these from an *a scatti* phone, or from the telephone company offices, called SIP (pronounced 'seep') or ASST. The addresses of many of these are listed throughout the book. Dial 00 and then the country code (for UK 44, for USA and Canada 1). Then dial the local code and number, dropping the first 0. So to dial London, it would be 0044-71 (or 81) and then the local number.
Telephone rates Peak rates are 8.30am-1pm Monday to Friday. Ordinary rates are 8-8.30am and 1-6.30pm Monday to Friday, 8am-1pm Saturday. There is a 30 per cent reduction 6.30pm-10pm Monday to Friday, 1pm-10pm Saturday and 8am-10pm Sunday. A night-time 50 per cent reduction operates from 10pm-8am every night.

Avoid telephoning long distance from your hotel; most hotels add a big charge for this service.

Calls to the UK cost about L5,000 for three minutes. Calls to the USA are about L10,000 for three minutes. A person-to-person call is *con preavviso*. To reverse the charges, say you want a *contassa a carico del destinatario*. Dial 170 for the USA and Canada; dial 15 for the UK. For general information about telephoning in Europe (in English), dial 176. An alarm (wake-up) call is 114. To dial Italy from London, dial 010 39 and then the local code.

NATIONAL HOLIDAYS

These are the days when offices, shops and

schools are closed. Museums and transport use Sunday operating times.

January 1 Capodanno

January Epiphany – La Befana is a kind witch who brings children toys on this day.

Easter Monday

April 25 (Liberation Day, Second World War). Many streets are called *via XXV Aprile.*

May 1 Labour Day.

August 15 The Ferragosto (Assumption). One of the biggest celebrations in Italy.

November 1 All Saints Day. People gather at the cemeteries.

December 8 Feast of the Immaculate Conception.

December 25 Christmas.

December 26 Feast of Santo Stefano, St Stephen. Our Boxing Day, and the day Good King Wenceslas set out.

MONEY

Currency is the *lira* (plural *lire*). Abbreviated to L, or Lit (*lira italiana*) and sometimes written £.

Coins come 50, 100, 500. Banknotes are 1,000, 5,000, 10,000, 50,000 and 100,000. The 100,000 note is hard to change. There are, very roughly, L2,000 to the pound. So for a quick conversion cross off the noughts and divide by two, to find the pound equivalent.

Spoken money can be confusing. Instead of saying one thousand five hundred, for example, *mille cinque cento*, shopkeepers may say simply *mille cinque*, and if it is two thousand and five hundred, simply *due cinque*, two five. So if in doubt, get all prices written down.

Best exchange rates are at larger banks and American Express offices. Hotels, restaurants and bars will take a big commission. Visa card cash dispensers are operated by the Banca d'America e d'Italia. Getting money from banks is very tedious. The afternoon hour is variable, and there are usually long waits. Also, be careful not to go through some of the banks' security doors with any metal appliance in your bag or pocket. You will have to go out again, dump your bag, or remove the item, and re-enter.

Travellers' cheques are the most sensible way to take money, but be careful to note the numbers, and keep that note separate from the cheques. Also note where to telephone in case of theft or loss. Some form of money belt is a good idea – if not for cash, then for credit cards.

Credit cards are not widely used by Italians, and therefore are only easily used in tourist restaurants (usually expensive ones) and the more expensive hotels and shops. Most one-star hotels don't like them, and even some two-star ones; they prefer Eurocheques, which clear faster. Don't try and use foreign currency if you can help it – it will be looked on with grave suspicion, and probably given an extortionate rate.

EATING OUT

Some of the best cooking is in the most unpretentious places – small places with no name but *Vini e Cucina*, meaning food and wine. For the best prices, avoid restaurants with elaborate food displays and fancy tablecloths. Tourist menus may mean decent food in some places (Venice for instance), but often they provide mundane food in mean portions.

A *tavola calda* is a self-service restaurant with hot and cold dishes either to eat there, or to take away. These can have very good food.

A *rosticceria* is similar, with mostly roasts, but less likely to have seating. A *pizzeria* obviously serves pizzas, a *pizzeria rustica* sells pizzas by weight. An *osteria* is, strictly speaking, a wine bar, with the accent on the drinks and some food to go with them. A genuine *trattoria* is often family-run, with good home cooking and possibly no menu, just the food of the day.

In most restaurants and *trattorias* you will pay a cover charge (*pane e coperto*) of between L1,500 and L2,000, and in addition there will be a service charge of up to 15 per cent. There's no need to tip if it is *servizio compreso*. If you have only a pizza in a *pizzeria*, there will probably be no cover charge.

Take care over items marked *SQ*, which means according to quantity, and often applies to fish and steak. You will not know the amount until you get the bill. Also food listed as costing, for example 'L4,000 hg', which is L4,000 an etto, or 3½ ounces.

Every restaurant has by law to give a receipt for the bill (*il conto*), and, by law, you have to carry it with you out of the restaurant into the street. All restaurants close one day a week.

Eye-catching shops sell produce of the area

Many people can't eat a large dish of pasta as well as the main course. If you only want a small portion, ask for *mezza porzione* (half portion).

The midday meal is the most elaborate, with *antipasti* (hors d' oeuvres), *primi piatti* (soup, pasta, risottos), *secondi piatti* (meat or fish), and *contorno* or *verdura* (vegetables). There's no need, obviously, to order all the courses, but it is confusing for waiters if some members of a group are having pasta as their main dish at the same time as others are having meat or fish. Fish is always more expensive than meat.

Bars are mostly breakfast time places, for a quick stand-up cup of espresso (small, black, very strong coffee). If you ask for *un caffè*, that's what you'll get. An *Americano* is a bigger cup, *cappuccino* with frothed up milk, *caffè latte* a large cup of white coffee, a

caffè macchiato has a dash of milk. To go with it you could ask for a *cornetto*, a sweet kind of croissant, or a *briosce*, more solid, also sweet. Ordinary bars don't usually do much savoury food. You must go to a bigger wine bar for that. Sitting down pushes the price of drinks up at least double. If you sit down at a table, a waiter or bar attendant will take your order and serve you. Otherwise, tell the cash desk what you want, pay, show your receipt to the fellow behind the bar, put L100 in the saucer on the bar top, and collect your drink and food.

Some average prices at the bar are beer L1,700; wine L800; fruit juice L1,300; hot chocolate L1,600; espresso L800; brandy L2,000; whisky L2,800 (large measure). If you want a freshly squeezed fruit drink, ask for a *spremuta di arancia* (orange), otherwise a *limonata* or *aranciata* will bring you a bottle of fizzy lemonade or orangeade. Small bottles of real fruit juices, pear, apricot, peach (*succo* is juice) are delicious but can be pricey, up to L1,700. A *granita* is a drink full of crushed ice (coffee flavoured and mint, *menta*, are particularly good).

Italy is the largest wine-producing country in the world, making a fifth of all the world's wine, with Apulia and then Sicily having the most vineyards. The best wines are classified as DOC (Denominazione di Origine Controllata), and the very best DOCG (as Brunello di Montalcino). An *enoteca* is a wine shop where you can sample wine by the glass, and some serve food as well.

After-meal drinks (*digestivo*) vary locally. Fernet Branca and Grappa are powerful spirits; *Amaro* is a herb-based drink. *Punt e Mes* is a bitter vermouth. *Viparo* is another herbal drink from Umbria, *Sambuca* is made from anise, *Amaretto* from almonds.

Picnic food for a budget meal can be bought at markets, supermarkets and *alimentari*, where you can get meat or cheese put in a roll to take away. *Prosciutto crudo* is the raw, expensive, very tasty, thinly cut ham, *cotto* is cooked. *Francetta* is a cheaper cut of raw ham. *Porchetta*, roast pork usually stuffed with fennel, makes delicious sandwiches, and is a speciality of Tuscany and

Umbria. *Panicoteche* are bread shops.

As it's awkward to take metal knives and picnic cutlery through airport security, don't forget to carry away those useful plastic utensils from airline meals. You'll need a corkscrew, though. Most bars will sell you a bottle of mineral water to take away. It can be fizzy (*gassata*) or still (*non gassata*).

ORGANISATIONS

TOURIST OFFICES IN ITALY

ENIT Ente Nazionale per il Turismo offices are state tourist offices dealing with large areas and found at the frontiers and in major cities, and are also represented in all major capitals. The head office in Italy is at via Marghera 2, 00185 Rome. Telephone 06/4971282.

EPT and APT are provincial tourist boards in all 95 provincial capitals providing useful local area tourist information, maps, time-tables, lists of hotels etc. There are also local tourist and information offices in larger towns dealing with the one locality. And in smaller towns, there will be just one office, sometimes called *Pro Loco*, sometimes housed in the local council offices, referred to as an *Azienda*. (An *Agenzia di Turismo* is a travel agency for Italians going abroad.)

ITALIAN TOURIST OFFICES (ENIT) ABROAD

UK 1 Princes Street, London W1R 8AY. Telephone 071-408 1254, telex 22402.   - -
Ireland 47 Merrion Square, Dublin 2, Eire. Telephone 001-766397, telex 31682.
USA 630 Fifth Avenue, Suite 1565, New York, NY 10111. Telephone 212-2454961, telex 236024.

500 N Michigan Avenue, Chicago, Illinois 60611. Telephone 312-6440990/1, telex 0255160.

360 Post Street, Suite 801, San Francisco, California 94108. Telephone 415-3926206, telex 67623.
Canada Store 56, Plaza 3, Place Ville Marie, Montreal, Quebec. Telephone 514-866 7667, telex 525607.

UK EMBASSY AND CONSULATES

EMBASSY
British Embassy via XX Settembre 80a, Rome. Telephone 06/4765441 (open 24 hours). The Rome Consulate is at the same address with the same telephone number, usually open 9.30am-12 noon and 2-4pm.

CONSULATES
Florence Palazzo Castelbarco, Lungarno Corsini 2. Telephone 055/284133. Open Monday to Friday 9.30am-12.30pm and 2.30-4.30pm.
Milan via San Paolo 7, telephone 02/803442. Open Monday to Friday 9am-1pm and 2-5pm.
Naples via Francesco Crispi 122. Telephone 081/663511. Open Monday to Friday 8.30am-1pm. Mid September to June 9am-12.30pm and 3-5.30pm.
Venice Dorsoduro 1051. Telephone 041/5227207.

USA EMBASSY AND CONSULATES

EMBASSY
United States Embassy 119a via Veneto, Rome. The consulate is next door at 121. Open 9.30am-5.30pm. Telephone for both 06/46741.

CONSULATES
Florence Lungarno Vespucci 38. Telephone 055/298276. Open Monday to Friday 8.30am-12 noon and 2-4pm.
Genoa piazza Portello, 6/16124. Telephone 10/282741.

Milan piazza Carlo Donegani 1. Telephone 02/652841, after-hours emergencies 02/653131, code 700. Open Monday to Friday 9am-12 noon and 2-4pm.

Naples piazza della Repubblica. Telephone 081/660966. Lines open 24 hours. Office open Monday to Friday 8am-12 noon and 2-4pm.

Palermo via Vaccarini 1. Telephone 091/291532.

Venice Nearest office is at Trieste, via dei Pellegrini 42. Telephone 040/911780.

CANADIAN EMBASSY AND CONSULATE

EMBASSY
Canadian Embassy via G B de Rossi 27, Rome. Telephone 06/855341/2/3.

CONSULATE
Milan via Vittor Pisani 19. Telephone 055/6697451, after hours 055/66980600. There are no Canadian consulates in Florence or Venice.

HEALTH AND EMERGENCIES

You need no special innoculations or injections for Italy. The most dangerous things you'll encounter will be sun (don't lie out in the midday sun); thirst (sightseeing can lead to dehydration, so do carry water with you); mosquitos (take repellant); blisters (take plasters); stomach upset (bring some mild digestive cures), though Italian food is very healthy, and drinking wine will counteract oiliness. If you are sensitive or allergic, avoid raw seafood.

All EEC members are entitled to the same state medical and dental care as the Italians. Before you go, get leaflet SA30 from the DHSS (Department of Health and Social Security) and complete form CM1. The DHSS will then send you form E111 to take with you. This protects you from having to pay part of the cost of treatment. But even so, you will not be entirely covered, so take out insurance as well.

First aid (*pronto soccorso*) is efficient, and emergency departments in big hospitals will provide X-rays or urgent injections for a small sum. Telephone 113 for Red Cross ambulance.

Private hospital rates are high, but not as high as Germany or France. Injured or sick visitors often go to the Salvator Mundi hospital in Rome or the Ospedali Riuniti di Santa Chiara in Pisa.

Chemists (*farmacia*) will often try and replace your prescribed pills or ointment without a prescription, but take one with you if you can. If closed, they will list an after-hours chemist near by. Apply to IAMAT (International Association for Medical Assistance to Travellers) if you want a list of English-speaking doctors. In the USA contact them at 736 Center Street, Lewiston, NY 14092. In Europe the address is Gotthard-strasse 17, 6300 Zug, Switzerland. Free membership; there is a scale of charges for treatment.

If you lose any valuables (lost = *perso*) or have them stolen (stolen = *rubato*), call the police on 113, or go to the offices of the local Polizia Urbana or Pubblica Sicurezza. (The Carabinieri, telephone 112, are part of the army and deal with very serious crime.) Always get a form signed for your insurance purposes. Consulates will help with lost or stolen passports – take extra photos with you. (Help! = *Aiuto!* Can you help me? = *Può aiutarmi?* My bag has been stolen = *La mia borsa è stata rubata*)

You may encounter a few unfamiliar creatures on your travels in Italy. In country areas there are sometimes adders in the long grass and a bite needs medical treatment; little lizards (harmless) run up and down the walks of houses, but mosquitoes (*le zanzare*) are probably the commonest hazard.

Treat undernourished, unaccompanied dogs and cats with caution as rabies is prevalent in Europe.

ITALIAN PHRASES

SOME PRONUNCIATION TIPS

Most Italian words are pronounced as they are written. The words which are often mispronounced are those including single or double *c*s or *g*s.

A single *c* or *g* is soft (as in church or gentle):

- *dodici* (twelve) is pronounced doh'dee-chee
- *gentile* (kind) is pronounced jen-tee'lay

but hard (as in cap or gold) before an *a*, *o* or *u* :

- *caro* (expensive) is pronounced kah'roh

Both a double *cc* or a double *gg* is soft before an *e* or *i*:

- *formaggio* (cheese) is pronounced forr-mah'djoh

h is never pronounced

Ch and *gh* are hard:

- *chiesa* (church) is pronounced kee-ay'zah
- *laghi* (lakes) is pronounced lah'gee

In words including *qu*, the *u* is pronounced as in squat, but the consonants *gl* or *gn*, when they occur in the middle of words, are pronounced in a special way:

- *Si sbaglia* (you are mistaken) is pronounced see sbahl'yah
- *bagno* (bath) is pronounced bahn'yoh

Vowels that differ from English are:

- *i* which is pronounced as English *ee*:

fine (the end) is pronounced fee'nay

- *e* at the end of a word is pronounced:

grande (large) is pronounced grahn'day

BUDGET HELP

Have you got something cheaper? *Ha qualcosa meno caro?*

Can you give me a discount? *Può darmi uno sconto?*

That's too expensive. *Costa troppo.*

I don't want to spend more than . . . lire. *Non voglio spendere più di . . . lire.*

I'd like a refund. *Desidero essere rimborsato.*

Have you anything smaller? *Ha qualcosa più piccolo?*

Do I have to pay VAT? *Devo pagare l'IVA?*

Do you accept credit cards? *Accettate carte di credito?*

I want to return this. *Desidero rendere questo.*

Can you give me an estimate of the cost? *Può farmi un preventivo?*

I'm just looking, thank you. *Sto guardando, solo, grazie.*

Is there a reduction for students/senior citizens? *Si fa una riduzione per studenti/cittadini anziani?*

You've given me the wrong change. *Il resto è sbagliato.*

Is service included? *È compreso il servizio?*

There's a mistake here. *C'è un errore qui.*

TRANSPORT

I'd like a booklet of tickets. *Vorrei un blocchetto di biglietti.*

A one-day ticket. *Biglietto giornaliero.*

I want to book a seat. *Vorrei prenotare un posto.*

A single to Rome, please. *Uno andata per Roma, per favore.*

A child's return ticket. *Uno andata e ritorno ridotto.*

half-price *metà tariffa*

Is there a connection? *C'e una coincidenza?*

Do I need to pay a supplement? *Bisogna pagare un supplemento?*

Where do I get off for . . .? *Dove scendo per . . .?*

Railway station *la stazione, la ferrovia,*

29

(also the initials FS)
Bus   *Autobus, pullman*

ACCOMMODATION

I'd like a double/single room.   *Vorrei una camera doppia/singola.*
With double bed, twin beds.   *Matrimoniale, a due letti.*
With a lake/canal view.   *con vista sul lago/canale.*
Does one pay extra for this?   *C'è un supplemento?*
Is there a reduction for children/low season?   *Ci sono riduzioni per bambini/ bassa stagione?*
I'd like the cheapest room.   *Vorrei la camera la più economica.*
Have you a cheaper room?   *Ha una camera meno cara?*
Is breakfast included?   *Include la prima colazione?*
Room with shower/without shower.   *Camera con doccia/senza doccia.*
I would like to book.   *Vorrei prenotare.*
Please send me your brochure/price list.   *Vi prego di inviarmi il vostro depliant/tariffario.*
I asked for/I booked.   *Ho chiesto/Ho prenotato.*
Have you a room with three beds/a child's bed?/a cot?   *Ha una camera tripla/con un lettino da bambino/una culla?*
Tax and service included.   *Tasse e servizio compresi.*
Double with shower and lavatory.   *Doppia con doccia e wc.*
I don't want full board/half board/ breakfast.   *Non voglio pensione completa/mezza pensione/colazione.*

EATING OUT

House wine.   *Vino di casa.*
A small child's portion.   *Una piccola porzione per il bambino.*
Have you a set menu?   *Ha un menu a prezzo fisso?*

Is there an inexpensive restaurant near here?   *C'e un ristorante economico qui vicino?*
Local dishes.   *Le specialità locali.*
The bill, please.   *Il conto, per favore.*
A bottle/cup/glass of . . .   *Una bottiglia/ una tazza/un bicchiere di . . .*
One portion between two people, please.   *Una porzione fra due persone, per piacere.*
Is service included?   *È compreso il servizio?*
Does it include wine?   *Include il vino?*
A half-bottle of wine.   *Una mezza bottiglia di vino.*
Tap water, please.   *Acqua semplice, per favore.*
I would like something without meat/ onions/garlic.   *Vorrei qualcosa senza carne/cipolle/aglio.*

CAR HIRE AND DRIVING

car hire   *autonoleggio*
I want to hire a small/economical car.   *Voglio noleggiare una macchina piccola/economica.*
Is that the cheapest car?   *È la macchina la meno cara?*
Does it include VAT?   *È incluso l'IVA?*
A full tank, please.   *Il pieno, per favore.*
unleaded   *senza piombo*
petrol   *la benzina*
Can you put some air in my tyres?   *Mi può gonfiare le gomme?*
Check the oil/brakes/battery.   *Controllare l'olio/i freni/la batteria.*

TELEPHONES

To make a phone call.   *Fare una telefonata.*
Telephone exchange, or operator (dial 13).   *Il centralino.*
Telephone directory.   *L'elenco telefonico.*
code.   *Il prefisso.*
The line is engaged.   *La linea è occupata.*
Just a moment, hold on.   *Un attimo.*
What is the code for . . .?   *Qual'è il*

prefisso per . . .?
Can I phone direct? *Posso telefonare direttamente?*
To England? *In Inghilterra?*

SHOPPING

I'm just looking, thank you. *Guardo solo, grazie.*
I want to buy. *Vorrei comprare.*
All wool/all silk. *Pura lana/pura seta.*
Leather. *Vero cuoio* (usually printed on the sole of shoes).
Is it genuine leather? *È vera pelle?*
Is it real silver? *È vero argento?*
Is it hand-made? *È fatto a mano?*
Can I try it on? *Posso provarlo?*
I don't like it, thank you. *Non mi piace, grazie.*
Have you got anything a little cheaper? *Ha qualcosa un po' meno caro?*
How much is it? *Quanto costa?*
It's too expensive, I'm afraid. *Mi dispiace, è troppo caro.*
A little less, please. *Un po' di meno, per favore.*
That's enough, thank you. *Basta così, grazie.*
Can you make me a sandwich? *Mi può fare un panino?*
One salami and one ham sandwich, please. *Mi fa due panini, uno con salame e l'altro con prosciutto cotto.*
I'd like a bit of this, please. *Mi dà per piacere un po' di questo.*
I want to take it away. *Voglio portarlo via.*
Can you wrap it up for me? *Mi può incartare tutto?*
Can I have two portions, not too big. *Mi faccia due porzioni, non troppo grandi.*
That's enough, thank you. *Basta, grazie*
A quarter of smoked ham, please. *Un etto di prosciutto crudo, per favore.*
Four slices of cooked ham. *Quattro fette di prosciutto cotto.*
Half a pound of cheese, please. *Due etti di formaggio, per piacere.*
I take size 38. *La mia taglia è il trentotto.*

BANKS AND POST OFFICES

Is there any mail for me? My name is . . . *C'e della posta per me? Mi chiamo . . .*
I want to send this express. *Desidero inviare questo per espresso.*
registered mail *raccomandata*
airmail *via aerea*
What's the exchange rate for a dollar/pound? *Qual'è il cambio del dollaro/della sterlina?*
I want to cash a traveller's cheque/Eurocheque. *Voglio incassare un traveller's cheque/Eurocheque.*
Please give me notes and some small change. *Per favore, mi dia banconote e della moneta.*
I want to change some dollars/pounds. *Voglio cambiare dei dollari/delle sterline.*
You have made a mistake. *Scusi, ha sbagliato.*
How much commission do you charge? *Quanto trattiene di commissione?*

MEDICAL AND DOCTORS

I feel ill. *Mi sento male.*
Can I have a painkiller/some sleeping pills? *Posso avere un calmante/dei sonniferi?*
Can you recommend a good dentist? *Può consigliarmi un buon dentista?*
I've got toothache. *Ho mal di denti.*
broken *rotto*
Can you repair this? *Può ripararmi questo?*
There's been an accident. *C'è stato un incidente.*
I need a doctor, quickly. *Mi serve un medico, presto.*
Can I have an appointment? *Può fissarmi un appuntamento?*
right now *subito*
Today. *Oggi.*
As soon as possible. *Il più presto possibile.*
I've got a sore throat. *Ho mal di gola.*

I'm allergic to . . . *Sono allergico a . . .*
I need something for a cold. *Desidero qualcosa per un raffreddore.*
a cough *una tosse*
insect bites *le punture d'insetti*
travel sickness *il mal d'auto*
upset stomach *il mal di stomaco*
I'd like some plasters, please. *Vorrei dei cerotti, per favore.*
toilet paper *carta igienica*

ART AND ARCHITECTURE

trecento the 14th century (1300s)
quattrocento the 15th century (1400s)
cinquecento the 16th century (1500s)
bottega artist's studio
campanile church's bell-tower, usually separate
camposanto cemetery
Certosa Carthusian abbey
ciboro ciborium or pyx, the canopy over the high altar

Baroque architecture, ornate as in this church in Lecce

dipinto su tavola painted on wood
dipinto su tela painted on canvas
duomo cathedral
intarsia mosaic woodwork
majolica earthenware with painted colour decoration on white background glaze.
museo dell' opera museum attached to church, with art belonging to it.
palazzo any large building
pietà picture or sculpture of the Virgin Mary with the dead Christ
pinacoteca art gallery
predella panel of paintings below an altarpiece
putto cherub
ritratto portrait
stucco plaster covering a wall, or used for moulding
tempera egg-yolk based paint, used for easel painting until oil was used in the Renaissance
tessera small piece of marble or glass used in mosaic
Tiziano Vecello Italian for Titian
triptych alter piece with three panels
Barocco Baroque, the type of architecture following after the Renaissance, in the 17th century, heavier, more elaborate and ornate in style.
Rinascimento Renaissance, the 'rebirth' or rediscovery of the art forms, some based on classical literature and humanist thought in the 14th, 15th and 16th centuries, set in motion by artists such as Cimabue, Nicola, Pisano and Giotto.
Romantico Romanesque. Architectural church style, from the 11th to 12th century.

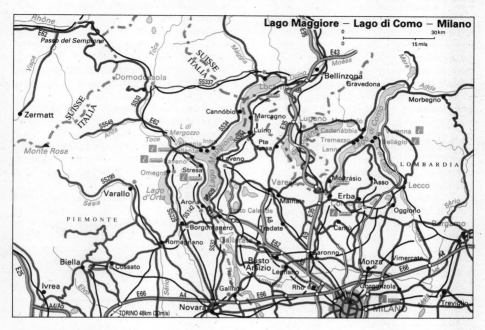

A holiday in the Italian Lakes usually means either a trip by car, touring the lakesides with an occasional foray into the mountains, or a holiday without a car, somewhat stuck in a resort and obliged to pay for expensive coach excursions to get away occasionally. There's a lot to be said for staying put; the scenery of Lake Maggiore with its islands and mountains behind, or the more dramatic Lake Como with its high-hilled sides, is splendid. Boating on the lakes and zigzagging on the ferry is very pleasant, but it is possible, even without private transport, to get about using local buses and the train (even only short distances) to explore the surrounding countryside. Just go a few miles into the hills behind Stresa or Baveno, and you are in a rural world far removed from the resorts. Bring your comfortable shoes and your tolerance; Italian buses run on time, but sometimes the times have been changed and not notified.

The lakes have been a playground for northern Europeans and Americans for more than a century, and the rich industrialists from Milan, Bérgamo and Turin have long built villas here to enjoy the peace and lakeside views. The long thin blue fingers of the lakes point down from the high Alps to the plains of Lombardy and Piedmont and to Milan. Trains, planes and roads all converge, via the lakes, on Milan, and to move from one lake to another without a car, it is easiest to go to Milan and then set off again.

Local flavour

Buy train tickets in advance at most travel agents, saving worries about last-minute queueing at the station. Tickets are valid for three days.

So in this chapter, as well as discovering some of the less well known lake spots and describing some popular ones, there is a section on Milan, as a very full day trip up from the quiet lakes, for a short stay taking in the sights, or as a stopover in transit. Although Milan has the justifiable reputation of being an industrial and somewhat grim city, it has more important art collections to see than any other Italian city outside Florence and Rome.

The main base on Lake Maggiore is the group of towns on the west side, halfway up, surrounding the Borromean islands – Stresa, Baveno and Pallanza (sometimes called Verbánia-Pollanza). There are three towns close together; further north is Intra, a more industrial town, then comes the smaller Verbánia, and round the Point of Castagnola, the town of Pallanza. All three are sometimes lumped together and called Verbánia. Verbánia railway station is 15km (9¼ miles) west of the town.

> **Moneysaver**
> Remember the quick calculation of lire to sterling – knock off the last three noughts and divide by two. So L32,000 is £16. Dollars are easier – knock off the lire noughts and you have the approximate equivalent in dollars (at time of going to press).

Stresa is on the main railway line (so is Verbánia), down through the Alps via the Simplon tunnel and Domodóssola. A lovely way to arrive at the lakes it to travel overnight by train, waking to snow-covered mountains and then blue waters, as the train runs along the lakeside. The price of a rail ticket plus couchette (bunk bed) return to Milan is £153 (Stresa a few pounds less), about the same as the scheduled air fair out of season, and less for students and over 60s. The rail fare remains the same all the year round, while charter fares and scheduled fares are more expensive than rail in peak months. However, by going direct to Stresa by rail, you avoid transfers and rail journey from Milan.

This part of the lake around the islands is well known and popular with many tour operators who arrange economical half-board deals with hotel owners, especially out of season. If you do go on your own you are less likely to be surrounded by other English people, and you will probably be staying in smaller hotels – perhaps less well equipped but also less anonymous.

> **Moneysaver**
> Always check the price of the room written on the door of your hotel bedroom and see that you are charged no more.

All three towns have beautiful views across the lakes to the nearby Borromean islands, with access by train and bus to other parts, to Milan, over the hills west to Lake Orta, and just near by to the remote little Lake Mergozzo (best for swimming), and with access, via Milan, to Lake Como and even Lake Iseo. The disadvantage of this part of the lake is exactly what makes it useful for holiday-makers who like mobility – the road and the railway line which both skirt the lake and run through the centre of the towns. Poor Stresa and Baveno are plagued by the main Simplon road (built by Napoleon) which pours cars through their centres. All the grand hotels with their grand gardens have the main road between them and the lake, with traffic noise roaring up to their windows.

The Simplon tunnel, built in 1906, funnels more and more people down to the lake, bringing fame to Stresa in particular. They have begun to build a bypass behind the towns, due to be completed by 1991–92, a date unlikely to be met. In 1990 work stopped because one of the tiny mountain villages they were skirting began to fall down the mountainside. No one is certain when the bypass will be finished, but in the meantime it is better to stay in a hotel well back from the main road or right down on the shore. Pallanza escapes the worst of this blight, because the road which continues up the west shore to Locarno is not as busy as the

Simplon road, and runs behind the lake-front gardens and lake-side part of town.

Springtime on the Italian Lakes, when the villa gardens are at their best

The best time to come here is April and May, when the azaleas, rhododendrons and magnolias are out and the villa gardens are at their most colourful, and not so many Italians themselves are holidaying yet. Lake Garda is most popular with Germans, but Como and Maggiore can be thronged with Italians, far outnumbering foreigners. You'll find all the tourist offices staffed with English speakers and very helpful – tourism is, after all, their main industry.

Part of one lake is probably all you will manage to see during one holiday because there are so many walks, boat rides and bus trips within a small area. But it is possible to see something of Como as well on a two-week holiday, staying either at Como or further north, where the island forks at Bellágio. Bellágio is one of the most beautifully situated towns on any of the lakes, and though a tourist town, is still unspoiled.

Activities on the lakes include swimming (though Lake Maggiore is somewhat polluted), waterskiing and serious hill walking.

You can fill an entire week and more with an organised bus excursion every day: to the mountains, to Milan and to other lakes, but these cost more than you need pay.

Certain destinations and trips are hard to do on your own – either because there is no public transport, or because they would take too long. So it might be worth L33,000 to visit Lugano and Como in one day in a coach with no hassle.

There is not much nightlife here. Most holiday-makers are middle aged or couples with young children; the young and trendy tend not to come to the lakes. Lake Maggiore is quite sedate; apart from trips, people sit at cafés, televisions come on in the evenings. You might find it utterly boring, or you might be so tired by a day's sightseeing or trekking in the hills that you wouldn't want to do a thing in the evening but eat and have a local *digestivo*, grappa, perhaps, or the local Fernet Branca. The Branca family own the Villa Branca down the road from Stresa, and the drink is made in Milan.

Hotels are reasonable here, though the best become full early. If you want to book in the high season you may have to resort to a more expensive hotel. There are plenty of camp sites – 40 along Lake Maggiore alone, and two right down by the lake in the centre of Baveno. Eating out can be a problem, with plenty of expensive tourist cafés. Walk away from the main streets and look at menus carefully, or consider settling for half-board terms.

The lakes can be very hazy in summer; those bright blue lake pictures with snowy summits reflected in the water are taken in the spring and autumn. And there can be occasional spectacular storms that thunder round the mountains and lash the lakes with rain, so bring some rain protection whenever you come.

Cheap passes are available on the lake ferries for unlimited travel, (children can travel for half price) and for daily and weekly periods.

Local flavour

Queen Victoria was a tourist here once. In 1879 she stayed at the Villa Branca, a noticeable neo-Gothic pile in the hills between Stresa and Baveno, visible from the road. A rich Mrs Henfrey also once lived there (so the story goes), married to the poor Mr Henfrey. When she got bored with him she made him sleep in a little hut in the garden, then she built herself a decorative ruin from which to observe her poor husband in his hovel.

LAKE MAGGIORE

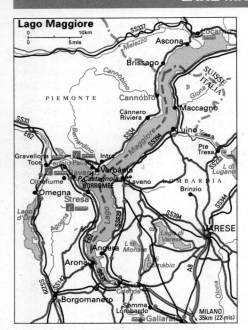

train and road from the Simplon pass run south by the lake from Feriolo down to Sesto Calende and on to Milan. The rest of the west bank, up to Locarno, is served by buses and ferries but no trains. In winter and spring the lake is surrounded by snow-covered peaks, a sharp contrast to the wooded hills. In high summer only Monte Rosa, far over to the west and just visible, second highest mountain in the Alps (4,633 metres, 15,190ft) is white with snow, and the lake views are a bit diminished.

Ferries zigzag up the lake; a regular service crosses from Intra to Laveno, where you can take the bucket lift up for views westwards, and eastwards towards Lake Lugano.

Local flavour

The water in the lake is never really warm because the lake is so deep (380 metres, 1,245ft) and fed by glaciers higher up.

Lake Maggiore lies partly in Switzerland and is split down the middle between two Italian regions, Piedmont on the west bank and Lombardy on the east. This division is very clear whenever Piedmont tourist offices provide maps – the east bank is left blank, nonexistent because it's another region. The

Maggiore is 60km (37¼ miles) long and no wider than 5km (3 miles) at most. The mild weather allows figs, olives and pomegranates to grow, oleander trees line the promenades, and mammoth waxy-leaved magnolias adorn old gardens.

Arriving by air at Milan Malpensa, take a

bus to Gallarate, from where a train will take you to Stresa or Baveno (there are more frequent trains to Stresa). Stresa is the bigger resort, its lake-side road lined with ornate grand hotels with long promenade gardens, many restaurants and cafés. Baveno is not so grand and ornamental, but it has some nice small hotels, one (the Rigoli) particularly attractive down on the lake, away from the road and the railway line, and it has some wonderful walks in the hills behind.

STRESA

Stresa is the biggest, most established and opulent resort on the Gulf of Pallanza in the centre of the lake. The high-balconied hotels are fringed with lawns and flower beds with magnolias and monkey-puzzle trees; across the busy road are more flowers, standard oleanders, and a gravel promenade (hopeless for open sandals). From the lake and boat landing-stages look beyond to the islands, the far shore and the wooded mountains beyond – a romantic setting (except for the road). The old grandeur and glamour have gone a bit, now that everyone can come here so easily, and conferences, groups and package tours fill the Regina Palace. But fortunately, and paradoxically, it is not too popular; maybe the lakes seem a little tame when the whole world is more accessible, and the British in particular don't come here in the numbers they used to.

Away from the lakeside, there are lots of

Stresa, the most established resort on Lake Maggiore

pizzerias and restaurants. Walk up the hill to piazza Luigi Cadorna, full of cafés and the smell of lime blossom (L5,000 for a cappuccino and small beer, sitting down). The tourist office (signposted) is beyond here, and just off the square there's a market on Friday mornings, also an inexpensive hotel and restaurant, the Fiorentino.

> **Local flavour**
> The American writer Ernest Hemingway stayed at Stresa, and sent his hero Frederick Henry to recuperate from the war at the Grand Hotel des Iles Barromees in *A Farewell to Arms*. (Recuperation now would cost you L269,000 for a single room per night with bath: sufficient to cause relapse.)

The station is further up the hill on via Carducci. The view of the islands from the train to Milan, by the way, is the most romantic of all.

Stresa runs an international music festival, the Settimane Musicali di Stresa, during last week of August and first two weeks in September. Well-known performers are featured (the English Chamber Orchestra has been among them); some concerts are held on Ísola Bella. Prices L38,000 upwards (students L10,000), but some at L20,000 for concerts by young performers. For information contact Settimane Musicali, Palazzo dei Congressi, via R Bonghi 4, 28049 Stresa. Telephone 0323/31095.

> **Moneysaver**
> Good local buys – available from Stresa market – are full-size tartan umbrellas with wooden handles L10,000, and jars of local acacia honey.

A good place to visit in Stresa is the Villa Pallavicino, south along the via Sempione (telephone 0323/31533). There are 40 acres of park and gardens, views of the lake, and animals and birds (ostriches, deer, llamas) roaming around the grounds. Open daily 9am-6pm from March to the end of October. L6,500, children 4-14 L5,000.

ORIENTATION IN STRESA

INFORMATION
TOURIST OFFICE
Via Principe Tomaso 70/72.
☎ 0323/30150.
POST OFFICE
Via Roma. ☎ 0323/30065.
Postal code 28049.
BANK
Change money at Banco Popolare di Intra, Corso Umberto 1.
PUBLIC TELEPHONE
In piazza Imbarcadero, on the lake front. ☎ code 0323.
CHEMIST
Farmicia Americana, via Cavour (behind the church).
PUBLIC LAVATORIES
Take the steps down near the public phones, piazza Imbarcadero.
TRAVEL AGENTS
For day excursions, exchanging money and arranging car hire.
Borroni corso Umberto 1.
☎ 0323/30251.
Tomassucci piazza Marconi 3. ☎ 0323/30341

TRANSPORT
TRAINS
Railway Station via Carducci. Many English newspapers on sale here.

ACCOMMODATION
Fiorentino via Anna Maria Bolongaro 8, central and away from main road off piazza Cadorna. ☎ 0323/30254. One-star, basic, eight rooms. Garden, restaurant. No singles. Double L50,000 with bath, L35,000 without. Breakfast L4,500. Open from the end of March to the end of October.
Hotel du Parc via Gignous 1. ☎ 0323/30335. Three-star, 22 rooms. Garden. Parking. Double L82,400 with bath, L61,800 without.
Hotel Mon Toc via Duchessa di Genova 69, above the station. ☎ 0323/30282. One-star, 15 rooms. Small garden and views. Restaurant. All rooms with shower. Half board required from June to September, L55,000 double, L60,000 full board. October to May double bed and breakfast L62,000. Parking space.
Italie et Suisse piazza Marconi 1, facing the lake. ☎ 0323/30540, fax 32621. Two-star, 31 rooms. Front rooms with view (noisy); rooms at the back with no view are quieter. Double L65,900 with bath, L50,000 without.
Luina via Garibaldi 21. ☎ 0323/30285. One-star, seven rooms. Open March 15 to the end of October. Double L50,000 with bath, L35,000 without. Half board L55,000 per person. Small restaurant, charming owner.

ENTERTAINMENT
WATERSKIING AND WINDSURFING
Club Nautico Stresa via Sempione Sud 17 – località Le Sale, 28049 Stresa. ☎ 0323/30551. Motor boats and sailing boats for hire.
SWIMMING
Stresa Lido is along the west end of the promenade.

Moneysaver
For a fair deal on local car hire, consult Liliana Borroni (something of a local celebrity, having featured in a BBC television Italian language series) at Viaggi Turismo Borroni, corso Umberto, along the promenade in Stresa. ☎0323/30251. (L480,000 for a Peugeot 205 per week, including VAT and insurance.)

Local flavour
Be sure to carry your driving licence, written permission from the owner if you have been lent a car, and the car documents whenever you drive. You may be asked to show them.

BAVENO

BUDGET FOR A DAY

Cable car return ticket	
STRESA LIDO to MONTE MOTTARONE	12,000
Picnic lunch –	
rolls, local salami, cheese and a drink	4,000
Boat trip, return ticket	
BAVENO to ISOLA BELLA	5,400
Admission to Palace and gardens	
on ISOLA BELLA	8,000
Dinner in BAVENO	15,000
	L 44,400
plus accommodation	

Local sculptor working in pink granite from Monte Comoscio

Baveno lies in front of Monte Camoscio, 698 metres (2,290ft) high, famous for its pink granite quarries containing a rare mineral, Bavenite. Baveno granite has travelled the world, and has been used in St Paul's Rome, the Opera House in Paris, and monuments to Columbus in New York and Chicago. The town once belonged to the Viscontis who allocated it to the Borromeo family in 1441; all of this corner of the lake is linked to the Borromeos.

Don't miss the church of SS Gervasio and Protasio (up via Monte Grappa), and especially the octagonal baptistry which may date back as far as the 5th century, with 15th-century frescoes (seats to sit and picnic here). Also see the four-storey Casa Morandi with its interwoven outside staircase.

A quiet spot is the public gardens, via Garibaldi, in Villa Fedora along the coast road away from Stresa, over the bridge. It has a small beach with pedalos and a bar, and you can swim from the gravelly shore, but the water is somewhat polluted. Open Monday to Saturday 9am-12.30pm, 3-6pm. Sunday only open in the morning out of season, but open daily 9am-7pm July and August.

Local flavour

If you are a walker, be sure to call in at the tourist office for a map and leaflet of walks in the hills.

ORIENTATION IN BAVENO

INFORMATION

TOURIST OFFICE
Via Garibaldi 16 ☎ *0323/ 924632. Open May to September Monday to Saturday 9am-12.30pm and 3-6pm. Sunday 9am-12 noon. October to April open 9am-12.30pm Saturday and shut Sunday. Very helpful, English speaking. Lists of hotels, walks, bus and train times.*
POST OFFICE

Opposite the tourist office. Open Monday to Friday 8.15am-6.30pm, Saturday 8.15-11.30am. Postal code 28042 (NO).
TRAVEL AGENT
Verbano Viaggi, via Garibaldi 27. ☎ *0323/ 923196. Organises excursions.*
TELEPHONE
☎ *at the post office. Code 0323. Buy phone cards at the Bar Regina.*

ACCOMMODATION
Elvezia via Monte Grappa

15, above the church. ☎ *0323/924106. One-star, 17 rooms. Pleasant modern rooms, quiet, small garden. Open March to October. Double bed and breakfast L60,000 with bath or shower. Half board L45,000 per person.*
Rigoli via Piave 48, very good position on the lake. ☎ *0323/924756. Quiet. Double bed and breakfast L40,000 per person with bath, L35,000 without. Two-star, restaurant, small beach. Open Easter to the*

end of October. Book in January or February for July and August.
La Ripa via Sempione 11, on the main road but with a lake view. ☎ 0323/924589. One-star, double L46,000 with bath, L36,000 without. Breakfast L5,000. Restaurant, 11 rooms. Open April to September.

Villa Ruscello via Sempione 62. ☎ 0323/923006. Two-star, 12 rooms, beach. Double L55,000, all rooms with bath.

CAMPSITES
Cala Speranza St Sempione 24. ☎ 0323/924179. Beach.
Camping Lido via Piave 66. ☎ 0323/924775. Beach.
Lago delle Fate via Pallanza 22, Mergozzo. ☎ 0323/80326. Beach.
Parisi via Piave 50. ☎ 0323/923156. Beach.
La Quiete via Turati 71, Verbánia-Fondotoce. ☎ 0323/416013. Beach.
Tranquilla via delle Cave 2 (at Oltrefiume). ☎ 0323/923452. Inland. Swimming pool.

THE BORROMEAN ISLANDS

These islands belong to the Borromeo family; there are three main islands, and a little one called La Malghera or Ísola d'Amore, because apparently it is only big enough for two people.

Ísola Bella   Ísola Bella was a flat rocky island with a few fishermen's houses and little chapels when, in about 1630, Count Carlo III (Borromeo) began importing soil to build a terraced garden for his wife (he wanted the island to look like an anchored ship). After his death, Carlo's sons, Renato and Vitaliano, built a baroque palace to fill the rest of the island, which was renamed Ísola Isabella after Carlo's wife. The name has since shortened itself to Bella. Perhaps it's because the whole island has been man made that there can be something unnatural, intimidating and almost gloomy about it. Though some people think it is very beautiful: John Ruskin called the islands the 'Eden of Italy', and Stendhal, the French writer, called them 'one of the most beautiful places in the world'.

One of the three Borromean islands, Ísola Bella, with grand Palazzo and theatrical gardens

Ísola Bella is open from the end of March to the end of October, 9am-12 noon and 1.30-5pm, L8,000, children 6-15, L4,000. The palace is more amazing than beautiful. It's main points include Napoleon's bed (Napoleon and Josephine slept here in 1797); a ceiling by Tiepolo; enormous 16th-century Flemish tapestries; marble-walled rooms; beautiful Gobelin tapestry-upholstered chairs; incredibly weird basement grottoes decorated in black and white pebbles, where the rich were entertained and watched marionette shows. You can look out of the window of this grand over-decorated palace and see in the garden below the Borromean family motto *Humilitas* (humility), picked out in stone and surmounted with a crown. The gardens, where they held plays, are monstrous and elaborate, with theatrical ornaments and statues. The only natural things about are the white peacocks and doves that strut about, and even they look a bit artificial. The ship that Duke Borromeo built is a top-heavy galleon, overloaded and bristling with statues, weighed down with obelisks and stone figureheads waving black iron flowers.

Ísola dei Pescatori   The next island, Ísola dei Pescatori, also called Ísola Superiore, is still partly a working island with awning-covered fishing boats (called *lucie*) and little lived-in houses. However it is also commercialised, with numerous tourist stalls selling Hong Kong fans. Walk up to the end, to the Church of San Vittore, and look inside to see the paintings and then the little cemetery with its unfading photos and (Ruffoni) family graves. There are two hotels on the island.

Ísola Madre   Ísola Madre has an elegant 16th-century villa and garden. There is a famous doll and marionette collection, and a botanical garden with an enormous collection of trees and plants, informally laid out. The Ísola Madre gardens are spectacular in May, with great swathes of azaleas and rhododendrons. Come in April for the camellias, and from June to September for the lotus blossom. Open end of March to end of October. 9am-12 and 1.30-5.30pm, L8,000. Children 6-15, L4,000.

ORIENTATION IN THE BORROMEAN ISLANDS

ACCOMMODATION
Ísola Bella
Elvezia Lungolago V Emanuele 18. ☎ 0323/ 30043. One-star, 9 rooms, no private baths. Double L37,100. Open Easter, and end of May to mid November.

Ísola dei Pescatori
Belvedere via di Mezzo 20. ☎ 0323/30047. One-star, double L46,000 with bath, L35,000 without.
Verbano via Ugo Ara 2. ☎ 0323/30408, telex 200269. Three-star, double L82,400, all rooms with bath. (Full board is expensive.) Garden, beach.

BOAT TRIPS ON THE LAKES

Boats leave frequently for the islands from Stresa, Baveno and Pallanza. If you are going to do a lot of hopping about the islands, you can buy an unlimited travel pass (for one day's travel). Between Stresa and Pallanza – L8,000, children L4,200. Between Stresa and Baveno – L6,000, children L3,000. A single trip from Baveno to Stresa (including Ísola Bella and Pescatori on the way) costs L2,700.

Ferries run about every half hour between Stresa and Pallanza. The boat from Stresa to Baveno, including Ísola Bella and Ísola dei Pescatori on its route, costs L5,400 return. Ísola Madre is on the route between Baveno and Pallanza. Round-trip fare from Stresa to Pallanza, including three islands, L7,600. Pick up a schedule from the tourist office.

Other outings you can take from Baveno and Stresa:

1 Orta San Giúlio, on Lake Orta. Take the 12.30pm weekday bus from Stresa, returning 3.45pm. (1 July to the end of August). Also coach excursions.
2 By bus or boat to Pallanza, walking on to Villa Táranto. Or take the hourly ferries (on the hour) direct to the Villa Táranto landing stage.
3 Take the bus to Intra, then the boat across to Laveno for the bucket-ride up the Sasso del Ferro.
4 Train ride to Mergozzo for a swim.
5 Numerous walks up in the hills behind Baveno. Visit Gignese, Alpino, etc.
6 Cable-car to Mount Mottarone.

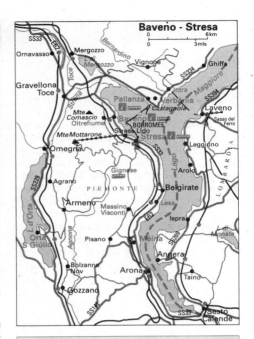

Baveno - Stresa

Local flavour
San Carlo Borromeo, born at Arona in 1538, was made a cardinal by his uncle, Pope Pius IV, when he was only 22. Later he was ordained a priest and became Archbishop of Milan. He was a renowned persecutor of heretics, and once complained there were not enough executions. An enormous 31-metre (102ft) statue of him in bronze and lead, called *San Carlone* (a monstrosity) stands outside Arona. His thumb is one metre (3ft) long. Walk up the steps inside the colossus and look through his Borromean eyes and earholes down to Lake Maggiore.

OUTINGS FROM LAKE MAGGIORE

MILAN

Not all trains on the Milan-Domodóssola line stop at Stresa, Baveno and Verbánia. The faster trains go to Milano Centrale station, stopping trains to Milano Porta Garibaldi (before the Centrale station, after Milano Certosa and Milano Bovisa), which is also quite central, on the MM2 underground line. (To get to the Duomo in Milan, go two stops east on the MM2 to Stazione Centrale, and then take the yellow MM3 line four stops south to piazza del Duomo.)

Stresa is about five minutes nearer to Milan, and Verbánia about five minutes further from Milan than Baveno. (The 7.11am commuter train from Baveno arrives at Milan Porta Garibaldi station at 8.48am). Check all times with the Stresa and Baveno tourist offices, who will photocopy timetables for you. A return train ticket from Baveno to Milan costs L11,600.

For more information on Milan, see page 56.

Moneysaver

Although most traders are honest, always count your change, however slowly, just in case someone is holding back a note. If you stand your ground, it will appear.

LESA AND MÉINA

Southwards, buses, trains and boats go to Belgirate, the pleasant old ports of Lesa and Méina (famous for the Villa Feraggina and its park). A bus leaves Baveno 12.55pm. Last bus back from Lesa leaves at 6.31pm (weekdays). From Lesa and Méina a road leads up into the mountains to Massimo Visconti, with remains of the old Visconti family castle, and at the end of the hill path San Salvatore, with a restaurant, views, and a

group of 13th-century monks' cells, some with their original frescoes.

LOCARNO AND DOMODÓSSOLA

For a day trip take the boat, hydrofoil (more expensive and faster), or ordinary ferry to Locarno. The hydrofoil, leaving Stresa at 10am Wednesday or Sunday, arrives at Locarno at 11.35am. The ordinary ferry leaves 11.50am, arrives at Locarno 2.35pm daily except Wednesday (food available on board). Book seats in advance, and remember to take your passport with you.

From Locarno, take the Vigezzo train across the mountains to Domodóssola along what is one of the finest short rail journeys in Europe. From Domodóssola return by train to Stresa (or Baveno or Verbánia). The 5.01pm train from Locarno arrives Domodóssola 6.48pm and leaves for Stresa at 7.17pm, arriving Stresa 7.47pm (for other times consult tourist offices). If you travel by boat check the times, they run less frequently in spring. This journey can be done in reverse. In April and May on Tuesdays, Thursday and Saturday a ferry runs from Locarno 4.30pm, arriving Stresa 6.50pm. From the end of May to the end of September the hydrofoil (booking compulsory) leaves Locarno 5.15pm, arriving at Stresa (only) 6.41pm.

WALKS IN THE HILLS

The mountainous area between Lake Maggiore and Lake Orta to the west is secret, wooded country with walks along paths smelling of privet, chestnuts and bracken, with small remote villages and occasional breathtaking views across the lake. The Baveno tourist office issues an essential guide and map for walkers, describing seven routes from $1\frac{1}{2}$ to $5\frac{1}{2}$ hours long. All the walks are signed in colour codes, but as the map supplied is rather sketchy it is better to get a detailed large-scale map. The paths go to the small lake-side village of Feriolo (also reached by bus); up Monte Camoscio; near the granite quarries in one direction and the alpine gardens and Gignese in the other; following mule tracks across alpine meadows past ruins of mountain huts (*cambretto*), with running water inside where farmers kept their cheese and butter cool in summer. A week's walking here is an attractive prospect but in the summer's heat requires careful timing and a supply of water.

Local flavour
Near Gignese is the Pope's Stone, a glacier-deposited single stone, 1,540 cubic metres (55,000 cubic ft) and weighing about 8,500 tons (8,636 tonnes), which is described as an 'erratic monolith'.

Just up the hill from the public park in Baveno, Oltrefiume is a curious old village to explore, with unexpectedly grand granite archways. Granite workers lived here in the 19th century when 1,000 people worked in the quarries. Follow via M Grappa and via Due Riviere to Romanico; its village festival is held on 19 March. Roncaro is a picturesque little village with a little porched church and panoramic views, and holds its festival 15 September.

The highest hamlet, on the edge of woods is Lóita, with a festival on 8 August.

Local flavour
Typical Piedmont local meat is donkey – *tapulon* is minced donkey in red wine; *stu' a' d' asnin cünt la pulenta* is lake country language for stewed donkey with polenta, and pretty unappetising it sounds too. If you want to avoid eating donkey, the word is *asino*.

Moneysaver
For thirst-quenching, note the difference – at the station bar, a large litre bottle of *acqua minerale* plus plastic mug is L1,650; one tiny bottle (a small glass full) of pear juice (*succo di pera*) costs L1,700.

GIGNESE

A small village on the hill behind Stresa, Gignese is a two-hour walk from the Alpinia garden and the Alpino cable-car stop, on the bus route to Orta. An 11am bus leaves Stresa on Fridays from the far left side of the embarkation square (facing the lake), 12.05 daily, returning 2.09pm weekdays, or 4.50pm daily (L3,200 return). The bus stops round the corner from the Tea Bar in Gignese (L1,700 to sit outside under umbrellas with two glasses of wine and eat a picnic lunch). Walk up to the church. Gignese is famous for its little umbrella museum – more lacy parasols than rain-proof umbrellas, a tribute and history to all the umbrella makers who lived around here, and then left to make and sell umbrellas all over Italy. It's not worth a special trip to see, but interesting, and would combine with a hill walk. Open 10am-12 noon and 2-6pm, closed Mondays. L2,500, children L1,000. Curious items include a 19th-century silk and ostrich feather, and tiny little black lace parasols with sword and parrot handles; one is made of horsehair. It was only in the 1890s that parasols turned into *parapioggia* against the rain. Note for linguists – pick up a leaflet on the umbrella-makers' own curious dialect.

LAKE MERGOZZO

This little lake, picturesquely set at the mouth of the Val d'Ossola, was once joined to Lake Maggiore. There is good (unpolluted) swimming and windsurfing here, and, though it is popular with locals, it is off the tourist track. The valley narrows here enclosing the small town, and Mount Órfano looms up behind it.

Lake Mergozzo – picturesquely set at the mouth of the Val d'Ossola

There's a 10-minute walk from the station: from the station turn right on to the main road, then first left down the *strada vecchia* to avoid the traffic, down to the front and turn left along the lake's edge for the usual small gravelly bathing place in a romantic setting.

Trains to Mergozzo leave Stresa 10.53am and 3.09pm (with stops at Baveno at 10.57am and 3.15pm), arriving at Mergozzo at 11.06am and 3.29pm. L1,200 return. Returning trains leave Mergozzo at 12.44, 2.38, 5.03, 6.36 and 7.33pm.

LAVENO

Frequent boats cross from Intra to the Lombardy side of the lake and Laveno. Take the *funivia* (an open two-person bucket) the 959 metres (3,144ft) up the Sasso del Ferro for a view across to Monte Rosa and the lake. (The grass swathe cut below the cable lines is a haven for butterflies.) From the station there's a half-hour walk up to the summit at 1,062 metres (3,482ft). *Funivia*, telephone 0323/668012. There is a restaurant near the top of the lift. Intrepid people hang-glide down from here.

MOTTARONE

A conventional cable car goes from Stresa Lido (on the road towards Baveno) up to the top of Mottarone (1,491 metres, 4,889ft), stopping halfway at Alpino. A winter sports centre, there are walks all over the mountain in summer. From the Alpino stop, a short walk along the hillside brings you to the Alpinia garden – an alpine garden (free) with wonderful views but disappointingly few flowers. Open April to October 9.30am-6.30pm, shut Mondays. From the summit of Mottarone on a very clear day it is possible to see the spires of Milan Cathedral, the Jungfrau in Switzerland, and seven lakes.

Mottarone Park is open all year; for information telephone 0323/20432.

The *funivia* runs every 30 minutes from 9am-12 noon and 1.30-5pm, returning from Mottarone, 9.10am-12.10pm and 1.50-5.10pm. The return fare to Mottarone is L12,000, children L7,000. Return fare to Alpino L6,000, children L4,000. For information telephone 0323/30295.

Contact the Italian Alpine Club for information on refuges on mountain trails providing basic accommodation and sometimes food at an average cost of L10,000 per night (more in winter). Club Alpino Italiano, via Ugo Foscolo 3, Milano. Telephone 02/802554.

Save going to the top of Mottarone for a beautiful clear day when you can see far away beyond the lake.

Located at the top of the cable car, small hotel with restaurant, only open at Christmas, Easter, and July 15 through August.
Case della Neve Telephone 0323/923516. Double L40,000.
Eden Telephone 0323/924873. Double L33,000 without bath.
Miramonti Frazione Mottarone, Stresa. Telephone 0323/924822. Double L50,000.

PALLANZA

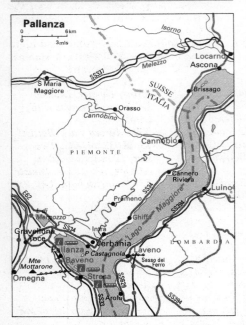

Down by the lakeside in Pallanza the avenues of standard pink and white oleanders, huge magnolia grandiflora and grassy lawns with flower beds are backed by elegant yellow and cream hotels. You can sit in comparative peace here by the lake edge. There's a good bar by the embarkation point. (Get key at the bar for the lavatory along the front). Pay L4,000 for a couple of cappuccinos, with a view up to Monte Rosa covered in snow, and a curious sweeping boat which trawls past with a giant's shrimping net to catch leaves.

and plastic bags.

The island almost joined up at the point is the Isolino di San Giovanni, with its 17th-century palace, private home of the Borromeo family (now a summer retreat of Prince Borromeo) where the conductor Arturo Toscanini lived.

Nerini (blue) buses connect Baveno and Stresa with Pallanza. The 10.35am from Stresa (five minutes later from Baveno) arrives in Pallanza at 10.55am. The last bus back from Pallanza is at 5.35pm. From Pallanza half-hourly Aspan buses go to Omegna on Lake Orta. Ísola Madre is the nearest island to Pallanza (L2,100).

Places to visit in Pallanza include the Romanesque Church of San Remigio with 15th-century frescoes (beyond the Castagnola headland). The Paesaggio (Landscape) Museum (open 9am-12 noon and 3-5pm daily, shut Mondays, telephone 0323/502418), and Palazzo Dugnani in piazza Cavour, the museum of peasant costume.

Villa Táranto, on the Castagnola promontory, has 16 hectares (39½ acres) of gardens with 7km (4⅓ miles) of avenues, terrace gardens, lotus pools, unique and rare plants, dahlia gardens (300 varieties), camellia and azalea avenues and innumerable botanical treasures. The garden was created by a Scotsman, Captain Neil McEacharn, member of the Queen's Bodyguard in Scotland, a descendant of Marshal McDonald whom Napoleon created Duke of Táranto, and after whom this garden is named. Captain McEacharn died in 1964 (he is buried in the garden) and gave it to the Italian state. A must for garden lovers; open 1 April to 31 October 8.30am-7.30pm. L6,000, children 6-14 L5,000.

Northwards from Pallanza by bus or car, visit Ghiffa, a little resort clustering round the Castello di Frino (the best view of the lake is from here); Cánnero, with its two castles on islets a short distance from the shore, little harbour, good beach, and gorge, the Torrento Cánnero, rushing under an old bridge; and Cannóbio, industrial town and resort, its old town full of arches, old stone houses and among its churches, the ornate Church of Madonna della Pietà. By boat, the 9.40am and 2.15pm from Intra calls in at all three towns.

Inland, follow the panoramic road up to Premeno (808 metres, 2,649ft), a summer holiday and winter sports centre.

ORIENTATION IN PALLANZA

INFORMATION
TOURIST OFFICE
Corso Zanitello 8. ☎ *0323/ 53249. Open Monday to Saturday 9am-12.30pm and 3-6pm, Sunday 9am-12 noon.*
POSTAL CODE
28048. Verbánia – Intra 28044.
TELEPHONE CODE
0323 (as Stresa).

ACCOMMODATION
Villa Azalea via Salita San Remigio 4. A walk up from the lakeside, but worth it. ☎ *0323/556692. Garden. Two-star, no restaurant. Top floors with lake view. Double L61,000 with bath, breakfast L4,500. Open Easter to end of October.*
Bella Pallanza via Manzoni 12, central. ☎ *0323/506332. Double bed and breakfast L50,000 with bath, L45,000 without. One-star, good*
restaurant. Basic rooms.
Belvedere viale Magnolie 6, on the lake, by ferry stop. Three-star, 52 rooms, all with bath. ☎ *0323/503202, fax 504466. Double L82,400.*
Italia viale Magnolie 10 central, near the lake. ☎ *0323/503206. Two-star, 14 rooms. Open March to October. Double L65,000 with bath. No restaurant.*
Novara via Garibaldi 30, central, near lake. ☎ *0323/ 503527. One-star, open March to mid November. Bed and breakfast per person L27,000-L31,000. Double half board L39,000-L45,000.*
Villa Petronio via Crocetta 26. ☎ *0323/556015. One-star, eight rooms. No private baths. Garden, restaurant. Double L37,000.*
VERBÁNIA – LUTRA
Il Chiostro via dei Ceretti. ☎ *0323/53151, fax 41231. Three-star, 20 rooms in*
former cloister. Double L82,400. All rooms with bath.
Villa Aurora via C Battisti 15. ☎ *0323/41482. Two-star, 12 rooms. Garden, parking, restaurant. Double L65,900 with bath, L49,400 without.*

SHOPPING
Biggest and best markets are the all-day ones in Luino, Omegna and Intra.
Sunday – Cannóbio 8am-1pm.
Monday – Baveno 8am-1pm, via 17 Martiri, above the station.
Tuesday – Laveno 9am-12pm.
Wednesday – Luino 9am-5pm.
Thursday – Omegna, on Lake Orta 7am-3pm.
Friday – Cánnero 8am-12 noon. Pallanza 8am-12 noon. Stresa, piazza Cadorna, 8am-1pm.
Saturday – Intra 8am-5pm.

LAKE ORTA

Lake Orta is a small lake only 12 miles long, surrounded by wooded hills, with the sizeable commercial town of Omegna at its northern end. Its most famous small town of Orta San Giúlio is about a third of the way up the eastern shore, with the island of San Giúlio opposite.

One bus a day (12.30pm) leaves Stresa for Orta, giving you a couple of hours to see the town of Orta San Giúlio, the island and the lake, before returning at 3.45pm (July 1 to end of August – ask at other times). Return

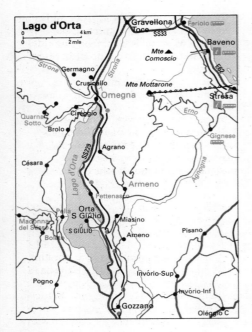

Lago d'Orta

town with painted buildings (including the Palazzo Comunale, 1582, in the square) and interesting nooks and crannies. It is also quite touristy. L2,000 will take you to the island opposite, or L4,000 for a lake trip.

bus fare L5,000. An excursion bus leaves at 2pm for Orta, going along the lake to Arona, returning at 6pm (L21,000).

The bus winds over the hills via Gignese and Armeno, among remote wooded valleys where a few tiny stone farmsteads stand in alpine pastures. Truffles grow here under the chestnut trees, and beehives are set among the robinia (false acacia) which grows everywhere at the edge of the chestnut woods and along the roads. Orta San Giúlia is a pretty

Orta S Giúlio, the main piazza from where you can survey the island of San Giúlio

On Ísola San Giúlio, the Basilica was built in the 9th century on the site of San Giúlio's cell and contains a black pulpit, three carved lecterns and walnut choir stalls. Next to it, the 14th-century Palazzo dei Vescovi is now a Benedictine monastery. Every inch of the island is built over with arcaded houses and little alleys. It can seem magical depending on the light, time of day, if the island floats on mist or just sits in the water looking overbuilt and prosaic. (As on the Borromean islands, the windows on many of the buildings are small.)

In the piazza Motta, where the boats come and go, sit and survey the island, and wander over to the Casa Morgarani, the 'House of Dwarves', another frescoed building.

Up in the hills beyond Orta San Giúlio, walk up through the beech and pine woods to

48

Sacro Monte, dedicated to St Francis of Assisi, with 21 frescoed chapels (mostly built in the 17th century), and 376 lifesize terracotta statues (numbers 11 and 16 are supposed to be best, and there is a view from 15).

> **Local flavour**
> The German philosopher Friedrich Nietzsche came to Orta in 1882 and climbed the Sacro Monte with the Russian poet Lou Salome, declaring his love for her there 'where the nightingales sing'. To no avail; she rejected him. Nietzsche, utterly dashed, sat down to write, *Thus Spake Zarathustra*, dating it 'von Orta an' – from Orta onwards. . .

Events and festivals you might like to see in Orta San Giúlio are:
January 31 Feast of San Giúlio, with a boat procession on the lake.
End of April – first week in May Ortafiori, flower festival.
June Festival Cusiano di Musica Antica.
Last week of August Feast of San Vito. Firework displays at Omegna.
There is more to Orta than Orta San Giúlio and the island, but you need a car to

> **Local flavour**
> For the best view of the whole lake go to the Punta di Crabbia, a small headland past the pretty lake village of Pettenasco.

explore the lake edge. Omegna, the industrial town on the north point, can be reached by Aspan bus every half hour (30-minute ride) from Pallanza. (Excursions run from Stresa on market day.)

> **Local flavour**
> A curiosity is the little river Nigoglia which joins the lake to the Strona river and runs north – the only river that runs *towards* the Alps. Omegna people are proud of their independent river; it suits them.

Omegna's old town has balconied houses, wrought-iron work, and a view of almost the whole lake. Quarna Sotto (with a museum of musical instruments) and Quarna Sopra lie westwards up in the hills among chestnut woods. Further south by the lake, Pella has a medieval tower and an old bridge over the Torrente Pellino, and galleried houses. Above Pella, Madonna del Sasso is worth seeing – a group of hamlets and a church with frescoes on a rock above Boleto village.

> **Local flavour**
> Comparative temperatures show Lake Orta is the warmest lake.
>
> | | May | Jun | Jul | Aug | Sep |
> |---|---|---|---|---|---|
> | Maggiore | 64 | 70 | 78 | 80 | 69 |
> | Orta | 68 | 72 | 80 | 82 | 76 |
> | Como | 68 | 70 | 78 | 80 | 70 |
> | Garda | 66 | 74 | 80 | 80 | 72 |

ORIENTATION IN LAKE ORTA

ACCOMMODATION
ORTA SAN GIÚLIO
Antica Agnello *piazzetta Regazzoni.* ☎ *0322/90259. One-star, double L37,000, no private bathrooms. Good restaurant.*
Leon d'Oro *in the centre.*

☎ *0322/90254. Three-star, beach and parking. Double L75,000 with bath.*
Ristoro Olina *via Olina 40.* ☎ *0322/905656. Closed November to mid December. Restaurant closed Tuesday. Just a few rooms with bath and view. Double L60,000, with breakfast L70,000.*
MIASINO
Albergo Bellavista ☎ *0322/*

980053. Two-star, garden, all rooms with bath. Double L55,000.
PETENNASCO
Hotel Giardinetto *via Provinciale.* ☎ *0323/89118. Three-star, pool and beach, all rooms with bath or shower. Double L65,000-L78,000 with breakfast. Restaurant meals L40,000. Open April to October.*

MADONNA DEL SASSO BOLETO, ABOVE PELLA
Panoramico ☎ *0322/981109.*
One-star, seven rooms. View

of lake. Double L40,000
with bath.
QUARNA SOPRA, ABOVE OMEGNA

Belvedere ☎ *0323/826197.*
Lake views. Two-star, all
rooms double with bath
L40,000.

LAKE COMO

BUDGET FOR A DAY

Bus return ticket - COMO to BELLÁGIO	5,700
Tour of Villa Serbelloni (approx. price)	4,000
Lunch - fresh trout, wine	15,000
Buy silk tie for present	24,000
Evening meal	8,000
	L56,700

plus accommodation

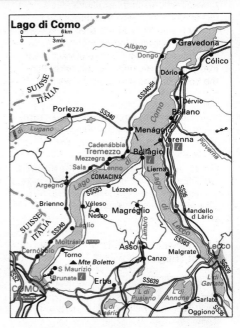

Fifty kilometres (31 miles) long, but only 4.4km (2¾ miles) wide at its widest point, Como is one of the deepest lakes in Europe (410 metres, 1,344ft).

Narrow, high-sided, wooded, wild and tame, with villas and gardens sweeping to the shore, Como was a favourite haunt of 19th-century romantic musicians yearning for inspiration – Verdi, Bellini, Liszt, Rossini all were here. And the English romantic poets Shelley and Wordsworth wandered these hills and shores too. The impressionable French writer Stendhal was here as well (he who nearly expired in Florence through excitement), going once more over the top, finding Como 'the most beautiful place in the world'. The British don't come to these lakes as much as they used, but as always, rich Milanese use it as their summer playground. Como is only a 40-minute train ride from Milan.

The lake was named Lacus Larius by the Romans, and it is still sometimes referred to as Lago Lario. Shaped like an inverted Y, the south-eastern arm, going past the town of Lecco, is known as Lago Lecco. Along the shores are many exuberant and luxuriant gardens, a few open to the public, while there are walks (some really stiff climbs) up into the mountains to the west and into the

central highland between the two southern arms of the lake. A cable car will do some of the work, taking you from Como town up to Brunate, where tracks lead up into the mountains.

COMO

Como town is a bustling small city full of speeding traffic. But it also has charm, with open squares, yellow shuttered buildings, flower gardens, yachts riding at anchor, and an air of sophistication, of wealth and pleasure, of having been a smart resort.

The train station is near the centre. Walk down via Gallio and via Garibaldi to piazza

*The Broletto 13th-century law court of black,
pink-and-white striped marble*

Cavour near the waterfront (the tourist
office is here). Buses leave from round the
corner, in piazza Matteotti, for Varese,
Bellágio etc.

Hotels in Como are rather a disappointment. There are no charming cheap hotels
with a view up the lake. However, there are a
couple conveniently in the centre of town,
where you can lodge reasonably comfortably
as a base for excursions. The information
office is very helpful, with lots of leaflets and
plenty of (English) advice.

Piazza Cavour, near the lake, with the
ferry landing, is the busy centre. Walking left
along the lake side, is the Giardini Pubblici,
with the Tempio Voltiano and scientific
Volta museum recalling Alessandro Volta,
native of Como – volts are his namesake.
Three kilometres (2 miles) along the lake, the
Villa Olmo, with its large formal garden, is
open to view.

In the centre of town, don't miss the black,
pink-and-white striped marble Broletto
(13th-century law court), or the Torre del
Commune in the Piazza Duomo. The

Duomo itself is a wonderful mixture of
Gothic (the west front) and Renaissance
architecture and art; the Rodari brothers
(Tommaso and Iacopo) embellished the
doors (late 15th-century). The Plinys, Elder
and Younger, are upstanding there, looking
saintly. Inside are Romanesque lions and
16th-century tapestries.

Along via Vittorio Emanuele, right and
then left, is piazza San Fedele, once a corn
market, its pillared houses dating back to the
15th century. The church is 12th century.
Near by is the civic museum, and down via
Giovio is the 12th-century Porta Vittoria.
Not far from here see the basilica of Sant'
Abbondio, the work of an earlier group of
the same Maestri Comacini who built San
Fedele.

Local folklore relates the fishermen's tale
that 9 kilo (20lb) trout can be caught in the
lake.

ORIENTATION IN COMO

INFORMATION

TOURIST OFFICE
Piazza Cavour 17. ☎ *031/ 262091 and 031/274064. Hotel information and boat timetables. English spoken. Open Monday to Saturday 9.30am-12.30pm and 2.30-6pm. They also exchange money here.*

POST OFFICE
Via T Gallio 4. Open Monday to Friday 8.30am-8pm, Saturday 8.15am-1pm. Postal code 22100.

TELEPHONE
SIP, via Bianchi-Giovini 41, off piazza Cavour. Open daily 8am-9.40pm. Telephone code 031.

POLICE
Viale Roosevelt 7. ☎ *031/272366.*

TRANSPORT

TRAINS
Principal station is San Giovanni, with frequent trains to Milano Centrale and Porta Garibaldi. (About 40 minutes, L4,000 return.) Another station, the Como Lago, on via Manzoni, off lungo Lario Trieste, only serves trains to Milano Nord (half hourly, takes an hour).

BUSES
Buses leave from near piazza Matteotti, along lungo Lario Trieste. Bellágio (L3,000 single, one hour) buses go to Cadenábbia, Menággio etc.

BOATS
*Leave from the lungo Lario Trieste, in front of piazza Cavour. Como to Bellágio L6,600 single.
Summer ferry excursions from Como, 17 June to 30 September:
To Argegno, including a trip on the funivia, with views over the Val d'Intelvi and the lake. Daily, L11,300 return.
To Ísola Comacina, Como's only island, almost uninhabited. Daily, L11,000 return.*

BICYCLE HIRE
On the lungo Lario Trieste, between bus station and piazza Cavour. March to September. 9am-12 noon and 2-6pm. L3,000 per hour, L10,000 per day.

ACCOMMODATION

All in the centre of town – no lake views.
Canova *via Gallio 5.* ☎ *031/ 273485. Double L50,000 with bath, L33,000 without. No restaurant, 13 rooms.*

Fontana *via D Fontana 19.* ☎ *031/263266. Restaurant. Two-star, 8 rooms. Modern furniture. Double L65,000 with bath, L48,000 without. One suite L90,000.*

Posta *via Garibaldi 2.* ☎ *031/266012. Two-star, 17 rooms. Newly decorated, all rooms with bath. Restaurant, terrace. Double L74,000.*

Protezione della Giovane *via Borgo Vico 182.* ☎ *031/ 558449. Take bus 1, 2 or 6. Basic, rather shabby rooms, women only. L7,000 per person. Meals 12.30 and 7pm. L13,000.*

Teatro Sociale *via Maestri Comacini 8.* ☎ *031/264042. One-star, six basic rooms above the restaurant in the arcade near the Duomo. Double L52,000 with bath, L33,000 without.*

EATING OUT

Ristorante Sant' Antonio *via Coloniola 10.* ☎ *031/ 262042. Not so much a restaurant, more a trattoria. Meal about L16,000. Open 11am-3pm and 6-11pm, shut Fridays.*

Taverna Messicana *piazza Mazzini 5.* ☎ *031/262463. All kinds of pizzas, L3,500 to L12,000.*

BRUNATE

Como is very proud of its cable car – new in 1989 with a capacity for 80 passengers, it takes a precise six minutes, 30 seconds, so they say. The service operates every half hour, leaving at the same time from Como and Brunate, 9am, 9.30 etc, but varying times at midday and from 4–5pm. It leaves from piazza de Gasperi, along the lake front past piazza Matteotti (telephone 031/269311). There are many walks from Brunate (the tourist office has a map). One footpath goes from the end of the lane through San Maurízio to the summit of Monte Boletto, 1,237 metres (4,055ft). There are wonderful views right over to Monte Rosa and Milan.

It is 2½km (1¾ miles) from Brunate to San Maurízio (871 metres, 2,856ft). The footpath to Monte Boletto (1,234 metres, 4,046ft) takes a good two hours; there is serious hiking up here.

Up in the hills above Brunate, several *baite* (*baita* = shepherd's alpine hut) are in fact eating places with a few rooms to let. Always telephone in advance to check on rooms. The usual charge is L25,000 per person for bed and breakfast. Baita Bondella (telephone 031/220307) has meals and rooms

and is open at weekends and all of August. To book, Tuesday to Friday, telephone 031/263304. It is 1,100 metres (3,606ft) up. Baita Carla, at S Maurízio, is a restaurant and hotel with views of lake. Specialities include polenta and mushrooms, closed Tuesdays (telephone 031/220186). A short distance from the top of Mount Boletto, Baita Fabrizio has good local cooking and has views both to the lake and towards the hills of Brianza. Telephone 031/220235, closed Fridays,

---

ORIENTATION IN BRUNATE

ACCOMMODATION ·
These are one-star, small inexpensive hotels, mostly without private baths, all with hot water in

bedrooms.
Bellavista ☎ *031/220260.*
12 rooms (one with bathroom, one with shower). Garden, restaurant. Double L32,000.
Capanna Cao ☎ *031/220264. Nine rooms (two with bathrooms, one with shower). Restaurant.*

Double L30,000-L36,000.
Del Moro ☎ *031/221003. Four rooms (one with bathroom, one with shower). Restaurant. Double L33,000.*
Milanino ☎ *031/221022. Six rooms, three with showers. Double L33,500, L45,000 with shower.*

VILLAS NEAR COMO

There are a number of worthwhile possible excursions to villas on the west shore, north of Como.

At Moltrásio is the Villa Passalacqua, an 18th-century palace, and nearby Villa Satterio, where the composer Vincenzo Bellini stayed in 1831 while he composed the opera *Norma*. It is open to the public on Tuesdays from May to October. There are fine walks in the woods and near the gorge; Santa Ágata has a Romanesque church.

Láglio, a walk of about 1½ hours, goes up to the Bear's Den, where bear bones have been excavated.

Ísola Comacina, Como's only island, is reached by ferry from nearby Sala, Ospedaletto or Spurano.

Around midsummer day, 24 June, St John's day, there are spectacular celebrations round the tiny island, less than a kilometre (half a mile) long and 366 metres (400yds) wide. On the Saturday following there are fireworks, on Sunday a procession

of priests and parade of boats round the island, and a special Mass in the ruins of Santa Eufemia, and afterwards a huge fair.

Northwards, at Lenno, the Tremezzina or Azalean Riviera begins, with luxuriant orange groves, lemons, olives, magnolias and azaleas growing. The Younger Pliny had a villa here, where he said you could 'fish from your bed'. The Villa Balbianello has

---

Local flavour

Silk is still one of Como's principal industries, though nowadays they also weave Chinese yarn. Lombardy has always been famous for silk – avenues of white mulberries grow on the plains, introduced by Lodovico Sforza (Il Moro). South of Lecco at Garlate, the Abegg silk mill is a silk museum (open first Sunday of each month, or enquire at Garlate's municipio). At Abbadia Lariana, another silk museum is due to open in 1991 in the Monti mill, with weaving demonstrations.

---

panoramic views and a fine garden. Between Tremezzo and Cadenábbia, the Villa Carlotta is the most visited villa on Como; built for the Clerici family in 1747, it was given to Princess Charlotte of Prussia when she married the Prince of Saxe-Meinigen. The villa has elaborately plastered and decorated ceilings, a famous marble table, and sculptures including works by Canova (his *Cupid and Psyche* is a copy). The garden includes 150 species of rhododendron and azalea, so April and May are the months to come. Open March and October 9am-12 noon and 2-4.30pm, and April to September 9am-6pm.

Up the hill from Cadenábbia is a 305-metre (1,000ft) walk up to a little chapel, San Martino, (for keen walkers) where goats scramble about with tinkling bells, and there's a picnic table and a view. From here you can walk along the ridge on a well shaded track.

In Cernóbbio, a big town with a beach, and the most famous villa on the lake is the Villa D'Este, now a hotel. You can stay for 10 nights at the two-star Terzo Crotto, via Volta 21 (telephone 031/512304, a double room with bath L53,000), for the price of one night at the Grande Hotel Villa d' Este. It

was built in 1557 for Cardinal Tolomeo Gallio, once the son of a local fisherman, who had another seven villas built for him along the road to Rome. It has a remarkable garden.

BELLÁGIO

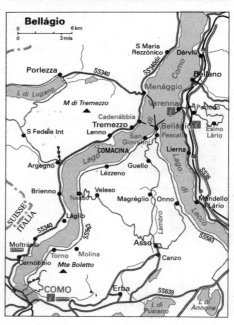

Bellágio lies just behind the headland where the lake forks, an area called the Punta Spartivento – the point that divides the wind. No one comes to Bellágio by chance because the road ends here. People come because of its position, its views and its quietness, despite being a tourist centre.

Not only is it exceptionally pretty, but there are some reasonable lodgings here as

well (the Spiaggia, the Roma). Ferries shuttle
to and fro connecting Bellágio with Menággio, Varenna and Cadenábbia, so plenty of
other towns and walks are easy to get to.

Take the bus from Como (L3,000 single)
for a bumpy, twisting scenic drive among the
woods, winding through small villages with
occasional glimpses to the lake. The road
takes a right angle bend at Torno (wonderful
view north), the interesting old town of San
Giovanni with a church worth seeing, past
Molina and a waterfall, on to Nesso with its
castle and gorge, the Torrento Nesso. A road
from here leads up to the Piano del Tivano
and the winter sports area of the High
Brianza. Our road leads on to Lézzone (more
views, and a lake cave, the Buco dei Carpi,
reached only by boat) and, just before
Bellágio, the Villa Melzi d'Eryl, a neo-
classical villa with gardens, open April to
October 9am–6pm.

Go over the promontory by bus, or walk,
to the Villa Serbelloni, now belonging to the

*One of the pleasures of a holiday in the Lakes,
eating out overlooking the water and hills*

Rockefeller Foundation and restored, the
garden (terrace, formal Italian) is open to
view. Two-hour guided tours are available
from April to October, Tuesday to Sunday
10am-4pm – not cheap, but proceeds go to
charity. The villa is reputed to have been
built on the site of Pliny's villa 'Tragedia'.

From the villa follow a walled path down
to the other side of the tongue of land, to
Pescallo, where you can sit and eat fresh
trout not too expensively (L10,000) in a
restaurant shaded by vines. The Miralago in
Pescallo lets rooms (double L45,000).

Enquire at the tourist office, the gardens of
the nearby villas of Balzaretti, Trotti and
Giulia may be open to the public.

ORIENTATION IN BELLÁGIO

INFORMATION
TOURIST OFFICE
Lungolago A Manzoni.
☎ *031/950201.*

ACCOMMODATION
Du Lac piazza Manzini 32.
☎ *031/950320, telex 326299
DU LAC. Three-star, 47
rooms. Roof terrace,
restaurant. All rooms with*
bath. Open 1 April to 14
October. Double
L75,000-L84,000.
Excelsior Splendide ☎ *031/
950225. Swimming pool
(opens May), 47 rooms.
Open March to October.
Some cheaper attic rooms,
restaurant. Double
L65,000-L80,000.*
*Fiorini Up in the hills, 20-
minute walk from the town
centre.* ☎ *031/950392. Two-
star, 14 rooms. Restaurant,
bicycle hire, sports centre*
with swimming near by.
Double L50,000-L65,000.
Roma In centre. ☎ *031/
950424. Basic and rather
shabby, good views and
balconies on top floors.
Restaurant. Open April to
October. L45,000-L56,000
with bath, L32,000–L37,000
without, breakfast L5,000.*
La Spiggia Near the lake.
☎ *031/950313. One-star,
eight rooms, none with
private bath. Double
L33,000.*

VARENNA

Varenna has the most lovely gardens and views. The villa Monastero, once a Cistercian convent, was suppressed by San Carlo Borromeo because of the scandalous behaviour of its nuns. It is now a conference centre for astrophysicists, open 10am-12 noon and 3-6pm April to November, L1,500. On the hill above the town (15 minutes' walk) are the ruins of good queen Theodolinda's castle (Queen of the Lombards, she died early in the 7th century).

Local flavour
G Pirelli, of tyre fame, was born in Varenna.

Also see the Villa Cipressi on via 4 Novembre, with views across the lake to Bellágio from its terraced gardens, and the Museo civico Ornitologico 'L Scanagatta', a bird museum showing hundreds of species which come down to Lake Como on their annual migrations.

From Varenna, buses follow the river Esino to Perledo, about 3km (2 miles) along and up 409 metres (1,342ft), and to Esino, higher up. From here long climbs lead up to Cainallo. More demanding and mountainous tracks lead right up to the Monza Refuge at nearly 1,830 metres (6,000ft). Quarries near here produce black and green shell marble. For enquiries to the tourist office in Varenna, telephone 0341/830367.

Local flavour
Near by is the Fiumelatte, a milk-white foaming river which crashes down from its cavern at the end of March and stops suddenly at the end of October. Leonardo da Vinci is known to have studied it, and possibly used its surroundings for his painting the *Virgin of the Rocks* (in the National Gallery in London).

MILAN

Although Rome is Italy's capital, Milan is its first commercial, industrial and banking city. Badly bombed in 1943, with much of its centre destroyed, Milan was rebuilt in modern style.

Architecturally it is not a very uplifting city, though some of the streets and squares are grand and impressive, and some of the old palazzos (now very often banks) still remain. It was a free commune until the 13th century, when first the Visconti family, and then the Sforzas took power and ruled Milan, bringing great riches and patronising great artists, like Leonardo da Vinci and Bramante, until the end of the 15th century. Nowadays industry has brought wealth and smog to the city (really clear days are rare in Milan), but it is an exciting, fashionable and prosperous city; the art is great, the food is good, the shops are fantastic, and it's a powerhouse of Italian design and invention.

Local flavour
The word milliner first meant a native of Milan and 'vendor of fancy wares and articles of apparel'. That was in 1529.

If you only have one sightseeing day and are mainly interested in art, go to the Brera Gallery, the nearby Poldi Pezzoli, and to Leonardo's *Last Supper* (take the MM – Metropolitana – or bus). If you have time return to the station via the Castello Sforzesco to see a *Pietà* by Michelangelo. These are basic essentials, and enough to take in in one day, but there are many other museums and churches.

If you are more interested in music and fashion, then look at the shops in the Galleria Vittorio Emanuele, the Scala Opera House which, though bombed and rebuilt, still has an aura of glamour and luxury as one of the most famous opera houses in the world. Not far away, window-shop at via Montenapoleone, Sant' Andrea and della Spiga for high fashion, and to actually buy, go to via Torino or corso Buenos Aires (see *Shopping*).

Local flavour

Don't expect shopkeepers and restaurateurs to fall over themselves with pleasure at serving you in Milan. It is not Italy's most polite city.

Moneysaver

Stylish Milan supermarkets and chain stores for affordable clothes include La Rinascente in piazza Duomo (open all day); Coin, on corso Vercelli, and piazza Loreto; also in the piazza, La Standa.

Most of the essential sights of the city are within walking distance of the Duomo, which is at the centre of a web of streets which spreads to an inner circle, and then an outer circle of roads. These follow the line of filled-in canals. One remains, the Naviglio Grande with its basin south of the Duomo along viale D'Annunzio (MM2 Porta Genova), the old port area with markets and artists' workshops where the old warehouses used to be (there are boat trips and bike rides along the canal). The canal goes westwards, past elegant Milanese villas.

Milan has a very useful underground, the Metropolitana (the MM) with three lines. The Red Line 1 comes southwards to the east of the Central train station, connecting the public gardens, corso Venézia (the good shopping area) with the Duomo, and then turns west towards Sforza Castle. The Green Line 2 connects Stazione Centrale (Central station), the Porta Garibaldi station, crossing the Red Line near the Sforza Castle and corso Magenta (near the Santa Maria della Grazie). The Yellow Line 3 comes south

from Central station to piazza Cavour and then piazza Duomo. It costs L800 for one ride or for 75 minutes by bus. An all-day pass (L3,200) valid on all public transport can be bought at the Duomo and Stazione Centrale stations (ATM office). Most of the important sights are contained within the central ring of the city, in walking distance with a litle help from the MM.

Local flavour

The Metropolitana is generally clearly signed, but destination boards never mention the station you are actually in. The first name on the bottom of the list will be your next station.

Local flavour

Useful buses and trams: from Central train station, tram 1 to piazza Scala. Tram 33 to Porta Garibaldi station. Bus 60 to piazza Duomo and Castello Sforzesco. Bus 65 goes down corso Buenos Aires. From piazza Cavour (near the public garden) bus 96/97 goes to Castello Sforzesco and near Santa Maria delle Grazie and Sant' Ambrogio.

Don't drive into Milan if you can help it. Yellow Milan taxis with honest drivers can be hailed in the streets, or telephone 8585. They're not cheap; taxi prices start at L4,000, with a L4,000 supplement at night. Stands are located at piazza Scala, piazza del Duomo, and largo Cairoli near the Sforza Castle.

Local flavour

The writer HV Morton said this was the only city where you could give a taxi driver a picture as a destination. '*L' ultima cena, per favore.*' To *The Last Supper*, please.

To try and keep Milan traffic free, the town hires out bicycles for a small fee from yellow bicycle stands. You can rent a bicycle at piazza Castello, piazza Cardona, and corso Venezia in front of ACI office.

Pick up a town map from the tourist office, to the right of the Duomo as you face it. The piazzá Duomo is the best place to start a day's tour. (To go there take Yellow Line 3 of the MM from Central station). From here go up the covered Galleria V Emanuele (good place to sit and see the smart business world go by, but expensive – have a coffee at the least ostentatious bar you can find. L4,000 sitting down).

Galleria V Emanuele   The Galleria is sometimes called *Il Salotto* (the drawing room). The architect Giuseppe Mengoni slipped and fell to his death on his own marble floor here a few days before it opened in 1878. Milanesi step on the Bull's testicles in the central ring of mosaic figures under the big dome for good luck!

The Comune di Milano office at the far end is packed with information on cultural events. Milano d' Estate, mid June to mid August, sponsors various events. Outside the Galleria you are in the piazza Scala (statue of Leonardo), with La Scala in front of you, and going from there up via Verdi you will come into via Brera, with fascinating houses and shops (at no 16, look in at the Fornasetti shop). The Brera Gallery is on the right, at the end of this street. The Poldo Pozzoli gallery is on via Manzoni, leading off piazza Scala.

Walking down via Borgo Nuovo from behind the Brera towards via Manzoni, look through the archways to the gardens behind. At the Croce Rossa there are benches to sit on and a modern gold triangular fountain. You are now in the exclusive shopping area, with via Montenapoleone in front of you.

Setting out from the Duomo, walking south west along via Torino (or you can hop on bus 15), you can see the curious Church of San Satirò by Bramante, and have a look at several affordable boutiques and department stores.

The Duomo   The Duomo is the fourth largest church in the world after St Peter's Rome, Seville Cathedral and the new African cathedral. It's a church that is more amazing than likeable. To climb it go outside the north transept to the west side for 158 steps up (L2,000), or to the east side for the lift

(L4,000) plus 73 steps to the dome and 139 steps to the tower. The figure at the top, the *Madonnina*, is four metres (13ft) high and 107 metres (350ft) up. There's a wonderful view from up there on a clear day (pious hope) to the Matterhorn and the plains of Lombardy.

Milan Cathedral has 135 spires and 2,245 statues

The Gothic Duomo, begun in 1386, has been added to ever since – the last bronze door was fitted in 1965. On the outside it is embellished (or confused) by 2,245 statues, 135 little spires, and 96 gargoyles. Inside, the huge church has 52 columns and a capacity for 40,000, but it is usually almost empty. Don't miss the stained glass windows in the apse. Open daily 9am-5pm (cover your arms, and no shorts).

La Scala Theatre   La Scala Theatre was built 1776 and almost destroyed by bombs in 1943. It has been rebuilt, keeping the double hollow ceiling which provides its special accoustics. There used to be dances and fencing tournaments here, as well as gambling in the boxes in the old days.

The theatre is open for visits, enter through the theatre museum, the Museo alla Scala which is open Monday to Saturday 9am-12 noon and 2-6pm, Sunday 9.30am-12 noon and 2.30-8pm. Not open on Sundays October to April (L4,000). The museum has

an intriguing collection in pretty rooms – Verdi's piano, top hat, lock of hair, cast of his right hand; a desperate, black painting of Maria Callas; Eleanore Duse looking dramatic; Theatre Guignol; hand puppets; Meissen and Chelsea figurines; musical instruments; playbills.

La Scala opera season runs from December to early June; June and September there are ballet and concerts. The theatre closes mid July to the end of August. Front-row seats cost L180,000, gallery L15,000 and standing is L4,000. Unsold gallery seats and standing room are offered an hour before curtain time. Box office telephone 02/809126, Tuesday to Sunday 10am-1pm and 3.30-5.30pm. For information telephone 02/809160.

The Brera Art Gallery   The Pinacoteca di Brera (Brera Art Gallery) at via Brera 28 has a wonderful collection. Don't miss the Bonnard (*Woman in Hat*) on your right as you enter, and Marino Marini, and Giorgio Morandi among the modern artists. Among many extraordinary paintings – the dead Christ, *Christo Moro*, foreshortened, lying feet foremost, by Andrea Mantegna (room

18); Piero della Francesca's *Madonna and Child*, taken from Urbino, with hook-nosed Duke Federico di Montefeltro kneeling in armour; Raphael's flowing *Marriage of the Virgin* (room 22), painted when he was 22; a Bellini *Madonna*; *Supper at Emmaus* by Caravaggio. And afterwards – lunch at the bar on the térrace. For gallery information, telephone 02/808387. Open Tuesday to Saturday 9am-1.45pm, Sunday 9am-12.45pm. Closed Mondays. Times vary considerably; it might be open some afternoons. And various halls close for no apparent reason, possibly staff shortages. L4,000. (Transport, MM2 Lanza, bus 61). Free for EC members over 60, under 18.

Santa Maria della Grazie Santa Maria della Grazie, in the same-named piazza off corso Magenta, is a brick-built Gothic church with a choir and 16-sided dome designed by Bramante. Next to it, in the refectory (*cenacolo*), is Leonardo da Vinci's fresco the *Last Supper* (open every day 9am-1.15pm plus 2-6.15pm Tuesday to Saturday, transport MM1 and 2, Cadorna). Telephone 02/4987588. Bring change for L1,000 for the commentary (or read this and save your money), and binoculars if you have them, because you have to stand some way back.

The figures of the Apostles are in turmoil, talking, gesturing around the quiet figure of Christ. Judas is the dark figure, fourth from left, leaning forward on the table in front of Peter, talking to John. St Matthew is in profile, third from right. It is said to portray the moment Christ said, 'One of you will betray me'. According to Vasari, Leonardo left the figure of Christ deliberately unfinished, as he could not presume to do it justice. The *Last Supper* was painted 1495–1498 in tempera on a glue and plaster base on the coldest wall (so that the artist could take time and give more depth of tone than is usual in a fresco), it soon began to flake. At one point the monks cut a door through it, to pass food through. Then in 1943 the building was gutted by bombing, but both end walls had been protected and survived. Since 1978 specialists have been trying to remove all the layers of restoring and repainting. It remains only a shadow, but full of power – don't miss it. And spare a look at Donato Montorfano's fresco of the *Crucifixion* (1495) on the other end wall. L4,000 but free to nationals of European Community countries who are over 60 and under 18. (Reproduction cards cost L700).

Local flavour

While Leonardo was still alive, and the picture was obviously disintegrating, a full-size copy was made which is now in the Royal Academy in London, and this has been used as a reference by the Italian conservators working on the original. The copy is so huge and takes up so much valuable wall space that it is usually kept boarded up out of sight.

The Poldi Pezzoli Museum The Poldi Pezzoli Museum, via Manzoni 12, is a nobleman's outstanding collection displayed in a noble house (rebuilt after wartime bombing). There is a famous portrait by Pollaiolo, paintings by Botticelli, Piero della Francesca, Bellini, Guardi etc, and Islamic rugs, Merano glass, tapestries and bronzes. Telephone 02/794889. Open Tuesday to Sunday 9.30am-12.30pm and 2.30-6pm (7.30pm Saturday). Closed Sunday afternoon April to September. L4,000.

Originally built in the 14th century, most of the massive structure of Sforza Castle (Castello Sforzesco) has been rebuilt from 1450 onwards. The central Filarete Tower was struck by lightning in 1521, igniting the gunpowder stored inside and causing a big explosion. The castle fell into bad repair but was mostly restored from 1880 on – the Torre Umberto is a 1905 reproduction. Transport (subway) MM1, Cairoli, MM1 and 2, Cadorna.

The castle museums inside are free; Egyptian, prehistoric and Etruscan artefacts are in the basement, while the castle contains a mixed collection including sculpture, musical instruments and ceramics. It also includes the masterpiece by Michelangelo, the *Pietà*

Rondanini, a carving of long suffering (his last work, done when he was nearly 90). Open Tuesday to Sunday 9.30am-12.15pm and 2.30-5.15pm.

Moneysaver
Milan is packed with free museums – wax, ethnographic, an aquarium, a planetarium. Consult the free handout *Museums in Milan* for full details.

In the public gardens region, near piazza Cavour and via Palestro, is a mixed bag of free museums; the Natural History Museum, corso Venezia 55 (shut Mondays), home of the Madagascar aye-aye, the colossal European lobster and the 36kg (80lb) topaz, two million insects, 100,000 fossils, 30,000 birds and a life-size dinosaur.

The Modern Art Gallery and the Marino Marini Museum The Modern Art Gallery and the Marino Marini Museum, via Palestro 16, (shut Tuesdays). Transport (subway) MM1, Palestro. Open 9.30am-12 noon and 2.30-5.30pm. Italian and French painters, 19th and 20th century – Morandi, Modigliani, Picasso, Cezanne and Bonnard.

In the public gardens themselves there are children's amusements, a zoo, a lake, and an informal 'English' garden (as opposed to the formal Italian grass and statuary garden).

The Contemporary Art Museum The Contemporary Art Museum, which is in the Palazzo Reale in the piazza del Duomo, is also free and houses Italian Futurist painting and Modigliani, De Chirico and many modern Italian painters.

The Ambrosiana Art Gallery The Ambrosiana Art Gallery piazza Pio XI 2, contains more outstanding paintings – Botticelli, Leonardo, Raphael, Caravaggio,

---

Local flavour
Il Giornale Nuovo newspaper lists all restaurants and shops still open during the great August shutdown.

Breughel, Titian. Telephone 02/800146. Transport (subway) MM1, Cordusio or Duomo. Open Sunday to Friday 9.30am-5pm. L4,000, L3,000 on Sundays. (Along via Torino, take via Spadari, then right to via Cantu.)

Local flavour
Church of San Satiro in via Torino was designed by Bramante and contains an octagonal baptistery. In the church, behind the altar, there seems to be a deep choir. A closer look reveals a *trompe l' oeil* painting, a trick to fool the eye.

The Church of Sant' Ambrogio The Church of Sant' Ambrogio, via Carducci (MM1, S Ambrogio) is Romanesque, parts dating from the 10th century, and near Sant' Ambrogio, is the Leonardo da Vinci Science Museum at via San Vittore 21. Telephone 02/48010040. Open Tuesday to Sunday 9.30am-4.50pm, L6,000. Transport, technology and Leonardo Gallery, with models of his inventions.

The Four Wheel Museum and the Alfa Romeo Historical Museum For car fanatics there are two car museums outside Milan, both with free entry. First is the Quattrorote, Four Wheel Museum, via Grandi 5/7, Rozzano, telephone 02/824721 (Domus Publishing). There are 30 vintage cars and engines, including an Isotta Fraschini, a Lancia *Lambda I serie*. Book a visit; it is closed during August. Take an ATM bus (10km, 6¼ miles).

Also see the Alfa Romeo Historical Museum at Alfa-Lancia, via Alfa Romeo, Arese (14km, 8¾ miles by bus from Milan), telephone 02/93392119. They have Alfa commercial and sports cars, from 1910 to the present. Open Monday to Friday 9am-12 noon and 2.30-4.30pm, telephone 02/93392303 for a booking.

The Wax Museum Napoleon, Dr Schweitzer, and others, in theatrical settings. Conveniently situated near Central station. Open 8am-11pm.

ORIENTATION IN MILAN

INFORMATION
TOURIST OFFICE
APT, via Marconi 1, in piazza Duomo, parallel with the Duomo and to the right, facing. ☎ 02/809662. Pick up vital maps, including underground maps, the Red Line walks through the city, and excellent Museums in Milan *leaflets* with up to the minute information (for example what's in restauro and can't be seen).
ALBERGO DIURNO
Day hotel in the Central train station (Stazione Centrale). Open 7am-8pm.
POST OFFICE
Via Cordusio 4, near piazza Duomo. ☎ 02/160. Monday to Friday 8.15am-7.40pm, Saturday 8.15am-5.40pm. Post code 20100.
TELEPHONE
ASST in the post office, 7am-12.45am. SIP, Galleria V Emanuele. 8.10am-9.30pm, and Central train station, 7am-8pm. Telephone code 02.
CHEMIST
The one in the Central station never closes. ☎ 02/6690735.

POLICE
Via Fatebenefratelli 11. ☎ 02/62261, extension 327. English spoken. Emergency ☎ 113 or 112.

TRANSPORT
TRAINS
Milan is a main line stop for all trains going south from Paris. The overnight train will get you there conveniently mid morning. It could hardly be more accessible, the Stazione Centrale (Central station) is right in the middle of the city on Metropolitana Line 2.
Stazione Centrale piazza Duca d'Aosta (☎ 02/67500) on MM2 and MM3. Information office open Monday to Saturday 7.30am-8.50pm, Sunday 7.30am-12 noon and 6.30-9pm. Direct trains to Venice, L15,700 single, and every hour to Florence, L18,600 single. Fast trains to Domodóssola and Stresa.
Porta Garibaldi piazza Sigmund Freud. ☎ 02/6551078. Slower trains to Stresa, Baveno.
Lambrate at piazza Bottini.
Porta Vittoria at viale Umbria.

Stazione Nord at piazza Cadorna.
AIRPORTS
Milan has two airports, Malpensa, 45km (28 miles) north west of the city, and Linate, 7km (4⅓ miles) east. From Malpensa, buses go to piazza Luigi di Savoia on the east side of the Central train station. Buses connect with particular flights. Check the schedule at the Agenzia Doria (☎ 02/268028). Or take a bus from Malpensa to Gallarate railway station on the main Milan-Stresa-Dommodóssola line. The bus to Linate leaves the Central station every 20 minutes. Or take bus 73 from piazza San Babila. For flight information at both airports ☎ 02/7482200.
Linate Information on international arrivals ☎ 02/7380723. Lost luggage, 02/7384451. SIP phone at the airport is open 7am-12 midnight.
Malpensa Lost luggage ☎ 02/74854215. SIP telephone at the airport is open 8am-8pm.

ACCOMMODATION
Giulio Cesare via Roverlo

Local flavour
At (MM), the subway station at Central station, follow signs for Ferrovie FS to find the main line trains. Buy your ticket in the hall downstairs and take the escalator to trains and departure boards. For Stresa and Lake Maggiore, take the Domodóssola train. For Como, direction is Zurich.

Local flavour
Panettone, a brioche-type cake/bread found all over Italy, originated in Milan. Subtly flavoured with vanilla and orange peel, it can be chocolate coated or baked in a dove shape (*colomba*) for Easter. Large and light, *panettoni* are sold in boxes (a bit unwieldy) but keep well for weeks.

Moneysaver
If you are not in a hurry, avoid the Rapido and Super-Rapido (TEE IC and EC) trains, for which you must pay a supplement (the fine is L10,000 if you are travelling without one). The Free Shop in the Central station is very expensive, you pay for the convenience; avoid it.

Local flavour
Milanese specialities – the famous breaded veal cutlet, *cotoletta alla milanese*; the delicious *risotto alla milanese*, scented with saffron; and *osso buco alla milanese*, knuckle of veal in white wine and tomatoes, served with risotto.

10. ☎ *02/876250. Double L67,000 with bath, L50,000 without.*
Hotel Brera *via Pontaccio 9, off via Brera, near the museum.* ☎ *02/873509. An old hotel in decline, large rooms, shabby. Rooms with and without shower.*
Hotel Cesare Correnti *via C Correnti 14, on a continuation of via Torino, south west of the Duomo.* ☎ *02/870725. Double L40,000.*
Hotel Valley *via Soperga 19, near the central train station.* ☎ *02/6692777. English spoken. Double L52,000 with bath, L38,000 without.*
Pensione Rovello *via Rovello 18a, off via Dante, very central. On MM1, Cairoli or Cordusio.* ☎ *02/ 873956. Tiny, spartan, you must book. Double L60,000 with bath.*
Vecchia Milano *via Borromei 4, central, between*

via Torino and corso Magenta. ☎ *02/875042. 17th-century building. Closed 1-21 August.*

EATING OUT
If you are on a day's sightseeing tour, a most convenient and pleasant place to eat at midday is the bar at the Brera art gallery, via Brera, but get there in good time because it shuts at 2pm. Very good pasta. Pasta, salad, wine, coffee for two L28,500.
Cheapest places are the fast-food Burghy and Wendy chains, and snack bars serving panini, *filled rolls.*
Spaghetteria Taverna da Emilio *via Solferino 3, in the Brera area, for 100 kinds of spaghetti.* ☎ *02/872735. Closed Sundays.*
Topkapi *via ponte Vetero, also in the Brera area.* ☎ *02/ 808282. Pizzas, risottos and homemade pies.*
Grand' Italia *via Palermo 5.*

☎ *02/877759. Pizzas, small choice of other dishes; good value.*

SHOPPING
Expensive but interesting areas are around via Brera and Montenapoleone. More affordable areas are down corso Buenos Aires, a continuation of the smarter corso Venezia. Also shop at via Torino, south west of piazza Duomo, and the chain stores Coin, Upim, Standa.
Window-shop at Missoni's knitwear, Montenapoleone 1; Valentino, via Santo Spirito 3; Krizia, via della Spiga 23; Armani, via Sant' Andrea 9; Gianni Versace, via della Spiga 4; Gaultier, via della Spiga 20; Ferragamo, Montenapoleone 3; and Beltrami, Montenapoleone 16.
In the Brera area are Naj Oleari, via Brera 8, for

Local flavour
Milan hosts the Italian fashion collection during all of March and October (models will bag best cheap accommodation. The Navigli festival is 4 June, with historical pageants and flag-throwing.

Moneysaver
If you don't want to buy, but feel pressured, say '*guardo solo, grazie*'. I'm only looking, thank you. If you haven't understood a question, say '*non la capisco*'. I don't understand.

children's clothes and household things. For colourful modern design, go upstairs at via Manzoni 46, to the Memphis shop.

MARKETS
All around the Navigli area, near the canal.
Tuesday and Saturday market (designer bargains) in vialo Papiniano (MM2, S Agostino).
Thursday, via Santa Croce.
Saturday, Fiera di Sinigallia, via Calatafini (near Santa Croce).

ENTERTAINMENT
Milan is a rock music centre, home to jazz, folk, discos, lots of cinemas and theatre. The pre-Lent carnival is getting increasingly popular.
The artists' quarter around via Brera is a safe place to find evening entertainment in clubs and restaurants.
Consult the Corriere della Sera or the Repubblica newspapers for what's on, especially the Thursday entertainment supplements.

Moneysaver
In June you can sit at long tables by the canale Darsena, near piazza XXIV Maggio, while the local volunteers serve you local specialities for only L10,000 a meal. Most restaurant owners, like everyone else in Milan, shut down and go fishing in August, so the city runs an outdoor cafeteria in Parco Sempione, near the Arco della Pace. Meals are about L10,000.

Moneysaver
Last season's designer names can be bought from wholesale outlets, (*blochisti*); Monitor, viale Monte Nero (MM2 to Porta Genova, then bus 9); La Vela, via Porpora 89 (MM1 or MM2, Loreto, then bus 93); Il Salvagente, via Bronzetti, off Corso XXII Marzo (bus 60). The end of July sales have genuine bargains in most shops (20 to 50 per cent off).

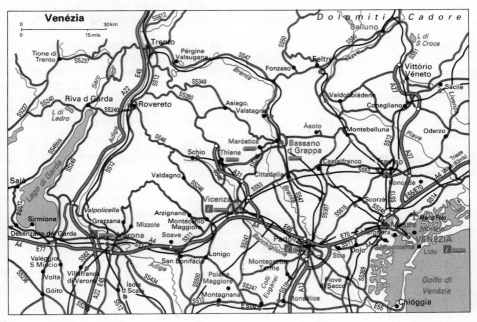

Don't miss Venice (Venézia) because of tales of how expensive it is. It *is* expensive, but it's possible to find cheap lodgings, and if you have to forgo a few creature comforts, that's a small price to pay to see the most beautiful city in Italy.

Tour operators are beginning to realize that visitors don't necessarily want to pay extortionate prices for the Gritti Palace or the Danieli, or be packed off to the Lido for cheaper hotels. They are now offering three, four, or seven-night trips to central hotels, with better deals extracted from hoteliers than individuals could manage. Good value is available especially out of season, November to March – excluding the 10 days' pre-Lent carnival time (Thomson and *Magic of Italy* catalogues are worth close scrutiny). Nevertheless, if a private bath is not a necessity, then one-star *pensioni*, and some two-star hotels are still a cheaper option, with a charter plane flight or student rail travel, than package deals.

It might seem a good idea to lodge in a nearby town, such as Treviso or Padua and commute, but that would be a pity, because you then join the army of day-trippers, arriving with everyone else flooding the city. You'd miss the best part of Venice, the early hours before the sightseers are abroad, and the chance to wander about in the evening, especially around St Mark's (San Marco) when all the coaches and trains have left. Venice at night is eery, theatrical, a bit spooky, but not threatening; crime is low.

Moneysaver

Hoteliers are often open to bargaining in out-of-season months. Low season is *bassa stagione*.

The area around Venice, westwards to Verona and Lake Garda and north to the foothills of the Dolomites, is full of interesting small towns – Ásolo, Bassano, Marós-tica, Cittadella – as well as being ringed with a series of hills, from the Euganean hills with thermal springs to the south, westwards to the Valpolicella and Soave vineyard region, round to the Alps in the north. The merchants of Venice built over 3,000 villas in this countryside. Some you can see both inside and out, some can only be glimpsed, some were built by Palladio himself.

Local flavour

La Grappa is a fiery spirit made by distilling the pulp left after the grapes have been pressed. Made in several regions, the best known comes from Bassano del Grappa, 35km (21¾ miles) north east of Vicenza.

To make a tour of more than a handful of villas you need a car. A good base would be either Vicenza or Padua (Padova).

However, based on Vicenza without a car, convenient buses make it possible to visit a couple of villas a day and to reach as far as Masèr. The Palladian villas, at Stra and Malcontenta for instance, between Venice and Padua can easily be visited by bus from Venice itself, as can Padua and Vicenza. Verona is only a two-hour train ride from Venice, but to spend all of a visit to Venice going out of the city is not only a culture shock (running the gauntlet of the hideous industrial towns of Mestre and Marghera just on the mainland) but a waste of Venetian time. If you want to make a study of the Veneto as well as Venice, first spend time outside on terra ferma, and then visit Venice itself.

FARM HOLIDAYS IN THE EUGANEAN HILLS AND THE VENETO

For inexpensive accommodation in the country, stay on farms which provide an insight into local life as well as local food and wine. All of these rooms and apartments are on local transport routes, and English is spoken. Charges vary (and some owners ask for a minimum seven-day stay), but are approximately L20,000 per night per person.
Az Agr Santa Lucia Loc Ca' Barbaro 35030 Baone (PD). Telephone 0429/4480.
Az Agr Sito degli Uccellai Montegrotto Terme (south of Padua). Contact Filippo Giacomello, via R Ardigo 3, 35126 Padova. Telephone 049/794132.
Az Agr Castello di Roncade 31056 Roncade (TV). North of Venice and east of Treviso. Telephone 0422/708736.
Az Agr Santa Mattia Loc S Mattia Verona. Contact Francésco Ederle, Strada Sant Fermo 13, 37121 Verona. Telephone 045/38698.
Residence La Pace 37030 Mizzole (VR), north east of Verona. Telephone 045/557658. Gianni Amaini.

If you need more information, contact the following local agriturist offices. Tourist offices will also give help. UPA is the Unione Provinciale Agricoltori.
Padua c/o UPA, piazza Martiri Libertà 9, 35137 Padova. Telephone 049/661655.
Treviso c/o UPA viale Cadorna 10, 31100 Treviso. Telephone 0422/548266.
Verona c/o UPA via Locatelli 3, 37122 Verona. Telephone 045/594707.
Vicenza c/o UPA viale Trento 193. 36100 Vicenza. Telephone 0444/960685.

VENICE

A car is useless in Venice and must be left either in piazzale Roma or on the island of Tronchetto. There are no cars, no vespas, no scooters in Venice; the main roads are canals, while the smaller streets are paved, dry, twisting, turning, crossing the canals by innumerable different bridges. You can walk everywhere in Venice and need never take a boat. Deliveries are by boat and then either hauled up in baskets or trundled on barrows.

BUDGET FOR A DAY

Vaporetto return ticket VENICE to Island of MURANO to visit glass shops and factory	3,600
Lunch: spaghetti, salad, cappuccino	11,000
Visit Peggy Guggenheim collection	5,000
Glass of draught beer (una birra alla spina)	1,700
Pizza at trattoria	4,500
Concert at La Fenice - 1 ticket	10,000
	L35,800
plus accommodation	

Local flavour

The sounds of Venice are bells clanging at 7am, cats and mosquitos at all hours, shouts of gondoliers, cooing doves, ambulances and fire boats hooting by, water lapping and gasps of tourists (pleasure at the sights, pain at the cost). Bring insect repellent with you, or buy Autan (a spray for the skin) at the chemist (*farmacia*). Mosquitoes are *zanzare*, an apt name.

(The American humourist Robert Benchley telegraphed home from Venice that the roads were flooded, 'Please advise'.)

For 10 months of the year it rains as much in Venice as it does in London. In winter it can be misty, cold, grim, wet, romantic, empty (and cheaper), with shorter days to sightsee and less light and warmth to picnic in.

November 21 is the feast of Santa Maria della Salute, and if you come to Venice in the winter, combine it with this festival. In a few hours a wooden bridge appears suddenly across the water from San Marco to the Salute, and it seems the whole of Venice presses across, everyone buying a candle on the way to light in the church, while behind the church there's an enormous funfair.

Occasional flooding in the winter at high tides (*acque alte*) may mean planks laid down in St Mark's Square, and water slopping about ankle-high at other places, so bring boots. Every season has something to be said for and against it. Before May it can be cold,

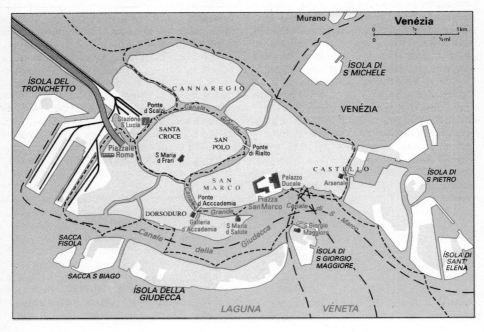

67

Smaller streets of Venice are paved, crossing canals by innumerable bridges

but the city will be emptier, and the opera season will be on. Late May and early June may be a good bet, with long daylight hours and not too many visitors. July and August are peak tourist months, hot and smelly, but lots going on, and it's perfectly easy to escape the crowds. September is when the hotels are fullest, with the film festival at the Lido, Vivaldi concerts, and the historic regatta, so be sure to book in advance.

Venice is served by two airports. Marco Polo is the nearest and most used, just north of Venice, on the Lagoon. Some charter flights go to Treviso, 32km (20 miles) north.

To get to and from Marco Polo airport, bus ACTV 5 goes every half hour (10 and 40 minutes past the hour) from under the trees in piazzale Roma to Marco Polo. The bus returns from Marco Polo at the same times, L600 (little luggage space). ATVO buses leave much less frequently (there is a gap between 3.40 and 5.25pm, for example, so check times), also from piazzale Roma, L4,000 single fare, half hour trip. A *vaporetto* (waterbus) operates from Marco Polo, a 40-minute ride in a great sweep past Murano, coming finally right round the far eastern end of Venice and up the wide expanse of water to San Marco – more expensive than the bus, but a wonderful way to arrive in Venice

(L13,000 single). Buy the ticket in the airport. If you plan to visit the islands anyway, or your hotel is nearer piazzale Roma than San Marco, then skip this trip and take the bus. Water taxis cost not less than L80,000 for four people to San Marco. Taxi (by land) approximately L20,000 to piazzale Roma.

ACTV buses to and from Treviso run every half hour as well, the first bus is at 4.30am, last bus 12.45am from Venice, last bus from Treviso 11.40pm; journey time one hour, L2,000. The Lamarca bus also leaves piazzale Roma two hours before each flight, L5,000. By train – regular trains go to Treviso Centrale (L3,000) with bus connection (L500) to the airport.

Porter stands (including the Accademia, the train station, piazzale Roma, the Rialto, San Marco) are listed in *Un Ospite in Venezia*. Flat rate for one or two pieces L8,000; for every other piece of luggage add about L2,200.

The first thing to do in Venice is to buy a really detailed map. The hand-out tourist map is not good enough. A good one is published by *edizione ezio tedeschi*, L4,000, showing the boat stops, the *traghetto* crossings, the islands, and it has a good index of streets. Keep the tourist map as well, because it has a useful list of where each boat line goes.

Keep your map with you at all times. Just when you are absolutely sure you know where you are going is the time you take just one wrong turning and end in a complete muddle. Not that it matters if you lose your way; the way you find will probably be just as interesting as the one you lost.

Venetian addresses can be confusing: there are only numbers, not streets, on most addresses. Venice is divided into six districts or *sestriere* – Cannaregio; San Marco; Castello; Santa Croce; San Polo and the Dorsoduro.

The long island to the south is Giudecca, a working and suburban district.

Within these six districts every house is numbered consecutively. The Doge's Palace is San Marco 1, and the San Marco numbers go on to no 5562 by the Rialto, where the Cannaregio numbers begin. But as to their exact route, up which street and round which convoluted alley they go, only God, and presumably the Venetian postman, knows. Always ask for the nearest well known church or landmark, as well as the street of places you want to find.

All the streets, squares and bridges are clearly marked high up, in the same large white stencilled lettering (spelling varies). Yellow signs direct you to the Rialto, San Marco, Ferrovia (the train station), and sometimes *vaporetto* (waterbus).

The Arsenal in the Castello district

more than 100 canals, totalling 45km (72½ miles) of water, crossed by over 400 bridges. It only takes about half an hour to walk from one end to the other, as long as you don't choose to go down each of the 2,300 alleyways. Venice extends about 1½km (a mile) by 3km (2 miles), and is built on millions of larch and pine tree trunks embedded in a layer of clay which rests on quicksand. Over the years this clay has become compressed, so Venice sinks, gradually into the water.

Be sure to see the piazza San Marco, the

Moneysaver

For a cheap sample ride in a gondola – take the *traghetto*, the gondolas which ply across the Grand Canal. L300 (pay the gondolier as you get on) a ride, but you will probably have to stand, and the crossing can be choppy.

There are only three bridges over the Grand Canal – at the train station, the Scalzi bridge; halfway along, the Rialto with shops along it; and round the bend, the wooden Accademia.

There is only one piazza in Venice – the piazza San Marco, with a couple of *piazzettas* off it (the bus station is called the piazzale Roma, never the piazza). All other squares are called *campo* (field), because that's what they were before they were paved over.

The islands of the lagoon first sheltered refugees from Atilla and the Lombards, sweeping down from the north, and in 697 the 12 towns elected their first Doge. Now Venice is made up of 117 little islands and

---

Local flavour

A Venetian vocabulary:

Calle – street
Campiello – a small square
Corte – courtyard
Fondamenta – paved walk along canal
Ramo – side street
Rio – any canal except the Grand, Cannaregio and Giudecca canals
Rio terrà – a filled in canal, now a wide street
Riva – wide fondamenta, for example Riva degli Schiavoni beyond St Mark's (*riva* = bank)
Ruga and *merceria* – a street lined with shops, for example the Ruga degli Orefici near the Rialto (*orefici* = goldsmiths)
Salizzada – the earliest paved street, made of flint flagstones
Sottoportego – alley under an arch
Zattere – landing stages along the south bank of the Dorsoduro

cathedral and the Doge's Palace. See inside the buildings by day, but come back again at night. Also see the Accademia gallery and the view from the bridge, Ponte dell' Accademia.

Take a slow boat trip (*vaporetto* 1) sitting right in the front of the boat up the Grand Canal. Venice has its rush hour like any other city, and the boats get very full about 12 noon and later between 4-5pm. Take a boat towards the station early in the morning, and away from it in the evening. It's the only way you can see the buildings along the canal, as there are virtually no canal-side roads except around the Rialto bridge. Don't forget churches shut at midday and open again (with luck) about 4pm. If you can, go to a concert at La Fenice, and visit an island by *vaporetto*.

Every street, bridge, twisting, turning path of this city reveals a pleasure to the eye. As you wander the streets look out for Venetian chimneys, tall, bulging, peculiar; grotesque heads on walls; madonnas under their little awnings on corners of walls; patterned pavements in the Piazzetta, outside the Salute church and many other places in the city.

Gondola rides Prices vary for gondola rides, and are negotiable, from L50,000 for five people for the first 50 minutes, then L25,000-L30,000 for the next 25 minutes (see listed price in *Un Ospite di Venézia* – carry it with you as ammunition), between 8pm and 8am, L60,000. It is sometimes easier to establish terms by ordering a gondola through a tour operator's courier or the hotel staff. The best time to go is in the evening before 8pm; if you have seen the Grand Canal by *vaporetto*, ask to be taken down a *rio*, a side canal, and wander the secret backwaters. Don't ask your gondolier to sing *Come Back to Sorrento*. All the gondoliers got a severe reprimand from the Venetian authorities a few years ago for singing non-Venetian songs.

St Mark's Square (piazza San Marco) St Mark's cathedral was built between 1063 and 1094 to designs by a Greek architect, after the first 9th-century church had burnt down. The brick vaulting (an innovation) was covered by mosaics, which were added to until the 16th century. Under the main altar lie the remains of St Mark, stolen from

The shop-lined Rialto Bridge on the Grand Canal

Local flavour

Gondolas, 11 metres (36ft) long and less than 1½ metres (5ft) wide, speed elegantly along, the whole of the stern and half the prow out of the water. They are also asymmetrical, leaning to the right, making it easier for the gondolier to steer – they can turn on their axis. The rowlock, the *forcola*, is carved from a single piece of walnut (a group was recently exhibited in America as sculpture). The fin at the prow is called the *ferro*. Lots of gondolas collect in the Bac' Orseolo, north of piazza San Marco, a sort of gondola park, where they stay covered up at night.

See the Grand Canal by gondola

Local flavour

Mark Twain thought St Mark's was 'like a vast warty bug taking a meditative walk'.

Local flavour

An essential morning sight is the fruit and fish market near Ruga degli Orefici, on the south side of the Rialto bridge. Find yellow *zucchini* flowers in bunches; men expertly cutting the leaves off artichokes down to the heart; long tomatoes; all kinds of peaches, nectarines, *nespole* (Japanese medlars); green salad ready cleaned and chopped.

Moneysaver

The best free entertainment in Venice – an evening in the piazza being serenaded (free) by the café orchestras. But you must keep moving; sit down, and you'll have to pay.

Alexandria and smuggled past Arab officials under slices of pork. The cathedral's cruciform shape and domes are Byzantine, and the outside is embellished with looted marble panels and carvings, wrenched from Constantinople (now Istanbul) and plundered from the Crusades. The four bronze horses over the door are copies; the originals, first made in Rome and sent to Constantinople, subsequently snatched from there by Venetians, are in the church. Inside, the extraordinary marble walls are patterned like dark flames, with the dark golden domes and arches dimly glinting. The mosaic pieces are set at an angle, not flush, to catch the light. Look up as you go through the entrance for the best view of the mosaics; the inside is very dim, only lit at mass and on special holy days. Notice the mosaic floor too. The Pala d'Oro is a dazzling golden bas relief, an assembly of pieces made over three centuries, studded with 2,500 precious jewels. Behind it are illuminated alabaster pillars. When the Basilica is full it's worth the money to sit away from the crowds and have a good look up at the mosaics. A ticket (L2,000) will also take you into the treasury. To see the original bronze horses, and another closer view of walls and ceiling, and birds-eye view of the floors, go up to the Galleria, open daily 9.30am-5pm, L2,000.

Note: no shorts or sleeveless shirts are allowed in Venetian churches. High Mass in San Marco is at 10am on Sunday.

Moneysaver

Almost every church in Venice has at least one excellent painting by a famous painter, or sculptures or reliefs.

The bronze horses at St Mark's

The clock tower (Torre dell' Orologio)
The clock tower was designed by Mauro Codussi, 1496. Its brightly enamelled clock face and its digital clock are linked with automata: climb the tower to see the bell being struck hourly by two bronze Moors, but stand well back. Open 9am-12 noon and 3-5pm Tuesday to Saturday, 9am-12 noon Sunday.

Looking from St Mark's, the long building on the right is the Procuratie Vecchie, built 1512-26 for the Republic's offices, the State Procurators. The Procuratie Nuove on the left were built a century later. At the end facing you, the Ala Napoleonica built by Napoleon houses the Correr Museum.

The campanile was rebuilt in the early 1900's to the previous 1514 design after it suddenly collapsed on 14 July 1902, crumbling like a child's castle, killing the caretaker's cat. Take the lift to the top for a panoramic view of the city, the lagoon and on a clear day, the Alps. (The original tower had stairs wide enough for a nobleman on horseback to ascend). Open daily 10am-7.30pm, L3,000. (There is a better view from San Giorgio Maggiore, which is less crowded.)

The cafés in the square are venerable institutions. During the 18th century, Quadri's, under the Procuratie Vecchie, was frequented by supporters of the Austrian regime – loyal Venetians sat at Florian's, opposite (as did Henry James later).

The Doge's Palace   The present Doge's Palace (Palazzo Ducale) dates from the 14th and 15th centuries, built of pink Verona marble and white Istrian stone in Gothic style. See how the columns have gradually sunk, and the pavement level round it has been raised to offset the rising water level. Rizzo's Scala (staircase) dei Giganti leads from the courtyard to the first floor. The Scala d'Oro by Sansovino leads to the Senate Chamber and the council rooms with paintings by Tintoretto, Veronese and others. In the Grand Council Chamber (first floor), note an empty frame among the portraits of the doges – that is for Marin Falier, the doge who aimed too high and was executed for treason. Secret passages lead from here across the Bridge of Sighs (Ponte dei Sospiri) where prisoners (including the infamous womaniser Casanova, who managed to escape) were escorted groaning and sighing to the jails opposite. (One-hour tour, in Italian, twice a day; book at the ticket office or telephone 041/5204287). The palace is open daily 8.30am-6pm, L5,000. Over 60s and children L3,000.

On the second floor is one of the finest armouries in Europe. And in the Sala della Bussola, just beyond the Council of Ten room, is the Bocca di Leone, where people posted letters denouncing their neighbours in the lion's mouth. This room was once covered in paintings by all the outstanding Venetian painters, but they were destroyed by fire, and now, except for a painting by Tintoretto (*Paradise*, the largest oil painting in the world) and Veronese panels on the ceiling, all the works are inferior.

The Doge was the elected head of government in the Venetian Republic – a once powerful figure who over the centuries became a constitutional figurehead, living in luxury, flattered, crowned, honoured, but restricted by councils and senates.

After San Marco, if it is very crowded in the smart shopping streets around the

Local flavour
Just along the canal, by the San Marco *vaporetto* stop, is a public garden with benches.

square, escape to some quieter and cheaper areas, such as Dorsoduro and Castello. Or to see some great paintings, cross the river and visit the *scuole*.

The Scuole   The *scuole* (*scuola* = school) were groups of craftsmen, similar to London Guilds and Livery Companies, who practised the same craft, had common origins (Greeks, Slavs etc) and combined in charitable works. They commissioned important artists to decorate their headquarters.

The Scuola Grande di San Rocco, (the largest and grandest of the *scuole*) in the San Polo district at the east end behind the huge Frari church, campo San Rocco, are 50 paintings by Tintoretto, recently restored with the help of an American fund. Telephone 041/5234864. Open daily 9am-1pm and 3.30-6.30pm, L5,000.

Local flavour

In 1564 the Scuola Grande di San Rocco invited various artists, including Veronese and Tintoretto, to send in competing designs for the central ceiling panel in the Sala dell' Albergo. While the others toiled away at their drawings, Tintoretto painted the whole panel, had it surreptitiously installed and covered, and on judging day he revealed it in all its glory and offered it free to the *scuola*. Amid cries of 'shame' and 'cheating', Tintoretto won the commission to paint the whole series.

The carvings of armless figures and the *trompe l' oeil* bookcase under the Tintorettos are by Francesco Pianta.

While you are here, the Frari church is

open weekdays 9am-12 noon and 2.30-6pm, Sundays 3-5.30pm, L800, free Sundays. The large plain brick building was built for the Franciscans between 1330 and 1499, and houses, among much good sculpture, a wooden statue of St John by Donatello and an altarpiece by Giovanni Bellini, as well as two paintings by Titian, the famous *Assumption* on the high altar, and the *Madonna of Ca' Pesaro* on the left of the nave.

The Frari also contains Titian's tomb and a statue of St Jerome by Alessandro Vittorio and opposite, across the nave, the pyramid enclosing the sculptor Canova's heart.

Further south, in the Dorsoduro near the Rio Santa Margherita, off the southern end of the long campo Santa Margherita, is the Scuola dei Carmini, telephone 041/5289420. Open weekdays 9am-12 noon and 3-6pm, shut Sundays, L2,000. Principal sight here is G B Tiepolo's light and airy ceiling in the *salone* upstairs, painted in 1744.

Scuola di San Giorgio degli Schiavoni is a very interesting *scuola*, north of the Grand Canal, in Castello district. It contains a series of paintings by Carpaccio. Ponte dei Greci, Castello, telephone 041/5228828. Open weekdays 10am-12.30pm and 3.30-6pm, Sundays 10am-12.30pm, closed Mondays, L3,000.

Local flavour

Not far from campo San Polo, the Ponte delle Tette marks the area where prostitutes lived in the 16th century, often standing stripped to the waist in doorways. Then there were 11,654 registered, tax-paying prostitutes in Venice.

ORIENTATION IN VENICE

INFORMATION

TOURIST OFFICE
APT at the railway station, ☎ 041/715016. Open daily

8am-9pm. Carta Giovani (youth pass) for ages 16-26 is available here, giving various discounts. Bring a passport photo (photo machine in train station, L2,000). Make sure you get

Un Ospite di Venezia (hotels often give them), A Guest in Venice, very useful English/Italian booklet on trains, museums, entertainment, water transport etc. There is also a *tourist office in piazza San Marco, 71c in the far left corner (standing with your back to St Mark's).* ☎ *041/ 5226356, open Monday to Saturday 8.30am-7pm. Piazzale Roma* ☎ *041/5227402.*

AMERICAN EXPRESS *San Marco 1471, along Calle Seconda dell' Ascensione, from piazza San Marco.* ☎ *041/5200844. (Automatic machine for cardholders on Salizzanda San Moise.) Money exchange Monday to Saturday 8am-8pm; office hours Monday to Friday 9am-5.30pm, Saturday 9am-12.30pm.*

POST OFFICE *San Marco 5554, Salizzada Fontego dei Tedeschi, near the east end of the Rialto bridge.* ☎ *041/5289317. Open Monday to Saturday, 8.15am-7pm. Branch office at the end of piazza San Marco, Monday to Friday 8.15am-1.30pm, Saturday, 8.30am-12 noon. Also at the railway station, facing platform 10, Monday to Friday 1.40-7pm, Saturday 1.40-6pm. Postal code 30124.*

TELEPHONE *ASST San Marco 5551, next door to the main post office, open daily 8am-8pm. SIP in piazzale Roma, open daily 8am-9.30pm. Telephone code 041.*

ALBERGO DIURNO *Day hotel, San Marco 1266, off the west end of piazza San Marco. Showers open daily 8-11am and 4.30-7pm. Lavatories 8am-7.30pm.*

There is a left luggage department.

PUBLIC LAVATORIES *Piazzalle Roma, the railway station, the Rialto, the Accademia and the Albergo Diurno.*

TRANSPORT

AIRPORTS **Marco Polo** ☎ *041/661262. Lost luggage,* ☎ *041/ 661266. 13km (8¾ miles) north of the city.* **Treviso** *Used by some charter flights. 30km (18½ miles) north of the city.*

TRAINS *Santa Lucia railway station, right inside Venice at the end of the Grand Canal. (Vaporetti 1, 2, 4 and 5 all stop near by).* ☎ *041/ 715555. Lost property,* ☎ *041/716122. Trains to Padua (takes half an hour), Verona (1¾ hours, L12,000 return), Milan (3½ hours, L32,000 return). Left luggage, L1,500 per piece.*

BUSES *ACTV from piazzale Roma.* ☎ *041/5287886. To Padua, Treviso, along the Brenta canal, to Marco Polo airport etc. Information office open 8am-8pm. Ticket office open 6.15am-12 midnight. ATVO buses to Padua etc, from the same square. Office at number 597.* ☎ *041/5205530.*

CAR HIRE **Eurocar** *piazzale Roma 540.* ☎ *041/5238616. If you do not pay by credit card, a large deposit is needed. Monday to Friday 8am-7pm, Saturday 8am-2pm,*

Sunday 8am-12 noon. L428,000 plus insurance and 19 per cent VAT per week.

VAPORETTO *Getting about in Venice means walking or taking a vaporetto (waterbus). Vaporetto offices: ACTV 3880 Corte dell' Albero.*

Principal routes *No 1 stops at every stage both sides of the Grand Canal from the station to St Mark's and the public gardens, L800. Every 10 minutes, 7am-11pm (named Accelerato). No 2. Fewer stops, from the station to San Marco, L2,500. No 4. In summer, a tourist route, up Grand Canal. No 5. Two semi-circular routes, Destra and Sinistra, from the train station, Fondamente Nuove and San Marco, to the Giudecca, San Giorgio and Murano, L1,800. No 8. San Marco to San Giorgio Maggiore and the Giudecca, L1,800, till 8pm. No 12. From Fondamente Nuove, every hour 5am-11pm. To Murano, Burano, Torcello, L2,500. L1,200 between islands.*

ACCOMMODATION

Low season runs from 1 November to 31 March, with high season rates usually at Christmas and carnival time.

These are hotels with views over the main canals.

RIVA DEGLI SCHIAVONI *Facing the San Marco Basin.*

Bucintoro *Riva degli Schiavoni, Castello 2135.*

☎ *041/5223240, fax 5235224. All rooms with view, restaurant, two-star, 28 rooms. Double L64,000-L80,000 with bath, L44,000-L54,000 without, breakfast L12,000. No air conditioning. Closed December and January.*
Paganelli *Riva degli Schiavoni 4182, Arsenale stop.* ☎ *041/5224324. This is the house where Henry James stayed. Double L81,000 with bath, L54,000 without, breakfast L12,500. Air conditioning. Two-star, 15 rooms.*

GRAND CANAL
Locanda Sturion *San Polo 679.* ☎ *041/5236243, fax 5225702. Calle Sturione, fourth left from the Rialto bridge along Fondamenta del Vin. Only the breakfast room and a room for five people have a canal view. Ancient and popular guesthouse, up three long flights of stairs.*

One-star, eight rooms. Only one with bath L87,000, others L61,000 bed and breakfast. Showers L2,000. English spoken. No restaurant.

GIUDECCA CANAL
La Calcina *Zattere, Dorsoduro 780. Zattere stop.* ☎ *041/5206466, fax 5227045. The English writer John Ruskin stayed here. Double L71,000-L81,000 with bath, L44,500-L54,000 without bath, high season, plus breakfast L11,000 per person. No air conditioning. Two-star, 37 rooms, canal view. Closed January and February. Sit out on the waterfront at the bar next door.*

The following accommodation has either limited or no canal views.
CASTELLO
Locanda Sant' Anna *Castello 269, across the Sant' Anna bridge at the end of via Garibaldi.* ☎ *041/ 5286466. One-star, eight rooms in courtyard. The sitting room has a view over the canal to Isola San Pietro. Double L70,000 with bath, L44,000 without. Remote and peaceful. Breakfast L6,000. No restaurant.*
Locanda Silva *Fondamenta del Rimedio, Castello 4423,*

very central, behind San Marco. ☎ *041/5227643. One-star, 25 rooms. Very clean. Double bed and breakfast L58,000 without bath, L70,000 with shower. L84,000 shower and lavatory.*
Locanda Tiepolo *Castello 4510, very central, off campo SS Filippo e Giacomo.* ☎ *041/5231315. Scruffy entrance, but pleasant old-fashioned rooms with painted ceilings. Basic, one-star, seven rooms (two baths). Bed and breakfast, double L86,000 with bath, L60,000 without.*
La Residenza *campo Bandiera e Moro, Castello 3608.* ☎ *041/5285315, fax 5238859. Exceptionally attractive Gothic palace once owned by the Gritti family. Popular hotel, so you must book. Double L81,000 with bath, L54,000 without, plus compulsory breakfast L13,000 per person. Closed November to February. Air conditioning (10 per cent extra). Two-star, 17 rooms.*
SAN MARCO
All of this accommodation is

central. Prices are high in this part, and you are generally expected to have breakfast in the hotel. **Brooklyn** Calle dei Fabbri, San Marco 4712, on a smart shopping street. ☎ 041/ 23227. Pretty Venetian decoration; breakfast is not compulsory here. Double L81,000 with bath, L54,000 without. Breakfast L12,000 per person. No air conditioning, two-star, 12 rooms.

Centauro campo Manin, Calle della Vida 4297a. ☎ 041/5225832, fax 5239151. Large well decorated rooms, some with canal views; rooftop view from the third floor (no lift), usually space available here. English spoken. Two-star, 31 rooms, all with bath. Double bed and breakfast L105,000. No restaurant.

San Giorgio Calle della Mandola, near La Fenice, San Angelo vaporetto stop. San Marco 3781. Good decoration, but near a smelly canal in summer. Two-star, all rooms with bath. Double L60,000-L80,000 plus L12,000 breakfast per person. Air conditioning (10 per cent extra). Low season L48,000-L60,000.

San Stefano San Marco 2957. ☎ 041/5200166, fax 5224460. Two-star, good

position on quiet square. Double bed and breakfast (plus television and frigo (fridge) bar) with bath and lavatory L90,000-L110,000. Air conditioning L10,000 extra.

DORSODURO
Alla Salute da Cici Fondamenta di Cabala, Salute, Dorsoduro 222. ☎ 041/5235404. Nearest vaporetto Santa Maria della Salute. Old two-star family-run hotel on a canal. English spoken. Tiny garden. New baths, old furniture. Double L78,000 with bath, L46,000 without. Breakfast L10,000 per person. Ask for a canal view.

Casa de' Stefani San Barnaba, Dorsoduro 2786, near campo San Barnaba on Calle del Traghetto, vaporetto stop, Ca' Rezzonico. ☎ 041/5223337. Shut January. One-star, 17 rooms. Great atmosphere, old rooms with paintings. No private lavatories. Double L55,000 with shower, L44,000 without. No breakfast. Bars and cafés near by in campo San Barnaba. Room 6 has the best view on the garden.

Hotel Messner Madonna della Salute, Dorsoduro 216/217. ☎ 041/5227443. Some rooms are located down the road. Open-air restaurant. Newly decorated. Some

rooms with canal view. Double bed and breakfast with bath L85,000-L99,000, without bath L60,000-L70,000. One-star, 20 rooms.

CANNAREGIO
Near Fondamente Nuove:
Casa Boccassini Calle del Fuomo, Cannaregio 5295. ☎ 041/5229892. Rather confusing to find, between Rio della Panada and Rio dei Gesuiti, but worth searching. Antique furniture and a little garden. Double bed and breakfast L82,000 with bath, L56,000 without. One-star, one double room with adjoining children's room. Shut mid November to 26 December. Ten rooms.

CANNAREGIO
Near the train station:
Antica casa Carettoni Lista di Spagna, Cannaregio 130. ☎ 041/716231. Some rooms with character, for students mostly. One-star, 15 rooms, three with bath. The doors have been decoratively painted by the owner and there are some pretty bedsteads. Double L42,000, no breakfast. English spoken. Closed August and part of February.
Hotel Abbazia Calle Priuli, Cannaregio 66. ☎ 041/717333. Two-star, but being improved and possibly upgraded. A charming hotel in an old abbey building off the Lista di Spagna.

Local flavour

IVA = VAT = European Value Added Tax. In Italy it is 19 per cent on car hire.

Local flavour

Feriali are weekdays, and festivi are Sundays and holidays.

Overlooks central garden, two-star, 31 rooms. Double bed and breakfast L105,000, all with bath. English spoken.

Hotel ai due Fanali S Croce 946, over the Scalzi bridge on quiet campo San Simeon Grande. ☎ 041/718344, fax 718344. Tables outside. Double bed and breakfast L98,000 with bath, L71,500 without. (L64,000 and L44,000 winter rates, plus L8,500 breakfast per person). No air conditioning. Two-star, basic modern rooms. Shut mid November to mid December.

Hotel Rossi Calle delle Procuratie, Cannaregio 262, on quiet alley off Lista di Spagna. One-star, biggish, anonymous rooms in good order. Double bed and breakfast (breakfast in room) L80,000 with bath, L54,000 without. Closed from January until the end of carnival. Lower terms in November.

San Geremia campo Sant Geremia, Cannaregio 290a. ☎ 041/716245, fax 716260. In the square facing the church, with bar and breakfast room. Double bed and breakfast L88,000 with bath, L62,000 without.

SAN POLO, SANTA CROCE

Not far from San Rocco and the Frari:

Hotel Iris San Tomà, San Polo 2910a, near the San Toma landing stage. ☎ 041/5222882. Shut January. Vine-covered restaurant. On canal, Fondamenta de la Frescada. Uninspired décor. Double bed and breakfast L85,000 with bath, L66,000 without. Two-star, good value for money. Half board for two L100,000 (without bath).

Casa Peron Salizzada San Pantalon 84 Santa Croco, halfway between piazzalle Roma and San Tomà landing, but still quite a walk. ☎ 041/5286038. One-star, 11 rooms. Shut two weeks of November and January. Tiny terrace, small, neat rooms. Double L52,000 with shower, L65,000 with shower and lavatory. Breakfast L7,000.

EATING OUT

DORSODURO

Ai Cugnai Calle San Vio 857. ☎ 041/5289238. Open 12 noon-3pm and 7-10pm. Closed Mondays and January. Little trattoria run by three sisters, with a tiny back courtyard. Crowds

come for the good fish. L46,000 for two (pasta, fish, salad and wine).

Al Profeta Lunga San Barnaba 2729. Garden restaurant. Open midday and 7-11 pm. Shut Mondays. Pizza L4,000-L5,000.

Locanda Montin Fondamenta delle Eremite 1147, between Ognissanti and campo San Barnaba. ☎ 041/5227151. Closed Tuesday evening and Wednesday. Large open-air restaurant (Jimmy Carter and Modigliani ate here), popular, relaxed management (no obligation to eat a large meal). Spaghetti L7,000, good vegetables and salads L2,500. Recommended.

Osteria da Toni Fondamenta San Basegio 1642. Shut Mondays. Sit outside by the canal. Small simple trattoria.

Trattoria da Bruno Calle Lunga San Barnaba 2754a. ☎ 041/5206978. Simple local eating house. Menu written sardonically in lingua italiana. Good tagliatelle with cream and ham L5,000. Mixed seafood grill, L8,500, vegetables L3,500. Shut the first two weeks of August, Sunday,

and Thursday lunchtime.
SAN MARCO
Leon Branco *Salizzada San Luca 4153, between San Luca and campo Manin.* ☎ *041/5221180. Stand-up meals at the bar. Main dish L6,000. Risotto L3,500. Sandwiches (* tramezzini *) L1,200. Meals midday. Snacks Monday to Saturday 9am-8pm.*
Vino, Vino *Calle del Cafetier 2007a, near Ponte de Le Veste, towards La Fenice.* ☎ *041/5224121. This is a wine bar with food (meals till 11.30pm, drinks till 1am). It is one of the few reasonably priced eating places in this area. L20,000 for pasta, vegetables and wine for two, sitting at tables. Shut Tuesdays.*
CANNAREGIO
Antica Adelaide *Calle Priuli, off the strada Nova.* ☎ *041/5203451. Garden*

courtyard. Closed Mondays. Small menu, good fish, pasta alla gorgonzola.
Antica Mola *Fondamenta degli Ormesini, across the canal from the Ghetto. Simple meals lunchtime only.*
Gazebo *Rio Terra San Leonardo 1333a.* ☎ *041/716380. Garden courtyard. Closed Thursdays. On main route from the train station to the strada Nova.*
Hostaria ai Promessi Sposi *north of the strada Nova, off Calle del Duca at Calle dell' Oca (opposite the Bernardi-Semenzato which lets rooms). Cannaregio 4367.* ☎ *041/5228609. Wine bar with snacks and sit down meals. Spaghetti bigoli in salsa and vegetables, L7,000. Open daily summer at lunchtime, and in the evening till 10pm. Shut Wednesdays in winter.*

Paradiso Perduto *Fondamenta della Misericordia 2540, further along from the Antica Mola.* ☎ *041/21457. Shut Wednesdays. Inexpensive pasta.*

SHOPPING

The smartest shops (and the most expensive) for clothes, jewellery, glass, masks and lace (Venice's specialities) are in the streets around St Mark's: the Merceria, Frezzeria, Calle dei Fabbri and Calle Largo XXII Marzo. Calle della Mandola has paper, prints and a fascinating bread shop. There are interesting and less expensive shops in Dorsoduro and San Polo. strada Nova in Cannaregio is Venice's home high street.
MARKETS AND SUPERMARKETS
You must visit the Rialto markets – the Erberia for

fruit and vegetables, and the Pescheria, the fish market along the Grand Canal front beside the Rialto Bridge, active in the mornings. Just by the bridge and on it, souvenir and jewellery stalls are full of tourists all day. More off the beaten track, look on campo Santa Maria Formosa (in Castello, north east of San Marco) in the mornings for food and clothes. Also Rio Terra San Leonardo (in Cannaregio, across the bridge from campo San Geremia, south of the Ghetto Nuovo) for all kinds of things.

DOGAL supermarket is on strada Vova; STANDA stores at campo San Luca, strada Nova and campo Manin. While there, walk through some tiny backstreets – signposted, but you have to look – to the Palazzo Contarini dal Bovolo with its amazing and elegant spiral staircase.

There's a morning fish and vegetable market in campo Santa Margherita.

MASKS
Ca' Macana 30123 Venezia, Dorsoduro 3171. ☎ 041/ 5203229. Between the Accademia and the Guggenheim. Particularly interesting large selection of hats and masks, run by a collective. Always open 9am-8pm with someone

working. Little mask brooches, L4,000. In Calle delle Boteghe, just across Ponte San Barnaba.

Mondonovo Rio Terra Canal, near campo Santa Margherita, in Dorsoduro.
Laboratorio Artigiano Maschere Barbaria delle Tole, near campo SS Giovanni and Paolo.

PAPER
Legatoria Piazzesi Ponte Zaguri, San Marco, Campiello della Fetrina 2511. Hand-blocked and marble papers. Cheapest buy, L2,500 one sheet of hand-made paper and initial (plus envelope).

LACE
More for-looking than buying because of the expense, the most genuine and interesting place to see lace being made is at Jesurum, behind St Mark's, near the Ponte della Canonica, housed in an old church. Old and new lace and embroidery is sold. San

Marco 4310, open daily 9am-7pm, closed Monday mornings in winter, free. In the mid 19th century, Jesurum relaunched the bobbin technique called al tombolo (small spools of thread woven round a grid of master threads). Special to Venice, and using threads as fine as hair, is the punto in aria. About 20 craftswomen work on the premises, but a lot of work for sale is made at home. (Many other lace shops in Venice sell lace from Hong Kong or China.) Visit Burano for its museum and lace stalls – see under islands, page 91. El Stringhesso, on campo San Provolo, near San Zaccaria has small pieces of genuine lace.

GLASS AND GLASS-BLOWING
Visit Murano for its glass museum and glass factories. See under islands, page 91.
Genedesi on Calle San Gregorio, in Dorsoduro.
Funcia degli Angeli (Angel's Forge), on Calle Corona, near campo SS Filippo e Giacomo.
Gianfranco Penzo campo del Ghetto Nuovo 2895, for Jewish vessels and plates.
Salviati showroom at piazza San Marco 78 and 110, also in Dorsoduro, at Calle San Gregorio 195.

FABRIC FACTORIES
Bevilacqua still using 18th-

century wooden looms, their specialist weavers each make only about 30cm (1ft) of cloth a day, some brocade patterns involving a warp of 10,000 threads. Offices and workshops on the Grand Canal in the San Zan Degola area, Santa Croce, nearest landing stage Riva de Biasio.

Fortuny San Biagio 804–6, Giudecca.

Rubelli makers of silk damasks and brocades, north of the Fondamenta Contarini, near the Church of Madonna dell' Orto.

ENTERTAINMENT

Wandering the streets in Venice at night (safe from muggers and bag-snatchers, no crooks in the nooks and alleyways), you'll find lights on and restaurants open and always something going on late around the Fenice, while other parts of the city shut down completely by 10pm. La Fenice Theatre is the

Venetian craftspeople at work
lace making
glass blowing
boat building
fabric making
wrought iron work
and picture framing and gilding

prettiest painted, decorated elegant little 18th-century theatre (rebuilt) with three rows of boxes (palchi L25,000), then two rows of balcony. Campo S Fantin, ☎ 041/5210161 and 5210336. Tickets and information 9.30am–12.30pm and 4-6pm. The opera season runs through the winter months, but in the summer there are concerts. It is usually closed during August; no need to wear evening dress. On summer evenings, people are still sitting out after midnight on the steps of the theatre, and the bars in the square are still open and serving.

There is a disco, El Souk, near the Accademia bridge, Calle Contarini 1056. ☎ 041/5200371. It is open daily 10pm-3am, but not many other places are open after dark, unless you go to the Casino, which operates on the Lido in summer. The Goldoni Theatre gives plays in Italian. There are concerts in several churches, including the Frari.

Consult Une Ospite di Venezia for details of concerts, plays and cinemas, also exhibitions in the modern art galleries (free).

St Mark's is a good place to wander in the evening. The tourist tat stalls are replaced by artists selling their pictures. You might pay L20,000 for a little evocative watercolour scene of Venice. Till midnight opposing orchestras serenade their clients in the cafés, alongside potted flowers with their standard lamps and grand pianos. Florian here, Quadri there, and round the corner opposite the Doge's Palace, couples who haven't paid a lira dance along outside the quadrangle of paying seats at Chioggia's. Sitting, L8,000 for a coffee and entertainment.

FESTIVALS
Venice has always been a city of shows and dancing, carnivals and masked figures, fireworks and regattas. The major carnival, which takes place the week before Shrove Tuesday, was spontaneously restarted in the 1970s. Now it's the main winter event, and hotels open, charge high rates and quickly become full. Grand palaces open up all along the Grand Canal. Check for events in the Ospite di Venezia or the

local paper, Il Gazzettino.
VENETIAN FESTIVAL CALENDAR
February or March
Carnival. Lasts about 10 days prior to Lent.
March One Sunday (different each year) there's a fun run called Su e zo per i ponti, up and over the bridges, from the Ponte della Paglia (in Cannaregio, near the train station) all round the city to San Marco.
April 25 St Mark's Day, patron saint of the city. Procession in the Basilica. Men give a rosebud un bocolo to their best-beloved, and the gondoliers race between Punta della Dogana and Sant' Elena.
May The Staffetta Remiera. Relay for five kinds of boats.
First Sunday after Ascension Day The Vogalonga, the long row. Non-competitive marathon race for any oar-propelled boat, starting in front of the Doge's Palace 9.30am, goes via Murano and Burano, finishing by the Dogana. (32km, 20 miles). L5,000 to enter.
June Regatta of the Four Maritime Republics: Amalfi, Genoa, Pisa and Venice, every four years. Venice is host in 1992.
June Even years. The Biennale modern art exhibition.
June 21 (nearest Sunday) Celebration for Burano's patron saints.
June 29 (nearest Sunday) Rowing races in honour of SS Peter and Paul.
July First Sunday. Gondola race at Murano.
July Second Sunday. Rowing races and fish-eating festival at Malamocco on the Lido.
July Third Sunday, Festa del Redentore. Two bridges are built across boats over the Grand and Giudecca canals to Palladio's Church of Il Redentore on Giudecca. The Saturday night before (the fresco), Venetians take their boats into the lagoon, watch the fireworks at midnight, and sometimes row over to the Lido for a quick swim to watch the dawn rise. On the Sunday, a gondola race along the Giudecca Canal.

On the same Sunday there are celebrations at Alberoni in honour of mussels, at the southern tip of the Lido. Music, dancing, and midnight fireworks.
August First Sunday. Regata di Pellestrina, a race between pupparini (rowing boats), and mascarete.
September First Sunday. Regata storica. Famous processions and races on the Grand Canal. Young people in pupparini, women in mascarete, men's pairs in gondolini, and teams in the big fat boats called caorline. A spectacular historical pageant includes a replica of the Doge's boat, the Bucintoro.

September Second Sunday. *Regata del Palio at Murano.*
September Third Sunday. A *regatta out at Burano.*
September For two weeks in September the International Film Festival is on at the Palazzo del Cinema, out at the Lido.
There is usually a musical fortnight in September, with concerts of Vivaldi and Monteverdi.
November 11 St Martin's Day. Buy a St Martin figure, with his cloak and sword made in pastry and icing sugar.
November 21 Festival of Madonna della Salute. Once more a floating bridge is built across the Grand Canal to the Salute church.

DISCOVERING VENICE

CANNAREGIO

From the station, follow the Lista di Spagna, an area full of hotels, including the Abbazia, Carettoni, Rossi, along the campo Santa Geremia (hotel here and large public garden behind).

For paintings by G B Tiepolo, see the frescoed room in the 16th-century Palazzo Labia on campo San Giovanni Nuovo. Exceptional paintings are hung in an exceptionally extravagant building, now the RAI (state broadcasting) headquarters. Open for visitors, 3–4pm, telephone 041/781111 before you go.

Now cross the bridge and turn left to the Ghetto (synagogue and museum). This is the first ghetto in the world: set apart for Jews in 1516, this small island is now called the Ghetto Nuovo. The word comes from the Italian *gettare*, meaning to cast in metal – and the district was named after iron foundries there.

Walking along the canal side (Fondamente della Misericordia), you pass several inexpensive eating places (including Paradiso Perduto). Take a left turn up the Calle Larga to see the church of Madonna dell' Orto, passing Tintoretto's house.

Returning south towards the Grand Canal, the main shopping street strada Nova, a wide filled-in canal, runs parallel to the Grand Canal. There are more everyday and less expensive shops here than around San Marco. Turn right down Calle Ca D' Oro for the Galleria Franchetti, an art collection housed in the Ca D' Oro, the most elaborate Gothic palazzo on the canal, once decorated with gold leaf, and once given as a present by the Russian Prince Troubetskoy to the ballerina Marina Taglioni. Gallery open 9am-2pm, L2,000. *Vaporetto* stop here.

DORSODURO – ST MARK'S TO CAMPO SANTO STEFANO

To get to the Dorsoduro from St Mark's, leave the square by the south-west corner near the information office in Calle dell' Ascensione (a kiosk sells foreign newspapers here). Cross over, through the arch, and next on your left the ritzy Calle Vallaresso leads down to the famous Harry's Bar. (Treat yourself to an expensive drink at Hemingway's 'local'.)

Drinks at the bar start at L6,000, service 20 per cent. L12,000 for their speciality, a Bellini (at the bar), peach juice and Prosecco. Mimosa is orange and Presecco (Venice's sparkling white wine). Closed Monday and

Carnival time in St Marks Square

during January, open 10.30am-11pm.

From the San Marco stop down on the canal, it is one stop across the canal on *vaporetto* 1 to the Salute stop, or three stops on to the Accademia. Or take a *traghetto* from campo del Traghetto, near the San Maria del Giglio stop. Or if you fancy a walk, continue along Salizzada San Moise into campo San Moise, along Calle Larga XXII Marzo (good window-shopping for antiques here). Continue on over several bridges, via campo Maria Zobenigo and campo Maurizio to campo San Stefano (also called Francesco Morosini). You'll know when you've arrived, because it is a large square with a big statue of writer Nicolo Tommaseo. The church is worth looking into, there are several fine palazzos, and many cafés to have a drink in. (Paolin is famous for ices.)

Moneysaver

On Sunday mornings there are often bookstalls in campo San Stefano selling cut-price art and other books.

Walk the length of the campo, past the church of San Vidale, and you will be at the temporary (since 1932!) wooden Accademia bridge.

DORSODURO – ALONG THE ZATTERE

When everywhere else is crowded on a Sunday morning in June, walk down the wide Rio Terra Sant' Antonio Foscarini to the Zattere, the long quayside facing south, and you will be far from crowds, with a view across to the Giudecca.

Just on your right is the Gesuati with a ceiling painted by Tiepolo. To your left by the Calcina bridge is the Calcina hotel, where the English writer John Ruskin once stayed. Ask for a room with view to the Giudecca. Sit out over the water in front of the next door bar. (The Seguso hotel behind is more expensive and only does half board).

Walk along the Zattere, past the Gesuati, and turn up right along Fondamenta Nani, running alongside the San Trovaso canal. Here are the oldest remaining boatyards (*squeri*) in Venice, dating from the 7th century. Not far away, on the Rio degli Ognissanti, the Tramontin family still make the 280 gondola components in the traditional way. The Montin *trattoria* is round the corner from here.

Moneysaver

Good sitting-down places, or seats for a picnic in the Dorsoduro area:

In campo Sant' Agnese south of the Accademia, along Rio Terra Rosarini, a few benches under trees.

On the steps of Santa Maria della Salute – shady at midday, a wonderful view across the Grand Canal with endless water activity – movement without noise.

On the canal-side platform outside the Guggenheim Museum.

Campo San Vio, between the Accademia and the Guggenheim, seats under trees and a view.

Ponte San Trovaso, at Fondamenta Toffetti, seats outside the church under trees by a canal.

DORSODURO – ACCADEMIA TO SANTA MARIA DELLA SALUTE

To visit the Accademia gallery, with its huge range of Venetian paintings, go early in the morning (only open mornings 9am-2pm, Sundays 9-1pm, L4,000). Note the big painting *Meal in the House of Levi* by Veronese, once called the *Last Supper*, but the Inquisition took exception – that jester and parrot, those German soldiers, the fellow with the nosebleed – was Veronese trying to be facetious? He was told to change it, which he did by changing the name.

From here follow the Calle Nuova Sant' Agnese and walk parallel to the canal, passing campo San Vio, a good place to sit out, until you reach the Peggy Guggenheim collection, well worth a visit for its modern art, her own collection of 20th-century mostly cubist and surrealist paintings (Kandinsky, Chagall, Klee, Max Ernst, Magritte), and also a chance to sit by the canal edge, down the steps in front of Marino Marini's *Angel of the City*. Open daily (except Tuesday) 11am-6pm, L5,000, Saturday open till 9pm.

There are interesting shops (glass-blowing at Genedesi on Calle San Gregorio, modern print shops, a gallery, L' Occhio, on Calle del Bastion, and the Salvati glass shop) and a few inexpensive restaurants in this area (the Ai Cugnai is one). When you finally reach the Church of Santa Maria della Salute, the whole of St Mark's and the canal basin is open to view before you (but stop to look at the paving outside the church as well).

Santa Maria della Salute (*salute* = health) was built as a thanksgiving after a terrible plague ended in 1630. Buildings were demolished and 1,156,627 wooden piles driven into the mud as foundation. Designed by Longhena, there are works by Titian and Tintoretto inside.

GIUDECCA

Walk along the unbeaten track here for a panoramic view of the Dorsoduro, St Mark's and the whole Grand Canal basin.

Take *vaporetto* 5 from San Zaccaria or the Dorsoduro or the *traghetto* across from the Zattere. The huge brick building along the end of the island on your right (looking like a mixture of Moscow University and a Lancashire cotton mill) was built in 1895 by a German and was a flour mill, the Stucky mill, now disused and waiting for transformation into a block of apartments.

Along the canal-side walk is the Palazzo Foscari (no 795), one of the Venetian country villas where households moved to in the summer months. Cross the Ponte Longo, and by the Redentore landing stage is the Palladian church of Il Redentore, the marvellous building that one looks across at from the piazzetta San Marco.

The Redentore was built as a thanksgiving to commemorate the end of a plague in 1576 which is still remembered every July. The church, consecrated in 1592, is built according to very precise arithmetical proportions. There's a *trattoria* near here (The Redentore), closed Thursday, pizzas L4,000-L6,000, and there are seats to sit near the landing stage (also called San Giacomo).

Walk south across the island from here to a little grassy area with seats and a view across the lagoon to the south. There are fruit and vegetable stalls in the mornings along this Fondamenta as well as little food shops. This is the working and suburban island, nothing fancy or touristy. Towards the Zitelle stop is the youth hostel (always crowded, book in advance), and the Casa Frollo, a lovely hotel, just renovated. And look out for no 43, a fantastic Gothic-style house built by a 20th-century painter. The church by the Zitelle landing stage, the Santa Maria della Presentazione was also designed by Palladio (only open for Mass on Sunday). Next to it, a convent where the nuns make the special *punto in aria*, fine Venetian lace, and further along the 15th-century house of explorer Alvise Da Mosto, with an interior courtyard you can visit. Round the corner is the only other hotel on the island, the very expensive Cipriani.

From the Zitelle landing, take *vaporetto* 5 to the Zaccaria stop, past the island (you can stop off) of San Giorgio Maggiore with the other large Palladian church and a campanile. This light and airy church houses two late paintings by Tintoretto (*The Last Supper* and *The Gathering of Manna*), and his last painting, *The Deposition* is in a chapel off the chancel. Take a lift up the campanile for the best view of Venice (and right to the Dolomites) L2,000. Open 9am-12.30pm and 2-6pm.

CASTELLO – THE ARSENAL

The Castello district is the east end of Venice (the tail of the big fish) and somewhat ignored. Turn eastwards along the Grand Canal from San Marco, look up the Rio di Palazzo beyond the Doge's Palace to see the Bridge of Sighs, and walk along the Riva

degli Schiavoni. Lots of boats come and go along here, and day-tripping Italians, well set up with their sandwiches and drinks, sit on marble benches by the water. Behind you at no 4196 is the Danieli hotel, once the Palazzo Dandolo, where the first opera was performed in Venice (Monteverdi's *Proserpina Rapita*). One of Venice's most opulent and famous hotels, Proust, Wagner, George Sand and Charles Dickens were among its customers.

Further along still, at number 2135, is the Bucintoro hotel, with wonderful views. Inland, just up the Rio dei Greci, the Church of San Zaccaria has a Bellini altarpiece.

Behind the Church of Santa Maria della Pietà, just before the next canal, in the Rio della Pietà, was an orphanage whose girls had Antonio Vivaldi himself as singing master from 1703 to 1745. Vivaldi concerts are given here; ask at the Agenzia Guetta, San Marco 1289, telephone 041/5209711. The church has a ceiling by Tiepolo as well as one of his paintings over the high altar.

For a short walk, turn up the Canale dell' Arsenale, but stop off at the naval museum before you go. It is housed in what were once the grain stores of the Republic of Venice. The Museum is one of the largest in the world, with cannons, anchors, models, and a replica of the Bucintoro. Just along the Riva di Ca di Dio are the old naval bakeries with battlemented walls, where millions of ships biscuits were hard baked.

At the end of the Arsenal canal is the

entrance to the Arsenal itself, a huge expanse of derelict boat-building yards where 16,000 shipworkers once worked, building a boat in a day, and where all the fame and fortune of Venice was founded. *Vaporetto 5* on its way to Fondamente Nuove and the islands goes right through the Arsenal, which is now under military control and cannot be entered by pedestrians.

In the southern part of the Arsenal, the Corderie (reconstructed by Antonio da Ponte, who built the Rialto bridge) was the rope-making building, 315 metres (1,033ft) long, 20 metres (65½ft) wide and 14 metres (46ft) high, where enormously thick hawsers and ropes for men-of-war and trading ships were made. Stone masks with open mouths show where the cables passed.

In campo Arsenale, admire the contrasting brick and stone, and the lion of St Mark over the gate, also the Greek lions that guard the entrance, the left hand one with ancient runes scratched on his side. There are benches (free) under small trees here near the bridge.

Turn westward towards the campo Bandiera e Moro, and then north up to the Calle dei Furlani and the Scuola di San Giorgio degli Schiavoni, open weekdays 10am-12.30pm and 3.30-6pm, Sundays 10am-12.30pm, closed Mondays, L3,000. This little building, once the headquarters of Dalma-

tian merchants trading with the east, houses a cycle of brilliantly coloured, fantastic scenes, landscapes and Venetian life by Carpaccio.

From here turn westwards again to campo Santa Maria Formosa (note the hideous stone face at the foot of the campanile). The square is pleasantly spread out, flanked by handsome buildings. Continue northwards to the campo SS Giovanni e Paolo, which is one of the most interesting and attractive of all Venice's squares to sit in. Treat yourself to a *tiramisù* – Venice's original chocolate pudding, but now popular all over Italy. In the centre is the splendid statue by Verocchio of Bartolomeo Colleoni, a mercenary general of no great importance.

Beside the canal is the Scuola di San Marco, now a hospital, with a *trompe l'oeil* façade by Pietro Lombardo. The huge brick

Gothic church, SS Giovanni e Paolo, known as San Zanipolo, was begun in 1333. Inside, there are five monuments by Pietro Lombardo and his sons; the second altar on the right has a polyptych by Giovanni Bellini.

As you approach the south end of the church from campo Santa Maria Formosa along Calle Lunga, look at the weird Ospedaletto church with its grotesque figures (17th-century), typical of a bizarre Venetian spirit that loves surrealist masks and *orrida bellezza* – ugly beauty.

From the campo SS Giovanni e Paolo cross the canal and follow Calle Larga Gallina (over the boundary of the Castello region, but there's no marking) to the Rio dei Miracoli, the campo Santa Maria Nova, and, just off it, along the canal side, the little church of Santa Maria dei Miracoli, a subtle piece of designing by Pietro Lombardi, using different coloured marble, placing of windows and pillars to extend and give depth and length to this small building (1481–1489).

North of Santa Maria dei Miracoli towards the Fondamente Nuove, just off the Calle del Fumo, is a very charming small hotel tucked away, with a little garden, the Casa Boccassini.

From here, follow signs to the Rialto, where the *vaporetto* will take you back to St Mark's. On the way to the Rialto take Salizzada San Canciano westwards out of campo Santa Maria Nova, turn left in Campiello Corner on to Salizzada San Giovanni Crisostomo where, at Cannaregio 5788, is the COIN department store, the biggest clothes shop in Venice, housed in a 15th-century palace. The church of San Giovanni Crisostomo, a Renaissance church, has the picture of *Three Saints* by Giovanni Bellini, and an altarpiece by Sebastiano del Piombo.

CASTELLO – RIVA DEGLI SCHIAVONI TO CAMPO SAN PIETRO

From the Riva degli Schiavoni, instead of going inland to the Arsenal, a longer walk takes you along via Giuseppe Garibaldi, a long wide road flanked by low houses. Further along the canal bank are the public gardens and the park where the Biennale, the modern art exhibition, is held on even years.

Up via Garibaldi there are plenty of little cheap *trattorie* to tempt you, and the little Trattoria alla Rampa at 1135, past garden and seats; the set meal prices drop, until at the Trattoria al Manca (shut Thursdays), number 1253, they offer a meal sitting outside without service and drinks, for L11,000. At 1341 look in at the home-made pasta shop (chocolate tagliatelle!). Continue along the Fondamenta Sant' Anna (well away from tourists now). A few streets along here, to the left, over the Sant' Anna bridge, the Locanda Sant' Anna is quiet and friendly in a courtyard, the long sitting room (lit by Murano lamps) looking over the Canale di San Pietro behind.

Back on the Fondamenta Sant' Anna, cross the bridge on to the Isola di San Pietro, looking across to the Locanda and boat workshops, and then walk on up campo San Pietro, and the big rather deserted area surrounding San Pietro with its remarkable white campanile – seats and plenty of quiet space here to picnic by the canal. San Pietro was the cathedral church of Venice until 1807. There are concerts and shows here at the end of June.

MUSIC AND PAINTING IN VENICE

Local flavour
Wagner used to sit at Florian's complaining that no one applauded his music. Proust sat there translating Ruskin. Henry James preferred it to Quadri's. It is on the shady side of the square.

Musical Venice   Famous Venetian composers include Claudio Monteverdi, born in Cremona 1567, died in Venice, 1643. He was director of music at St Mark's for the last 30 years of his life. The priest and composer Antonio Vivaldi, known as the 'red' priest because of his flaming red hair, was probably born in Venice about 1657; died 1741. For centuries Venice was famous for its concerts, musical boating parties on the lagoon, and its operas. The world premiere of Verdi's opera *La Traviata* was held in the Fenice – and was a failure then. A hundred years' later, Stravinsky's *Rake's Progress* caused a stir.

Local flavour
When the opera *Rigoletto* was premiered in the Fenice theatre in 1851, the composer Verdi kept the famous song *La Donna è mobile* a secret until the last moment, for fear that all the gondoliers of Venice would be singing the tune before the premiere.

Notes on a few Venetian painters
Jacopo Bellini (about 1400-70) was the father of Gentile Bellini (about 1429-1507), who was official painter to the Republic in 1474. Three large paintings of his are in the Accademia in room XX, and show wonderfully rich scenes of Venetian life. Giovanni Bellini (about 1430-1516) is Jacopo's youngest son, brother of Gentile, and the greatest painter of the three. First working in tempera, he later (after 1473) used the new medium – oil. See his paintings in churches all over Venice, including the Frari, Madonna del Orto, San Francesco della Vigna, San Giovanni Chrisostomo and San Pietro Martire on Murano. There are also many in the Accademia, including (room V) five small *Madonna and Child* paintings.

Canaletto (1697-1768), Antonio Canale, was born and brought up in Venice, first working as a scene painter. Of all his famous scenes of Venice, (two in the Ca' Rezzonico), only three remain in the city, all the rest were exported. Francesco Guardi was his pupil, and Bernardo Bellotto, sometimes called Canaletto as well (1724-80), was his nephew and pupil, painting in the same style.

Carpaccio (about 1450-1525), Vittore, was working in Venice between 1490 and 1523. All Venetian life is in his intricately patterned opulent pictures. See them in the Accademia, the Scuola degli Schiavoni, and Museo Correr. Carpaccio's son Benedetto was also a painter, but not very famous.

Very little is known about Giorgione (about 1478-1510), except that he was painting in Venice in 1506, died of the plague in 1510, was said to have been the first easel painter (art for its own sake), and had an enormous influence on other painters such as Titian. Hardly an authenticated painting by him exists, except for the two extraordinary paintings in the Accademia, the amazing *Tempesta* and the frightening *Old Woman* (*La Vecchia*), both in room V.

Tiepolo (1696-1770), Giovanni Battista (also known as Gianbattista), and his son Giovanni Domenico were primarily fresco painters. GB Tiepolo was the greatest Italian 18th-century painter, and his light and airy paintings embellish walls and ceilings all over Venice. See the Palazzo Labia, the Gesuati church in Dorsoduro, and the Scuola Grande del Carmini.

Tintoretto, 1518-94, was the nickname of Jacopo Robusti, whose father was a dyer (*tintore*). Unworldly, devout, a musician and family man, Tintoretto was so keen on religion and art that he would paint religious pictures for free. For the last 20 years of his life, he lived near the Ponte dei Mori at Cannaregio 3399, giving musical parties with his daughter Marietta (also a painter, her self-portrait is in the Uffizi). The nearby Church of Madonna dell' Orto, his parish church where he is buried, was recently restored with the help of British funds. See his works there, in the Scuola di San Rocco and the Palazzo Ducale.

Titian (about 1480-1576) (real name Tiziano Veccellio) studied under the Bellini brothers and is said to have lived to 95 before dying of the Plague. He lived the last 40 years of his life just beyond the east end of the Gesuiti church in Cannaregio, with a garden which stretched down to the water. (The Fondamente Nuove was built in 1589 along the water's edge.) A visitor described an evening supper party there with Titian and Sansovino, one August night in 1540, the lagoon swarming with gondolas full of beautiful women, and music and singing long into the summer night. For nearly 60 years Titian was the outstanding Venetian painter, and the first fashionable portrait painter. In old age he was said to paint more with his fingers than his brush. See his work in the Accademia and the Frari church, and the *Martyrdom of St Lawrence* in the Gesuiti church

(Santa Maria Assunta), first chapel on the left (the light switch is behind the column on the right), painted in the 1540s, one of his finest works.

Veronese (1528-88) alias Paolo Caliari, was born in Verona (hence his nickname), but came to Venice in 1553 and lived near the Church of San Sebastiano (in Dorsoduro, just north west of the San Basilio landing-stage), which is full of his sensuous paintings, and where he is buried. Also see his work in the Palazzo Ducale and the Accademia.

There are plenty of places around Venice to see some of the wonderful fabrics, lace, furniture, and aspects of Venetian life.

The Museo Civico Correr   The Museo Civico Correr is in piazza San Marco (facing the cathedral) in the Procuratie Nuove. Usually uncrowded, this is a museum of Venetian life and times from the 14th to the 18th centuries. There is a historical collection of ships, letters, flags, coins; paintings include the well known *The Courtesans* by Carpaccio, works by all the Bellini family and sculptures by Antonio Canova.

Carpaccio's courtesans have very blond hair which was very fashionable in Venice (and unusual, presumably). Women spent hours sitting on their rooftops bleaching their hair in the sunshine, but shading their faces under crownless straw hats. The very high shoes Carpaccio's courtesans are wearing were in fact only worn by respectable married women. When someone remarked to a Venetian that the high soles must make it very difficult for his wife to walk, 'So much the better', replied the Venetian. Telephone 041/5225625. Open weekdays 10am-4pm, Sunday 9am-12.30pm, closed Tuesdays. L3,000.

Fortuny Museum   The Fortuny Museum, campo San Benedetto (or Beneto) 3780, off Calle Pésaro (nearest stop Sant' Angelo), for Fortuny and fashion fans. Palazzo Pesaro degli Orfei was the home of Mariano Fortuny, a Spaniard (1876-1949) who worked in this building, painting, sculpting, designing and making damask and silk fabrics and clothes. Everything here was made by him, but the factory is now on the Giudecca.

Also included in the entrance price are occasional photographic and other exhibitions. Telephone 041/700995. Open every day except Monday, 9am-7pm. L5,000.

Ca' Rezzonico   Ca' Rezzonico (Palazzo Rezzonico), is a museum of the 18th century at San Barnaba, on the Grand Canal, corner of Rio San Barnaba. To get there take *vaporetto* 1 to Ca' Rezzonico stop, or *traghetto* across from campo San Samuele. Telephone 041/5224543, open weekdys 10am-4pm, closed Fridays, Sunday 9am-12.30pm, L3,000. There is a collection of 18th-century art and furniture, all in a grand palazzo built in 1752. The poet Robert Browning lived here (he called it 'a corner for my old age') and died here in 1889; his son Pen continued to live here for a while. The paintings are not always ones which were in the house originally, but there are two Venetian scenes by Canaletto, oddly enough the only ones in this city. The Grand Tourists (especially British) bought Canaletto's pictures and carried them away; many of his best are abroad, including a series in Windsor Castle near London. Also here are the typically Venetian *black servant* figure vase holders carved by Andrea Brustolon, architectural cabinets, as well as lacquering, gilding, carving, all the skills of inlay work and picture framing, which peaked in mid 18th-century Venice and are still carried on today.

Centre for fabric and costume   The Centre for Fabric and Costume (Centro studi di storia del Tessuto e del Costume) is at Ca' Mocenigo, San Stae. This is not in the large Palazzo Mocenigo on the Grand Canal, but down Salizzada di San Stae (no 1992), just inland from the San Stae landing stage. See silks, velvets, cottons and clothes in a palace with painted ceilings, very little changed since the 18th century. Open Tuesday, Wednesday, Saturday, 8.30am-1pm, free entrance.

ISLANDS

Scattered across nearly 200 square miles of the Venetian lagoon are some 40 islands.

San Michele is a beautiful sight and first stop en route to Murano. Venice's Renaissance cemetery, with a church built by Mauro Codussi. Ezra Pound, Diaghilev and Stravinsky are buried here. The Jewish cemetery is on the Lido.

Murano comprises several islands. From first (Faro) or second (Colonna) *vaporetto* stops, walk down Fondamenta Manin, where there are glass shops and factories, and look in at the Church of San Pietro Martire, with its two great Giovanni Bellini paintings, or stay on the boat to Canale degli Angeli. Near by the Museo Vetrario, Fondamenta Giustinian 8, on the Canale di San Donato is open weekdays 10am-4pm (shut Wednesdays), Sunday 9am-12.30pm, L3,000. This is a large glass museum, but glass is no cheaper here than in Venice. Beyond the museum is the handsome church of Santa Maria e Donato.

Local flavour

Glass factories were sent here from Venice in 1291 for safety. Glass was an important export; any glass-blower who left was condemned to death in his absence. The making of clear crystal glass was perfected here early in the 16th century.

Burano is served by *vaporetto* 12 from the Fondamente Nuove, L5,000 return (half an hour). This bright and colourful island of little flower-trimmed houses painted in blues, yellows, orchres and reds is inhabited by fishermen and lace-making wives. There are *trattorias*, shops, stalls and a lace museum, Scuola di Merletti di Burano, telephone 041/730034, open Monday to Saturday 9am-6pm. Sunday 10am-4pm. L2,000, half price for students, children and over 60s.

Torcello This trip takes about 40 minutes on *vaporetto* 12 (every hour, 9.05am, 9.55am, 10.55am, then 35 minutes past the hour) from Fondamente Nuove, stopping at Murano and Burano on the way, L5,400 return. There are no shops, and only an expensive restaurant, the Locanda Cipriani (owned by Harry's Bar) on the island, so bring a picnic. In the 16th century, 20,000 people lived here, working in the wool trade and fishing, and there were 10 churches. But malaria and Venetian competition ruined them, the buildings fell down, the materials were re-used, and now only about 100 people live on this little island out in the lagoon. Come to see the 11th-century Church of Santa Fosca and the Venetian-Byzantine Cathedral of Santa Maria Assunta founded in the 7th century and partly rebuilt in the 11th, with vast, beautiful mosaics. Open 10am-12.30pm and 2-6.30pm daily, L1,000. Adjacent is a museum, closed Monday.

The Lido *Vaporetto* lines 1 and 2 go to the Lido, with its long sandy beaches and grand hotels evoking memories of Visconti's film of *Death in Venice*, is strictly a place to go if you want to watch other people sitting on the beach (the water is polluted). Saunter down the viale Santa Maria Elisabetta, or have lunch at a *trattoria* (very full on Sundays, shut on Mondays). In September the film festival brings film people and journalists.

VILLAS BETWEEN VENICE AND PADUA

There are several interesting villas, reached by bus from along the Brenta canal. ACTV buses go from piazzale Roma.

From the 16th century, all wealthy Venetians owned a house on *terra firma* (the mainland). Families, servants, furniture moved out from June until the end of July while courts and Senate shut down and piazza San Marco became deserted. They returned to the country from October to mid November for more rural life – gambling, balls, feasting and entertainments – *villeggiatura* it was called, and such extravagances ruined many Venetian families.

ACTV buses go from piazzale Roma. For the villas at Mira and Stra, take the yellow, slow bus to Padua along the Brenta canal (not the motorway). A lot of this ride goes through grim industrial areas. These villas all have several names because of their changing owners, which can be confusing.

Villa Malcontenta (also called Villa Foscari), built by Palladio, this is one of the most famous of all his villas. Take bus 16, L1,200 return. Telephone 041/969012. Open Tues-day, Saturday and first Sunday of the month from May to October, 9am-12 noon, admission L5,000.

Villa Widmann-Foscari-Rezzonico at Mira. Telephone 041/423552. Open Tuesday to Sunday 9am-12 noon and 2-6pm. Admission with guided tour L6,000, over 65s, L3,500.

Stra, also called Villa Pisani, is further along the bus route towards Padua. This immensely grand villa and garden, begun in 1735, has frescoes by Urbani and Tiepolo. Tsars, emperors and kings stayed here, and in 1934 Mussolini first met Hitler here. Telephone 049/502074, open Tuesday to Sunday 9am-6pm, admission L3,000.

All the villas have large gardens with picnic space. For villa information contact the Ente per le Ville Venete, piazza San Marco 63, Venice.

VERONA

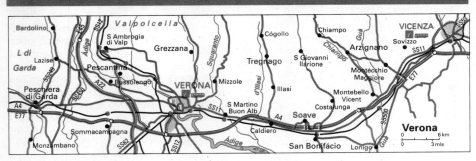

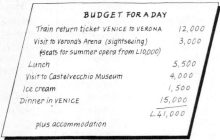

BUDGET FOR A DAY	
Train return ticket VENICE to VERONA	12,000
Visit to Verona's Arena (sightseeing)	3,000
(seats for summer opera from L10,000)	
Lunch	5,500
Visit to Castelvecchio Museum	4,000
Ice cream	1,500
Dinner in VENICE	15,000
	L41,000
plus accommodation	

40 trains a day (the last train back at 10.33 arrives in Venice at midnight). APT buses as well as trains will take you on from here to Lake Garda. Originally a Roman city on the banks of the Ádige river, Verona, although industrialised and built up, is still a picturesque city not to be missed. It is liable to fill up, especially at Easter and mid-summer with visiting Germans and Austrians coming down through the Brenner Pass.

From Porta Nuova train station, take AMT bus 2 to piazza Brà (L800 from the ticket office outside the station). For a day's sightseeing, this is the place to start.

Pick up a map of the city and the leaflet

Reached from Venice in 1½ hours by train (L12,000 return), Verona is about midway between Milan and Venice, linked by about

Verona for You and explore Verona's Arena, built in the 1st century AD, and one of the largest and most complete amphitheatres in existence. Open Tuesday to Sunday, 8.30am-6.30pm (closes 5.30pm in winter), L3,000. On July and August afternoons it is sometimes shut for rehearsals for the operas staged here. The Arena holds over 20,000 on stone seats (bring your cushion or rent one). Some tickets are usually returned before the performance. Box office is under Arch 6. Information (you can't book by telephone) 045/590109 or 045/590966.

Verona's Arena, an amphitheatre built in 1st century AD

From the Arena, follow via Mazzini in piazza delle Erbe, site of the old Roman forum, and a modern market in the morning. Nearby piazza dei Signori contains the 12th-century Pallazzo della Ragione, the Loggia del Consiglio and the Governor's Palace. At the end of the square the Arche Scaligere are Gothic tombs of the Scala dynasty, who ruled here for centuries, a violent crew with violent names (*Cangrande* 'big dog' was head of the family, and *Mastino* 'mastiff' another member).

In via Capello 23 (open Tuesday to Sunday, 8am-6.45pm, L3,500) you can queue to look down from Juliet's balcony in the Casa Giuletta (with crowds of pseudo-Romeos and trinket stalls below), or see Casa Romeo, now a coffee bar at via Arche Scaligare 2. Juliet's supposed tomb is south towards the river, off via Shakespeare, open 8am-7pm, L3,500. These may disappoint you, but the town itself won't.

Cross the Ponte Nuovo to the Giardino Giusti to visit an 18th-century garden (open daily 9am-8pm, L4,000). And if you can, visit the Castelvecchio Museum near Ponte Scaligero, north west of the Arena, a modern complex designed by Carlo Scarpa in an old (war-bombed) building, with paintings and sculpture. Open Tuesday to Saturday 8am-7pm, L4,000. Also see the church of San Zeno Maggiore with an altarpiece by Andrea Mantegna (stolen in 1973 but recovered). Open daily 7am-12 noon and 3-6pm.

ORIENTATION IN VERONA

INFORMATION
Tourist Office
Via Dietro Anfiteatreo 6.
☎ *045/592828, behind the Arena in piazza Brà. Helpful, English speaking, they exchange money (12 noon-7pm) and give hotel information. Open Monday to Saturday 8am-8pm. Sunday 9am-2pm.*
Postal Code
37100.
Telephone Code
045.

ACCOMMODATION
Note that Verona gets very full in July and August, as well as in March for the agricultural fair.
Aurora *via Pellicciai 2.*
☎ *045/594717. Two-star, 22 rooms. L39,000-L41,200 without bath, L51,000-*

L59,000 with, breakfast L8,000.
Castello *corso Cavour 43.* ☎ *045/8004403. One-star, eight rooms, Restaurant. L42,300 with bath, L30,300 without. Breakfast L5,500.*
Cavour *vicolo Chiodo 4, Verona 37121.* ☎ *045/ 590508. Two-star, 17 rooms.*

Doge *via C Abba 12b* ☎ *045/912491. One-star, 16 rooms.*
Volto Cittadella *vicolo Volto Citadella 8, within walking distance of the train station.* ☎ *045/8000077. One-star, 11 rooms, three bathrooms. No private bathrooms. Basin in room.*

L30,000-L40,000.

EATING OUT
Torre 5 *on corso Porta Nuova 9, near the Arena. Good pizzas.*
Al Cacciatore *via Seminario 4, across the Ponte Nuovo.* ☎ *045/594291. Closed Sundays.*

Local flavour

Gnocchi (small potato dumplings) are a speciality. On the last Friday of the carnival in spring, the Bacchanale of Gnocchi is celebrated, with Papa del Gnoco walking about with a huge dumpling on a fork.

Local flavour

The province of Verona produces some of Italy's best-known DOC wines. From Soave: Soave Classico (white), or sweet Recioto Soave. Bianco di Custoza is another white and from Valpolicella and Bardolino, reds.

VICENZA

Coming into Vicenza by train from Padua, passing fertile plains of maize and poplars with a backdrop of first the rolling green Euganean hills and then the Berici mountains, that dreamy rural feeling isn't interrupted by hideous city outskirts. The hills and woods with their Palladian villas come close to the leafy arcadian city, and rise right up behind the station as you arrive.

From the station, take a 1 or 7 AIM bus to the town centre and piazza Matteotti. Or walk through the gardens in front, up via Roma to the Giardino Salvi the other end. A right turn, and a walk down corso Andrea Palladio (the main street) will bring you to piazza Matteotti. Or turn right and right again into piazza Castello and continue along Contra Vescovado into piazza del Duomo, with the large Gothic brick cathedral and nearby APT office.

Just a street away from here is the architectural heart of Vicenza, the piazza dei Signori, which used to be the old Roman forum, and where Palladio's colonnaded Basilica surrounds the earlier Gothic town hall inside (the Basilica is not a church). In

the piazza opposite is the Loggia del Capitano, begun by Palladio but never finished. Turn back into corso Palladio from here. (There are two inexpensive hotels in this area.) Vicenza is a centre for goldsmithing, and has some good shops.

Don't miss the Palazzo da Schio, also called the Ca d'Oro, on corso Palladio. The best Palladian palaces are along the Contra Porti. (The streets are called *Contra*, which is Venetian dialect for *Contrada*, as in the Siena districts.)

The architecture of Andrea Palladio fills Vicenza: this is La Rotonda

94

Don't miss the Teatro Olimpico, in piazza Matteotti, Palladio's last work. Based on a Roman theatre with a permanent false perspective stage set, it is over-elaborate but unique. Admission L3,000, children under 10 free. Open all year Monday to Saturday 9.30am-12.30pm and 3-5.30pm (closes at 4.30pm in winter), Sundays 9.30-12.20pm.

In the church of Santa Corona, Contra Santa Corona off via Palladio, see a *Baptism of Christ* by Giovanni Bellini over an altar on the left, and amazing inlaid marble on the high altar.

The Villa Thiene, another Palladian villa (unfinished), now a municipal office at via IV Novembre, Quinto Vincentino (a suburb). Open office hours (not Saturday or Sunday). On Monte Berico is the baroque Basilica Monte Berico, with a Veronese painting and Montagna frescoes. Open daily.

Two villas not to be missed are within walking distance of the town (to the south east) in the hills behind the train station and near bus routes:

Villa Valmarana dei Nani is an 18th-century villa with frescoes by Giambattista Tiepolo. Take bus 8 from the corso Palladio or the station to via San Bastiano, then quarter of a mile gentle uphill walk. The guesthouse has frescoes by Tiepolo's son Domenico. Open March to November every afternoon 2.30-5.30pm. Also open morning 10am-12 noon on Thursday, Saturday and Sunday.

La Rotonda became the model for Jefferson's house, Monticello, and most US state capitol buildings. Begun by Palladio 1567, it was completed by Scamozzi 20 years later. Open March 15 to October 15, interior only open Wednesdays 10am-12 noon and 3-6pm, L5,000. The outside is most interesting; grounds are open Tuesday, Wednesday, Thursday at the same times, L3,000.

OUTINGS FROM VICENZA

There are several possibilities for excursions by bus from Vicenza. Buses go every hour to Bessano del Grappa (L6,000 return). Maróstica (L4,800 return), Thiene (L4,800 return). Change at Thiene for Lugo (five buses per day). Southwards, 10 buses a day go to Poiana Maggiore (Ł6,000 return). Bassano is famous for its Palladio-designed covered bridge over the Brenta river. Maróstica has a human chess game in 15th-century costumes in the town square, played the second weekend in September.

At Masèr the famous Villa Barbaro-Volpi, built by Palladio, houses Veronese

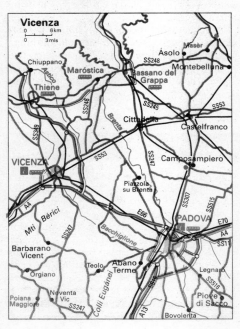

frescoes, with water gardens and a temple in the grounds. Telephone 0423/565002. Open afternoons, Tuesday, Saturday, Sunday. At

Lugo are the Villa Godi-Valmarana, and Villa Piovene (at the Villa Piovene only the park is open, daily 2.30-7pm, L2,000).

ORIENTATION IN VICENZA

INFORMATION
TOURIST OFFICES
APT, piazza Duomo 5.
☎ *0444/544122.*
Information office, piazza Matteotti 12, next to the Teatro Olimpico. ☎ *0444/ 320854. Very helpful, English spoken. Maps, opening times etc; ask for villa information. Open Monday to Saturday 8.30am-12.30pm and 2.30-6.30pm. Sundays, mornings only.*
APAT, via Gazzolle.
☎ *0444/399155 for more leaflets on villas.*
POST OFFICE
Contra Garibaldi, near the Duomo. Monday to Friday 8am-7.30pm, Saturday 8am-1pm. Postal code 36100.
TELEPHONE
SIP, via Napoli 11. Daily 8am-9.30pm. Telephone code 0444.

POLICE
Via Muggia 2 (pronounced Mooja, sounds better).
☎ *0444/504044.*

TRANSPORT
TRAINS
Railway station at end of viale Roma. ☎ *0444/324396.* Information ☎ *0444/325046.* Frequent trains to Venice, Padua, Verona.
BUSES
City buses, AIM. Out-of-town buses FTV, viale Milano 7, on the left as you come out of the railway station. ☎ *044/544333.*
CAR HIRE
Avis via Milano 88.
☎ *0444/321622.*
Maggiore Stazione F S.
☎ *0444/545962.*

ACCOMMODATION
All these are two-star hotels, recommended by the tourist office.
Casa S Raffaele viale X Giugno 10, up in the hills

behind the station, with views. ☎ *0444/323663.* City centre
Due Mori Contra 2 Ruote 26. ☎ *0444/221886. L38,000 with bath. Restaurant (where you can eat a Pizza Sophia Loren, decorated with two well placed eggs).*
Palladio via Oratorio Dei Servi 25. ☎ *0444/321072.*
Vicenza via dei Nodari 5.
☎ *0444/321512.*

EATING OUT
Tre Visi Contra Porte 6 (once home of the author of the original story of Romeo and Juliet). Fireplace, rustic surroundings, home-made pasta. L35,000 full meal (closed mid July to mid August).
Vecchia Gurada Contra Pescherie Vecchie 11, popular trattoria, for local pizza and local polenta with cod. Also try the Trattoria Pizzeria al Paradiso next door.

PADUA

Not to be missed in Padua (Padova) is the Cappella di Serovegni, entirely covered with frescoes by Giotto; other sights include a Donatello statue and a handsome basilica. Medieval yellow and cream classical buildings surround Padua's ancient and important university in the town centre (founded in 1222; Galileo was a professor here).

Padua is a large modern city as well, but the historic centre is easily accessible from the bus station or the railway station. Buses 3, 8 and 12 go from the railway station south

along via Garibaldi towards the centre. From the bus station cross the bridge and keep straight on to reach piazza Eremitani, where the information office, museum, Chiesa degli Eremitani (containing war-damaged paintings by Mantegna), Cappella and civic museum are all conveniently clustered together. The information office provides a wealth of material, a leaflet all about the town and maps. On request you can get maps with routes to all the villas in the vicinity and opening times.

The Cappella degli Scrovegni (also known as the Chapel of the Arena) was built 1303-1305, and in 1306 Giotto began covering the inside with scenes from the life of Christ, the largest series and best preserved (though decaying a bit) of all his paintings. Open daily 9am-7pm April to September, shut Mondays and open only until 6pm in winter. L5,000 (with civic museum), L2,500 ages 14-17, L1,500 ages 6-13, free under five and over 65.

In the centre of piazza delle Erbe, separating this market square from the Frutta, the other side, is the huge 12th-century Palazzo della Ragione, built as a law court, now a conference centre.

> **Moneysaver**
> In the university building there are guided visits (free) on weekdays, (9.30am, 11.20am, 3.30pm and 5.30pm, Saturday mornings only) to the round-tiered anatomy theatre (1594), the first of its kind, used by William Harvey, discoverer of blood circulation, among others.

ORIENTATION IN PADUA

INFORMATION
TOURIST OFFICE
At the railway station. ☎ 049/8752077. Also near the bus station and at the Museo Civico Eremitani, ☎ 049/8751153, open Monday to Saturday 9am-8pm, Sunday 8am-2pm. Economical money exchange office here 9.20am-12.30pm and 1.30-5.30pm.
POST OFFICE
Corso Garibaldi 25. Postal code 35100.
TELEPHONE
ASST, corso Garibaldi 31, open 24 hours. SIP, near Caffè Pedrocchi, 8am-9.30pm.

Telephone code 049.

TRANSPORT
TRAINS
Piazza Stazione. ☎ 049/8750667. To Venice every half hour, L4,000 return. Verona every hour. Vicenza every 10-20 minutes, 20-minute trip, L2,400 return. If you take a Rapido or IC train, you must pay a supplement. Departures also from Padua to Bassano, Castelfranco and Belluno.
BUSES
ATP via Trieste 40, near piazzale Boschetti. ☎ 049/8206844. Venice every half hour, L6,400 return.

ACCOMMODATION
Al Fagiano via Locatelli 45, right by Il Santo. ☎ 049/8753396. Newly refurbished 33 rooms, restaurant (closed Mondays and July). Double L65,000.
Pensione Bellevue via L Belludi 11, off Prato della Valle. ☎ 049/30434. One-star, 11 rooms. Double L43,000 with bath.
Tourismo via Santa Chiara 49, on quiet street near Il Santo. ☎ 049/651276. One-star, seven rooms. Simple. Double L38,000 with bath, L30,000 without.

EATING OUT
Vecchia Padova via Zabarella 14. ☎ 049/38679). Closed August and Mondays. Good cafeteria food midday.

97

BOLOGNA, FLORENCE AND NORTHERN TUSCANY

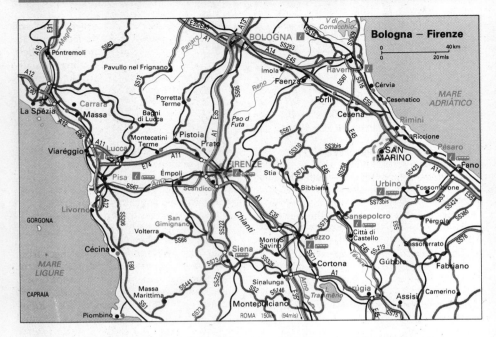

This is a true cross-section of Italy, stretching from the Adriatic to the Ligurian Sea (Mare Ligure), across three central regions easily accessed by car, train or plane. There are two main international airports in this area, Pisa and Bologna. You can fly in at one and out the other (Italy Sky Shuttle, for instance, does charter flights and fly-drive deals to both airports.) Starting from either Bologna or Pisa you can make a great arc over the whole region. In the summer there are flights to Rimini as well. Italian trains are inexpensive, ideal for the budget traveller. To cover this whole area by train need cost you not more than L35,000.

This is an area of great variety: Bologna has the cosmopolitan atmosphere of a big city (and is famous for its food); the early Byzantine mosaics at Ravenna are wonderful; and some call Urbino the most beautiful small Renaissance city of all. If you make Florence (Firenze) your centre, the Chianti hills and valleys (not to mention the wine) are easily reached by bus, and Arezzo and Siena are not too far by bus or train. (Siena is described in the next chapter.)

Local flavour

In the mid 19th century, when many intrepid foreigners visited Italy, it took 36 hours to go by stagecoach from Florence to Rome, five or six days by carriage via Siena, and about seven days via Arezzo and Perúgia. There were 27 posts along the route, where travellers could change horses, eat, or spend the night. Teams of oxen were hired to pull the coaches up mountains in Umbria.

If you are travelling with children or in a large group, it might be more convenient (but not necessarily more economical) to rent a villa or farmhouse. Against this you have to calculate the cost of hiring a car (unless you drive down), which will be at least £220 a week, booked in this country. (See the traveller's handbook from the Italian Tourist Office for lists of villa agents.) Both hire car rates and villa rates rise steeply at school holiday time.

Local flavour

Around and to the west of Florence, US and British connections are very strong. Elizabeth and Robert Browning lived in Florence until Elizabeth's death. D H Lawrence finished writing *Lady Chatterley's Lover* at the Villa Miranda in Scandicci. Keats, Shelley and Byron lived on the Ligurian coast where Shelley died. Henry Moore came for his marble to the quarries near Carrara, as had Michelangelo before him. And in the Chianti country a sea captain called Giovanni de Verrazzano was born in Castello di Verrazzano. It was he who landed on the American coast in February 1524 and discovered Manhattan Island and the Hudson River.

Monday is the best day for travelling, because many museums are closed then. Do watch out for museum opening times; most large national museums such as the Bargello and Accademia in Florence are closed all day Monday, and shut at 2pm on other weekdays.

It is best to start early in the day and see the indoor sights first. Have a late lunch (with food bought *before* the midday closing), eat out of doors in a park, and then spend the afternoon looking at the outsides of things. And when the wild hordes of schoolchildren come pushing their noisy way into the same museum as you, especially in Florence, don't take it personally – wait for the storm to subside and slip in later.

You could, however, spend an entire holiday here without entering a single museum, and still enjoy a visual feast – little villages perched on hills, one house and a pine tree on the horizon, hills and cypresses and valleys folding into a blue distance. . . .

There are wines to feast on too, of course, such as Chianti Classico with its black cockerel symbol denoting the best quality, or Vin Santo, a strong, usually sweetish wine, best drunk with an *amaretto* (a macaroon) perhaps, or a slice of *panforte* (fruit cake).

Moneysaver

Remember that it is cheaper to drink coffee or wine standing at the bar. It can cost double to sit in or outside a café. At most bars you pay at the till first, then show your receipt to the barman and collect your drink.

The food in this varied area ranges from the famous fish soup from Livorno in the west – *cacciucco*, to the *brodetto*, another fish soup, found on the east coast. Anything *alla livornese* on the menu is usually fishy. *Ribollita* is a local Tuscan soup, chiefly bread and vegetables and oil. *Crostini* are starters, slices of bread covered with chicken liver paste or mayonnaise. *Bistecca alla Fiorentina* is a rather expensive Florentine speciality – a thick rare steak. *Pecorino*, sheep cheese; *pappa*, bread soaked in olive oil or tomato, *fagioli*, dried beans, are all common here. *Porcini*, one of many kinds of mushroom, have a rich and unforgettable taste. Revel in the cheeses, the smoked hams (expensive, but you only need a few thin slices), and look for homemade pasta.

Local flavour

Confetti di Pistoia are sugar-coated almonds given as mementoes at weddings.

Zuppa inglese is a kind of sweet and rather sloppy trifle.

Coniglio umbriaco al Chianti is 'rabbit drunk on Chianti'. Not a bad way for a rabbit to go.

The best free shows are markets, festivals and the evening *passeggiata*. Some of the festivals are spectacular, jousting on land, and on water as at Pisa, flag-waving everywhere, and several towns have crossbow contests. And last but not least, in a region which stretches from the birthplace of Puccini (in Lucca) in the west, to Rossini (at Pésaro) in the east, there are all the music festivals held in towns large and small. Enquire about them at local tourist offices.

> **Moneysaver**
> Not expensive or hard to carry, posters, reproductions and postcards are a good buy. Always buy a few more than you think you need, you won't regret it. They make wonderful presents, framed, and you may never find them again outside the region. Town guides usually have good pictures too. In Florence, Alinari, via della Vigna Nuova 46-48, is *the* shop. Rizzoli's *Maestri dei Colori* series is a good buy.

FARMHOUSE HOLIDAYS

Agriturist is the Italian agency renting rooms in farmhouses. Prices range from L11,000 to L30,000 per night. Regional offices are at:

Arezzo c/o UPA, corso Italia 205, 52100 Arezzo, telephone 0575/22280.

Bologna via delle Lame 15, 40123 Bologna, telephone 051/233321.

Florence piazza Santa Firenze 3, 50122 Florence, telephone 055/287838.

Lucca c/o UPA, via le Barsanti e Matteuci, 55100 Lucca, telephone 0583/332044.

Pésaro c/o UPA, piazzale le Matteotti 28, 61100 Pésaro, telephone 0721/33168.

Pisa c/o UPA, via B Croce 62, 56100 Pisa, telephone 050/26221.

Ravenna c/o UPA, via M d'Azeglio 38, 4800 Ravenna, telephone 0544/22002.

Siena c/o UPA, piazza G Matteotti 3, 53100 Siena, telephone 0577/46194.

Write to the head office at corso Emanuele 101, Rome, (telephone 06/6512342) for a *Rural Hospitality Guide*.

The local tourist offices can also advise about renting villas and boarding with local families. See under each town for the address.

BOLOGNA

The airport, G Marconi, is 6km (3¾ miles) north west of the city at borgo Panigale. Take a blue bus 91 to the train station. The tourist office at the station will book rooms for you free, telephone 051/246541.

Bologna, capital of the Emilia-Romagna region, is a large commercial city, hosting many conferences and exhibitions. It is also home to Europe's oldest university, founded in 1088. It is famous for its arcaded buildings, leaning towers, a bronze fountain by Giambologna, and also for its pasta, sausage, and all kinds of food. Hotels tend to fill up with business people, though not so much in July and August.

From the train station, take bus 25 or 30 to go straight to piazza Maggiore, the centre of the city. There the main tourist office, in the Palazzo Comunale (on your right facing the cathedral) will give you all the train schedules, in English. The palazzo itself is open to visitors.

In piazza Maggiore is the Basilica di San Petronio, with marble reliefs by Jacopo della Quercia (1367-1438). Charles V was crowned

Bologna, famous for its arcaded buildings

Holy Roman Emperor here in 1530. Near by is the piazza del Nettuno, with its famous bronze fountain – the giant Neptune with four Sirens riding on dolphins. In piazza Porta Ravegnana are the two remaining towers of the 200 built in the 12th and 13th

centuries. The Garisenda family built in haste and repented at leisure when their tower leaned over and lost its top section. The Torre degli Asinelli 100 metres (320ft), built by the rival family, was shorter but more durable, and you can climb it for a wonderful birds-eye view of the city (open 9am-6pm, L2,000).

Visit the Church of San Giacomo Maggiore in piazza Rossini, and the Church of San Domenico in piazza San Domenico which contains three small statues by the young Michelangelo and reliefs by Nicola Pisano. The Pinacoteca Nazionale, via delle Belle Arti 56 (closed Mondays, open Tuesday to Saturday until 2pm, Sundays 1pm), contains a fine collection of Bolognese art.

Outside the city, and visible from the train, on Monte della Guardia, is the Santuario della Madonna di San Luca, with a walkway of 665 arches connecting it with the south-west city gate, Porta Saragozza. It contains a Byzantine Madonna.

ORIENTATION IN BOLOGNA

INFORMATION
POST OFFICE
Piazza Minghetti. Postal code 40100.
TELEPHONES
ASST, piazza VIII Agosto 24. Open 24 hours. Telephone code 051.

TRANSPORT
TRAINS
Bologna station, viale Pietro Pietra.
TAXI
☎ 051/372727 or 051/534141.

ACCOMMODATION
Accademia via delle Belle Arti 6, near the Pinacoteca. ☎ 051/232318.
Albergo Il Guernico via L Serra 7, behind the train station. ☎ 051/369893. English spoken. Double with bath L53,000.
Elisea via Testoni 3.

☎ 051/2777738.
Orologio via IV Novembre 10. ☎ 051/231253. Rather more expensive than the others, double L77,000, breakfast L10,000, but very central, by the clock tower of the town hall.
Pensione Marconi via Marconi 22 (walk up via Amendola to the right of the train station, through piazza dei Martiri). ☎ 051/262832. Double with shower L55,000.

OUTINGS FROM BOLOGNA

This section takes in the ancient university town of Bologna, the flat country of the Marches and miles of orchards of almond blossom in the spring, and Ravenna with its Byzantine mosaics. Coming inland and turning west is the great Renaissance city of Urbino. From here it is possible to go by bus (or car) westwards again across the valley of the Tiber (Tévere) to the Arno river and the town of Arezzo.

Pésaro, an ancient and interesting town, is also in this region though not covered in this book. Its good communications make it easy to get to for enjoying its Adriatic beaches, the Rossini museum, concert programmes and the opera festival in late August.

RAVENNA

BUDGET FOR A DAY

Train return ticket - BOLOGNA to RAVENNA	9,000
Bus return fare to CLASSE to see mosaics	2,000
Entrance to Basilica S Apollinare Nuovo	1,000
Public lavatory	400
Lunch at Mensa Il Duomo	10,000
Visit covered market to buy presents	10,000
Hot chocolate	1,600
Supper in BOLOGNA - piazza Verdi	5,000
	L 39,000
plus accommodation	

From Bologna, take a day trip to Ravenna by train (return fare L9,000), or by car from Bologna take the SS253, via Lugo, or motorway A14.

Although it's inland now, Ravenna used to be a Roman port. Augustus built the Castle of Classe and constructed 250 boats here, and Julius Caesar tarried here wondering whether to cross the Rubicon, a little river further south; later the swamps filled up, and the sea receded. Then, in the 5th and 6th centuries, Ravenna became the centre of Byzantine rule in the West. The wonderful mosaics here date from that time – the greatest to be seen outside Istanbul. The glorious colours and the gilt of these Ravenna mosaics are far more vivid than the rather pale Roman mosaics we are used to in Britain.

Ravenna is a small city, the centre is old, and there is a handsome square, the piazza del Popolo, with a colonnade. The town is level, it is easy to walk about, and there are many public gardens and open spaces with benches and places where you can sit on the grass. It can easily be seen in a day, but it is a pleasant place to stay, and the mosaics are worth seeing more than once.

Dante died here, and his bones are interred next to the Church of San Francesco. There are no mosaics on the walls, but there is a beautifully quiet atmosphere, and alabaster windows give a dim, amber light. The Archbishop's Museum, Museo Arcivescovile, in piazza Arcivescovado houses the famous carved ivory Throne of Maximilian. Open 9am-7pm, L1,000.

There are mosaics in many of the churches; the largest is the Basilica di San Vitale, a simple octagonal-shaped church on via San Vitale. The very small Mausoleum of Galla Placida behind the basilica holds the oldest mosaics. The ancient, glowing mosaics are lit up. Open the amazingly generous hours of 8.30am-7pm, and even more generously, it is free.

The Basilica Sant'Apollinare Nuovo on the via di Roma is a huge bare church, with a procession of 22 virgins on one side, and 26 martyrs on the other, all depicted in mosaic. It has a pleasant cloister. Open 9am-7pm, L1,000.

There are other churches with fine mosaics all over the town and the Battistero Ariani on the via degli Ariani, off via Diaz, is particularly worthy of note, it has wonderful representations of the baptism of Christ and a procession of the 12 Apostles.

The glowing mosaics of Ravenna are worth seeing more than once

The most beautiful mosaics of all are in the Church of Sant' Apollinare in Classe, where the apse and the choir are filled with a blue, green and gold heaven full of gentle animals and peaceful countryside. It is open from 8am-12 noon, and from 2-6.30pm. The church is 5km (3 miles) south on route SS16 and is almost all that remains of the 6th-century port of Classis. Bus 4 goes there every half hour from opposite the railway station. This is a sight absolutely not to be missed.

ORIENTATION IN RAVENNA

INFORMATION

TOURIST OFFICE
Via Salara 8.
☎ 0544/35404.
TELEPHONE
SIP, via Rasponi, off piazza
XX Settembre. Open every
day 8am-8pm. Telephone
code 0544.
POST OFFICE
Piazza Garibaldi 1, off via
Diaz near the piazza del
Popolo.
PUBLIC LAVATORIES
In the via Pasolini off via

Cavour, just along the road
from the tourist office
(L400, and spotless).

ACCOMMODATION

Argentario via Roma 45.
Comfortable, no restaurant.
It is in an old merchant's
house. ☎ 0544/22555
Centrale Byron via 4
Novembre 14, no restaurant.
☎ 0544/39164.
Hotel Trieste via Trieste 11.
☎ 0544/421566.

EATING OUT

Bella Venezia via IV

Novembre. Has good food
and atmosphere, but not
very cheap. Closed
Mondays.
Pizzeria Valentino via
Salara 5, opposite the
tourist office. Closed
Mondays. Open at
lunchtime and 6.30-11pm.

SHOPPING

MARKET
There is a covered market in
piazza Andrea Costa along
the via IV Novembre.
(Closed at midday
Thursday, otherwise open
mornings and 3.30-6pm.)

Moneysaver
You can get an entire meal plus a glass
of wine for L10,000 at lunchtime (12
noon-2.15pm, come early) at the Mensa
Il Duomo Self-service, via Oberdan 8, off
the piazza del Duomo. Closed Saturday
and Sunday, and all of August.

Local flavour
The Ravenna Festival of opera, music and
drama runs from the first week of July to
the first week of August.
  The Dante Festival, with readings from
his works, is held during the second week
of September.

URBINO

Urbino is a wonderfully steep city. The buses
stop in the car park at borgo Mercatale, from
where the lift, *ascensore*, will take you to the
end of via Garibaldi (shuts at 8.45pm). The
railway station is at the very bottom of the
hill, deep in the valley, but a bus (L600) will
take you to the piazza della Repubblica.
  The splendour of Urbino is due to Duke

Federico da Montefeltro, a great Renaissance prince and patron of all the arts who
built his great palazzo in the middle of the
15th century and filled it with art treasures.
After his time, Urbino lost its importance as
a ducal state, and came under the control of
Rome. Because it became a backwater,
Urbino has remained almost unchanged for
500 years, and is now a university town
surrounded by little hills of olives and vines,
an exemplar of the finest Renaissance archi-

Local flavour
Look for Duke Federico's portrait by Piero
della Francesca when you are in the Uffizi
in Florence. He is the man in the flat red
hat, red gown, hooded-eyed and hooked-
nosed, standing resolutely in front of a
landscape of little hills.

Moneysaver
There is nearly always plenty of free car
parking space at the top of the hill, near
the Fortezza Albornoz and the piazzale
Roma. Take the left turning off the
SS73bis from Sansepolcro *before* you go
down into the centre of town.

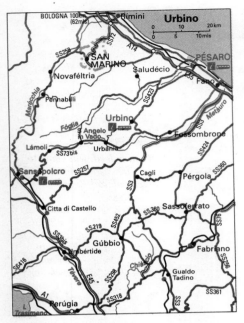

terious geometry; a Raphael lady, her necklace throwing shadows on her neck; a long horizontal Uccello with brilliant reds. Don't miss the little chapel, which you will find down a flight of 40 steps.

It's a collection which deserves several hours' study, and luckily there are central and window seats to rest on. (Raphael and Bramante looked out of these windows.) The Duke's study, with its wooden inlay, is reputed to have been designed by Botticelli. (There's something extraordinarily like a television set depicted on the left of the door as you go out.)

The painter Raphael (Raffaello Santi, 1483-1520) was born here. Raphael's house is at via Raffaello 57, and has one of his earliest frescoes. Admission L3,000; open Monday to Saturday 9am-1pm and 3-7pm. Sunday 9am-1pm.

In the via Bramante, off via Raffaello, are Urbino's botanical gardens, with a famous collection of over 4,000 species. The gardens are open 8am-12 noon and 2-7pm.

The best view of the Ducal Palace is from the public gardens of the Fortezza Albornoz. Turn left at the end of via Raffaello, or climb the steep path opposite the car park at borgo Mercatale. A good picnic place (and free), though it can be crowded, it is open every day 8am-7pm.

In the evening the townspeople and the students, who come from all over the world, congregate in the piazza della Repubblica to talk. It is then just like a large outdoor drawing room.

tecture. Hot in summer, its steep streets hard to walk, a little remote, it is nevertheless not to be missed.

The Ducal Palace   The principal attraction in Urbino is the Ducal Palace, which houses the National Gallery of the region. Entrance to the Archeological Museum across the courtyard is included in the National Gallery admission of L4,000. The Ducal Palace is open in summer (10 July to 9 October), Tuesday to Saturday 9am-7pm, Monday 9am-2pm, Sunday 9am-1pm. Do check before setting out on a Monday, when it may be shut out of season. Times do vary. Palazzo Ducale: Superintendent, piazza Rinascimento 13, telephone 0722/2760. If you get no reply from the tourist office, try another office at piazza Rinascimento 1, telephone 722/2613.

The palace has enormous rooms, ceilings arched and curved, and painted stark white, with only blue and gold or grey decoration round the doors and mammoth fireplaces. It is the perfect background for a myriad madonnas and Piero della Francesca's mys-

ORIENTATION IN URBINO

INFORMATION
TOURIST OFFICE
Piazza Duca Federico 35.
☎ 722/2441.
TELEPHONES
SIP piazza Rinascimento 4,
off piazza Duca Federico.
Monday to Saturday 8am-
10pm, Sunday 3-9pm.
Telephone code 0722.
PUBLIC LAVATORIES
(Clean) Albergo Diurno, via
C Battisti 2. Open 7am-12
noon, and 2-7.30pm. L200.
Shower L1,500.

TRANSPORT
BUSES
Frequent buses to and from
Pésaro; to Sansepolcro on
weekdays only at 12
noon; to Arezzo weekdays
at 6.50am (arrives Arezzo
9.45am) and 12 noon
(arrives 3.30pm). From
Arezzo the 3pm bus arrives
in Urbino at 5.30pm. Buses
leave from borgo Mercatale.
Buy tickets at the café.
Timetables are displayed at
the top of corso Garibaldi

*near piazza della
Repubblica.*

ACCOMMODATION
*Urbino is only a small town
and doesn't have many
hotels in the centre, so try
and book in advance.*

Fosca via Raffaello 67.
☎ *0722/329622. Rooms
only, no private baths. (The
old Pensione Fosca is no
more, but the Fosca
restaurant still exists at 62
via Budassi). Double room
L34,000.*

Italia corso Garibaldi 32.
☎ *0722/2701. Large and
old-fashioned, with bar and
breakfast terrace. Double
rooms with and without bath
L36,000-L47,000.*

*Rafaello via Santa
Margherita 38/40. Just up
the hill off via Rafaello.*
☎ *0722/4784. All rooms
with shower, double
L45,000-L62,000.*

*San Giovanni via Barocci
13.* ☎ *0722/2827. Newly
redecorated. Double rooms
with and without bath
L36,000-L46,000. Separate*

restaurant next door.

EATING OUT
*Il Girarrosto piazza San
Francesco 3, off the via
Raffaello does takeaway
pasta, or food and wine at
the bar (L5,000 for wine
and one dish). Half a roast
chicken and two special flat
pastry-cum-bread circles –
called crescia sfogliata, very
good indeed, will come to
L7,700. Closed Friday.
Open all day 8am to
midnight.
Pizzeria le Tre Piante via
Foro Posterula 1, off via
Budassi for a pizza lunch or
dinner. Closed Monday.
Open 12 noon-3pm and
7pm-2am. Sit outside for the
view.
Ristorante Ragno d'Oro on
piazza Roma, is open in July
and August. Good pasta
(L4,500). Open every day,
12 noon-3pm and 7pm-12
midnight.
Tavola Calda via Garibaldi,
is inexpensive and serves
good pasta, pizzas, and à
delicious homemade
tiramisù.*

Local flavour
From Urbino, look out for Sant' Ángelo in
Vado. The annual national truffle
exhibition is held here – the last week in
October and first week of November. Just
before Lámoli (about 20km, 12½ miles
on, after Sompiano) look out for
encampments of charcoal-burners by the
road and up in the chestnut covered hills.
You'll see steam rising after rain, and the
great circular mounds which cover the
slow-burning wood.

Local flavour
The countryside between Pésaro and
Urbino is famous for black and white
truffles.

It is possible to continue by bus from
Urbino to Sansepolcro or Arezzo. There may
only be one early morning bus to Arezzo in
winter, check at the tourist office. By car,
there is no swift road between Urbino and
Sansepolcro, only the most scenic, winding,
switchback climbing road (SS73 bis) among

the steep wooded hills. (Drive through one of the rumbling thunderstorms and torrential rain and you won't forget it). Allow at least 1½ hours to be on the safe side. The bus between Urbino and Arezzo takes three to 3½ hours.

FLORENCE (FIRENZE)

BUDGET FOR A DAY

Buy Firenze Spettacolo for what's on	1,800
Entrance Uffizi Gallery	5,000
Lunch at restaurant	12,000
Glass of fizzy fruit juice (limonata)	1,300
Film at the Astro Cinema	6,500
Supper in osteria - bar snack	4,000
Glass of wine	1,200
	L 31,800
plus accommodation	

here is a list of the essential sights, and some idea what the museums and churches hold, as well as tips, alternative sights, and ideas for survival, financial and otherwise.

Florentine doctors treat patients for *Stendhalismo*, a cultural shock illness which comes from a surfeit of Renaissance art. The French writer Stendhal was the first sufferer – he described how he simply couldn't walk after being dazzled by the beauty of the church of Santa Croce. So take it easy.

You might want to make Florence your only permanent home for a holiday, there's so much to see here. If so, there is a motorway and a very scenic non-motorway road via the Futa Pass from Bologna (trains as well, about L6,000). Pisa is slightly nearer, and trains to Florence go direct from Pisa airport. (The railway station is right in the centre of Florence.) If you can, go out of season. It's not only cheaper to fly and lodge, but Florence gets increasingly crowded.

Trains go about every hour to and from Arezzo, Pisa, Bologna, Rome and Lucca. The train station, Santa Maria Novella, is near the church of the same name, and within walking distance of the city centre along via Panzani. Florence has its own small airport, but international flights go to Pisa (Galileo Galilei airport) or Bologna, both about an hour away by train.

By car, Florence is on the main A1 Milan-Rome motorway via Bologna and Arezzo, and the A11 connects with Pisa and Lucca. A car is more of a hindrance than help in Florence itself, where local buses are adequate, and the main sights can be visited on foot. Leave your car at the Fortezza da Basso car park, north east of the train station, and walk, or take the free bus into town.

Art in Florence is long, this book is short;

Local flavour

The English novelist Aldous Huxley said, 'We came back through Florence, and the spectacle of that second-rate provincial town with its repulsive Gothic architecture and its acres of Christmas-card primitives made me almost sick. The only points about Florence are the country outside it, the Michelangelo tombs, Brunelleschi's dome, and a few rare pictures.'(!)

Florence is so popular and all its sights are so tightly crammed into so few narrow streets that it seems even more crowded than Venice or Rome. From Easter to May, schoolchildren flood in on day trips. July and August is peak holiday time and hot for sightseeing (holiday time for the Florentines too: lots of shops and restaurants are shut). Florence is a fashion centre, and in March and October there are fashion shows in the Pitti Palace. The Maggio Musicale, a range of musical shows and concerts, runs through May and into June. Spring is a very popular time for visitors. September and October might be better, or you might consider the winter; it can be cold, but many sights of Florence are indoors (and the opera season begins in December). Views of Florence vary, depending on whether you are looking down from Fiésole on a misty morning, or are stuck in the hot depth of summer in a jam along the Lungarno.

Don't try to see too many museums, churches and galleries, you don't have to see inside anything. The places to sit down (without paying for it at a café) are the piazza Santa Maria Novella in front of the church, where there's grass, benches and pigeons; in the piazza della SS Annunciata, off the via Battisti, among the lovely della Robbia terracottas; or (especially good) across the river in the Boboli Gardens. There are public lavatories in the Pitti Palace, at the Palazzo Vecchio, upstairs in the Mercato Centrale, and at the train station. Armed with a detailed map, a small water bottle, and comfortable shoes, you'll enjoy Florence (and the ice cream and the Chianti wine and the food. . .).

Among the essential sights is the view of

Brunelleschi's dome and all the brown roofs of the city from high up across the river. This will set the city in perspective for you. Besides, Florence looks her best from up here. There are several viewpoints:

Walk across the Ponte Vecchio and up via Guicciardini, through the Pitti Palace into the Boboli Gardens (there's quite a steep walk up) to sit on the grass or at a café at the top. Picnic below the café.

Or else turn left across the bridge, and walk along the costa San Giorgio to the Belvedere Fort, where there is free entry to a picnic space and a fine view.

Another alternative is to take a 13 bus across the Ponte alle Grazie, up to the piazzale Michelangelo (lit at night). A further walk from there takes you up to the Church of San Miniato. If you are there at 11.45am on a Sunday morning the valley will be full of the sound of church bells.

The Cathedral dome designed by Brunelleschi

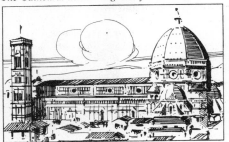

The Uffizi Gallery, designed by Vasari and built between 1560 and 1574 as public offices (uffizi), houses the best collection of 14th to 16th-century painting in Italy. Centrally situated between the piazza Signoria and the Ponte Vecchio, it contains paintings by Paolo Uccello, Fra Filippo Lippi, Sandro Botticelli, Leonardo da Vinci, Raphael, Piero della Francesca, Michelangelo, Rembrandt, Titian and Caravaggio. You may have to queue here. Both this gallery and the Palazzo Vecchio in piazza Signoria stay open till 7pm (last entrance 6.15pm). Your best hope of avoiding the big groups is to visit later in the day. If you find yourself hungry go east to Santa Croce to find a *trattoria*. The Uffizi Gallery is open Tuesday to Saturday 9am-7pm, Sundays and holidays 9am-1pm, closed Mondays. L5,000, free for nationals of EEC countries who are over 60 and under 18.

Next after these essential sights come the Duomo, the chic shops, the statuary and a really good Tuscan meal.

> **Moneysaver**
> The cheapest areas to eat in lie between the train station and the Church of San Lorenzo, where many local workers gather, and in the streets around the Church of Santa Croce where little *trattorias* provide a decent meal of pasta and meat for L15,000. (Try Trattoria Santa Croce, open for lunch. Shut Sundays.)

ORIENTATION IN FLORENCE

INFORMATION
The streets are numbered in red and black, red numbers are commercial, and black are residential addresses.
TOURIST OFFICE
AAST via Tornabuoni 15.
☎ *055/216544. First floor up. Monday to Saturday 9am-1pm.*
EPT via A Manzoni 16.
☎ *055/2478141. Information on Tuscany. Monday to Saturday 8.30am-1.30pm.*
Information Office in red and white booth outside the railway station. Maps and hotel lists. 8am-9pm every day.
Informazione Turistiche Alberghiere in the train station, near platform 16.
☎ *055/283500. Will book rooms, L1,800 commission charge. Information on Pisa flights from the air terminal office on platform 5.*
Esercizio Promozione Turismo via Condotta 42r near piazza Signoria. ☎ 055/294551. Maps, guides, and currency exchange at official rates (commission at least L3,000). Monday to

Saturday 10am-7pm and Sunday 10am-6pm.
POST OFFICE
Via Pellicceria, off piazza della Repubblica. ☎ 055/216122. Monday to Friday 8.15-7pm. Saturday 8.15-12 noon. Postal codes number from 50121 to 50129.
TELEPHONES
At the post office, also SIP phones near platform 5 at the train station. Telephone code 055.
INTERNATIONAL PHARMACY
Piazza della Repubblica 23r. English spoken. US and English products.
ALBERGO DIURNO
Near platform 16 at the train station. Showers, lavatory, barber. Monday to Saturday 6am-8pm, Sunday 6am-1pm.
PUBLIC LAVATORIES
At the Palazzo Vecchio, Palazzo Pitti, upstairs in the Mercato Centrale.
POLICE
Ufficio Stranieri, for foreigners. English speaking, via Zara 2, ☎ 055/49771. 9am-2pm. Emergency ☎ 113.

TRANSPORT
BUSES

ATAF city buses, piazza del Duomo 57r. ☎ 055/580528. Buy tickets at station or tabacchi shops. Route map at ATAF in the station. SITA buses, via Santa Caterina da Siena 15r.
☎ *055/211487. For buses to Arezzo, Siena, Volterra, San Gimignano, Pisa. CAT buses, via Fiume 2.*
☎ *055/283400. Buy tickets at via Nazionale 4. LAZZI buses, via della Stazione 1r. ☎ 055/215154. For buses to Lucca, Pisa, Prato, Pistóia.*
CAR HIRE
All south west of the station. Hertz via Fininguerra 17.
☎ *055/282260. Avis borgo Ognissanti 128r.*
☎ *055/213629. Budget borgo Ognissanti 134r. ☎ 055/293021. MOPED HIRE Excelsior, via della Scala 48. ☎ 055/298639. Mopeds and bicycles can be hired from via Alamanni, near the station. ☎ 055/213307.*

ACCOMMODATION
The old category of pensione, so particularly linked with Florence, has officially disappeared, and

not many of the less expensive hotels now provide evening meals. This at least gives one freedom of movement in the evening. There are hundreds of hotels in Florence, but it is still advisable to book between April and November. If you arrive without a room the ITA near platform 16 at the station will ring round and find one for you. As always, the cheaper places will be round the station on via Faenze and via Nazionale and via della Scala. Here is a selection of decent places spread over the city. Many of the simplest hotels are in old, unmodernised buildings, do not provide private baths and are mostly small establishments.

Not many of the more modest hotels take credit cards. They sometimes accept Eurocheques.

Some three-star hotels have rooms without baths which are within our budget.

HOTELS

Aprile via della Scala 6, near the train station. ☎ 055/216237. Telex 575840. Three-star.

Cestelli borgo SS Apostoli 25, near the Ponte Vecchio. ☎ 055/214213. Post code 05123. Some rooms with bath. Breakfast only. Double L37,000-L48,000. One-star.

Consigli Lungarno Vespucci 50, on the river. ☎ 055/214172. Post code 50123. Parking. Some rooms with bath. Breakfast provided. Two-star.

Hermitage vicolo Marzio 1, near the Ponte Vecchio. ☎ 055/287216. Three-star.

Hotel Bandini piazza Santo Spirito 9, across the river. ☎ 055/215308. Post code 50125. Some rooms with bath. Meals. Double L58,000-L67,000. One-star.

The Hotel Porta Rossa via Porta Rossa 19, very central. ☎ 055/287551. Plenty of public sitting-space. Three-star.

Liana via Vittorio Alfieri 18, former British Embassy, north east of centre, near piazza Donatello. ☎ 055/245785. Post code 50123. Parking, garden, breakfast. Two-star.

Locanda Rosy via Pandolfine 22, north of Santa Croce. ☎ 055/263083. One-star.

Locanda Scoti via Tornabuoni 7, in the central smart shopping street. ☎ 055/292128. Post code 50123. No private bath or breakfast. One-star.

Madrid via della Scala 59, south west of the train station. ☎ 055/282776. Post code 50123. Rooms with and without bath. Breakfast. Two-star.

Medici via de' Medici 6. ☎ 055/284818. Post code 50123. Rooms with and without bath. Breakfast. Car parking space. Two-star.

Orcagna via Orcagna 57, near the river, east of city centre. ☎ 055/669959. Post code 50121. All rooms with bath. Breakfast. Garden. Two-star.

Orchidea borgo degli Albizi 11, north of Santa Croce. ☎ 055/2480346. Post code 50122. No private baths or breakfast. Double L39,000. One-star.

Palazzo Vecchio via Cennini 4, just east of the station. ☎ 055/212182. Post code 50123. Most rooms with bath. Breakfast. Parking. Garden. Two-star.

Rigatti Lungarno Diaz 2, central, on the river. ☎ 055/213022. Post code 50122. Rooms with and without bath. Breakfast. Two-star.

La Scaletta via Guicciardini 13, across Ponte Vecchio going up to the Pitti Palace.

Moneysaver

The Comune (town council) of Florence now hires out bicycles at various points in the city: at the railway station, near the Biblioteca Nationale (south of Santa Croce), at piazza Pitti and piazza della Repubblica. You can hire from one and leave the bike at another.

Local flavour

E M Forster's *pensione* that offered a *Room with a View*, is said to be the Jennings-Riccioli, corso dei Tintori 7 (off via dei Benci, north of Lungarno delle Grazie) ☎ 055/244751. It is very changed; a hotel, no meals, 44 rooms, and a charge of L12,000 for breakfast.

☎ 055/283028. Post code 50125. Most rooms with bath. Breakfast provided. Two-star.
Silla via dei Renai 5, just across the river. ☎ 055/2342888. With garden and restaurant. Three-star.
Souvenir via XXVII Aprile 9, near piazza San Marco, north east of the station. ☎ 055/472194. Post code 50129. No private baths. Terrace, garden, meals. One-star.
Splendour via San Gallo 30, near San Marco. ☎ 055/483427. Post code 50129. Rooms with and without bath. Breakfast. Terrace. Two-star.
Varsavia via Panzani 5, south east of the train station. ☎ 055/215615. Post code 50123. Some rooms with bath. Breakfast. One-star.

EATING OUT

The best value eating places in Florence are often small and unprepossessing from the outside. Beware of ordinary tourist menus, and menus in many languages. A local trattoria will probably have communal tables, and either a short menu, or none at all (the owner will tell

you what's good), so join in and take pot luck.
TRATTORIAS
Acqua al Due via dell'Acqua 2r, near the Bargello. Shut Mondays and during August. ☎ 055/284170. Very good pasta.
I Latini via Palchetti 6r, near piazza Goldoni. Closed Mondays and Tuesday lunchtime. ☎ 055/210916. Serious eating at communal tables.
Trattoria Capponi borgo San Frediano, over the Vespucci bridge. ☎ 055/292130. Closed Tuesdays.
Trattoria Coco Lezzone via Parioncino 26, near piazza Santa Trinità. ☎ 055/287178. Very popular. Closed Tuesday evenings and Sundays.
Trattoria Nello borgo Tegolaio 21r, near Santo Spirito. Closed Sundays and during August. ☎ 055/218511.
Za-Za piazza Mercato Centrale 26r. Closed Sundays and during August. ☎ 055/215411.
In the old city – near the river:
Cibero via dei Macci 118.
La Maremmana via dei Macci 77. ☎ 055/241226. Shut Sundays and August.

Open midday and evening.
EATING OUT IN OLTRARNO
Oltrarno is a good area in which to eat. Florentines come here to escape the crowds and prices across the river.
I Tarocchi via dei Renai 14, for pizza or pasta. ☎ 055/217850. 7pm-1am. Closed Mondays.
La Taverna Mescitá via dei Michelozzi 15.
Trattoria Casalinga via dei Michelozzi 9.
Trattoria Jerragli via dei Serragli 108.

WINE BARS

Borgioli piazza dell' Olio.
Fiaschetteria via dei Neri.
Fratellini via dei Cimatori.
Niccolino volta dei Mercanti.
Piccolo Vinaio via Castellani
Cantinone del Gallo Nero across the river in via Santo Spirito 6.

SHOPPING

Florence is world-famous for its clothes, leather goods, special flower-decorated paper, art books and reproductions, jewellery, and general chic and style. Window-shop at the pricy places, but buy at the

---

Local flavour

According to tradition in Florence, when Catherine de Medici went to France to become queen in the 16th century, she took her Florentine chefs with her and taught the French how to cook – in fact Italian cooking was the basis of all French cuisine.

Moneysaver

In recent years, 30 restaurants have agreed to offer special low-price but good menus for tourists in the summer. Highest prices are L20,000 (including fish dishes), and even locals commend them as good value. Ask at the tourist office on via Tornabuoni for details.

The Ponte Vecchio, from where you can look along the Arno and browse in the old shops

supermarkets and markets. Go to Alinari's in via dell Vigna Nuova for prints.

MOSTLY WINDOW-SHOPPING
Via Tornabuoni for Gucci, 73r, 57r; Ferragamo (shoes), 16r; Ugolini (gloves) 20r.

Via dell Vigna Nuova
Alinari (prints etc), 46r; Antico Setificio Fiorentino (fabrics), 97r; Et Cetera (papermakers), 82r; Ungaro (fashion house), 30r.

IN THE DUOMO AREA
Bartolini via dei Servi 30r for household goods.

Calamai via Cavour 78r for stationery and household goods.

Casa dello Sport via dei Tosinghi 8r, sports clothes.

Emilio Pucci via dei Pucci 6r for silks and wines.

IN SANTA CROCE
Leather Guild piazza Santa Croce 20r for leather goods.

Ponte Vecchio along the bridge for shops selling coral and all kinds of jewellery.

ACROSS THE RIVER IN OLTRANO
Giannini piazza Pitti 37r for marbled papers.

Via Maggio window-shopping for antiques.

Sabens via Tornabuoni and **Centro Di**, piazza de' Mozzi, for books. Antiques are sold around via dei Fossi and borgo Ognissanti.

MARKETS
Open-air clothes market every Tuesday morning in the Cascine park. (Take bus 9, 17c, 26 or 27 from the Duomo or station.) Good for shoes, etc. There are also stalls selling old lace.

Mercato Nuovo off via porta Santa Maria (touch the pig for luck here). But be careful what you buy, there's a lot of tourist tat and souvenir stalls. Not bad for linen and straw goods.

San Lorenzo market in the streets between San Lorenzo and the central market. All kinds of stalls. Famous brand name imitations. Well worth browsing.

Mercato Centrale via dell' Ariento. Food market, and upstairs bar for coffee and a view.

Flea market piazza Ciompi, off via Pietrapana. Tuesday to Saturday. For all kinds of bric-a-brac. The best market is 10am-7pm on the last Sunday of the month.

Local flavour

If you crave a film in English, go to the Astro Cinema, piazza Simone, near Santa Croce. Tickets L6,500, two shows an evening. Closed Mondays and during July.

Moneysaver

Posters advertise free, all-year-round concerts in the city churches.

Local flavour

Picnic places with room for children to run about: in the Cascine Park (bus 17, or walk west along the river); in the fortezza da Basso, viale Strozzi, a quiet park with a pond and swans; in the Boboli gardens, on the grass below the café. Not a picnic place, but a green oasis – the Orto Botanico, the botanical gardens (founded by Cosimo I in 1545), open Monday, Wednesday, Friday 9am-12 noon.

Piazza Santo Spirito daily food market. 7am-1pm, Monday to Saturday. Also wooden articles and second-hand items.

SECOND-HAND AND ANTIQUE CLOTHES

La Belle Epoque volta di San Piero 8r, off piazza San Piero Maggiore.

Lord Brummel Store, via del Purgatorio 26r, off via Tornabuoni.

Paperback exchange via Fiesolana 31r (Santa Croce). New and used English-language paperbacks.

ENTERTAINMENT

Firenze Spettacolo *(L1,800) and* Firenze la Sera *(L2,500) list what's on. There's not a great deal going on at night in Florence, though there is live jazz at the Jazz Club, via Nuova de'Caccini 3, at borgo Pinti most nights (closed Monday and mid July to mid September). Jazz at weekends at Salt Peanuts, piazza Santa Maria Novella 26r.*

Large discos for a young

crowd are Space Electronic, via Palazzuolo near Santa Maria Novella, open every day (shut Mondays, October to February) and Yab Yum, at via Sassetti 5, off piazza della Repubblica (shut Mondays). In summer they run a disco in the Cascine Park (bus 17c) in front of the Hotel Michelangelo (open daily). Smaller hot spots are Jackie O', via Erta Canina 24, and Full Up, via della Vigna Vecchia (cost about L20,000 Monday-Thursday, L25,000 Friday and Saturday).

The evening passeggiata *is along via dei Calzaiuoli.*

LOCAL FESTIVALS

The Scoppio del Carro *(explosion of the cart) takes place on Easter Sunday at the Duomo after a procession featuring an enormous decorated firework-filled cart. During Mass, a rocket from the high altar shoots towards the cart and sets it alight.*

June 24, feast day of St John the Baptist patron saint of Florence. Fireworks at about 10pm, fired from

piazzale Michelangelo and visible along the Arno. In the day (and two other variable dates) the calcio storico, *traditional wild and fearsome football, 27 a side, in costume, takes place in a central city square (tickets from Chiosco degli Sportivi, via de'Anselmi).*

September 7, Festa della Rificolone when the city is lit in the evening with glowing paper lanterns.

There is a film festival in spring at the Forte Belvedere, and a documentary film festival in December in the Fortezza da Basso.

MUSIC

The Maggio Musicale Fiorentino is a series of concerts and recitals which now stretch from late April to June. Held in the Teatro Comunale, corso Italia 16, ☎ *055/277931.*

The opera season (also in the Teatro Comunale) runs from December to February.

There is a concert season by the local Orchestra Regionale Toscana in the church of Santo Stefano al Ponte, ☎ *055/2420.*

DISCOVERING FLORENCE

FROM SANTA MARIA NOVELLA END UP AT THE PONTE VECCHIO

To sample old and new Florence, begin by looking at the façade of the church of Santa Maria Novella (inside is a fresco by Masaccio, the Strozzi chapel and the cloisters). Look in at Bagman, via dell'Alberto 19 off via della Scala 19, to see a craftsman working in leather. After that, via de Banchi and via de Carretani will bring you to the Duomo and the Baptistery.

The bronze panels on the north and east doors of the Baptistery, which Michelangelo said were so beautiful they could be the gates to Paradise, were made by Lorenzo Ghiberti from 1403 to 1452. When he was 20, and Brunelleschi was 23, they each made a sample panel in competition for the commission, and these hang in the Bargello. On the east door, below and left of the Jacob and Esau panel, is a tiny self-portrait bust of Ghiberti. These east door panels are being removed to the museum to protect them from pollution damage.

Climb the separate bell tower, Giotto's Campanile, named after the painter who designed it, for an even better view than from the top of the Duomo. Loiter along the via Calzaiuoli, looking at shops, and potter into the piazza Signoria.

Signoria means Sire, the political boss, and this square was the centre of Florence's political life in the Middle Ages. The tall-towered Palazzo Vecchio (old palace) is now the town hall. Don't waste admiration on the copy of the statue of David on the steps. The original, by Michelangelo, which stood here from 1504 to 1882, is now in the Accademia gallery.

Local flavour

Michelangelo was only 26 when he carved this statue of David out of a huge chunk of discarded marble left lying about in the yard of the cathedral works office. It was intended for the Duomo, and designed to be viewed from far below.

Look at the statues in the Loggia dei Lanzi, under the arches, which include Benvenuto Cellini's bronze of Perseus holding Medusa's head. From here walk past the Uffizi Gallery, and then on to the Ponte Vecchio for a look along the river, especially towards the elegant Trinita bridge, and a browse among the jewellery shops. In 1500, Duke Cosimo I passed an order decreeing all shops on the bridge were to be goldsmiths. Above the shops there's a passage connecting the Uffizi with the Pitti Palace, containing an exhibition of painters' self-portraits (entry is from the Uffizi).

Straw hat making, a local craft

Local flavour

Some of the great merchants' and bankers' palaces in the centre of town are open to view. Palazzo Strozzi, via Tornabuoni (built 1489) is open Monday, Wednesday and Friday, 4-7pm, free. Palazzo Davanzati, via Porta Rossa 13, is now a museum of 15th-century life. Guided tours (in Italian) Tuesday to Saturday, every hour 9am-2pm, Sunday 9am-1pm. L2,000.

If you saunter along the river west to the Trinita bridge, looking in on Raffaello Romanetti, sculptor in marble, and down the via Tornabuoni (the tourist office is upstairs at number 15), past more smart shops, you will have got a good sense of the past and present of the city.

FROM THE DUOMO TO THE ACCADEMIA

This walk mixes the old and new taking you from the Duomo to the Church of San Lorenzo (designed by Brunelleschi). Near by is the Palazzo Medici with a private chapel (free entrance, closed Wednesdays) decorated vividly by Benozzo Gozzoli. Round behind San Lorenzo are the Cappelle dei Medici and the New Sacristy with tombs by Michelangelo (which Huxley praised so highly) while next door, in the Biblioteca Mediceo-Laurenzina, (also free) is an exceptional and curious building designed by Michelangelo. Behind here, visit the Mercato Centrale for appetizing fruit, meat and vege-

tables, and a coffee at the bar upstairs.

Continue to piazza San Marco by way of via Cavour. There the museum at number 3 is an ancient monastery full of Fra Angelico frescoes and with a *Last Supper* by Ghirlandaio. Just up the via Ricasoli is the Accademia Gallery, absolutely not to be missed, for sculptures by Michelangelo. Open until 2pm on weekdays, 1pm Sunday – closed Monday. Returning, continue along via Battisti to the piazza della SS Annunziata, the prettiest square in Florence. The arched building, a foundling hospital, the Ospedale degli Innocenti, was built by Brunelleschi in 1419, the first truly Renaissance lay building. The terracottas are by Andrea della Robbia. Under the arcades on the left is a sort of rotating letter box for depositing babies.

Just down the via della Colonna from here is the Archeological Museum, with a large Etruscan collection – artefacts brought from Volterra and all over Tuscany. The Museum is open until 2pm on weekdays, 1pm Sunday – closed Monday. Return to the Duomo along via de Servi.

FROM THE DUOMO TO SANTA CROCE

From the Duomo, south along the via Proconsolo to the Bargello National Museum, another towered building. This rather intimidating building was once a jail, (*bargello* means chief of police) and now houses a wonderful collection of sculpture by Michelangelo, Donatello (a *David*) and many others. The Bargello is open until 2pm on weekdays, 1pm Sunday – closed on Monday.

Local flavour
The sculptor Donatello (1386-1466) was only 22 when he carved his marble *David*, but lived to the ripe age of 80, a favourite of Cosimo de Medici. He was always in work and well paid, but was generous, keeping some money in a basket hung from the ceiling so his friends could help themselves.

Opposite, on the other side of via del Proconsolo, the Badia church has famous paintings by Filippino Lippi (on the left as you go in). Walking eastward from the Bargello, along via Ghibellina, you will find Casa Buonarroti at number 70, with Michelangelo memorabilia (closed Tuesday). Return down via Ghibellina and turn left into piazza Santa Croce.

Santa Croce is a Franciscan church, and one which stunned Stendhal with its beauty. It contains the tombs of many of Florence's famous sons – Michelangelo, Machiavelli, Rossini, Galileo, and the empty tomb of Dante. The Florentines banished him from their city, so he died and was buried in Ravenna, despite Florence's pleas to return his body. Visit the museum (closed Wednesdays), the cloister and, next door, the Pazzi Chapel, one of Brunelleschi's finest buildings.

Local flavour
Be sure to see Giotto's frescoes (painted in tempera) in the Peruzzi and Bardi chapels. Giotto, when asked to submit a sample of his work to the Pope, drew one single perfect freehand circle in red chalk.

From here, depending on the time of day, your capacity for more art, your hunger or exhaustion, go west along the borgo dei Greci to visit the Uffizi; go round the corner for a meal or an ice cream; visit the leather school behind the church to buy leather goods; catch the 13 bus from via dei Benci, cross the river to piazzale Michelangelo. You can also hire a city bike from near here (near the Biblioteca Nazionale) and pedal your way along the river or into the centre of town.

Local flavour
The Horne Museum, via dei Benci 6, has a small collection of paintings (by Giotto and others) collected by an Englishman, Herbert Horne, and displayed in the 15th-century palazzo he restored and furnished. An undiscovered delight.

FROM THE PONTE VECCHIO TO THE OLTRARNO

Oltrarno means the south bank of Florence, on the other side of the Arno. Cross the Ponte Vecchio and walk up via Guicciardini, past lots of interesting antique shops, to the Pitti Palace. The Pitti contains a modern art gallery, collections of silver, porcelain, costumes, ceramics, historical carriages, and an important picture collection in the sumptuous rooms of the Palatine Gallery (includes

Local flavour
The Casa Guidi, where Robert and Elizabeth Barrett Browning spent years of their married life, and where Elizabeth died, is at piazza San Felice 8, at the corner of via Maggio and via Mazzetta. It is owned by the English public school, Eton College, and is occasionally open free to visitors. Ring the bell to enquire. Elizabeth is buried in the Protestant cemetery, and during her funeral (1 July 1861) all the shops on via Maggio closed in respect. (Their son Pen is also buried there.)

works of Titian, Raphael, Rubens and Caravaggio). From there walk toward the via
Maggio, stopping to look at Giannini's
paper shop opposite the palace, and the Casa
Guidi on the way.

There are a host of antique and restoration shops around here, with the expensive
antique shops on via Maggio. From piazza

Santo Spirito walk along via Sant' Agostino
and via Santa Monaca to the Church of
Santa Maria in Carmine. The Masaccio
frescoes in the Brancacci Chapel, revolution-
ary early three-dimensional painting, should
not be missed.

For a complete list of opening times go to
the tourist office on via Tornabuoni 15.

OUTINGS FROM FLORENCE

SHORT TRIPS BY BUS

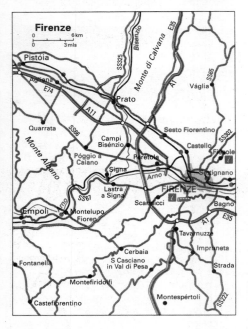

Even if one doesn't go very far, it's good to
get up into the hills around Florence for a
change of air. The nearby villages offer more
peace, views, shady trees and often stately
formal gardens to visit. South of Florence,
the Chianti countryside is famously beautiful, hilly, wooded, vine-covered slopes, little
villages perched, dark cypresses, grey olives.
SITA buses will take you there; there's no

need for expensive guided tours. With a car,
you can wander the Chianti-tasting route,
which is well sign-posted.

It is always a good idea to check opening
times with the tourist office before making a
special journey.

To Fiésole A 25-minute bus ride
(number 7 from via Cerretani, near the
cathedral or San Marco) up through olive
groves and umbrella pines, Fiésole sits high
on a hill, 14km ($8\frac{3}{4}$ miles) away and 295
metres (967ft) up above the heat and mayhem of Florence. Come up for the view and
the day, and to visit the beautiful amphitheatre, or you could make it your base for a

> **Local flavour**
> From June to August, concerts, opera,
> ballet and plays fill the Roman Theatre in
> Fiésole as part of the Estate Fiesolana.
> Get tickets and information from the
> Teatro Comunale, corso Italia 16,
> telephone 055/215253; at
> Universalturismo, via degli Speziali 7r,
> telephone 055/217241, near piazza
> della Repubblica; or the EPT office, via
> Manzoni in Florence.

> **Moneysaver**
> Look out for, and enquire at the tourist
> office for a list of local *sagre*, festivals of
> food and wine, where you can get cheap
> wine-tasting and meals.

few days' sightseeing below. Unfortunately there are not many inexpensive hotels in the town. On the south side is the Villa Bonelli (two-star), via Francesco Poeti 1, some rooms with bath, some without. Telephone 055/598941.

To Settignano   Take bus 10 from the station or the Duomo for another nearby hill village, Settignano. The 17th-century Villa Gameraia and the Villa i Tatti (once home of art historian Bernard Berenson, now a Harvard research institute) both have beautiful formal gardens.

To Castello   At the villas in Castello there are two gardens to visit, with free entry. Take bus 28 from the train station.

Villa Castello is a Medici villa which once housed Botticelli's *Birth of Venus* (now in the Uffizi); it still retains sculptures, a grotto and an orangery. Open 9am-4.30pm in winter, till 5.30pm March, April, September, October, and till 7pm from May to August. Closed Mondays. Telephone 055/454791.

Villa della Petraia is another Medici villa, open from 9am-2pm weekdays, 9am-1pm on Sundays. The gardens are open at the same times as the Villa di Castello.

To Sesto Fiorentino   Bus number 28 continues on to Sesto Fiorentino. Visit the Villa Corsi-Salviati, and also the Museo di Doccia at the Richard-Ginori porcelain factory, via Pratese 31. For the villa, telephone 055/4489150. Open 9.30am-1pm and 3.30-6.30pm, closed Sunday and Monday.

To Impruneta   Impruneta, a little Chianti hill town is only a 30-minute bus ride away.

Wine festivals are held here on the third Sunday in September, and St Luke's Horse and Mule Fair in mid-October. Also see the Della Robbia terracottas in the Basilica of Santa Maria.

To Póggio a Caiano   Take the CoPiT bus marked 'Quarrata' from Piazza Santa Maria Novella for a 30-minute ride to Póggio a Caiano, a famous Medici villa rebuilt for Lorenzo the Magnificent in 1480. A century later, Duke Francesco Medici and his wife both died here on the same night. The gardens are open from 9am-4.30pm in winter, to 5.30pm March, April, September and October, and till 6.30pm May to August. Free entry. Telephone 055/877012.

CHIANTI WINES

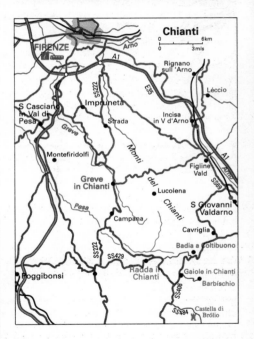

From Florence, cross the river at Ponte Carraia, make for Porta Romana and take the SS222, the Chiantigiana. The wine-growing estates will be signed, but you can only taste the wine if they advertise *vendita diretta*, direct sale. In the towns, look out for the *enoteca*, wine shop. Greve, 25km (15½ miles) south, has wine tasting and buying. Further south, turn east on the 429 to Radda (two *enoteche* here). From Radda, take the SS429 on to Badia a Coltibuono (restaurant here), then right along the SS408 to Gaiole. From here a winding stretch on the SS484 leads to the Castello di Brólio, a Renaissance fortress, with wine tasting and guided tours.

Local flavour

In the last century, the cross-eyed Baron Bettino Ricasoli dragged his wife from a ball in Florence because a young man had made a pass at her, drove her through the snow to this castle, and kept her here in (cross-eyed) sight to the end of her days. To while away the time, he developed a rather fine brand of wine.

Just after Gaiole, if you have time, take a left turn up to Barbíschio for a view of the assembled hills. No wine – just a stunning view.

AREZZO

Arezzo is a good centre for a short visit, with bus connections across to Sansepolcro (home of Piero della Francesca and the Buitoni pasta industry), or, only 1½ hours by train, 77km (48 miles) and L1,000 return (*andata e ritorno*) to Florence. Except when the big antique fairs are on, there is usually accommodation available in Arezzo, though, as with other places in this area, it is always wise to book in advance for the high season in July and August.

The motorway or train go from Florence to both Pisa, which is well worth a visit or short stay, and Lucca, which is a marvellously complete walled city.

Arezzo was a great Etruscan city, famous for pottery and metalwork, rich and warlike,

a rival to Florence in the Middle Ages, then decimated by the plague and the French. Now it's a rich city full of jewellers, antiques and furniture makers. It is also busy, modern and tough to drive into, but the historical centre is traffic-free.

The choir chapel of the church of San Francisco houses a series of frescoes, *The Legend of the Cross*, by Piero della Francesca, (open 7am-12 noon and 2.30-7pm). For some this is the principal glory of Arezzo. They are under restoration (della Francesca's 500th anniversary is in 1992) but should still be visible. The piazza Grande, a few streets away, is a curious and interesting square, tilted at an angle and surrounded by ancient houses.

Up the hill is the Passeggio del Prato, a beautiful park with the cathedral at one end and the Fortezza, a ruined Medici castle, at the other. From here there are wide views (you can see Florence and Urbino), benches and a café.

There are several terracotta works by Andrea della Robbia in Arezzo, in Santa

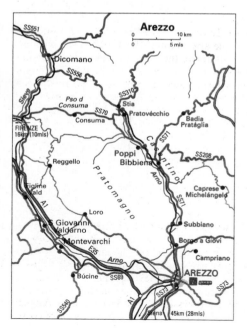

118

Maria in Gradi, in the Palazzo Bruni-Ciocchi, and Santa Maria delle Grazie. Also visit the chronicler and painter Vasari's house on via XX Settembre.

Don't miss Santa Maria del Pieve, a plain Romanesque church inside, with steps up to the original gold-painted altarpiece (by Pietro Lorenzetti) shining in front of the bare stone apse. Notice the 11th-century carving right above the postcard table, and, outside in the piazza Grande, looking at the pillars on the rounded apse, there is a curiously bent stone pillar under the carving of a cow.

The first Sunday of every month the Fiera Antiquaria (Antiques Fair) fills the piazza Grande with antiques, and the town with people. Also in this square a spectacular medieval jousting tournament, the Giostra del Saracino is held on the first Sunday in September (and another one in the summer), with processions. The last week of August there is a singing festival, the Concorso Polifonico.

The *passeggiata* takes place in the Corso Italia.

If you have a car, try a restaurant out of town, the Osteria La Capannaccia in Capriano (telephone 0575/361759) for local specialities, L24,000. You can eat eels and homemade spaghetti at Al Principe (telephone 0575/362046) in Borgo a Giovi north of the town. Go out on SS71. Closed Monday. L28,000.

There is a pretty drive from Arezzo to Caprese Michelángelo, the home of Michelangelo, and his supposed birthplace and museum (only reproductions of his work). Michelangelo's father was Mayor of Caprese, and his small son was sent into the country to be nursed by the wife of a mason.

Caprese Michelángelo, home of the painter

The quickest route by car to Florence is on the autostrada. The prettiest is on SS70 through the Passo della Consuma among the forests of the Cassentino hills.

If you are travelling by public transport, consider one of these:

Arezzo is on the main Florence-Rome railway line, a $1\frac{1}{2}$ hour's ride into Florence costs L4,700.

The CAT bus goes to Sansepolcro (L2,900) once an hour. The last bus back from Sansepolcro is at 8pm.

SITA/TRA-IN has four buses every morning to Siena (L4,000), returning in the afternoon. Useful, but doesn't really give enough time to see such an important city.

LFU has a railway line up the Arno valley to Subbiano, and then on by bus north towards Stia. (Check with the tourist office for details.) There are signed trails for a day's hiking from there. More trails go from Badia Pratáglia.

Pratovécchio on the SS310 and Poppi on the SS370 are both small towns well worth a visit, going south from Stia to Arezzo.

ORIENTATION IN AREZZO

INFORMATION
TOURIST OFFICE
EPT, piazza Risorgimento, near the piazza Repubblica (not open Saturday afternoon). There is also an information booth at the train station in July and August.
TELEPHONE
SIP, piazza Guido Monaco 2, in the shopping arcade. Open 8am to 12 midnight. Telephone code 0575.
PUBLIC LAVATORIES
In piazza Grande. L200. Closed Wednesday. You can ask in a hotel for il bagno per favore.

TRANSPORT
BUSES
Buses go from the viale Piero della Francesca in

front of the railway station. From here it is not far (but uphill) to walk up to the old town, along the via Guido Monaco.

ACCOMMODATION
Hotel Cecco corso Italia 215. ☎ 0575/20986. Double L44,000 without shower, L60,000 with shower.
Hotel Continental piazza Guido Monaco 7. ☎ 0575/ 20251. Double L89,000 with shower. Recently refurbished.
Hotel Milano via Madonna del Parto 83, not far from the station. ☎ 0575/26836. Large double rooms with shower L42,000, L34,500 without shower. Next door is an excellent trattoria.
Hotel Truciolini via Pacinotti 6, some way from the centre. ☎ 0575/380219. Has parking, air-

conditioning and private bath, double L57,000.
Michelangelo viale Michelangelo 26, turn right from the train station. ☎ 0575/20673. Double L40,000 with bath, L34,500 without.

EATING OUT
La Piazzetta piazza Risorgimento 16, in front of the tourist office. Very good food, reasonably priced, 12.30-2pm and 7.30-11pm. Closed Tuesday.
Ristorante La Tagliatella viale Giotto 45. Open 12 noon-3pm and 7pm to 12 midnight. Closed Tuesday.
La Torre piazza Grande 5, for pasta and pizzas. Open lunchtime and 7pm to midnight. Closed Monday.
The bar at the train station has Tuscany's best railway food.

SANSEPOLCRO

Sansepolcro is reached by CAT bus from Arezzo – 1 hour, L2,900. (Last bus back to Arezzo at 8pm.) By car about 65km (40 miles) on the SS73 bis from Urbino or about 40km (25 miles) from Arezzo via Anghiari. (Worth a visit – there is a beautiful view, even from the bus.) On this route make a detour to Monterchi on road SS221 to see a Piero della Francesca fresco there, in the chapel in the cemetery, *The Madonna del Parto.*

Although the Museo Civico houses other good paintings, the reason for the pilgrimage here is to see the room of Piero della Francesca paintings. There are so few to be seen outside this part of Italy (though the National Gallery in London has the centre-piece of a triptych). He was born just up the road from the museum at via Aggiunti 71. The Museo Civico, via Aggiunti 65, is open 9.30am-1pm and 2.30-6pm. L3,000. It is within easy walking distance of the bus terminal.

The tourist office is in via della Fonte, off the piazza Garibaldi, telephone 0575/730-231, open 9.30am-12.30pm, 3.30-6.30pm.

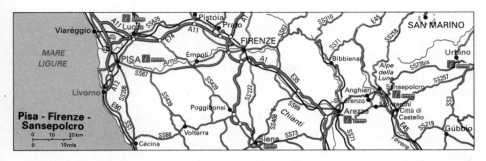

Pisa - Firenze - Sansepolcro

Also in via Aggiunti, at number 30, the Ristorante Da Ventura is recommended by Italians for its Tuscan cooking, especially the *crostini neri, ravioli* and *funghi* (mushrooms) cooked in all kinds of ways. It has a few rooms and is closed Saturday. Less expensive is the Trattoria Ricci, via della Fraternità, off the piazza Torre di Berta (closed Tuesday).

If you need accommodation, try the Albergo Fiorentino, via Luca Pacioli 60, telephone 05751/76033. It has a garage and a good restaurant.

A worthwhile short trip by car is to Anghiari, 8km (5 miles) south west on the road to Arezzo. And near by, at San Lorenzo, is the Locanda al Castello di Sorci (telephone 05751/789066) which serves good local food and wine. Northwards above the town is the Pian della Luna, or Alpe della Luna (the mountains of the moon). Drive to the *rifugio* (mountain hut) Pian della

Capanna. From here it is about an hour's walk up to the top of the mountain through scrubby country bedecked with wild orchids, and roamed by boar, deer and (so the Italians say) the occasional wolf. From the top, if the weather is clear, you can see the sea.

PISA

The old city of Pisa, once a Roman colony, is built on the same river as Florence. In the Middle Ages it was a great seafaring republic. Pisa lost her independence to Florence in 1405, but prospered under the Medici, becoming a great cultural centre with an admired university.

Now Pisa seems a somewhat sad place, a city of wonderful colours – ochres, yellows, with the famous River Arno, but the handsome houses which line it seem retired, resting, as if the whole town had been overcome by its dazzling white showpieces. Tourists mill around the Leaning Tower and the tourist tat, the jointed Pinocchios, the little leaning towers, the kitsch 'toadstools from Pisa'. Nevertheless the buildings on the piazza del Duomo are wonderful, and walk only a few yards on, to piazza Vescovado, and then to the piazza Cavalieri, and you will soon be off the tourist track.

The piazza del Duomo is also called the Campo dei Miracoli, and there is something miraculous about the four shining white buildings that sit on the wide green lawns. (You get a good view from the train to Lucca.)

The Cathedral The cathedral was designed by Buscheto (who is buried behind the last blind arch of the façade on the left), and was begun to commemorate the successful Pisan campaigns against the Saracens in Sicily in 1063. The design, called Pisan-Romanesque, with its triangular façade, upper pillared galleries and marble stripes, influenced other buildings all over Tuscany and even as far south as Amalfi.

> **Local flavour**
> Fourth column from the right in the second gallery up is a small red column, brought from Majorca, made of porphyry. Legend says, whoever looks on it will not be betrayed in love for at least one day! Notice how people have worn shiny the little figures of the dog, frog and two lizards on the central bronze doors, believing touching them makes dreams come true.

The dome was added in 1380. The main doors were made by a Florentine, after a fire in 1595 had destroyed three of the original ones designed by Bonanno Pisano in 1180. One survived, and is now the door to the St Ranieri chapel at the east end of the cathedral – don't miss it. The modelling of the figures and the whole design is very direct and vivid. Is it chance that Bonanno, who was the first architect of the Leaning Tower, should have depicted so many leaning palms? Looking along the side of the cathedral, and at the huge pillars inside, you can see that it too was built on sloping ground.

Inside, the upper galleries, called *matronei*, were reserved for female worshippers. The large 16th-century chandelier is called Galileo's lamp. The mosaics over the apse are early 14th-century. The most important work is the pulpit by Giovanni Pisano, showing scenes from the life of Christ, with some extraordinary crowd scenes.

> **Local flavour**
> There are several important sculptors surnamed Pisano; to avoid confusion:
> **Bonanno**, started building the Leaning Tower in 1173; sculpted the bronze door to the San Ranieri chapel in Pisa Cathedral, and a door in Monreale Cathedral, Sicily.
> **Nicola** (*circa* 1225-1278) made the pulpits in both the Pisan Baptistery and in Siena Cathedral, and also, with his son Giovanni, the great fountain in Perúgia.
> **Giovanni** (*circa* 1249-1314) designed the façade of Siena Cathedral and sculpted the pulpit in Pisa Cathedral (reconstructed 1926).
> **Andrea** (*circa* 1270-1348) worked mainly in Florence, where he made one of the bronze doors on the Baptistery. In 1347 he was appointed architect of the Duomo in Orvieto (already designed by Lorenzo Maitani). He had two sons, Nino and Tommaso.
> **Tommaso**, son of Andrea, finished the bell chamber on top of the Leaning Tower.

The Baptistery Building started on the Baptistery in August 1152, to designs by Diotisalvi. But it was only partly built, and building only resumed in 1278. Consequently, it is a mixture of Romanesque with Gothic decoration. The hexagonal pulpit was sculpted by Nicola Pisano and his pupils in 1260. The statues round the walls are by Nicola and his son Giovanni. Nicola's pulpit is considered one of the greatest and latest works of Romanesque art.

The Leaning Tower Bonanno Pisano began building the Leaning Tower in 1173, and it had got to about 10½ metres (35ft) when the ground subsided and the tower tilted 15cm (6in). Bonanno tried to correct the tilt from above and built up to the fourth floor. No luck – it leaned again. Bonanno retired with a red face and work stopped. Building resumed in 1234 up to the seventh floor, and finally Tommaso Pisano perched the bell chamber on the very top in 1350. At the time of writing, no one may climb the 294 steps to the top, while committees think what to do. Should they remove the 750-ton belfry? Cut off the top? Prop it up with buttresses? Shore it up underneath? Every year for the past 60 years it has leaned a further 1.29mm (about $\frac{1}{20}$ of an inch). Experts expect it will be another 200 years before it keels over, which should be almost enough time for one committee or another to agree on a solution.

Note: the Leaning Tower is not open to the public.

The Camposanto   The huge cloistered cemetery, the Camposanto, which encloses the Campo to the north, contains earth which was brought from Mount Calvary in Palestine on a ship back from the Crusades in about 1200. The little tabernacle perched on top is late 14th-century. Inside, the cloisters are calm and monumental, with restored remains of the 14th and 15th-century frescoes destroyed in 1944.

Other sights include the brick building (1263) opposite the cathedral which houses the **Museo delle Sinopie** (*sinopie* are the outline paintings sketched on the wall as a guide to the finished fresco); these come from the Camposanto. The **piazza dei Cavalieri** is the site of the old Roman forum, with a church by Giorgio Vasari (mid 16th-century) who also remodelled the great Palazzo with its central staircase. The **Church of Santa Maria della Spina** is the little spiky white Gothic church on the south bank of the river, near the ponte Citadella. The *spina* (thorn) from Christ's crown was once kept inside this miniature cathedral whose elaborate decorative exterior is more interesting than its inside.

Local flavour

Galileo, the astronomer and philosopher, was born in Pisa on 15 February 1564, and died in his villa outside Florence on 8 January 1642. He evolved the pendulum theory from watching the big bronze lamp swinging over the nave of the cathedral; proved that two equal weights will fall at the same speed, after experiments dropping weights from the Leaning Tower; and published a work confirming that the earth is round and revolves round the sun. On June 22, 1633, after an infamous trial, Galileo recanted.

Local flavour

The San Ranieri boat race takes place on 17 June for a mile along the Arno. Eight oarsmen in 16th-century costumes row boats representing different quarters of the city. If you can, stay in Pisa the night before to see the Luminaria, when lights (*lampanini*) float and shimmer on the water. All this is to celebrate the feast day of San Ranieri, patron saint of Pisa.

ORIENTATION IN PISA

INFORMATION

Tourist Office
Piazza Duomo 27, behind the Leaning Tower. 9.30am-1pm, 3.30pm-7pm. ☎ 050/560464. Another office is just beside the train station, at piazza della Stazione 11, open in summer from 8am-10pm.

Post Office
Piazza Vittorio Emanuele 8, near the station. ☎ 050/24297. Monday to Friday 8.15am-7pm. Saturday 8.15am-12 noon. Postal code 56100.

Telephones
Open day and night at the train station. Telephone code 050.

Public Lavatories
In piazza Duomo, along from the tourist office.

TRANSPORT

Airport
The airport (Galileo Galilei) is used by the military, and is less liable to

strikes than other Italian airports. ☎ 050/28088. Left luggage costs L2,500 per piece per day. (Only L1,500 at the central train station.) And they charge a disgraceful L1,000 for a trolley. No need for coins, there are plenty of attendants waiting to take your money.

Trains go direct to and from the airport, once an hour (via the central train station) to Florence. Change at Émpoli for Siena. Buy a ticket in the airport for L600, the price to Pisa central train station, but with this you can buy the rest of the ticket on the train without incurring any penalty. (Curiously, you can't buy a full ticket to Florence.)

If you just want to get into town, or to the central train staion for more frequent trains (and trains to other destinations), buy a L600 bus ticket in the airport (at the tobacconist, newsstand) and take bus 7 just outside which leaves every 15 minutes for the central train station (five-minute ride).

TRAINS
The central train station is south of the river. The Leaning Tower and other sights are north, across the river.

From Pisa Centrale station trains go about every half hour to Florence (L5,000 single, about 1 hour). Change at Émpoli for Siena (L7,000 single, takes 1¾ hours). Trains to Lucca every half hour (L3,000 return, 20 minutes.)

BUSES
Local yellow buses from in front of the train station, go to the Duomo (number 1) and airport (number 7).

Long-distance coaches: LAZZI pullmans from piazza Vittorio Emanuele 11, (☎ 050/46288) go to Lucca, Pistóia, Prato and Florence.

APT coaches from piazza Sant'Antonio go to Livorno and Volterra (☎ 050/ 23384).

Bus 1, in front of the train station, takes you on a round trip through the city to the Duomo, Leaning Tower, etc, and back by another route. A good sightseeing trip of the city. The city buses are frequent and efficient.

RADIO TAXI
☎ 050/541600.

ACCOMMODATION
Albergo Gronchi piazza Arcivescovado 1. ☎ 050/ 561823. Basic rooms. No private baths, but good position. Double L36,000.
Bologna via Mazzini 57, in

the centre of town. ☎ 050/ 14449. Double L45,000 without bath, L62,000 with bath. Car park.
Roseto via Mascagni 24, near the train station. ☎ 050/42596. Respectable rooms, a stand-up bar for breakfast coffee. (Bar near by down the road.) Double L45,000 without bath, L60,000 with bath.
Royal Victoria Lungarno Pacinotti 12. ☎ 050/502130. Prices of double rooms vary widely according to position and season, from L30,000 (without bath) up to L95,000. This is an enormous 19th-century hotel, worth staying at for the 19th-century spaciousness and (somewhat dilapidated) style. Its river front is impressive, there are large public rooms, long corridors to vast washrooms and loos. The Duke of Wellington once stayed in room 212.
La Torre via Cesare Battisti 17, near the station. ☎ 050/ 25220. Simple hotel, with modern fittings. Breakfast available, L5,000. Double from L40,000 without bath to L62,000 with bath. Garage.
Villa Kinzica piazza Arcivescovado 4. ☎ 050/ 560419. Double L90,000 including air-conditioning, breakfast and bath.

LUCCA

Lucca is a prosperous, leafy self-contained city, surrounded by great thick intact ramparts (30 metres, 98ft at their base), built of thin red bricks. Below lies a wide green grass moat, and you can cycle or walk along the top, or sit on the grass that covers the walls, shaded by huge plane and lime trees, and look across to the hills.

Lucca with its rampart walls

Lucca has always been wealthy (silk and banking), conservative, never Communist; the only city in Tuscany never to submit to Florence. Surrounded by hills of chestnut trees, olives and vines, where mulberries grow, it is a quiet place off the beaten track. Don't expect great things of Lucca, but take the time to explore and enjoy its narrow streets and shuttered houses.

A short walk from the station across the piazza Ricasoli in front, and left along viale Regina Margherita, will bring you to piaz-

zale Umberto I, and through Porta San Pietro into the city centre. Turn left along via F Carrara, and right up via Vittorio Veneto, to the tourist office on the left at number 40 for a map of the city. On the way, stop at the café Bei and Nannini on the corner of the corso Garibaldi. (A lemon tea, a *caffè lungo* and a glass of *acqua minerale* only costs L2,900, sitting outside.)

From piazza Napoleone, one side of via Vittorio Veneto, turn right along the via Duomo for the cathedral, or continue straight up via Veneto to piazza San Michele for the astonishing white church with its carved and twisted pillars, the façade eventually running out of church two stories up, surmounted by the Archangel Michael.

> **Local flavour**
> Buy *buccellato*, a special local sweetish cake, flavoured with aniseed, from the Pasticceria Taddeucci behind the church of San Michele. Sample coffee and ice cream at Puccini's favourite spot, the Caffè di Simo on via Fillungo.

> **Local flavour**
> The composer Puccini (1858-1924), who wrote *La Bohème*, *Tosca*, and *Madame Butterfly* was born in Lucca. His birthplace is open to the public, Corte San Lorenzo 9, off via di Poggio. Telephone 0583/584028. October 1-March 31, 10am-4pm. April to September. 10am-6pm. Closed Monday. L3,000.

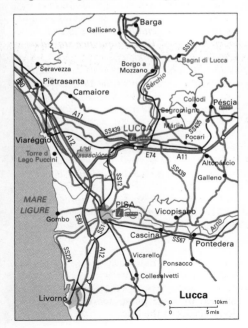

Principal sights include the churches of San Michele and San Frediano, and in the cathedral don't miss the beautiful tomb of Ilaria del Caretto, by Jacopo della Quercia (1374-1438). The 11th-century wooden Christ in the nave is called the *Holy Face*, the *volto sacro*, said to have reached the nearby shore from the east in a ship without sails or crew. It is paraded through the town on 13 September.

Trees grow on the top of the Torre Guinigi!

Torre Guinigi, in via Sant' Andrea, is a tower with the trees growing on top. Open October to March 10am-4pm, April to September 9am-7pm.

Notice all the old filled-in arches of narrow bricks on the outside walls of the Roman amphitheatre, piazza Antifeatro. In fact the whole of Lucca is full of arches.

AROUND LUCCA – THE VILLAS

From the beginning of the 16th century, many merchants built themselves country villas at the foot of the hills surrounding Lucca. Several are open to view and make a very pleasant outing by car. The Villa Mansi, at Segromigno is accessible by bus as well.

First built in the 16th century by Muzio Oddi, the Villa Mansi, at Segromigno in Monte, was enlarged and transformed in the next two centuries, the front adorned with figures, arches and staircases. The formal garden was transformed in the 19th century *all' inglese*, meaning to a more natural look, with pools, forests and statues of nymphs. Telephone 0583/928114. Open winter, 10am-12.30pm and 3.30-5pm; summer, 9am-1pm and 3.30-8pm. Closed Monday. L4,000 park and villa, L3,000 park. It is accessible by bus from Lucca.

Another worthwhile trip is to Villa Torrigiani, Camigliano, about 3km (2 miles) from Villa Mansi. First built at the same time as the Villa Mansi, and similar in appearance, it has grottoes, pools, balustrades, a lemon garden and lots of *giochi d'acqua* – fountains and water-jets. Inside is baroque decoration, ceiling paintings, rich hangings and luxurious furniture. Telephone: porter's lodge 0583/928889, villa 0583/928114. Villa open March to November 9am-12pm and 2.30-6pm. Park open on Sundays all year – see the custodian. Park and villa L5,000, park L3,000.

Only the park is open at the Villa Reale, Márlia (also known as the Villa Orsetti), but it is exceptionally large and varied. Napoleon's sister Elisa bought it from the Orsetti family in 1806. The grounds include a water garden, the Bishop's villa, and an open-air theatre, where, while Elisa lay on a chaise-longue, her musical director, Paganini, played the violin for her behind the yew trees so powerfully, so wonderfully, that she fainted clean away. Telephone 0583/30108. Open July-September, Tuesday, Wednesday, Thursday, Sunday 10-11am and 4-6pm, L4,000. October to June, every day except Monday, 10-11am and 3-6pm, L3,000. Guided tours on the hour.

The Villa Garzoni at Collodi, near Péscia, is the biggest and grandest *palazzo in villa* (palace in the country) outside Lucca. The village stretches up the hill behind it, and until recently the villagers had to go through the palace door to reach their homes. The garden, with cascades and terraces, pools and statues, and a little open-air theatre, climbs up and down the hill. Collodi is a tourist spot because it is also the birthplace of Carlo Lorenzini, who wrote the story of Pinocchio, and there's a children's playground here, Parco di Pinocchio. Telephone: 0572/429342. Open 8.30am to sunset. Adults L4,000, children L3,000.

West of Lucca, within easy reach for a day's excursion, lies Torre del Lago Puccini, along the via Aurelia between Pisa and Viaréggio, home for a long time of Giacomo Puccini, the composer, whose house you can visit. Nearby is the little lake Massaciúccoli, an important bird and wildlife sanctuary belonging to the LIPU, the Italian Birds' Protection League. Telephone 0584/975567.

From Pievelago, in the direction of Monte Giovo, is the Lago Santo, surrounded by mountains which echo like a huge bell.

ORIENTATION IN LUCCA

INFORMATION
TOURIST OFFICE
APT, via Vittorio Veneto 40, off piazza Napoleone. ☎ 0583/43639. English spoken. Monday to Saturday 9am-12.15pm and 3-7pm. Sunday 10am-12.30pm and 3-6pm. The tourist office has a list of private rooms to rent for the night.

CIV EX travel agency, via V Veneto 28, (☎ 0583/56741, telex 0501501) will help with accommodation.

Centro Accoglienza Turistica, Porta San Donato, piazzale Verdi. Open 9am-7pm in summer, 9am-2pm in winter. ☎ 0583/53592.

POST OFFICE
Via Vallisneri. North of the piazza San Martino near the cathedral. Monday to Friday 8.15am-7pm, Saturday 8.15am-12 noon. Postal code 55100. Telephone code 0583.

TRANSPORT
BUSES
City buses leave from piazza Napoleone.

LAZZI coaches leave from piazzale Verdi to Florence, Viaréggio, Bagni di Lucca, Pisa, Torre del Lago Puccini, Livorno; ☎ 0583/584876.

CLAP buses from piazzale Verdi for Castelnuovo,

Garfagnale, Segromigno; ☎ 0583/587897.
BICYCLE RENTAL
Casermetta San Croce, on the north-west ramparts, along from Porta San Donato. Open 9am-7pm daily in summer, Monday to Saturday 10am-6pm, Sunday 9am-7pm. L1,500 per hour, L9,000 per day.

ACCOMMODATION
Diana via del Molinetto 11, near piazza San Martino and the Duomo. ☎ 0583/42202. Fax 0583/47795. Single without shower L22,000-L32,000. All doubles with shower L42,000-L65,000.
Ilaria via del Fosso 20, on a street with a canal down the centre, east of the cathedral. ☎ 0583/47558. Double L65,000 with shower.
La Luna Corte Compagni 12, just off via Fillungo near the amphitheatre. ☎ 0583/43634. Double with shower L80,000, L65,000 without. Fax 0583/490021.

EATING OUT
Antico Caffè delle Mura piazzale V Emanuele 2. ☎ 0583/4792. Closed Tuesday. The restaurant itself, right up on the south walls, is not cheap but has a pizzeria open in the evenings.
Trattoria da Giulio via San Tommaso 29, near the north-west Santa Croce walls off via Galli Tassi. ☎ 0583/55948. Renowned for inexpensive local food.

Closed August, and every Sunday and Monday.
Trattoria da Leo via Tegrimi 1, north of piazza San Michele. ☎ 0583/42236. Closed Sunday. More local cooking.

ENTERTAINMENT
MUSEUMS
Palazzo Mansi via Galli Tassi. Pinacoteca Nazionale. Art Gallery and Museum. ☎ 0583/55570. Closed Monday. Open weekdays, 9am-7pm. Sunday 9am-1pm. L3,000.
Palazzo Pfanner via degli Asili 33. Gardens and exhibition of Costume of the 18th and 19th century. April to September 10am-5pm. Closed Monday. Other months, ask at the Comune di Lucca. ☎ 0583/41449.
Villa Giunigi Museo Nazionale, via della Quarquonia. ☎ 0583/46033. Open weekdays 9am-2pm. Sunday 9am-1pm. Closed Monday. L2,000.

SHOPPING
MARKETS
There is an open-air market every Wednesday and Saturday in piazza Antifeatro from 8am-1pm. A permanent market is in piazza del Carmine, near the amphitheatre, Monday to Saturday, 7am-1pm and 4-7.30pm. An antiques market is held on the third Sunday in every month, by the cathedral.

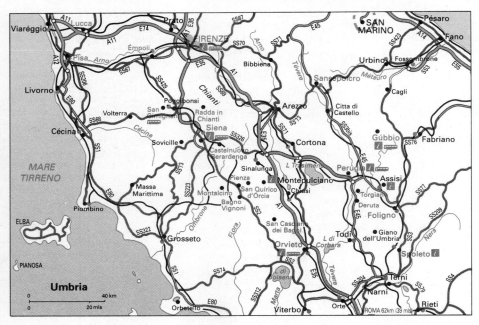

The Tuscan province of Siena is a self-contained small world, accessible by air from Pisa, by motorway or train from the north via Florence, and by motorway or the old via Cassia up from Rome. For the budget traveller expecting to use public transport, a charter flight to Pisa, and then train to Siena via Émpoli is an obvious choice. (For flight and rail details, see information for Pisa in the previous chapter.)

Local flavour

Prince Charles has been a keen visitor to Tuscany, painting watercolours of Brolio, visiting the Collegiata church at San Quírico d' Órcia. In his book *A Vision of Britain*, he describes Siena – pedestrianised, its old buildings protected, with a real city heart and centre to it (the Campo) – as an example of how a city should be.

Siena is a wonderfully unspoiled and compact city, built at the meeting point of three hills, stretching along the ridges, its tall towers and black-and-white striped cathedral visible from miles away. Make it your centre for trips, not only to some of the famous small towns nearby, like San Gimignano and Pienza, but also for seeing the countryside itself.

The Chianti hills north of Siena towards Florence are covered in woods, vineyards, castles, farmhouses, self-catering holiday accommodation, and have become so popular that prices have risen accordingly. But southwards the landscape is different, much barer and less wooded. These low, rolling hills are called the *crete*; the soil is volcanic clay, coloured grey, yellow, varying browns (burnt Sienna, raw Sienna), all blending and revealed when the wheatfields are ploughed.

This is the countryside you see in the background of the paintings of the Lorenzetti brothers in Siena, but in the 14th century, and right up till recent times, it was covered with shrubby bushes and much less cultivated. Once oxen laboriously pulled a few ploughs; now a new form of land ownership (not the old *mezzadria*) and combine-harvesters have transformed much of the country into undulating golden waves of wheatfields, punctuated along the skyline by lone cypresses or occasional groups or avenues of cypresses, and farmhouses crowning the hilltops. There are still sheep, some olive trees, and tightly packed ancient hill-towns guarding the valleys. Bring your camera – it's irresistibly photogenic.

Local landowning farmers are now leaving some land unploughed, or planting cover for animals and birds. There is talk of a large sweep of country around Pienza, San Quírico and Montalcino being made a national park.

Even without a car you could spend a few days out in the country, at Bagno Vignoni, a tiny hamlet south of San Quírico. Use this as a walking centre to explore nearby hill villages, or hire a mountain bike so you can go further.

Come to this part of Italy for an unstressful time. Siena is (almost) traffic free. You can walk about the narrow streets without fear of speeding vespas. There's room to move, and not too many tourists, except at Palio time, when the place is completely packed and out of its mind with excitement (the weeks leading up to 2 July and 16 August). The best work of art in Siena is the city itself. It's full of surprises; suddenly you are facing the huge striped cathedral, or you turn a corner and glimpse a tower, or an alleyway breaks through the protecting rim of houses, and you are in the piazza Il Campo. And that's surprising too, a shell-shaped, sloping meeting-place. You can get withdrawal symptoms after leaving Siena, though at first you may find it too enclosed. Take your time and wander around. It is well served with buses to Florence, buses and trains to Rome, as well as good public transport to interesting places near by, so you need never feel trapped without a car.

Self-catering farmhouses can be booked from agencies in Britain, or keep an eye open for advertisements in the Sunday newspapers. Agriturist will provide lists of accommodation. The Montepulciano tourist office is run by an exceptionally alert, English-speaking cooperative who organise a catalogue of houses to rent, advise on walks, festivals and even learning Italian. Called Il Sasso, the address and details are on page 140.

Umbria, less well-known and explored than Tuscany, is now also being searched for country properties for holiday accommodation, and more agencies now provide it. You need a car if you stay in the country, and Umbria has wonderful river valleys – the

Valnerina in the south east, and the northern reaches of the Tiber (Tévere) especially – which can't really be covered by local transport. However, based in Perúgia or Orvieto, two centres with good local buses and train connections, you can reach the beaches and islands of Lake Trasimeno; the towns of Assisi, Gúbbio, Spoleto; the ceramic town of Deruta; the wine museum at Torgiano; several small country towns; the two cities themselves need a day or two to explore. A visit to Orvieto is very worthwhile.

Local flavour

Only 6 per cent of Umbria is level ground, and it is the only region of central and southern Italy without a sea coast.

Umbria has some very picturesque camp sites, on mountain tops (like Giano dell' Umbria) or by lakes (Lake Corbara). May and June or September would be good months for a camping holiday. Umbria is called 'the green heart of Italy', which means it rains here – especially in April and late October – though nothing is certain about the weather, even in Italy. There can be terrific downpours.

Local flavour

There is much good food in Tuscany – try *anatra all' uva*, duck; or *coniglio con capperi*, rabbit with capers; *affettato Toscano*, a mixed first course of salamis; *cinghiale* is wild boar (many still roam the hills).

Peak summer months of July and August are hot for sightseeing and climbing around the medieval hill towns, but it is also festival time – jazz in Perúgia, international music and drama (Dei Due Mondi, Festival of the Two Worlds) in Spoleto. In September come the ancient jousting and crossbow festivals (Gúbbio, Foligno, and Arezzo and Sansepolcro further north). These mock fights and

cockerel displays of brilliant costumes are the relics and reminders, still full of powerful meaning, for the inhabitants. They are reminiscent of the wicked power struggles between the Guelphs (supporters of the Pope) and the Ghibellines (supporters of the emperor), which ruined much of central Italy from the 10th to the 13th centuries. City states and communes would wage battle, and factions within those would quarrel among themselves. No wonder the hilltop towns have such thick walls and high towers.

Local flavour

Spot the battlements . . . Members of the Guelph party in the Middle Ages (10th to 13th centuries), supporters of the Pope and usually merchants, built their castles and palaces with square battlements. The Ghibellines, pro-emperor and aristocratic, built fish-tail shaped ones.

From a budget traveller's point of view, all these Umbrian and Tuscan festivals are a bonus, a free show worth arranging dates for, though they also mean booking accommodation in advance. In general, hotels are not expensive here, though prices are creeping up in Perúgia. Orvieto has old-fashioned cheap hotels.

Moneysavers

There is a 30 per cent reduction on phone calls between 6.30-10pm weekdays, 1-10pm Saturdays and 8am-10pm Sundays and holidays. The cheapest time of all (50 per cent reduction on normal tariff) is every day between 10pm and 8am next morning.

AGRITURIST AND FARMHOUSE HOLIDAYS

Az Agr means *Azienda Agricola* = agricultural estate.

Radda in Chianti, unofficial capital of the Chianti area, has its own Agriturist office. Apply to Centro Chiantitourist – Sezione Agriturismo, telephone 0577/738215. English is spoken.

The Siena Agriturist office is at piazza G Matteotti 3, 53100 Siena, telephone 0577/46194.

Az Agr Cosona 53026 **Pienza** (SI). Near Pienza. Telephone 0578/7905893. English spoken. Two apartments, eight rooms. Board, half-board or bed and breakfast. Riding, painting and sculpture courses.

Fattoria Pagliarese Loc S Giusmè, 53019 **Castelnuovo Berardenga** (SI). Alma Sanguineti. Telephone 0577/359070. Vines and olives. Pool and nearby river Arbia. Chianti Classico wine. English spoken. Four apartments.

Az Agr di Selvole (east of Siena), Vagliagli, 53010 **Castelnuovo Berardenga** (SI). Marco Toti. Telephone 0577/322662. Chianti vineyard, olives and lavender. English spoken. Pool, tennis, guided visits of farm, 26 apartments. Chianti Classico wine. Meals on request.

Az Agr Cantanio, San Casciano di Bagni 53040 **Celle sul Rigo** (SI). Telephone 0578/53625. English spoken. Trekking organised.

Two apartments.

Fattoria dei Barbi 53024 **Montalcino** (SI). Telephone 0577/848277. English spoken. Bicycles. Riding near by. Three apartments. Brunello wine.

Az Agr Casanove di Pescille 53037 **San Gimignano** (SI). Telephone 0577/941902. Nine rooms. Bed and breakfast. Views of San Gimignano. Riding.

Az Agr Il Rigo Loc Casa Bianca 53027. **San Quírico d' Órcia**, (SI). Organic farming. Telephone 0577/897575, 0577/897291. Four double rooms. Bed and breakfast, L50,000 for two, L60,000 for three people.

Az Agr Il Colle, 53027 **San Quírico d' Órcia**, (SI). Telephone 0577/897562. Farmhouse with three double rooms. L430,000 per week.

At Trequanda (south east of Siena.) Cereal farm. Swimming. Nine apartments. English spoken. Apply to Duccio Pometti, via Socino 4, 53100 **Siena**. Telephone 0577/662017.

Az Agr La Torre alle Tolfe strada alle Tolfe 12, 53100 **Siena**. 3km from Siena. Telephone 0577/44322. English spoken. Six apartments. Swimming pool, bicycles.

Az Agr Montestigliano Massimo Donati. 53010 **Sovicille** (SI). Telephone 0577/342013. English spoken. Swimming, lake, riding available. Three apartments.

SIENA

The city, capital of its province, 70 kilometres (43½ miles) south of Florence, is intact and unchanged within its walls, despite new building on the hills outside. In medieval times it was governed by the Ghilbelline nobles and warred constantly with Florence, stronghold of the Guelphs. Siena has a university, founded in the 13th century, a remarkable cathedral, many fine Gothic palaces, and was the centre of its own school of painting (Sienese) in the 13th and 14th centuries. Since the Middle Ages it has been divided into districts (*contrade*) which have a strong civic and social life of their own.

Siena is also an old banking city, with the oldest bank in Italy, the Monte dei Paschi in piazza Salimbeni.

Local flavour

For centuries in the Middle Ages, Siena and Florence were deadly rivals. In 1230 the Florentines even catapulted dead donkeys over Siena's walls, trying to cause plague. It didn't work; Siena later trounced Florence at the battle of Montaperti in 1260, but did eventually fall to the Florentine Medicis in the 16th century. The rivalry persists.

The districts of Siena   The districts of Siena, the Contrade, were first divided at the beginning of the 13th century, with final boundaries set in 1729. There are 17 districts, each with its own church, museum, meeting house, bar, kitchens and fountains. Most important is the feast day of its patron saint, and the night before, with processions and games, a 'children's palio' and singing and feasting in the streets. The birth of the Virgin, 8 September, is another special occasion. From the end of April until the middle of September, not a week passes but one or another Contrada such as the Unicorn, the Snail, the Owl or the Caterpillar will be celebrating – often noisily and often gastronomically, with food fairs, ice cream fairs or dinners. Look out for the Torre (elephant) district celebrations in via di Salicotto at the end of July. The tourist leaflet, *Siena 91* (or *92*), lists the Contrade's festivities, and times and dates of the Palio trial races; also telephone numbers and addresses of the various museums (best to telephone in advance).

Moneysaver

If you are lucky, you may come across a street specially lit with wall-torches (*braccialetti*) and trestle tables and chairs set out – it's one of the Contrade having a *mangia e bevi* evening. Sit down and be wonderfully fed for very little, for instance *zuppa lombarda* (bean soup), or *crostini*, stuffed rabbit, with beans or radicchio, cheese, good wine, all for L24,000 for two, with the added pleasure of dining outside among friendly people, with the towers and churches of Siena profiling themselves against the night sky. A great, inexpensive Sienese night out.

The best sights are to be seen just wandering around, or sitting on the marble bench in piazza del Duomo (beware of pigeon-droppings), with the cathedral to your right and the Santa Maria della Scala hospital on your left (especially at sunset), or having a cup of coffee at the Costa in the Campo.

Siena is very well provided with *osterie* and *trattorie* for inexpensive eating. In the

Campo, the Costa is the best value. (Be careful not to sit at the café next door, which is very expensive.) The self-service restaurant along from the Palazzo Pubblico – Il Barbero – is good value, clinical but pleasant with no cover charge, and you can see exactly what you are getting. Less expensive eating places are in the little side streets, and down in the piazza del Mercato, behind the Campo, around the via di Porrione and Salicotto.

The Duomo   The Duomo is open all day in summer, till 7.15pm. Many of the 52 marble inlaid panels on the floor are covered for protection, the best ones are exposed from August 15 to September 15. The cathedral's pillars need cleaning and ghoulish popes and emperors look down from above, but there is a wonderful pulpit by Nicola and Giovanni Pisano. The Libreria Piccolomini has frescoes by Pinturicchio. A Donatello statue stands in the St John the Baptist chapel.

The Duomo was consecrated in 1179, then enlarged, and in 1339 it was decided to build a new vast church, including the existing Duomo as part of it. But in 1348 came the Plague, and parts of the building collapsed, as did the whole project, and so the megalomanic walls in the piazza outside house nothing.

Don't miss the museum of the cathedral (Museo dell' Opera Metropolitana). Open 9am-7.30pm in summer, 9am-1.30pm in winter. L4,000. Downstairs are all the statues by Giovanni Pisano which used to be on the front of the cathedral. Upstairs is the *Maestà* by Duccio Buoninsegna, (painted both sides), and a *Birth of the Virgin* by Pietro Lorenzetti. Upstairs, at the end of a room of copes, a short stairway leads up and out for an expansive view over the city.

In the Baptistery (open 9am-1pm and 5.30-6pm) the font has panels by Jacopo della Quercia, Donatello and Lorenzo Ghiberti.

The Pinacoteca   The Pinacoteca, via San Pietro 29, has a dazzling collection of Sienese golden paintings, with too many *Madonnas* to take in at one go. It is best to start on the second floor. (The top floor has non-Sienese paintings, including a self-portrait by Albrecht Dürer.)

Among the highlights here are in room 5, *Adoration of the Magi* by Bartolo di Fredi; room 6, large triptych by Pietro Lorenzetti; room 7, little landscapes by Ambrogio Lorenzetti, and the long *compianto*, also the *Assumption of the Virgin* by Maestro d' Ovile; room 13, Giovanni de Paolo's *Madonna dell' umilità* among the fruit trees. The gallery is open 1 July to the end of September on Mondays 8.30am-1.45pm, but is shut Mondays in winter. (The postcard stall is shut Mondays, so go to Lombardi – via di Città – instead.) Open Tuesday to Saturday, 8.30am-7pm, Sunday, 8.30am-1pm. L3,000.)

Piazza del Campo Siena's centre is the Campo. The fountain, Fonte di Gaia, here has copies of statues by Jacopo di Quercia, now moved to the Palazzo Pubblico, Siena's town hall since medieval times. The brick floor of the Campo is divided by nine strips of travertine, to represent the nine lords who ruled Siena from 1285-1355. The palazzo and civic museum in it are open Monday to Saturday 9.30am-6.45pm. Sunday, 9.30am-12.45pm (closed in the afternoon, November to March), L5,000. Separate admission to the tower L3,000.

In the civic museum see Taddeo di Bartolo's frescoes in the Cappella dei Signori, the *Maestà* and *Guidoriccio* (the Knight on the

The Campo, its brick floor divided by nine strips of travertine

Horse), supposedly by Simone Martini, *Allegories of Good and Bad Government* by Ambrogio Lorenzetti, all in lovely rooms.

Local flavour

The Torre del Mangia, in the Campo, is named after its first bellman who was nicknamed *Mangiaguadagni* (money-gobbler) or *Mangia* for short. The city built the tower to balance the cathedral tower – Siena versus the Church. You can climb the tower, 102 metres (334ft) high.

The Palazzo Chigi Saracini, via di Città 89, houses a musical academy, the Chigiana. Look in at the courtyard. Parts of the art collection upstairs are sometimes on view, and there are occasional concerts in the elegant concert hall.

Local flavour

In piazza Posteria, at the end of via di Città, a modern bronze fountain, topped by an eagle, is one of the 17 fountains belonging to the Contrade. This is the Contrada of the Aquila, the eagle, and every baby born here is given a 'baptism' in the fountain.

Local flavour

It's odd to see Rome's wolf with Romulus and Remus depicted all over Siena, but Siena adopted the she-wolf. The story is that Senius, the son of Remus, founded the city. It is also said that Siena's wolf always holds her head straight in front, while Rome's bends hers, but maybe that is not entirely true.

State Archives A fascinating and usually quite empty exhibition is in the state archives, Palazzo Piccolomini. (From the Campo go up via Rinaldini, turn right and through the archway across to the left hand corner of the courtyard and up four flights.) Ask to see the *tavolette della Biccherna*, and a civil servant will escort you to a series of very decorative small painted wooden panels, once the covers of the city account books, painted by famous Sienese painters from the 13th century, showing scenes of the city's history. Free, no need to tip. Buy cards of the pictures in Lombardi (via di Città).

Flag bearer from the Wave Contrada at the Palio

The Palio The Palio, a horse race for the prize of a silk banner, has been a Sienese tradition since the 11th century. More a small war than a sport, it takes place on 2 July and 16 August in the piazza Il Campo, and is tremendously important to all Sienese. Each of the 17 Contrade practise their flag-throwing and their music for weeks before. On 27 May lots are drawn to see which 10 Contrade will compete. On 29 June the horses are shown at the Palazzo Pubblico, tried out, and 10 are chosen. These are allotted to the Contrade. At 7.45pm the first trial race takes place in the Campo. The jockeys, who come from the Maremma, south of Rome, or Sicily as mercenaries are despised and deemed untrustworthy, but necessary pawns (a jockey to a Sienese means a cheat). If a horse dies, he cannot be replaced, but a horse may win without a rider.

From 29 June till 2 July there are trial races, scheming, plotting, bribing, threats and even beatings. At 9am on 2 July, after the square has been covered with a thick layer of tufa, and stands have been built for spectators (40,000 can stand in the sloping square), the last trial race is run. The horses and jockeys are blessed in each Contrada's church. At 5.20pm the pageant begins. At 7.30pm the mounted jockeys are handed the crops with which they may beat their opponents and their horses, and, riding bareback, they career three times round the Campo at top speed.

The next day the winning Contrada parades round the town ending a week of intense excitement, which will recur in August. And in October there is a great feast in honour of the winner – which is the horse.

If the Dragon Contrada wins, for instance, there will be a great open-air dinner in the piazza Matteotti, with a film of the race constantly shown, and in the central place of honour is the horse itself. The following year there are another 10 Contrade, more races, more good luck, bad luck, and more cunning. The July Palio began in the 17th century, the August race was first held in 1147 in honour of the Virgin's Assumption.

Seats for the Palio cost from L150,000-L300,000, are hard to get and need to be ordered a year in advance, so join the other 39,999 standing in the centre.

ORIENTATION IN SIENA

INFORMATION
Tourist Offices
Via di Città 43. ☎ *0577/ 42209. Monday to Friday 9am-12.30pm and 3.30-7pm. Also at piazza del Campo 56 (usually very crowded).* ☎ *0577/280551. A booth near the bus stop in piazza San Domenico will find rooms, change money and sell city maps, open Monday to Saturday 9am-8pm June to September; other months 9am-1pm and 3.30-6.30pm.*
Post Office
Piazza Matteotti 37 (for telex, fax etc). Monday to Saturday 8.15am-7pm. Postal code 53100.
Telephone
SIP, via dei Termini 40, weekdays 8am-9pm, Sundays 9am-1pm and 3-8pm; via Cecco Angiolieri 7am-10pm; via Pantaneto 44, 7am-11pm; viale Vittorio Emanuele II 21, 7am-12 midnight. Telephone code 0577.
Police
Questura, via del Castoro,

near the Duomo. Open 24 hours. Foreigners' office, piazza Jacopo della Quercia. Monday to Saturday 10am-12 noon.
Public Lavatories
Piazza San Domenico; via di Beccheria, off via di Città, near the Campo.

TRANSPORT
Railway Station
Piazzale Fratelli Rosselli. Information office 7.30am-8pm daily. Left luggage open 24 hours.
Buses
SITA/TRA-IN buses (out of town excursions), piazza San Domenico 1. ☎ *0577/ 221221. Open daily 5.50am-8.15pm. Computerised information machine in booking office.*

TRA-IN local buses (to railway station, etc), piazza Gramsci. TRA-IN is pronounced 'trah een'.
Radio Taxi
☎ *0577/49222. June to October 7am-11pm. Other months 7am-9pm.*
Taxi Stands
Piazza Matteotti. ☎ *0577/ 289350; and at the railway*

station, 0577/44504.
Car Hire
Autoneleggi Sartini via di Pantaneto 27.
☎ *0577/281074.*
Intercar Eurodrive – Hertz Agency, via San Marco 96.
☎ *0577/41148. Both rent cars, minibuses and scooters. SENA via del Rustichetto 12.* ☎ *0577/283203 provide minibuses with driver for day or half-day trips.*

ACCOMMODATION
Central, near the Campo
Canon d' Oro via Montanini 28. ☎ *0577/44321. Fax 280869. Double L61,000 with bath, L48,000 without. Two-star, small breakfast room. Pleasant.*
Centrale via Cecco Angolieri 26. ☎ *0577/ 280379. Double L71,000 bed and breakfast with bath. Two-star, third floor, no lift, 7 rooms. Breakfast in rooms. Hair-dryers, television, frigo-bar.*
Chiusarelli via Curtatone 9. ☎ *0577/280562. Two-star, double with bath L62,000, without L41,000. Terrace, restaurant. Faded, not much*

charm, but near piazza San
Domenico buses.
Tre Donzelle via delle
Donzelle 5. ☎ 0577/280358.
Double L49,000 with bath,
L38,500 without. One-star,
basic. No breakfast.
La Perla via delle Terme 25,
off piazza Independenza.
One-star, second floor.
Small rooms with minute
shower. Double L49,000.
La Toscana via Cecco
Angiolieri 12. ☎ 0577/
46097. Three-star, double
with bath L81,000, without
L61,000. Fourth-floor rooms
have good views (especially
number 441).
DUOMO
Duomo via Stalloreggi 38.
☎ 0577/289088, telex
58035, fax 44043. All rooms
with bath L83,500. There
are cheaper rooms in the
annex (dipendenza).
Duomo via Stalloreggi 34.
Same phone number. Double
L61,500 with bath.
Two-star.
Palazzo Ravizza Pian dei

Mantellini 34. ☎ 0577/
280462, telex 575304.
Double room with bath
L83,500, without L63,000.
Three-star, restaurant,
garden, lift. Old and
spacious.
PRIVATE ROOMS
Bagnai via Bianchi di Sopra
6. ☎ 0577/40100.
Bencini via Roma 3.
Telephone 0577/222747.
Masignani via Pantaneto
105. ☎ 0577/220142.
Rauch via del Giglio 14.
☎ 0577/289195,
0577/291912.
NORTH WEST OF SIENA
In the Poggiarello area, for
those with a car
Garden hotel via Custoza 2.
☎ 0577/47056, telex
574239, fax 46050. Double
room with bath L73,000-
L83,000. With parking,
garden and swimming pool.
CAMPING
North of Siena, in the
Scacciapensieri area
Siena Colleverde strada
Scacciapensieri 47. ☎ 0577/

280044. Open mid-March to
mid-November. High season
prices, double: adults
L7,000, children (three to
12 years) L3,500 –
including car and tent. Bus
number 8 from piazza
Gramsci.
Convent via di Camporegio
31. ☎ 0577/44177. 'Casa del
Pellegrino'.

EATING OUT
NEAR THE CAMPO
Il Barbero piazza Il Campo
77-80. Open daily, self-
service. ☎ 0577/40187.
La Grotta del Gallo Nero
via del Porrione 65-67.
☎ 0577/220446. Very
popular. Can be crowded.
Closed Mondays in winter.
Osteria il Carrocio via
Casato di Sotto 32. Shut
Wednesdays. ☎ 0577/41165.
Osteria Le Logge via del
Porrione 33. ☎ 0577/48013.
Closed Sundays.
Pizzeria Costa piazza Il
Campo.
Ristorante Il Verrochio

logge del Papa 2. ☎ *0577/ 284062. Not very cheap, but local food and good value for money.*
Trattoria da Dino *via Casato di Sopra 73.*
BEHIND THE CAMPO
Trattoria Papei *piazza del Mercato.*
OFF THE PIAN DEI MANTELLINI
La Vecchia Osteria *via San Marco 8.* ☎ *0577/281133. Shut Tuesdays, stays open late. Recommended. Good plain food.*
NEAR THE DUOMO
Osteria dell' Artista *via Stalloreggi 11.* ☎ *0577/ 280306. Shut Thursdays. Menu includes truffle-flavoured tongue in a green sauce.*
Trattoria La Torre *via di Salicotto 7.* ☎ *0577/287548. Inexpensive. Closed Thursdays.*

There is a permanent Italian wine exhibition in the Enoteca Italia in the Fortezza Medicea, near the entrance, off via Cesare Maccari. ☎ *0577/288497. Open daily 3pm to midnight. In winter they organise special tastings on Tuesdays, called 'Martedi dell' Enoteco'.*

SHOPPING

The smart street is Banchi di Sopra for well known names. But there's also a useful UPIM in piazza Matteotti. You can buy panforte *everywhere with little price variation. The best, most comprehensive selection of cards and posters is at Lombardi, via di Città.*
MARKET DAY
Wednesday, La Lizza and viale XXV Aprile (against the fortress walls, walk up via dei Mille) 8am-1pm. The usual wide variety of market offerings here.

ENTERTAINMENT

There's not a lot going on at night in Siena, except for eating and drinking and walking about in the Campo and along the Banchi di Sopra. There are two discos, the Jet Set at via Pantaneto 13, ☎ *0577/288378, and Al Cambio at number 48,* ☎ *0577/43183. Also the Club Enoteca, Fortezza Medicea,* ☎ *0577/285466.*

At the end of August, the Settimane Musicali Senese, run by the Accademia Chigiana, hosts many concerts, and it's worth checking the posters at the Accademia for concerts at other times. They sometimes organise them in San Galgano and Sant' Antimo. And all summer, while the master classes are on, there are occasional performances. Accademia Musicale Chigiana, via di Città 89, ☎ *0577/46152.*

Moneysaver
Don't miss the Siena market, Wednesday 8am-1pm, and don't buy any shoes until you've been there. To find the shoe stalls, go up viale dei Mille, and they are straight in front of you against the walls – the best buy here. You can bargain, but stall-holders won't budge much. Real leather (*vero cuoio*) shoes for about L30,000.

Moneysaver
Siena Jazz, a series of courses, the last week in July and first week in August, provides some free jazz concerts. Look for posters. For information telephone 0577/220607. Otherwise the principal free entertainment is the Palio, the Contrade, and all the local festivals connected with them.

OUTINGS FROM SIENA

BUDGET FOR A DAY

Bus return ticket - SIENA to MONTALCINO	7,000
Entrance to Montalcino fortress	1,500
Glass of Brunello (DOC) wine	3,000
Lunch	8,000
Buy present, local pottery jug	15,000
Bus return ticket - MONTALCINO to SANT' ANTIMO	4,000
Supper ·	20,000
	L 58,500
plus accommodation	

Buses leave Siena from near **San Domenico.** Buy your ticket first at the office. Many buses fit in with working hours, running early in the morning, at midday, and again in the evening, and not at all **on Sundays.** Both buses and trains run every hour to Florence; buses take either the motorway, the via Cassia (route SS2), or the scenic Chiantigiana (route SS222).

SAN GIMIGNANO

Buses 1 and 2 run about every hour weekdays, every two hours on Sunday (L4,900 single). A town famous for its remaining 15 plain stone towers. There were once 72, built by warring factions in the 12th and 13th centuries who were trying to outdo each other, until finally, in the 14th century, San Gimignano came under Florence's power. Later economic decline meant the town has

stayed looking very much as it was then, though it's rather touristy now – big car parks outside the walls (no cars allowed inside), lots of pottery shops and places selling the local DOC white wine, Vernaccia.

Local flavour
Notice the slits high up in the towers where gangways once connected friendly tower-owners. If you come in March, there will be violets flowering on the towers as they first did, according to legend, when the town's patron saint Santa Fina died, and the angels rang all the bells in San Gimignano, and all the towers burst into flower.

Among the sights to see is the Collegiata church (Duomo). 12th-century Romanesque with frescoes by Ghirlandaio of Santa Fina's life, di Bartolo, Benozzo Gozzoli and wooden statues by Jacopo della Quercia. To the left is the Palazzo del Popolo with the Museo Civico on the second floor, open daily 9.30am-12.30pm and 3.30-6.30pm, shut Mondays, October to March. A L4,000 ticket for this museum gives you entrance to the Santa Fina chapel in the Duomo, the Etruscan Museum in the courtyard behind, and the Torre Grossa, the highest tower in San Gimignano, and the only one you can climb. More frescoes by Benozzo Gozzoli are in the Church of Sant' Agostino at the other end of the town near Porta San Matteo, where you can visit the Renaissance cloisters.

An open-air market is held in the piazza del Duomo on Thursday and Saturday mornings. There is good, cheap, quick food at the Vecchie Mura, via Piandornella 15, right off via San Giovanni (closed Tuesdays); the Pizzeria Chiribiri, first left off via San Giovanni (closed Wednesdays), or the Pizzeria da Nino, on via San Giovanni itself, number 38 (open daily). Gelateria Jolly in piazza Cisterna serves excellent home-made ice cream.

Buses arrive in Porta San Giovanni, and leave from Porta San Matteo. There is a public lavatory in via Arco dei Becci, behind the Palazzo del Podestà (shuts between 12 noon and 1pm).

SAN QUÍRICO D' ÓRCIA

Bus 17 goes south along the via Cassia through Buonconvento to San Quírico. Bus 112 connects San Quírico with Pienza and Montepulciano. In the afternoon three buses go to Bagno Vignoni from here.

San Quírico is an unspoiled remote small town in its own walls; an elegant little formal public garden off the square designed by Leoni in 1540 (called the orti Leonini) has a splendid statue of Cosimo de Medici. On your right, note the steps leading up to a flat within the very thickness of the walls (where, as it happens, an Englishwoman, Miss Molly, lived for many years). See the Romanesque Collegiata church with two splendid doorways, one with knotted columns supported by lions.

For an inexpensive meal try the Vecchio Forno, via della Piazzola 8. Closed Wednesdays, telephone 0577/897380. The nearby motel and *pizzeria* Patrizia, on via Cassia, telephone 0577/897715, is open all year, with double rooms with bath L40,000. The restaurant is closed Mondays.

San Quírico was the scene of a famous meeting between Frederick I, called Barbarossa (red-beard) and the Pope, to fix his coronation. Now, the third Sunday in June the Feast of Barbarossa is celebrated with parades, flag-throwing and an archery contest.

Buses connect here with Pienza, Montepulciano and Bagno Vignoni.

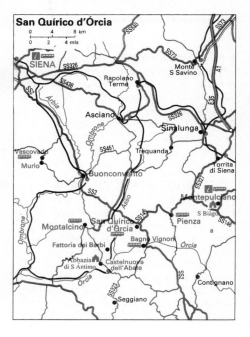

San Quírico d'Órcia

139

PIENZA

Take bus 17 on weekdays (not very frequent). After an early morning 7am, the next services are 10.45am, 1.55pm, 4.30pm and 5.30pm. The bus continues to Montepulciano, or take the 112 on from San Quirico.

Pienza was an 'ideal city' created for Pope Pius II Piccolomini by the architect Rossellino. Pope Pius was born at nearby Corsignano (where the parish church still stands, down in the valley), and he wanted it transformed into a Renaissance city. Work began in 1459, and stopped in 1462, with building costs three times their estimate. Each member of the papal court was compelled to build a house in Pienza.

The cathedral, which is slowly slipping down the hill, is light and elegant inside, with a beautiful ceiling. The Palazzo Piccolomini has a fine courtyard and a garden (guided tours, closed Monday, open 10am-12.30pm and 4-7pm, L2,500). In the museum of the cathedral, across the square (open 10am-1pm and 4-6pm in summer, 2-4pm in winter, closed Tuesdays, L2,000) are Flemish 16th-century tapestries and the Piviale, the cope given to Pius II in 1462. It is worth a close look to see how the different directions of the stitching show the folds of the cloak. It is English work (*scuola Inglese*), every centimetre of cloth stitched over, except the people's feet – quite rare, and a work of art.

Pienza is full of tempting wine, olive oil and cheese shops – great to browse among. *Pecorino*, a sheep's cheese, is a Pienza speciality.

Eat at the Ristorante Corsignano, via della Madonnina, before you go inside the walls (you can also stay there), telephone 0578/748501. Il Prato, just outside the entrance arch has good food at moderate prices, closed Wednesdays.

Before you leave, take a walk along the via d' Amore overlooking the valley.

MONTEPULCIANO

A two-hour (scenic) bus ride from Siena on the 17 bus goes to Montepulciano (L15,000). To have time to spend there, take the early 7am or the 10.45am bus. There's only one bus back in the afternoon at 6.05pm. (No buses Sundays.)

On the road in from Pienza, 2km (1¼ mile) down the hill before Montepulciano is the church of San Biagio, look left and you can't miss its white dome. Once in the town wind up the long street or cut up the steep alleys to the square at the top. The town is full of Renaissance palazzos, and the 15th-century Palazzo Comunale in the piazza Grande may have been designed by Michelozzi. There is a friendly tourist office on via Ricci 9, just off the piazza Grande, shut Mondays, open Tuesday to Saturday 10am-1pm and 4-7pm, Sunday 10.30am-1pm and 3.30-7pm.

The Cooperative Il Sasso, which provides information on houses to rent, walks, folklore etc, is at via de Voltaia nel Corso 74, telephone 0578/758311, open Monday to Friday 10.30am-12.30pm and 5-7pm, Saturday 10am-12 noon. Or write to the same address, 1-53045 Montepulciano (SI). English is spoken. Montepulciano has a well known summer arts festival, the Cantiere Internazionale d' Arte with many concerts and shows.

MONTALCINO AND THE ABBEY (ABBAZIA) OF SANT' ÁNTIMO

Sant' Ántimo, facing lines of cypresses

Buses run to and from Montalcino every other hour, with seven on Sundays as well. There is the usual morning gap between 7am and 10.45am (6am on Sundays). The last bus back is at 8.15pm, the journey takes an hour, L3,600 single.

Montalcino is an unchanged Sienese medieval hill fortress. You can climb the walls and turrets (L1,500, closed Mondays), and in the fortezza's main room there is an *enoteca* for wine tasting and sandwiches. The wine you taste here is the famous Brunello, a delicious DOC red wine, very expensive out of Italy, and not cheap here. The church of Sant' Agostino has 14th-century Sienese frescoes.

Moneysaver

The best place to buy Brunello di Montalcino is at the Coop Market, off piazza del Popolo. You can sample it in town bars for between L2,500 and L3,000 a glass.

To eat out in Montalcino, try Ristorante Il Giglio, via Soccorso Saloni 5, telephone 0577/848167, or the Ristorante Il Moro in via Mazzini.

From Montalcino, buses leave at 10.30am, 12.30pm, 3pm and 5.30pm for the Abbey of Sant' Ántimo, 9km (5½ miles) south on the road to Castelnuovo dell' Abate. This most beautiful, simple Romanesque church (begun in 1118) is all that remains of an abbey originally founded by Charlemagne in

781. Many pillars around the altar are made of translucent alabaster (onyx-marble). Bring a torch, or ask the custodian to shine a light through them. Walk round the outside to see the curious carvings, here a cat, there a horse. The setting is so peaceful, low in the valley facing lines of cypresses, among old grey olives and large white cattle. Open 10.30am-12.30pm and 3-6pm, but telephone 0577/835669 for further information, if you will arrive outside these times it is possible that they may still be open.

Local flavour

Since 1979, a community of Canons, St Augustinian brothers, has been established here, primarily to celebrate Mass in Gregorian chant. Hear it at 4pm every Sunday (from October to March) or 5pm in summer. Concerts are also held here on summer Sunday evenings at 6pm.

On the road between Montalcino and the Abbey of Sant' Ántimo, about 5km (3 miles) along (the bus stops there) you'll find the Fattoria dei Barbi, a Brunello-making vineyard that's open for wine-tasting and also has its own *taverna*, telephone 0577/848277. The *taverna* is shut Wednesdays and all of February, otherwise open 12.30-2.30pm and 7-9.30pm. The cellars are open Monday to Saturday 9.30am-12 noon and 2-5.30pm, Sunday 2-6pm. They also rent rooms.

covered hills of the Maremma. It is near the valley of the Ombrone river, which sweeps round and then flows south towards Grosseto. All this is an area where, from the 7th century BC, Etruscans lived in settlements among the hills.

Local flavour
Montalcino has two bloodthirsty festivals; on the second Sunday in August the usual costume parades celebrate the beginning of the shooting season; on the last Sunday in October is the Festival of the Thrush, *Sagra del Tordo*, with archery contests and feasts of local food including roast thrush, but also macaroni, *pinci*, and many elaborate dishes.

VESCOVADO AND MURLO

The next excursion is right off the beaten track and entails a bus trip to Vescovado, south of Siena, and then a walk on to the tiny, well preserved hilltop village of Murlo, with its Etruscan museum.

To Vescovado, take the 16 TRA-IN bus from San Domenico (Siena). Buses go at 10.45am, 12.45, 2.10 and 6.05pm Monday to Saturday, returning in the afternoon at 2.20pm, 4.20pm and 8pm (not Saturday). There are no buses on Sunday. The Etruscan museum in Murlo is closed on Monday. So organise your trip for Tuesday to Friday, returning late.

Local flavour
Where the Etruscans came from is uncertain, but they occupied Etruria, stretching from Florence down to Rome, over Tuscany and eastern Umbria, from the 8th century BC until finally, in 91BC, they were awarded Roman citizenship and were absorbed forever. They built their houses of wood, so none remain, but their life and art are recorded in their tombs, their sarcophagi, as well as pottery and wall-paintings.

Vescovado is up in hills of sheep pasture on the edge of two different landscapes – to the east, the small rolling hills of the *crete*, and to the west the larger, wilder, tree-

Local flavour
In the 6th century, the Tarquins, according to tradition, were kings of Rome. Their leader, Lars Porsena of Clusium, now Chiusi, was one of many who battled with the Romans. They left no literature, only their expressive art and their humorous sculptures to show what kind of people they were.

Picnic near Murlo, or eat at the Osteria da Deo in the centre of Vescovado, sitting outside at the back under an awning, with views across the hills (L30,000 for two with wine, pasta with *porcini*, *vitello*, *peperonata*). Closed Tuesdays, and from 16 August to 4 September.

From Vescovado it is about a 1½km (1 mile) walk to Murlo. In the centre, in the old Bishop's Palace, recently renovated, is the Etruscan museum. The artefacts in it come from nearby Poggio Civitate (*poggio* = hill), where excavations only began in 1966, first dug by archaeologists from Bryn Mawr College, and since the mid-1970s from Bowdoin College, USA.

There are some interesting insights into Etruscan civilisation, which included a curious mixture of savagery and refinement. The museum is very well displayed; an English catalogue is for sale. On the top floor are figures and faces which used to be on the ends of roof tiles, called 'Gorgon heads', they look like long-haired Billy Bunter vampires with grinning fangs and lolling tongues, horses' and leopards' heads, and unique to Poggio Civitate, a fellow in a curled Mexican hat with pointed crown. The museum is open Tuesday to Friday 9.30am-12.30pm and 2.30-5.30pm, Sundays 9.30am-12.30pm and 3-6pm, telephone 0577/814099.

BAGNO VIGNONI

The best way to get to Bagno Vignoni is by bus via San Quírico. By car, turn right off the via Cassia, 5km (3 miles) south of San Quírico.

The baths in this small hamlet date back to Roman times. The water emerges steaming at 50 degrees Celsius and gathers in a rectangular bath in the centre of the village, just opposite the Terme hotel. The more expensive Hotel Posta near by has an open-air pool full of this mineral water (calcium, iron, sodium and magnesium for arthritis and rheumatism), L15,000 a day. It is great in winter, with stunning views across the Órcia valley to the castle of the Rocca d' Órcia.

Bagno Vignoni

Until about five years ago, Bagno Vignoni was almost unknown, but now visitors and boutiques are arriving, and hotel prices have risen. However, it is still a peaceful place, with wonderful walks around, up the hill to the ruined castle of Vignoni, along the river to the startling viewpoint of Ripa d' Órcia, walking on rough paths among wild mint and thyme and blue chicory.

From Bagno Vignoni go up the long climb and the white road (*strada bianca*, meaning not made-up) to Vignoni Alto, along to Castello della Ripa, down to San Quírico, on the road to Pienza, turn left to the monastery of Sant' Anna in Caprena, on to Pienza, and then return back home by Spedaletto. You can drive this route too, bumping and slithering (very slippery after rain) on the rough track.

This is the only place in this area where you can hire mountain bikes. One day's mountain bike hire costs L30,000. For information contact Giancarlo Diodato, piazza del Moretto 40, 53020 Bagno Vignoni (SI), telephone 0577/887476; or c/o Speedcom, Piazza Peruzzi 2, Firenze, telephone 055/216901.

Local flavour

Some local dishes – *frittata con gli zoccoli*, a solid kind of omelette with bacon; *pappa col pomodoro*, soup of bread and tomatoes; *fagioli all' uccelletto*, bean and sausage stew flavoured with sage and garlic; *torta della nonna*, tart with cream, nuts, chocolate on top; *brutti e buoni*, macaroons with hazel nuts.

The Osteria del Leone, closed Mondays, serves genuine Tuscan dishes (*carpaccio*, boar, rabbit with capers). Main dish L10,000. It is popular, so book or get there early. Opens at 7.30pm in the evening. Telephone 0577/887300.

Moneysaver

The spring water also runs down the hillside, where you can sit and dangle your feet in it (free), and collects at the bottom of the hill in a natural pool (the Gorella), reached either by climbing down the hill or from the road up to the village off the via Cassia.

Moneysaver

The modern Posta hotel normally oversteps the budget range, but offers a cheap half-board midweek price in winter of L70,000 (double), including use of the hot-spring pool, for a minimum two-day stay, L60,000 if you stay a week. Telephone 0577/887112.

The Albergo Le Terme, Bagno Vignoni, 53027 San Quirico d' Órcia, telephone 0577/ 887150, was built in the 15th century by Rosselino as a summer house for Pope Pio II Piccolomini. It has a garden; double with bath costs L60,000. Half-board per person including wine L50,000-L55,000, depending on the season.

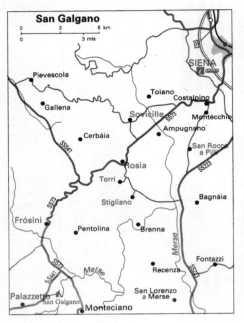

San Galgano

CAR OUTINGS

By car, explore the area towards Montepulciano, going east to Spedaletto (with its old castle) and Montichiello, a picturesque town. For three weeks in the summer there are local theatre productions in its little square, called Il Teatro Povero (or poor theatre); usually held from about 21 July-5 August, the performances start at 9.30pm. Tickets L7,000, telephone 0578/755118.

If you do have a car, it is worthwhile getting a leaflet published by the tourist office (free), called *Siena e la sua Provincia*, which describes 10 tours around Siena with mileages given.

Local flavour

For an unusual, rather more special meal in a delightful place, go to Le Torre di Stigliano, Stigliano, telephone 0577/ 342029, closed Mondays. (Turn south off the SS73 at Rosia, for about 2km, 1¼ miles). There are interesting antipasti – polenta with two hot sauces, aubergine fritters etc, and home-made *orecchiette* (pasta), ravioli filled with truffles. Not cheap, but not outrageous. Antipasto and pasta for two, with wine about L60,000. Eat outside in the garden.

PERÚGIA

Perúgia is capital of the Umbrian region, built on a hill 300 metres (984ft) above the Tiber valley, with wide views. It is also a university town twice over, with an old university, founded in 1276, and a newer university for foreigners. It is one of the 12 cities of the old Etruscan federation.

If you are driving to a hotel in Perúgia, be sure to find out which exit off the motorway to take, because the junctions and roundabouts round the base of the hill on which Perúgia stands can be quite confusing.

Arriving by train at the Fontivegge train station, piazza Vittorio Veneto down in the valley, a 33 or 36 bus leaves every 20 minutes, for piazza Matteotti. Or if you arrive by bus, in piazza dei Partigiani, take the escalator which goes up through the bowels of the rock fortress (Rocca Paolina) and deposits you under the arcade at the end of corso Vannucci.

From up here you can look over the parapet at the end and view all the new buildings and trunk roads below, and look across the hills and valleys of rural Umbria. Lake Trasimeno is to the west. Walk down corso Vanucci and you are at once in the thick of old Perúgia, with its tall massive Gothic buildings, and arched-over, dark winding lanes behind.

Perúgia gives the impression of an old moneyed, mercenary, warlike city, very close, and appropriately its most colourful monuments are the Moneychangers' Guild (Collegio del Cambio) and the Merchants' Hall (Collegio della Mercanzia). The wood-lined Merchants Hall, in the Palazzo dei Priori on corso Vannucci, enshrines its gods – Justizia, Fortezza, Prudenza, Temporenza (Justice, Strength, Prudence, Power), L2,000 entrance, with the Cambio. The elderly attendant will intone them for you with relish, implying that it is time we all returned to those old verities. In the Moneychangers' Guild there is a series of frescoes by Perugino (Perúgia's most famous painter), painted by him and his pupils, 1498–1500. He also included his self-portrait set in a painted frame.

The winding steps of Perúgia

Outside, in today's corso, the wide street is lined with smart shops like Gucci, and the Standa chain store opposite. The square at the end, piazza IV Novembre, is often full of students from the two universities, sitting on

the cathedral steps facing Perúgia's famous fountain – the Fonte Maggiore. It was carved to designs of a Perugian, Fra Bevignate, by Nicola and Giovanni Pisano. The tourist office is under the arches, below the staircase in Palazzo dei Priori. Pick up a rather sketchy map of the town, a leaflet of town walks, and a very useful list of bus and train times to nearby towns. Go up the steps to look at the great Hall of Notaries (dei Notari).

It's in the little streets behind the Palazzo dei Priori that you twist and turn, up and down stepped paths, with many odd archways and curious stonework to look up at. There are several cheap hotels in this area.

Visit the National Gallery of Umbria (Galleria Nazionale dell' Umbria) in the Priori Palace, entrance in corso Vannucci, (several flights of stairs up – lift is first right after foot of stairs). There is a large collection of Umbrian art, always being rearranged and restored. It should contain, as well as paintings by Perugino (real name Pietro Vannucci) and other Umbrian painters, a Fra Angelico *Virgin and Child*, and a Piero della Francesca altarpiece.

Also worthwhile to see are the Oratorio of San Bernadino, near the end of via dei Priori (early Renaissance building by Agostino de Duccio, about 1460), and the Archeological Museum in the corso Cavour, with prehistoric, Etruscan and Roman objects – interesting, but with very little information about the exhibits. Closed Mondays, open 9am-1pm, L2,000.

The Church of San Pietro, outside St Peter's Gate at the end of via Cavour (past Signa hotel) has a 10th-century bullet-shaped tower, and is part of a Benedictine monastery. In the sacristy, at the far right-hand corner, are panels by Perugino and his pupils. A door at the back of the choir leads to a terrace with a spectacular view across to Assisi. (Don't lock yourself out.)

The massive fortress of Rocca Paolina, along via Marzia, was built by Sangallo (1540–1543) on land where the Baglioni family had their houses, by order of the Pope. The Perugians, who loathed the papal

---

Local flavour

The Baglioni and Oddi families nearly exterminated each other in a series of vicious battles in the 15th and 16th centuries. After one bloody battle, priests put 35 altars up here in the piazza IV Novembre and celebrated Mass non-stop for three days, and after another they washed the whole square down with red wine.

---

regime, destroyed the interior 300 years later when the Kingdom of Italy was formed. Go through Porta Marzia to find via Bagliona, here you will be able to see where the old buried houses have been revealed (Tuesday to Saturday 8am-2pm, Sunday 9am-1pm, free).

The Church of San Severo is in piazzetta di San Severo, below piazza Michelotti. A small chapel next door contains a fresco by Perugino, and above it an early work by Raphael, the only attested work by Raphael in Perúgia. Open in summer 9am-12 noon and 3.30-6.30pm, Monday to Saturday; 8.30am-12.30pm Sunday. In winter telephone 075/284295.

Local flavour

Above the altar of the Cappella Sant' Anello in the left aisle of the cathedral in a safe locked by 15 locks and 15 keys, is the Reliquary of the Holy Ring, containing the wedding ring of the Virgin Mary, stolen by the Perugians from Chiusi. (Actually as big as a bangle and only revealed on 30 July.)

Local flavour

Perugian woven cotton cloth (called the Perugian veils) inspired by middle-eastern motifs, has been hand-woven here since the 13th century; also a fabric known as 'flame of Perúgia'. On Ísola Maggiore in Lake Trasimeno, they have revived a lace with a special crochet stitch known as *pizzo Irlanda*.

ORIENTATION IN PERÚGIA

INFORMATION

TOURIST OFFICE
In the Palazzo dei Priori, piazza IV Novembre. Open Monday to Saturday 8.30am-1.30pm and 4-7pm. Sunday 9am-1pm.

POST OFFICE
Piazza Matteotti. Open Monday to Friday 8am-7.30pm, and then Saturday 8am-2pm.

Postal code 06100.
TELEPHONE
ASST, next to the post office.

SIP, by the Tre Archi on corso Vanucci. Open daily 8am-8.30pm. Telephone code 075.

TRANSPORT

BUSES

Piazza dei Partigiani for out-of-town buses. Local buses (and the Rome bus) from piazza Italia and the piazza Matteotti.

There is one bus a day to and from Rome on weekdays. From Perúgia (piazza Italia) 6.30am, arrive Rome 9.30am (piazza della Repubblica). Depart Rome 4pm, arrive Perúgia 6.45pm. Perúgia to Rome Fiumicino Airport – 6.30am, arrives 10.05am. Rome Fiumicino Airport, 2.30pm, arrives Perúgia, 6.30pm. Daily 5.30pm from piazza Partigiani, arrives Rome 7.40pm, leaving Rome 7.15am, arrives Perúgia 10am.

One bus daily connects with services to Florence: leave Perúgia, piazza Partigiani 7.30am, arrive at Florence 9.30am. Return from Florence at 5pm, arrive Perúgia 7pm.

One bus each weekday from Siena, 12pm, arrives Perúgia 2.30pm. Leave Perúgia, piazza Partigiani 9.30am, arrive Siena 11.15am.

To Orvieto, depart piazza Partigiani, weekdays 2pm, arrive Orvieto 4.30pm. This journey is not advisable in reverse. Leave Orvieto 5.45am, arrive Perúgia 8.05am. Use the train: seven a day, change at Teróntola.

TRAINS

Fontivegge station, piazza Vittorio Veneto. By train from Florence, about 2½ hours, change at Teróntola, L9,900 single. From Rome, three hours, change at Foligno, L12,200 single. By car from Rome, take the A1 and turn off at Orte (SS204). From Florence, take the A1 and then the SS75bis. From Siena, the SS326, then the SS75bis.

ACCOMMODATION

Anna via dei Priori 48, off corso Vannucci. Up four flights of stairs. ☎ 075/ 66304. L48,000 with bath, L31,000 without. One-star, 11 rooms. Small sitting room crammed with heavy dark furniture. Meals available.

Excelsior Lilli via L Masi 9, large hotel near the car park. ☎ 075/20241. Telex 662074 ATT EXCELSIOR. Three-star, double L70,000- L80,000 with bath. Some cheaper rooms without bath. Own garage. No restaurant.

Palace Hotel Bellavista piazza Italia 12, large hotel in the centre of town. ☎ 075/ 20741. Telex 660274 PALACE. Garage, three-star, no restaurant. Double L66,000-L80,000, all with bath.

Pensione Paola via della Canapina 5, bus 26 or 27 from the station. From the corso Vannucci follow signs to Hotel Umbria and continue past it, go down the steps and turn right. ☎ 075/ 23816. One-star, nine rooms. Meals available. Near a town car park. Double L48,000 with bath, L31,000 without. Book if possible.

Piccolo Hotel via Bonazzi 25, central. ☎ 075/22987. Two-star, L48,000 with bath, L31,000 without. All double rooms, quiet but with no views. Book, especially in spring and September. Ten rooms.

Priori via Vermiglioli 3, central. ☎ 075/23378. Double L60,000 with bath, L38,000 without. L10,000 self-service breakfast. Two-star, large terrace, garage L15,000 extra.

Rosalba via del Circo 8. Near the escalator entrance and bus stop for the train station. ☎ 075/28285. L52,000-L60,000 all with bath. Two-star, no breakfast (bar very near).

Signa via del Grillo 9, just inside St Peter's Gate, off top of corso Cavour (bus route 29). ☎ 075/61080. L60,000, all with bath. Two-star, parking space, quiet, small patio garden, some rooms with terrace.

EATING OUT

With two universities in town there are plenty of good eating places here. For ice cream go to Gelateria 2,000, via Luigi Bonazzi 3, off piazza della Repubblica, and the Gelateria Veneta, corso Vannucci 20.

There is an open-air food market Tuesday and Saturday, and a covered market in piazza Matteotti, Tuesday to Sunday 8am-1pm. An outdoor café is here on summer evenings. *Lo Scalino* pizzeria on steps down from via Obadan. Pizzas L3,500 to L5,500. ***Ristorante del Sole*** via Obadan 28. ☎ 075/65031. Closed Mondays. Great

views over the hills. Good display of mixed antipasti, L6,500. First course L6,000-L7,000.
Ristorante XX Giugno
borgo XX Giugno 14, just outside the gates, at the end of corso Cavour, near Hotel Signa. ☎ 075/20959. Good plain local cooking (crema di carciofi, arista alla porchetta, *very tasty pork*) L20,000.

OUTINGS FROM PERÚGIA

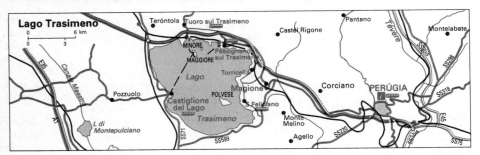

BUDGET FOR A DAY	
Train return ticket– PERUGIA to ASSISI	3,600
Light candle in Cathedral	1,000
Entrance fee to Rocca Maggiore	2,000
Porchetta sandwich	4,000
A beer	1,800
Return to PERUGIA	
Visit to National Gallery of Umbria- free	
Evening meal: Ristorante XX Giugno	20,000
	32,400
plus accommodation	

LAKE TRASIMENO

Famous as the site of a trouncing of the Roman army by Hannibal at Tuoro (24 June 217BC, it began at dawn, when a thick mist hung round the lake). Now the lake is Umbria's swimming pool, surrounded by low hills with three islands, lots of beaches,

reasonably clean water and the chance to windsurf and swim in the hot Umbrian summer. (Perúgia's public swimming pool is so heavily chlorinated it's eye-damaging.)

Buses from piazza Partigiani go to Magione, and San Feliciano, from where a boat crosses to the least frequented island, Ísola Polvese; Passignano, which is an established lake resort town, with several hotels, restaurants, a garden walkway beside the lake, boats and small beach; Tuoro, which is just a beach, camping, picnic place under trees (don't use the public lavatories, go to the restaurant), windsurfing school (L8,000 an hour), pedaloes and canoes. From both Passignano and Tuoro boats go to Ísola Maggiore and connect with boats to Castiglione del Lago on the west bank. There is plenty of free parking at Tuoro, and the beach attendants are obliging. The season in these parts runs from 1 May to 30 September

for umbrellas, sunbeds etc. Average cost is
L10,000 per day for umbrella, two sun beds,
use of cabin and shower.

From Tuoro, the bus continues round the
lake to Castiglione del Lago, a medieval
village with a walled castle, several hotels,
and beaches stretching along the shore.

Perugians also recommend Torricella,
between Magione and Passignano on the
railway line. Trains are more frequent to this
side of the lake, and the station at Tuoro is
within easy walking distance of the lake,
though at Passignano it is quite a trek to the
bathing beach.

Buses return in the afternoon from Castiglione at 4.45pm and 8.50pm (not on Saturday); from Tuoro at 2.35 and 8.45pm (not
Saturday), with Passignano 10 minutes later
and San Feliciano 20 minutes later. The train
fills in between times with a 4.42pm and
6.58pm returning from Tuoro, with Passignano and Toricella roughly five minutes
later. Sample cost of boat trips on lake
Trasimeno – all return trips:

Passignano to I Maggiore, L5,100
Castiglione to I Maggiore, L6,400
Tuoro to I Maggiore, L3,900
San Feliciano to I Polvese, L3,900
Passignano to I Maggiore to I Polvese,
L10,300
Toricella to I Maggiore, L7,000

ASSISI

A 9.30am bus from piazza dei Partigiani goes
daily direct to Assisi (piazza Matteotti),
arriving at 10.25am. (On some buses, change
at Santa Maria degli Ángeli.) The last bus
back is at 6.25pm. Trains leave about every
hour through the day (L3,600 return, takes
half an hour). From the station near Santa
Maria degli Ángeli, 5km (3 miles) below
Assisi, take the half-hourly bus (L600). The
last train back leaves at 10.53pm. Pick up a
town map and information from the tourist
office in piazza del Comune.

The Basilica of Santa Maria degli Ángeli
contains the Porziuncola, where St Francis'
order first worshipped: he died in the little
infirmary next door, now the Capella del
Transito. The Festa del Perdono on 2 August
was started by St Francis himself, when
anyone coming to the church gets an
indulgence.

Assisi is a beautiful town, built along the
side of Mount Subásio, but most people (2
million a year) come to Assisi because of St
Francis (and the painter Giotto). Of the
summer months, May and June are the
quietest, though not for three days starting
from the first Tuesday in May when the town
celebrates the Calendimaggio, a challenge
between two medieval factions, the Parte di
Sopra and the Parte di Sotto, with concerts,
dancing, processions, flags and singing.

The Basilica of San Francesco consists of
a lower church hacked out of the rock, and a
grander, elaborate church above it. Bring
plenty of 200 lire coins and be prepared to
look high up in the dim light of the lower
church to see Simone Martini's frescoes of

the life of St Martin in the first chapel on the left, Cimabue's *Madonna* and a possible portrait of St Francis in the right transept and Pietro Lorenzetti's paintings in the left, and above the altar four frescoes by Giotto. There is some doubt about the authenticity of the Giotto frescoes of the life of St Francis in the church above, which are glorious paintings nonetheless. St Francis is buried in the crypt below the lower church.

The churches are open from 6.30am to 7pm Monday to Saturday, but closed to visitors Sundays and holy days. Friars take guided tours round the upper church 9am-12 noon and 2-5pm, lower church 2-5pm. Mass in English is celebrated on Sundays at 8.30am.

In the piazza del Comune are the Tempio di Minerva (Temple of Minerva) and the 13th-century People's Tower.

The Church of Santa Chiara, with a façade similar to San Francesco, is dedicated to St Clare, daughter of a noble family who ran away to join St Francis, and founded the Order of the Poor Clares.

Local flavour

Porchetta is a central Italy speciality, a whole pig, boned, stuffed with rosemary, and spit-roasted. Many *porchetta* sellers travel around the markets with their vans, serving slices of meat and stuffing in a roll. Buy some here from a stand near San Rufino Cathedral.

The cathedral (San Rufino), begun in 1140, is more interesting outside than in, with some fascinating Romanesque sculptures. From here go up to the Rocca Maggiore (open 9am-7pm, L2,000). Below, along via della Rocca, are the Roman amphitheatre and the Teatro.

Local flavour

From the last fortnight in July to the first week in August, the Pro Mundo Uno musical festival organises concerts in Assisi's squares.

San Domiano is a 15-minute walk downhill through the Porta Nova. The interior is austere; the frescoes date from the 14th century, and the wooden Christ in the south chapel is 17th-century. Santa Chiara died here in 1253. In the refectory, which is just as it was then, the dying St Francis wrote his *Canticle of the Creatures.* Open daily 10am-6pm.

The Éremo delle Cárceri is outside the town, a good hour's walk up into the forest behind, or by car go from piazza Matteotti along via Santuario dei Cárceri. A monastery built round the little cave with its stone bed which was St Francis' retreat, and the stone altar is where he preached to the birds. There are trails where you can wander silently off into the woods around. The hermitage is open daily 6.20-8pm (5pm in winter).

ORIENTATION IN ASSISI

TOURIST OFFICE
Piazza del Comune,
☎ *075/812534.*

ACCOMMODATION
The tourist office will supply a list of religious institutions providing really cheap rooms.

Ascesi via Frate Elia 7, near *San Francesco.* ☎ *075/ 812420. Two-star, double L60,000 with bath. Restaurant.*
Dei Priori corso Mazzini 15, central. ☎ *075/812237. Three-star, double L80,000. Open mid-March to mid- November. Restaurant.*
Italia vicolo della Fortezza 2, near piazza del Comune.

☎ *075/81625. One-star, double L48,000 with bath, L31,000 without.*
Minerva piazzetta R Borghi 7, near San Francesco. ☎ *075/812416. Two-star, double L60,000 with bath. Restaurant. Open mid- March to mid-November.*
La Rocca via Porta Perlici 27. ☎ *057/812284. One-star, L42,000 with bath, L32,000*

without. Usually you have to have half board, L35,000-L38,000. **San Francesco** via San Francesco 48, near the basilica. ☎ 075/812281, telex 660122 SF AZITUR.

Double L74,000-L80,000. Restaurant, three-star. **St Anthony's Guesthouse** via G Alessi 10. ☎ 075/812542. Double bed and breakfast L56,000. Gardens, view. Run by American

Franciscan sisters. **Sole** corso Mazzini 35, near Santa Chiara. ☎ 075/812373, fax 813706. Two-star, double L53,000-L60,000 with bath. Restaurant.

Local flavour
Follow the Éremo dei Cárceri road for about 1km (⅝ mile) towards the mountains for La Stalla, a *trattoria* with big garden, self-service, reasonable prices and rustic cooking *alla brace*, on the spit. There is a camp site near by.

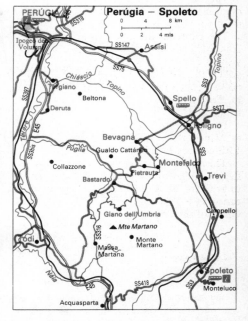

SPELLO

An interesting small medieval town, off the tourist beat, between Assisi and Spoleto. An 11am bus, leaving from piazza dei Partigiani, will get you there at 12 noon, but to have adequate time there you must return by train (4.39, 6.01, 6.38, 7.47, 8.38, 10.43pm), the same train that stops at Assisi before Perúgia. The railway station is in the valley, beyond the main road.

For 35km (56½ miles) the bus route follows the wide valley full of lines of poplars, the fields striped with vines and dotted with olive bushes. Market day in Spello is Wednesday, good for picnic food. This picturesque little town is built in terraces on the slopes of Monte Subásio. It's a little town to look up and down in, and through archways, you never know what you might find – a painted ceiling at the top of via Sant' Angelo, a flock of chickens, or an old paved street reminiscent of Erice in Sicily.

From the Roman Porta Consolare, walk

Spello – flowers pave the streets in the local festival

up via Consolare. The Pro Loco, with town map and information, is in piazza Matteotti 3, telephone 075/651408.

In the church of Santa Maria Maggiore is a frescoed chapel by Pintoricchio. You need a L1,000 note to light it up, but it's worth it – his best work (also paintings by Perugino). In the Church of San Andrea, up the road, still on via Cavour, there are more works by Pintoricchio and a little 13th-century painting. Pintoricchio was once sacked from a job for using 'too much gold, too much blue, and too much wine'.

TORGIANO AND DERUTA

Buses go mid-morning and early afternoon to Torgiano (wine-making museum) and Deruta (a ceramic centre). Both have specialist appeal and are only worth a special bus trip for pottery buffs or wine-making addicts, but worth popping to look at if you are driving near – on the SS3bis road south of Perúgia, towards Todi.

At Torgiano, the Museo del Vino shows all about wine cultivation (they used to manure the vines with dove and pigeon droppings), with tools, huge presses, wine in myth and medicine, and a large collection of ceramic jugs and pots, from the Etruscans to Jean Cocteau. All the descriptions are in Italian only. Among many curiosities are a 16th-century joke jug, *bevi se puoi* (drink if

Torgiano – a wine jug on display at the Museo del Vino

you can), which you can tip but can't pour, and wafer irons for making batter cakes laced with Vino Santo. They are ready in the time it takes to recite a *Pater* and an *Ave*, says the recipe. Next door see some of the real stuff – an *osteria* with local DOC Torgiano wine on sale. See the museum at Palazzo Baglioni, corso Emanuele, telephone 075/ 982129. Open every day 9am-1pm and 3-8pm, summer, 3-6pm, winter. L2,000.

Deruta has an Umbrian Ceramic Museum, at Palazzo del Comune, piazza dei Consoli (telephone 075/9711143), but also a great many workshops, mostly along the via Tiburtina, where you can buy and see the pots being made. Deruta is the biggest pottery centre in central Italy. Bright majolica ware, 16th-century scenes and heraldic decoration, pine cone shaped vases and big bulbous jars decorated in dark blues and oranges. There is a large choice of small plates etc for presents. The museum is open daily 10am-1pm and 3-6pm, L2,000. Shut Mondays.

Local flavour
Deruta pottery is renowned for yellow decoration on white ground, and firmly drawn figures on its majolica ware. Gúbbio, a strangely silent and remote town north east of Perúgia, was famous for the special iridescent gold and ruby red glazes of its master potter, Giorgi Andreoli. Since the 1920s Etruscan designs have been revived in local pottery.

Local flavour
The huge modern sculpture outside the train station is by the American sculptor, Alexander Calder.

Moneysaver
Small, inexpensive hotels fill up fast; book in advance or telephone a day before if you can.

TODI, TREVI AND SPOLETO

The Etruscan tomb, Ipogeo dei Volumni, lies 5km (3 miles) east of Perúgia, just before Ponte San Giovanni. It dates from the 2nd century, with nine rooms and many funeral chests on view. Closed Mondays.

Other towns within reach of Perúgia for a day's visit include Todi – 34km (21 miles) due south of Perúgia, a small medieval hill town with a famous central square, piazza del Popolo. Hosts a national craft show, last 10 days of June – first 10 days of July, and its own Festival of Music, the first 10 days of September. Famous for its woodcarving. Last bus back 5pm.

Trevi and Spoleto are both on the train line to Rome, changing at Foligno. A bus from Perúgia leaves 2pm for Spoleto, but the only Spoleto-Perúgia buses leave 6.20am and 7.10am.

Spoleto is an interesting medieval town, well worth a visit, with a fine Duomo, several Roman remains (arches, theatres), and near by is the papal fortress (Rocca), and the Ponte delle Torri, a 14th-century, 80 metre (262ft) high bridge over the river. The tourist office is at piazza della Libertà 7, telephone 0743/28111. The Festival of the Two Worlds, started by the composer Gian Carlo Menotti (the other world is Charleston, South Carolina, which has a similar festival), is held from mid-June to mid-July. About 1¾ hour's train ride.

THE BALCONY OF UMBRIA

If you have a car, here is an exceptionally varied long day's outing into the Umbrian hills. Take the route SS75, signposted Assisi, out of Perúgia. Continue on through Spello, and in the outskirts of Foligno turn right towards Bevagna. This is a very pleasant little town with a lovely square, worth the short detour. From Bevagna turn left up to Montefalco.

Local flavour
Sagrantina is the famous local sweet red wine (DOC), made with added raisins. Local eating places here are the Coccorone and the Falisco *trattorias*. But in the week before 17 August, the feast of Santa Chiara, you'll find people eating in the streets, with everybody dressed in medieval costumes and plenty of cheap food and good wine (which you can sample at the Cantina Antonelli on the road to Pietrauta, out of Montefalco).

Montefalco is called the Ringhiera dell' Umbria, the Balcony of Umbria, because it is 472 metres (1,548ft) up, with great views (though there's an even better view further on). There are 14th-century frescoes in the Santa Chiara church, 14th to 16th-century frescoes in Sant' Agostino, halfway up corso

Mameli, and in San Francesco, now the Pinacoteca, opposite via Ringhiera Umbria 19, are paintings by Perugino and a series of frescoes on the life of St Francis by Benozzo Gozzoli (1420–97). Walk along the via Ringhiera Umbria to the Belvedere for the view.

From Montefalco go west towards Pietrauta and on to Bastardo, a small town in the valley of the Púglia river. Take a left turn in the main street, marked 'Giano dell' Umbria', and 'Camping'. From here the road winds uphill again, with beautiful views all round. Keep going up to the little village of Giano dell' Umbria and follow the 'Camping' signs. You will find yourself up in the hills, with a camp site and swimming pool on your left, and a hotel, the Monte Cerreto, on your right (a bit of a roadhouse, with 10 basic bedrooms and a large restaurant area).

The camp site, Pineta di Giano crams its customers rather close together under pine trees, but is well equipped. The swimming pool opposite the hotel is open to outside visitors, L3,000 a day for campers, L6,000 for others. You could do worse on a hot Umbrian summer's day than swim in this pool, either before or after a walk in the hills. But you can drive further on, up Monte Martano (1,000 metres, 3,279ft). On the way up, just below the wireless station and before the animal crossing sign, turn right on a rough track for a picnic place on the edge of the mountain with the best and widest views of this part of Umbria.

Or continue a bit further to the Rifugio San Gaspare, a restaurant in a stone shelter with a wood fire always burning inside. The food is good and not expensive. Crisp grilled pizza folded round ham, home-made *strangozzi*, the local pasta with tomato sauce, two mixed salads, a glass of wine and coffee for L15,000, enough for a light lunch for two. Open from Easter to 31 October all week, and Saturday and Sunday in winter. It is a favourite haunt for the people of Bastardo; few tourists have heard of it. Marked nature trails up here are planned; meanwhile there are walks to be found.

Return down the hill to Bastardo and leave the town by the road you entered, forking left to Ponte di Ferro, following the river valley until you meet the main road, SS3bis, and turn right towards Perúgia. If there is time, you can look in at either Deruta or Torgiano on the way back.

Local flavour

More examples of delicious Umbrian food: black olives flavoured with orange – *arvoltolo*, hot pancakes sprinkled with salt and sugar — *brustengolo*, *polenta* with apples, pine nuts, lemon rind and sugar.

ORIENTATION IN THE BALCONY OF UMBRIA

ACCOMMODATION

With the freedom of a car, it's possible to lodge in smaller country towns, religious establishments, or more remote farmhouses. The following are in the area around Foligno, neatly placed between Perúgia, Assisi, Spoleto, Todi, and within reach of Orvieto (recommended by local tourist offices and agriturist).

BEVAGNA

Maria Bizzarri *via Santa Margherita 3, Bevagna.* ☎ *0741/360262. Double L35,000 with bath, three rooms.*

MONTEFALCO

Nuovo Mondo *viale delle Vittorie. Postal code 06036 (PG).* ☎ *0742/79243. Garden, restaurant, swimming pool, disco. Two-star, double L60,000 with bath.*

Ringhiera Umbria *via G Mameli.* ☎ *0742/79166. One-star, restaurant. Double L48,000 with bath, L31,000 without.*

Santa Chiara *via de Cuppis 18.* ☎ *0742/79114. No restaurant. Double L60,000 with bath, L38,000 without.*

GIANO DELL' UMBRIA

Park Montecerreto *Montecerreto, Giano dell' Umbria, 06030 (PG).* ☎ *0742/90186. Two-star, double with bath L53,000. Half board per person*

L40,000-L45,000.
RELIGIOUS INSTITUTIONS
Rooms per night from
L14,000 to L22,000.
P Carmelitani *via San Paolo*
13. Nocera Umbra. ☎
0742/818814.
San Martino *via Ciuffelli 4,*
Trevi 06039 (PG).
☎ *0742/78297.*
Santa Maria Del Monte

piazza Matteotti 15,
Bevagna. ☎ *0742/360133.*
Santa M Maddalena *via*
Consolare, Spello 06038
(PG). ☎ *0742/651156.*
CAMPSITES
Pineta di Giano, 06030
Giano dell' Umbria (PG).
☎ *0742/90178. Open 1 April*
to 30 September. Book for
August. L5,000 per person,

L5,000 per tent, a swimming
pool is located near by,
L3,000. Bar and restaurant,
mountain bikes L3,000 per
hour.
AGRITURIST OFFICE
Via Savonarola 38, 06100
Perúgia, ☎ *075/32028.*
c/o UPA, via di piazza del
Popolo 16, 05018 Orvieto.
☎ *0763/42820.*

ORVIETO

Orvieto is built high on a flat-topped hill, made of soft volcanic rock, riddled inside with old Etruscan and Roman tombs, cellars and sewers. For centuries it was a religious centre, and many popes lived here, finding refuge when Rome was threatened by foreign invaders. Now it's a relaxed, friendly and inviting place to stay.

Coming by car, take the Orvieto exit off the Florence–Rome A1 motorway.

From the railway station in Orvieto, bus number 1 (L600) goes every 20 minutes up the hill, to piazza Cahen, from where you can take the long walk up corso Cavour to the top, or take the half-hourly bus right up to the piazza del Duomo. All excursion buses go from piazza Cahen.

Orvieto Cathedral

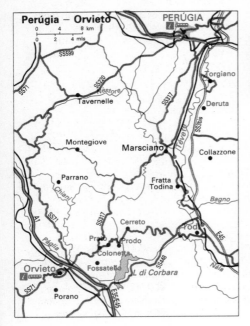

Orvieto's famous Gothic cathedral, the white Duomo, sits in its piazza like a white peacock in a crow's nest. Everyone gathers round it; the children roller skate down boards across its steps, and people sit at cafés or on the marble ledges of the building opposite, watching the light play on the mosaics and sculptures on the front. Its first stone was laid 12 November 1290, and it took more than 300 years to build. The façade was designed by Lorenzo Maitani, and he also carved the bas-reliefs on the bottom level in the early 14th century. The carvings are extraordinarily vivid. (Large black and white photos of them are for sale in the shop opposite.) The mosaics are copies,

155

the original ones were sent as a present to a pope. Inside, it's tremendous too, with great fat striped pillars (almost as good as Durham), high bottle-glass windows, and lower ones made in thin sliced alabaster, patterned in burnt sienna and Umbrian brown colours. (From the outside they look like any dirty old stone.) It is an effect altogether uncluttered and powerful. Further along on the right is the Cappella Nuova with frescoes of the Last Judgment, begun by Fra Angelico in 1447 and finished by Luca Signorelli – it was his masterpiece.

Local flavour
Signorelli was so obsessed with studying the nude figure that, when his 17-year-old son was killed in a duel, he had him stripped and spent the day drawing his body. On a lighter note, he had a clause written into his contract, saying 'that he be given as much as he wanted of the wine of Orvieto'. No wonder he painted his masterpiece here.

Signorelli's self-portrait is on the left of the door, a stern figure in black. A forerunner of Michelangelo, you can see here his mastery of anatomy and human form. The Duomo is open 7am-1pm and 2.30-5.30pm November to February, till 6pm March and October, till 7pm April and September and till 8pm May to August.

The Palazzo dei Papi (Palace of the Popes), on the right of the Duomo, is a museum of works from the Duomo, but at the time of writing is being restored. Beyond it, an archaeological museum (there is another opposite the Duomo) has a fascinating collection of Etruscan artefacts from around Orvieto, which was an important Etruscan city. There are shields and armory from the 4th-century Tomb of Settecamini, and don't miss a small room with original tomb-paintings of men and women dining on grapes and persimmons. Free, open Monday to Saturday 9am-1.30pm and 3-7pm, Sundays 9am-1pm.

Local flavour
Particular to Orvieto is a kind of lace (*merletto*=lace), called Ars Wetana, which is world famous, made by Orvietan women in their homes as piecework.

The other archaeological museum, the Museo Civico, in Palazzo Farina opposite the Duomo, has a scrappy collection with some Etruscan and Greek pieces. There are lots of black jugs with pinched mouths; downstairs a sarcophagus has weird people on it – some winged, some masked, one with a ram's head; see little 4th-century bronze figures from the Etruscan temple of Belvedere; and most memorable, a 6th-century BC fat stone head of a smiling warrior. Open summer 9am-1pm and 3-6.30pm, in winter 2.30-4.30pm. Closed Mondays.

Moneysaver
If you are not in a hurry, avoid the Rapido and Super-Rapido (TEE, IC and EC) trains, for which you have to pay a supplement.

Walking from the piazza Duomo down via Domo and corso Cavour towards piazza della Repubblica, you pass shops selling Orvieto's typical products, wine, lace and ceramics. Just on the left, Mastro Paolo makes plates with modern designs and plain circles of colour – L15,000 for a small plate (home address: via Felice Cavallotti). It's a refreshing change from all the flowery, heraldic pots. Orvieto also produces geometric designs, but not as skilfully painted as the Grottaglie (Apulia) versions. To see a potter at work, go to via L Mercati to see Mirella Ceconni (turn left off piazza della Repubblica).

Down the hill, near the Etruscan temple, and a shady picnic spot, is the Pozzo di San Patrizio, via Sangallo, an oddity worth visiting. It's a well, 58 metres (190ft) deep, built by Antonio da Sangallo in 1527. So that many people and their donkeys could go down at once to fetch water in times of siege, without impeding those coming up, he designed two concentric spiral staircases twisting round each other deep into the rock (248 steps). Open daily 8am-8pm, L4,000.

Trips from Orvieto   Orvieto itself makes a good base for outings: here are some suggestions. All excursions by bus leave from piazza Cahen. Check with the tourist office for up-to-date schedules of day and half-day trips to nearby towns using ACOTRAL and ATC buses, weekdays in the summer season.

ATC buses leave 11.30am southwards to the nearby small towns of Baschi and Montécchio. Also at 11.30am a day trip, returning to Orvieto at 6.15pm, includes the village of Alviano as well as Lugnano, with its outstanding Romanesque church, Santa Maria Assunta. Leaving at the same time, there is a day excursion to the hill town of Amélia (south east of Orvieto, towards Narni), a medieval thick-walled city which encloses some 16th-century palaces in its central piazza Marconi. The unusual thing about Amélia is that the walls were

built by the ancient Umbrians in the 5th century BC.

Lake of Bolsena and Viterbo, and further south, over the Umbrian border into Lazio.

Going out of Orvieto to the south west, look back for the best view of the town high on its hill.

You can either take an afternoon trip to Bolsena (leaving 1.10pm) or go for the whole day, changing buses at San Lorenzo on the way (leaving 8am). Another all day trip goes on to Montefiascone, near the south-east part of the lake.

Probably the most interesting trips south of Orvieto are the longer journey to Viterbo, and the short trip to Bagnorégio. The bus to Viterbo (ACOTRAL) leaves at 8.25, arriving at Viterbo 10.30am, returning either 2.15pm or 4.30pm (change at Montefiascone).

The trip to Bagnorégio leaves at 9.10am (ACOTRAL bus), returning either 2.30pm or 5.25pm. After a half-hour drive, there is a walk across a new bridge and a steep pull up to a rather extraordinary little town (becoming a bit of a tourist mecca) perched on a hill called the Cívita. All around are hills and valleys which dip away, and in the past a fair amount of the Cívita has fallen down into the valley too. However, it now has a new access road and enough visitors to help preserve it. It is just a little old town with a little *trattoria*, Al Forno, and a stupendous view, it makes an unusual outing.

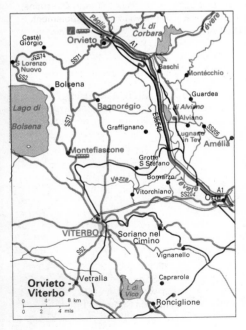

157

ORIENTATION IN ORVIETO

INFORMATION

TOURIST OFFICE
Piazza del Duomo 24.
☎ 0763/41772. Friendly and
helpful. Ask for the bus
excursion leaflet. English is
spoken. Open Monday to
Saturday 8am-2pm and 4-
7pm, Sunday 10am-1pm and
4-7pm.

POST OFFICE
Via Cesare Nebbia, off
corso Cavour 112, behind
the Luigi Mancinelli theatre.
Postal code 05018.

TELEPHONE
Bar Valentino, piazza
Fracassini 11, off corso
Cavour 127. Open 8am-
8.30pm, closed Friday.
Telephone code 0763.

POLICE
Piazza della Repubblica.
☎ 0763/40088.

PUBLIC LAVATORIES
In piazza Cahen; near
piazza della Repubblica; to
the left at the back of the
Duomo.

TRANSPORT

BUSES
There are two local bus
companies, ACOTRAL and
ATC. The three bus stations
are at piazza Cahen, above
the station, at the bottom of
corso Cavour; piazza
Marconi, south side, at the
end of via C Nebbia behind
the Duomo; and piazza
XXIX Marzo, north side, at
the end of via Cavalotti. One
bus on weekdays links
Perúgia with Orvieto,
leaving Perúgia at 2pm,
arriving Orvieto at 4.30pm.

TRAINS
Orvieto is on the main
Rome-Florence railway line,
about 2½ hours (150km, 93
miles) to Florence (trains
leave at about 30 minutes
past the odd hours), and
about 1¼ hours 100km, 62
miles) to Rome (trains leave
at about 20 minutes past the
odd hours). From Orvieto to
Siena a cross-country train
journey takes 2½ hours,
changing at Chiusi.
   Trains leave Assisi (and
Perúgia about 30 minutes
later) seven times a day for
Orvieto, change at
Teróntola. Journey time
from Perúgia is about two
hours. Leave Perúgia
8.25am, 11.03am, 12.34pm,
5.21pm, 7.18pm. Note: All
times are taken from the
summer timetable. Winter
times may vary.

ACCOMMODATION

Antico Zoppo via
Marabottinit 2, off piazza
Fracassini, on corso Cavour
531. ☎ 0763/40370. Two-
star, double L60,000 with
bath, L38,000 without.
Duomo via di Maurizio 7,
central, near the Duomo.
Two-star, double L60,000
with bath, L38,000 without.
Pleasant.
Posta via L Signorelli 18,
between corso Cavour and
piazza I Scalza. ☎ 0763/
41909. One-star, double
L48,000 with bath, L31,000
without. Very few
bathrooms.
Virgilio piazza del Duomo 5,
right beside the Duomo.
☎ 0763/41882. Three-star
hotel in an old building,

completely modernised with
the most incongruous latest
metal furniture inside.
Double L80,000, breakfast
L12,000 (café near by).
Budget accommodation at
the annexe, two rooms only,
L48,000. Ask for
dipendenza.

EATING OUT
Collect the list of wine shops
and restaurants from the
tourist office.

INEXPENSIVE RESTAURANTS
Del Cocco via Garibaldi 4.
☎ 0763/42319. Closed
Fridays.
Del Pino' Da Checco' via di
piazza di Popolo 15.
☎ 0763/42661. Closed
Tuesdays.

TRATTORIAS
Da Anna piazza Ippolito
Scalza 2. ☎ 0763/41098.
Closed Fridays.
Ricci via Magalotti 22.
☎ 0763/41119. Closed
Mondays. The cheapest
place in Orvieto, fixed meal
only L12,000.

ENTERTAINMENT
Check with the tourist office
for times of the many
concerts around town in the
summer.
   At 9.30pm on summer
evenings the small streets
are still lit by open shops full
of majolica, and residents
and visitors are ambling
about the streets, the
Duomo is floodlit. Groups of
young and old move towards
the public library in piazza I
Scalze, behind which, every
evening from 15 July to 4
September, there is an open-
air cinema at 9.45pm.

158

ROME AND ITS ENVIRONS

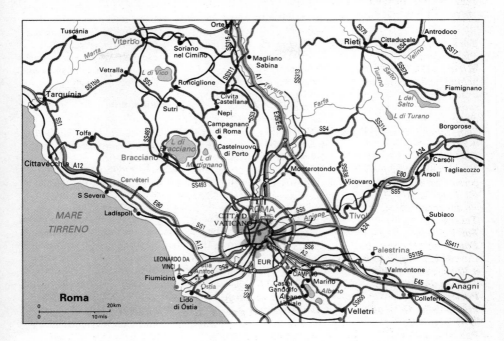

The American writer **Henry James** wrote of his first day in Rome in 1869. 'I went reeling and moaning through the streets in a fever of enjoyment. In the course of four or five hours I traversed almost the whole of Rome and got a glimpse of everything – the Forum, the Colosseum (*stupendissimo!*), the Pantheon, the Castle of Sant' Ángelo – all the *piazzas* and ruins and monuments. The effect is something indescribable.'

It's still the best idea – just to walk about Rome and enjoy the many sights, but with a little less of the reeling, and cutting down on the moaning. The usual sightseeing rules apply; don't try to see too much. Rome is bigger than you think, and the distances do seem large, even though in theory you could walk round it in a day. For hardy visitors short of time, we have charted a quick one-day dash taking in some of the major sights. But in general, allow a day for St Peter's and the Vatican if you are staying for some time.

Only spend time in the Forum if you are really interested in ancient Rome, otherwise go up on the Palatine for a picnic, and a stroll. Explore around piazza Navona and the campo dei Fiori and via dei Coronari especially. You could easily spend several days in this part, which is always referred to rather confusingly as 'old' Rome. The Rome of Julius Caesar is called Imperial or Ancient Rome; but of course, it is all mixed in together in most of the city.

For the budget traveller Rome can be expensive; especially accommodation in the

159

city centre. The tourist office provides a list of religious establishments, but none of these are right in the centre, they have curfew hours, and most cater for men and women separately. However there is one, the Domus Aurelia, near the Vatican, which is more of a hotel and very good value. Otherwise, lodgings near the train station are a bit rough (one little place, the Albergo Aurora, is cheap and clean and just like an English guesthouse).

North of the train station, the Nomentana district is a bit out of the centre but quieter (served by number 60 buses) and has several unpretentious two-star hotels. The few inexpensive (mostly two-star) hotels in the popular old part, near piazza Navona, get very full, so you must try and book these well in advance. Good places in Rome get snapped up very quickly. In the piazza di Spagna (the Spanish Steps), traditionally the English travellers' home from home, are one or two decent but not too expensive *pensioni*. Luckily, eating-out places are much more numerous, and relatively cheap.

Trastevere, the part across the Tiber south of the Vatican, is less well known and not too busy, but a lively place in the evening with lots of varied eating places, not expensive, and the streets around the church of Santa Maria are worth exploring for decent *trattorie*. It also has the only English-language cinema. There are also many trattorias off the main squares (Navona etc) in old Rome. Testaccio, the region further south, where the old slaughterhouses used to be, is where traditional Roman food is served, though you may not like the sound of it.

Eating around the Vatican is expensive, so move out of the area before sitting down to a meal, or have a snack in the Vatican cafeteria.

Traditionally, Romans leave town in August and many restaurants and bars shut. However, some Romans are staying home these days because Rome council has put so much effort into attractions for visitors in the summer – concerts, exhibitions, festivals along the Tiber etc. The heat is oppressive, though, making Rome still very much a tourist city in both July and August. The season in Rome begins at Easter and continues to the end of September. You will have to come either early or late to avoid the worst crowds in popular places like the Vatican.

It rains on average 80 days a year in Rome, mostly between October and December, July and August are the driest months. It can be windy in winter; the coldest month is January, when temperatures drop to an average 7.5 degrees Celsius, with December and February a little warmer. Average temperature in May is 18 degrees Celsius, just a bit warmer than in October. From June to September you can expect the weather to be very warm, with occasional unexpected downpours.

ROME

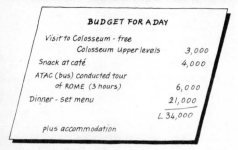

BUDGET FOR A DAY

Visit to Colosseum - free	
Colosseum upper levels	3,000
Snack at café	4,000
ATAC (bus) conducted tour	
of ROME (3 hours)	6,000
Dinner - set menu	21,000
	L 34,000
plus accommodation	

Rome has two airports, Fiumicíno is the most used. Fiumicíno airport is officially named Leonardo da Vinci airport, but is usually called after the city Fiumicíno. It is the most modern and best equipped of the two airports, with money exchange facilities and a tourist office. ACOTRAL buses shuttle every 15 minutes between the air terminal at via G Giolitti 36, on the west side of Termini station in Rome (8am-10pm), every 30 minutes between 10.30pm and 7.30am; journey time 45 minutes, L6,000. A metro line from Fiumicíno to the Piramide stop on line B is scheduled to open, which should cost the normal metro fare (L700).

Ciampino is a military airport used by many domestic and charter flights. An ACOTRAL bus runs between the airport and Anagnina station, the last stop on metro line A. Buses run every 30 minutes between 5.30am and 8pm, then every 45 to 50 minutes from 8-10.15pm. Bus and metro tickets, both L700 each, are sold from machines, so be sure to have change. A taxi to either airport costs L40,000-L50,000. Buses do *not* run through the night from Ciampino.

For train travellers, Naples, Bari, Milan, Verona and Sicily can all be reached direct from Rome. If you are travelling by train from Rome to Florence, and then on to Venice within three days, just buy one ticket to Venice, L33,500. The journey to Venice

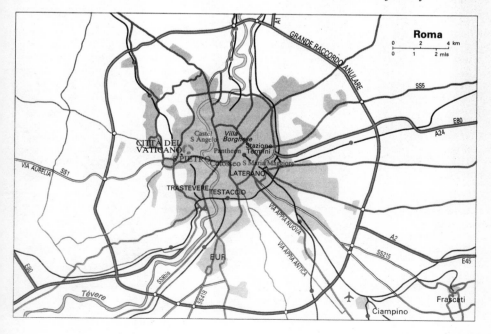

takes about 7½ hours. There are several routes to Florence, journey time about 3½ hours, L19,000. When the music festival is on in Spoleto there are special late weekend trains back after the performances, L10,000 return; journey time about two hours.

Warning! There are pickpockets about, especially on buses (number 64 is worst); purse and bag snatchers operate from vespas, and angelic looking children cover thieving hands with a piece of cardboard, so take care. Leave valuables in the hotel safe. Don't carry bags or cameras swinging loosely from your shoulder.

The Rome and Latium map provided by the tourist office is quite good and clear, showing the metro with a useful list of sights near each stop, and on the back another list of palaces, monuments and churches with a brief resumé of what they contain. The only thing missing is an index of streets and the bus routes.

Rome is split north to south by the long street, via del Corso, always referred to as the Corso, stretching from piazza del Popolo in

the north, down to the piazza Venezia and the landmark great white monument to Vittorio Emanuele (ex-king of Italy) in the south. East and south of this street cluster the seven hills of Rome, with the train station (always called Termini) over to the east. This eastern part is linked by two underground lines. To get to the great basilicas (papal churches) of Santa Maria Maggiore and San Giovanni in Laterano, and the market at piazza Vittorio Emanuele, take the metro. There are also useful stops at the Colosseum and piazza di Spagna. Get off at the piazza Repubblica stop to see the great National

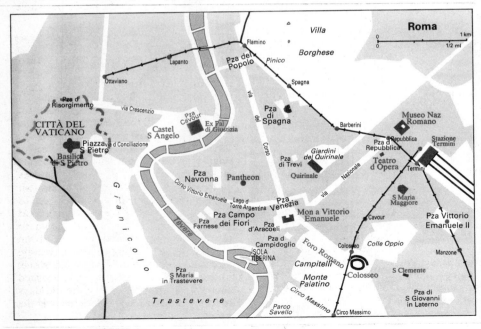

Umbrella pines and ancient buildings – a sight characteristic of Rome

Gallery (Museo Nazionale Romano) collection of Imperial Roman finds, housed in the old Baths of Diocletian.

South of piazza Venezia are the Palatine hill, the Forum and the Colosseum, with the Capitoline hill just up behind it. In the area of higgledy-piggledy streets west of the Corso, in the curve of the river, is old Renaissance Rome mixed in with some Imperial ruins. For centuries Rome has been recycling itself. The marble was stripped off the Colosseum to build a palace somewhere else, the Farnese family took urns and statues from the Baths of Caracalla for their palace; all over Rome you can see a bit of old column or a marble block embedded in later buildings. Rome isn't just a monument, it's a living, noisy, changing place, but essentially it's the same city. Julius Caesar banned chariots and carriages from the centre of Rome because they caused too much congestion, and though they've pedestrianised some streets in central Rome, it's mostly a maze of motors – honking through the streets and parking on the pavements.

When you get tired of the noise and streets and heat, escape to one of Rome's hills. Climb up the Pincio, above piazza del Popolo; walk up on the Quirinale, (behind and above the Trevi fountain) where the president lives (changing of the guard here daily at 4pm); find shade under the umbrella pines on the Palatine; or cross over past the Colosseum to the Colle Oppio. Across the river in Trastevere there are famous lovers' walks along the top of the Gianicolo hill. North of the city is the enormous Villa Borghese with enough to see for a whole day's walk or a bike ride.

One of the major sights is the Vatican, across the Tiber, with the great Cathedral of St Peter which houses the principal art collections, and the Sistine Chapel. Another sight, one of the most atmospheric of ancient Rome, is the old via Appia Antica (bus 118 goes along part of it), the long Roman road which eventually stretched right down to Brindisi and along which St Peter fled from Rome and returned again to his martyrdom. To this day it is littered with old stone, marble columns, shaded by pines and visited by lovers – probably just like the old days when the Roman carriages clattered over the same paving stones.

A day around Rome

To see Rome in a day you must be up at crack of dawn. Start early at St Peter's, after looking at Castèl Sant' Ángelo (in passing) and walking up via del Conciliazione (or if you can, get a 64 bus). St Peter's opens at 7am. Now walk (if it's before 9am) or take the Vatican bus to the Vatican museums (open 9am) and go round the shortest museum route (1½ hours), following brown letter A, switching to C to include the Raphael rooms and, of course, the Sistine Chapel. If you haven't got up as early as you intended, then don't attempt both St Peter's and the Vatican.

Take the 64 bus along corso Emanuele to largo di Torre Argentina and have a quick whirl round the Pantheon, venturing to piazza Navona, perhaps snatching some-thing to eat. From piazza Gesù, walk down via dell' Aracoeli to piazza Aracoeli. Climb the steps to the Campidoglio to admire Michelangelo's square and then the view behind over the Forum. If you are still in good shape, visit the Forum below and then walk on to the Colosseum.

From here walk up north to piazza San Pietro in Vincoli (by this time it should be around 4pm or later, and the church will be reopening for the afternoon) to see the statue of *Moses* by Michelangelo. Walk on to via Cavour to get the underground to Termini, change lines and go to Spagna. Here, if you are still in good fettle, the shops will be reopening for the evening, and you may forget your feet by doing some serious window-shopping.

Some practical help for day-trippers: in the Vatican the lavatory is just before the Sistine Chapel; the cafeteria is near the Pinacoteca and the exit.

ORIENTATION IN ROME

INFORMATION

TOURIST OFFICES

EPT *Termini train station, between lines 1 and 2,* ☎ *06/ 48254078. Open daily 8.15am-7.15pm. Main office is in via Parigi 5,* ☎ *06/ 463748. Cross the piazza in front of the station, take via Einaudi to piazza della Repubblica, then via G Romita into via Parigi. Open Monday to Saturday 8.15am-7.15pm. Pick up the* Rome and Latium *map,* Here's Rome, *and the newspaper,* Carnet di Roma. *Also the up-to-date*

list of museums with prices and opening hours, Musei e Monumenti di Roma, *and anything else you can glean. They also provide lists of hotels and religious institutions and will try and find you a room. There is also an information office at via Parigi 11.*

There is an American Express office in piazza di Spagna 38, ☎ *06/722801. Open Monday to Friday 9am-5.30pm, Saturday 9am-12.30pm.*

Centro Turistico Studentesco *via Genova 16.* ☎ *06/446791, for ISIC and YIEE card information and train, boat and bus*

discounts. Open Monday to Friday 9am-1pm and 4-7pm, and Saturday 9am-1pm. Also at via Nuova 434 and corso Vittorio Emanuele 297.

CIT *piazza della Repubblica 64,* ☎ *06/47941 for discount train tickets and tours. Open Monday to Friday 9am-1pm and 2.30-6pm. There is also an office in the train station which exchanges money.*

Transalpino *for discounts (for under 26-year-olds) on train tickets. Piazza Esquilino 8a, and platform 6 in the train station.*

POST OFFICE

Main office, piazza San Silvestro 19, between the

Corso and via del Tritone. ☎ 06/6771. Open Monday to Friday 8.25am-9.40pm and Saturday 8.25am-11.30pm. Postal codes from 00180 to 00190 mostly.

TELEPHONE
ASST piazza San Silvestro 20, next to the post office. Open Monday to Saturday 8am-11pm, Sunday 9am-10.30pm. Expect to queue. There is also an office at the train station.
SIP corso V Emanuele 201, near piazza Navona. Open 8am-9.30pm. Numbers in Rome are always changing, and may have any number of digits. Telephone code is 06.

POLICE
Ufficio Stranieri (Foreigners' Office) is at via Genova 2. ☎ 06/46862987 for reporting thefts or losses; English is spoken, open 24 hours. Police headquarters is at via S Vitale 15, ☎ 06/4686. Railway police, ☎ 06/4759561. Emergencies ☎ 113.

TRANSPORT
TRAINS
The main railway station is always called Termini. Booking office, ☎ 06/7280. Left luggage on platform 1, open 5am-1am, L1,500 per item per day. Also on platform 1 is a police station for reporting theft or loss on the train or in the station itself.

METROPOLITANA
(Underground) There are only two lines on the metro, line A from Ottaviano near the Vatican to piazza di Spagna, the Termini, and then southwards to Subaugusta and Anagnina from where buses leave for Ciampino airport and other southern destinations. Line B crosses line A at Termini, coming from the north east, and stopping at the Colosseum and Circus Maximus, open 5.30am and runs till 11.20pm, tickets L700 flat rate. There are not many stops in central Rome, but the A line between San Giovanni and Spagna, for instance, is useful, Line B shuts at 9pm Monday to Friday.

BUSES AND TRAINS
ATAC (orange local Rome buses) have an office at via Volturno 65, ☎ 06/46951, and in piazza dei Cinquecento near Termini, open daily 7.30am-7.30pm. Buy tickets for the daily city tour here.
ACOTRAL (blue out-of-town buses) have an office at via Ostiense 131, ☎ 06/57531, but ask the tourist office for information. Buses leave from various streets near the Termini for Óstia Antica, Tivoli etc as well as from the Subaugusta station on the underground.
Trams There are several tram lines; number 30 ambles all round Rome. For information see the Tuttocittà phone directory supplement, or buy bus and tram maps at the ATAC stand in piazza dei Cinquecento.

SOME USEFUL BUSES AND TRAMS
23 Vatican Museums – Castèl Sant' Ángelo – along the Tiber – Porta San Paolo – St Paul's Basilica.
27 Termini – via Cavour – Colosseum – Porta San Paolo.
30 Piazza Risorgimento (near Vatican) – viale della Milizia – Villa Borghese (passes the Villa Giulia and the zoo) – Viale Regina Margherita – Porta Maggiore – San Giovanni in Laterano – Colosseum – viale Aventino – Porta San Paolo – viale Trastevere (tram).
36 Termini – via Nomentana (for Sant' Agnese).
46 Piazza Venezia – corso Vittorio Emanuele – Vatican.
56 Piazza Sonnino (in Trastevere) – Argentina – via del Corso – via Tritone – via Vittorio Veneto.
60, 61 and 62 go along via XX Settembre to piazza San Silvestro, the Vatican and Trastevere.
64 Termini – via Nazionale – corso Vittorio Emanuele – Vatican.
115 Piazza del Popolo – villa Borghese – via Vittorio Veneto – via del Tritone – Augustus' Mausoleum – piazza del Popolo.
118 San Giovanni in Laterano – Colosseum – Baths of Caracalla – via Appia Antica (for catacombs and tombs).
170 Termini to Trastevere.
910 Termini to via Po and piazza Pitagora, near the Villa Borghese.

Night routes with conductors who sell tickets.
20 from Piramide to

Termini.
30 *from near Vatican to Termini.*
60 *from via Veneto to Trastevere.*
78 *As 30.*

TAXIS
Radio taxi, ☎ *06/3570; Cosmos,* ☎ *06/8433. Taxis cruise for hire in Rome, costing L3,000 one minute or 660 metres (722yds); L226 each extra minute or 300 metres (328yds), L3,000 extra 10pm to 7am.*

BICYCLE HIRE
Shops are at via del Pellegrino 82, near campo dei Fiori, and at piazza Navona 69. You can also hire bikes from near the metro stop at piazza di Spagna, in piazza del Popolo, largo San Silvestro, largo Argentina, and at viale della Pineta and viale del Bambino in the Villa Borghese; about L3,000 per hour.

SCOOTER AND BICYCLE HIRE
Scooters for Rent via della Purificazione 66, near piazza Barberini, ☎ *06/*

465485; open daily 9am-7.30pm. Mopeds L30,000 per day, bicycles L15,000 per day, vespas L35,000-L45,000; L300,000 deposit required.

ALBERGHI DIURNI
(day hotels) with baths, rest rooms etc.
Bertolini *via Conte Verde 43,* ☎ *06/7313304.*
Casa del Passaggero *via del Viminale 1, has Turkish baths and sauna,* ☎ *06/461795.*
Cobianchi *via Cola di Reinzo 136,* ☎ *06/312006.*
Diurno Stazione Termini ☎ *06/4755776, open 7.20am-8.30pm.*

LAVATORIES
Rinascente department store on via Corso has the best free lavatories, third floor.

ACCOMMODATION
Maximum prices listed by the authorities at time of writing:

TWO-STAR
Single room without bath L52,000, with bath L66,500. Double room without bath

L66,500, with bath L85,000.
ONE-STAR
Single room without bath L34,500, with bath L44,500. Double room without bath L44,500, with bath L57,000.
These prices do not include breakfast. Prices may be lower, but should not be more than 5 to 10 per cent higher.

NEAR THE TRAIN STATION
Albergo Aurora *via Magenta 39 (first floor).* ☎ *06/4957613. Only doubles without bath, L34,000. Breakfast L5,000. Bath L6,000. One-star, five rooms, all with basin. Clean, respectable, couldn't be cheaper.*
Hotel Stromboli *via Marsala 34, 00185 Roma.* ☎ *06/4451787, fax 4040320. Right beside the train station. Recently refurbished. Television and telephone in all rooms. Double with bath L103,000, without L68,000. Two-star, 40 rooms. English spoken. This hotel may seem a little expensive but it is very safe.*

Moneysaver
The cheapest way of getting an idea of the city is to take tram 30, which circles the city from piazzale Risorgimento near St Peter's, crossing the Tiber, passing the Coppede quarter near piazza Buenos Aires, then via the university, the cemetery, the church of St John Lateran, and on to the Colosseum, the Cestia Pyramid, and the Protestant cemetery (Keat's body and Shelley's heart are buried here), then across the Sublicio Bridge to Porta Portese. Get off around there for the Sunday morning flea market.

Moneysaver
A week's tourist pass (*biglietto settimanale*) gives eight days' unlimited bus travel for L10,000 – from ATAC in largo Giovanni Montemartini or in piazza dei Cinquecento.

Local flavour
Famous related local white wines are Frascati, Castèl Gandolfo, and other Castelli Romani. Local reds are from Marino, Velletri, Grottaferrata and Lunivio.

North of the Train Station, Nomentana Area

Hotel Flavia *via Flavia 42, 00187 Roma.* ☎ *06/463037. All rooms with bath. Double bed and breakfast L90,000. Two-star, 24 rooms, recently refurbished. Quiet, comfortable. Parking. English spoken.*

Hotel Galeno *via dei Villini 10, 00161 Roma.* ☎ *06/4402017, fax, same number. Double bed and breakfast with bath L95,000, without L75,000, 27 rooms. Parking, garden, bar, breakfast outside. English spoken.*

Pensione Claudia *via B Eustachio 7a, 00161 Roma.* ☎ *06/8551196. Double with bath L65,000, without L55,000. Breakfast L5,000 per person, 58 rooms. Quiet, unpretentious hotel with parking.*

Spanish Steps Area

Hotel Nerva *via Tor de' Conti 3, 00184 Roma. Two-star.* ☎ *06/6793764.*

Hotel Margutta *via Laurina 34, 00187 Roma.* ☎ *06/6798440. Two-star, 20 rooms. Recently renovated.*

Pensione Parlamento *via delle Convertite 5, 00187 Roma, just off the Corso.* ☎ *06/6787880. Up three flights of stairs, 18 rooms. Roof terrace. Double L78,000 with bath, L56,000 without.*

Pensione Suisse *via Gregoriana 56, 00187 Roma.* ☎ *06/6783649, fax 6781258. Double bed and breakfast with bath L108,000, without L83,000. Two-star, 30 rooms. Quiet, comfortable, popular. Visa*

credit card. Good value for the location.

Near the Vatican

Domus Aurelia *via Aurelia 218, 00165 Roma. Take bus 64 from Termini to largo Tassoni, then number 46 to near via Pio VIII.* ☎ *06/636784. Convent run by Orsoline sisters, very good value. All rooms with bath, single L27,000, double L50,000, triple L75,000. Cash preferred, 50 comfortable rooms. Bar in lobby. 11.30pm curfew.*

Old Rome

Due Torri *vicolo del Leonetto 23, 00186 Roma, north of piazza Navona. Two-star.* ☎ *06/6540956.*

Hotel Abruzzi *piazza della Rotonda 69, 00186 Roma.* ☎ *06/6792021. With view of the Pantheon. Two-star, decent small rooms.*

Hotel Mimosa *via Santa Chiara 61, 00186 Roma, near Pantheon.* ☎ *06/6541753. Good inexpensive lodgings, one-star.*

Rinascimento *via del Pellegrino 122, 00186 Roma, near campo dei Fiori.* ☎ *06/6874813.*

Sole *(one-star at time of writing, but being refurbished and possibly upgraded) via del Biscione 76, 00186 Roma, near campo dei Fiori.* ☎ *06/6540873. Garden terrace. Parking. Credit cards.*

Primavera *piazza San Pantaleo 3, 00186 Roma, just south west of piazza Navona.* ☎ *06/6543109. No private baths. One-star.*

Hotel Portoghesi *via dei Portoghesi 1, 00186 Roma.*

☎ *06/6864231, fax 6876976. Double bed and breakfast without bath L94,000, with bath L110,000. English spoken. Charming, comfortable and popular.*

Near the Forum

Casa Kolbe *via San Teodoro 44, 00185 Roma.* ☎ *06/67944974. All rooms with bath. Booking essential. Two-star.*

For Women Only

Instituto Madri Pie *via A De Gasperi 4, just south of St Peter's.* ☎ *06/631967.*

Santa Caterina da Siena *via degli Artisti 18, religious institute in the piazza di Spagna area.* ☎ *06/465974.*

EATING OUT

Old Rome

Hostaria La Capannina *piazza delle Coppelle 8, north of the Pantheon and east of piazza Navona.* ☎ *06/65453921. Small kitchen, limited choice, tasty pasta.*

Pizzeria Il Baffetto *via del Governo Vecchio 114, near piazza Navona.* ☎ *06/6861617. Open 6pm-1am. Very popular, get there early or late, or queue. Closed Sundays and August. Cover L500. First-rate pizzas.*

Ristorante da Gioacchino *via dei Coronari 233.* ☎ *06/6865890. Good family cooking, closed Sundays. Cover L2,000, pasta L5,000-L6,000, main dish L8,000-L10,000, vegetables L3,500. Wine litre L3,500.*

Trattoria della Stampa *via dei Maroniti 32.* ☎ *06/6789919. Closed Sunday.*

Local flavour

Some Roman specialities:
Saltimbocca alla romana – veal rolled round ham, butter and sage, cooked in white wine; *trippa alla romana* – sliced tripe, cooked with onions, carrots, meat sauce, mint and parmesan; *spaghetti* or *bucatini alla matriciana* – spaghetti with a sauce made of bacon, tomatoes, chillies and sheep's cheese; *pomodori con riso* – tomatoes stuffed with rice, garlic, basil, mint and oil.

Local Flavour

More Roman dishes:
Involtini di manzo alla romana – rolled stuffed beef slices; *misticanza* – a mixed salad, dressed with oil, vinegar and anchovies; *carciofi alla guidia* – artichokes; *bucatini all' amatriciana* – hollow pasta with a bacon and pecorino sauce – *pecorino romano* – cheese from Moliterna; *ricotta*, and for dessert *crostata di ricotta* – the Roman equivalent of cheesecake.

Trattoria del Pallaro largo del Pallaro 15, north of campo dei Fiori. ☎ 06/ 6541488. Set menu plus wine L21,000.

On campo dei Fiori itself are La Barese (closed Sunday), La Carbonara (closed Tuesdays).

Giolitti via degli Uffici del Vicario 40. Reputedly the best ice cream in the world. Packed out on Sunday afternoons.

Insalata Ricca Two places, one on largo di Chiavari 85 (closed Wednesdays and mid July to mid August), the other on piazza Pasquino 72, closed Mondays, open all year round. Salads and savouries.

NEAR THE TRAIN STATION

Hostaria da Dino via dei Mille 10, third street east of the Termini off piazza Independenza. ☎ 06/491425. Closed Sundays. Good simple food; two-course meal with wine and coffee L19,000. Try fettucine alla ciociara.

PIAZZA DI SPAGNA AREA

Not many good cheap places here.

Beltramme via della Croce 39. Simple and good.

Hostaria al 31 via delle Carrozze 31. ☎ 06/6786127. Small and inexpensive. Closed Sundays. Two courses, wine, coffee and tip L23,000.

Re degli Amici via della Croce 33b. ☎ 06/6795380. Not cheap, but good food. Cover L3,000, pasta L9,000. Closed Mondays.

It is better to cross over the Corso from via dei Condotti to via del Leoncino for the pizzeria at number 28 (closed Wednesdays), or to via dell' Arancio for the trattoria at number 50, closed Sundays. Both these close for most of August.

TRASTEVERE

Try the side streets around piazza Santa Maria and the Taverna della Scala on via della Scala.

La Canonica via della Paglia 6a. ☎ 06/5803845. Good for antipasti and seafood.

NEAR THE PIRAMIDE METRO STOP

Taverna Cestia via Piramide Cestia 65. ☎ 06/5743754.

Closed Monday.

Late in the evening, when pizzerie and rosticcerie are shut, there are still snack bars open.

Argentina largo di Torre Argentina 15. Open till 2am, closed Sundays.

Chez Toi via Cicerone 56a. Sandwiches till 3am, open daily.

Gran Caffè Adriano piazza Cavour 21. Sandwiches till 3am, closed Mondays.

La Spaghetteria via Arno 80. Spaghetti till 3am.

Nori piazza dei Cinquecento 51 (Termini train station). Open till 3.30am, closed Tuesdays.

Rosati Due piazza Clodio 25. Open till 2.30am, closed Wednesdays.

Settebello via dei Serviti 21. Sandwiches till 2.30am, closed Sundays.

Tritone via del Tritone 144. Open till 2.30am, closed Sundays.

WINE BARS

Bottiglieria Cavour via Cavour 313, open 8pm to midnight. Closed Sundays.

Buccone via di Ripetta 19, open till 9pm. Closed

Eating out, Roman style

Sundays.
Cul de Sac *piazza Pasquino 73, near piazza Navona.* Closed Sundays.
Da Giorgio *piazza Campo dei Fiori 15, till 9.30pm.* Closed Sundays.
Gamelino *via Frangipane 35, open till midnight. Closed Tuesdays.*
Il Piccolo *via del Governo Vecchio 74, open daily till 2am.*

SHOPPING

For second-hand clothes, inexpensive antiques, jewellery, there are shops near piazza Navona, in via del Pasquino and via del Governo Vecchio; there are furniture workshops on via del Cappellari and via del Pellegrino, off campo dei Fiori. For antiques of all kinds, there's a half mile of via dei Coronari (from north of piazza Navona towards the river) with nothing but antique shops, (Coronari means Rosary-makers.)

There is a good bookshop with an art department at Libreria San Silvestro, piazza San Silvestro 27, open 10am-1pm and 3.30-7.30pm, closed Monday morning.

Guido Pasquali at via Bocca di Leone 5, (same hours as above) has original shoes.

MARKETS
Fun to look at, not always as cheap as they look, Roman markets are found on both sides of the Tiber.
Porta Portese *in Trastevere every Sunday morning. Just about everything; Rome's biggest flea market is not the bargain or the bargaining place it used to be.*
Via Sannio market *near Porta San Giovanni. Every weekday, early morning to 1pm. The clothing part of Porta Portese market.*
Porta Vittorio *mostly food, but some other stalls.*
Piazza della Fontanella Borghese *near piazza di Spagna. Weekdays, small antiques market, look for old prints.*
Via Trionfale 47 *Tuesdays 10.30am-1pm. Flowers and seeds.*
Piazza campo dei Fiori *Flowers, food and clothing market. Morning, not Sundays.*
Piazza Vittorio Emanuele *daily market. Great variety.*
Piazza di San Cosimato *in Trastevere – food market.*
CHAIN STORES AND SUPERMARKETS
All open Tuesday to Saturday 9am-8pm (open through the lunch period), closed Monday morning.
Coin *piazzale Appio (San Giovanni metro stop). High-class department store;*

clothes and household items.
La Rinascente *Another top-class chain. Two branches in Rome – in piazza Colonna – clothes and accessories and toys; in piazza Fiume – household goods.*
Standa *at viale Trastevere 60 and via Cola di Rienzo 173. Household goods, also good food department in via Cola di Rienzo.*
Upim *at viale Tritone 172 and via Nazionale 211 for clothing and household goods.*

ENTERTAINMENT

OPERA
Teatro dell' Opera *via del Viminale.* ☎ *06/461755. Season from November to May. Tickets on sale two days before a performance, box office open 10am-1pm and 5-7pm. Prices from L8,000 to L44,000.*
Baths of Caracalla ☎ *06/ 5758300. Spectacular operas, huge casts, lavish sets, chariots, horses, a night to remember (with pleasure if you bring defence against hard seats and cold nights) from June to September. Performances 9pm-1am. (Buses L1,200 return to various spots afterwards.) Unreserved seats L20,000, numbered seats from L43,000. Advance sales at*

Teatro dell' Opera box office, ☎ *06/461755, otherwise at the Baths, between 8 and 9pm.*
MUSIC
In winter, concerts are held at the Accademia di Santa Cecilia, via della Conciliazione 4, and the Accademia Filarmonica, Teatro Olimpico, via Gentile da Fabriano 17. ☎ *06/3962635.*
In July, the Accademia di Santa Cecilia (☎ *06/ 6541044) gives concerts in the piazza del Campidoglio, and in June and July the Rome Festival orchestra performs regularly in piazza Collegio Romana.* ☎ *06/ 381550 or 3598196.*
The RAI (Italian radio), gives a series of concerts at Foro Italico, ☎ *06/36865625.*
Other organisations for music festivals and concerts are the Associazione Musicale Romana (☎ *06/ 6568441) and Il Tempietto (* ☎ *06/5136148).*
For tickets to rock, pop and jazz concerts go to Orbis, piazza Esquilino 37, near Santa Maria Maggiore. ☎ *06/4751403 and 4814721. Open Monday to Friday 9.30am-1pm and 4-7.30pm, Saturday 10am-1pm. Rock concerts are usually held at Palazzo dello*

Sport, in EUR, at the end of via C Colombo, ☎ *06/ 5925205. Tickets start at L12,000. Acoustics are apparently frightful, but bands are good. Concerts are also held at Stadio Flaminio.*
CINEMA
The only cinema showing English language, undubbed new films is the Pasquino in vicolo del Piede 19a, off piazza Santa Maria in Trastevere, ☎ *06/5803622. Two or three showings, starting 4pm, L5,000.*
FESTIVALS AND OTHER SPECTACULAR EVENTS
January 6 *Last days of toy fair in piazza Navona.*
March 19 *St Joseph's day (San Giuseppe). Open-air stalls in the Trionfale district, frying special cakes.*
Good Friday *The Way of the Cross, usually led by the Pope, from the Colosseum to the Palatine Hill.*
Easter Sunday *The Pope gives his* Urbi et Orbi *(to the city and the world) address in St Peter's Square, noon.*
Easter Monday *Traditionally everyone has a day out in the country. Many restaurants and eating-places are shut Easter weekend.*
April *Flower (azalea)*

Moneysaver
In May there is free entrance to contemporary music concerts at the Accademia d' Ungheria, Palazzo Falconieri (and possibly during other months). Consult the *Carnet di Roma*.

Local flavour
EUR stands for Roman Universal Exhibition, a new town built by Mussolini in the 1930s. It was built to house a festival of Fascism, never held because of World War II.

festival on the Spanish Steps.
Spring and autumn *Art festival in via Margutta, with pictures spread all over the street (about 8–11 May).*
End of April to beginning of May *International Horse Show in piazza di Siena in the Villa Borghese, including the Coppa delle Nazioni, show-jumping. Finishes with a dressy display by the Carabinieri and a cavalry charge. For information contact the Italian Federation of Equestrian Sports, viale Tiziano 70. ☎ 06/36858202.*

May *Antiques week in via dei Coronari (mid May).*
May to June *depending on the year. The Valle Murcia in the Aventino stays open for a month with a rose exhibition.*
May *Last 10 days, Italian Open Tennis Championship in Foro Italico.*
June 23 *Feast of St John. Songs, games, feasting and eating in the San Giovanni district.*
June–July *Tiber exhibition, musical events along the river.*
July, last two weeks *Festa de Noantri in Trastevere to celebrate the Madonna del*

Carmine. A chance to find an interesting cheap outdoor meal, and assorted revelry.
June–September *The Estate Romana. Rome's summer season of shows.*
Discos and night spots *These can be expensive – those that are not include*
Piper *via Tagliamento 9, disco and live bands, opens from 4pm at weekends. Closed Mondays and Tuesdays. ☎ 06/854459.*
Folkstudio *has jazz, country and folk music. Via Gaetano Sacchi 3. ☎ 06/5892374.*
Le Stelle *via C Beccaria 22.*
New Life *via XX Settembre 92.*

Local flavour
A tunnel connects the Baths of Caracalla with Palazzo Venezia, once used for transporting wood to keep the baths hot. Mussolini liked to drive his sports car along it, to pop up dramatically on stage just before a performance.

Moneysaver
Children get in free at the zoo in Villa Borghese. Open all year except 1 May, 8am-6.15pm in summer, till 5pm in winter. See monkeys, chimps, giraffes, seals, elephants, also birds and a reptile house.

DISCOVERING ROME

PIAZZA DEL POPOLO TO PIAZZA DI SPAGNA AND THE TREVI FOUNTAIN

Just above the piazza, and overlooking it, the Pincio gardens have one of the best views over Rome. Look at the church of Santa Maria del Popolo in the square. In the left-hand chapel are two of Caravaggio's paint-ings (*Conversion of St Paul* and *Crucifixion of St Peter*) hiding in the darkness (light switch on right wall). Don't miss Pintoricchio's frescoes and the Chigi chapel, designed by Raphael. From here, going towards the Spanish Steps, either go window shopping

BUDGET FOR A DAY	
Visit to piazza di Spagna	
Entrance to Keats/Shelley Museum	3,500
Lunch at Hostaria al 31 (2 courses, wine, coffee and tip)	23,000
Visit to St Peter's - entrance fee	2,000
lift	1,000
Snack supper	5,000
Ticket for Teatro dell' Opera	10,000
	L 44,500
plus accommodation	

down the Corso or look at the antiques along via del Babuino.

The Spanish Steps are so-called because the Spanish Embassy is housed in a palazzo

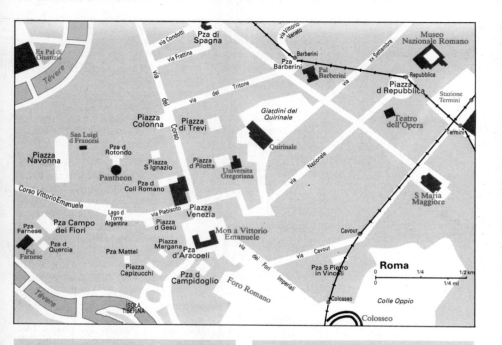

here. This is a great cosmopolitan meeting place and has been for hundreds of years; the steps are always thronged with people.

The Spanish Steps – a great cosmopolitan meeting place

Walk up to the church (138 steps) to look down and along the via Condotti, a famous smart shopping street. On the right of the steps at number 26 is the Keats-Shelley Museum (open Monday to Friday 9am-1pm and 3-6pm, L3,500) where the English poet John Keats died (23 February 1821), and you can go into the tiny room and see his death mask as well as many letters and mementoes of Keats, Shelley and their circle.

In the Babington Tea Rooms, another Roman institution near the Spanish Steps, shepherd's pie *pasticcio di manzo* costs L24,000! When in Rome, eat as the Romans do, not the British. The nearest inexpensive eating place is Hostaria al 31 on via delle Carozze (closed Sundays).

Curiously the smallest state in the world is not the Vatican, but the Sovereign Military Order of Malta (the Knights of St John), with their headquarters here at via Condotti 68, their own numberplates SMOM, passports and merchant fleet. Their Grand Master takes the traditional vows of chastity, poverty and obedience in the same way as his knights.

Several parallel streets running down to the Corso have interesting shops; via delle Croce for all kinds of food, via Frattina for boutiques, handbags and tassles, and look in at Micci (number 68).

From via Condotti turn left into via del Corso, passing the best department store, La Rinascente (lavatory on the third floor) and reaching piazza Colonna, with Marcus Aurelius' column celebrating his victories in a horror comic strip cartoon spiral (200 metres, 656ft tall) of vicious reliefs (190 stairs inside lead to the top).

Piazza Colonna is now virtually a car park, but in the 18th century Marcus Aurelius' column was entirely surrounded by stoves, roasting the whole city of Rome's coffee supply. This was ordered by law, because in those days people didn't like smells, even coffee or flowers, wafting all over the place, and contained them in one area. In the 19th century booths for drinks and smart cafés replaced the coffee ovens; now it is the centre of Rome's main restaurant area.

Turn left at via delle Muratte to piazza di Trevi, a small square with the startlingly large and ornate fountain (built 1762 by Nicola Salvi). You used to have to drink the water in order to ensure your return to Rome, now throwing a coin in is supposed to

The Trevi fountain, depicting Neptune with seahorses, tritons and shells

do the trick. (You may have to throw a coin into a dried-up basin because of renovation.)

TREVI FOUNTAIN TO PIAZZA NAVONA

From the Trevi fountain, via San Vincenzo and via Lucchesi lead to piazza della Pilotta. Turn right along via del Vaccaro and continue back to the Corso past the Palazzo Colonna.

Just up the Corso, turn left at via Lata, and at 1a piazza Collegio Romano you can visit some of the rooms and art collection in the huge Doria Pamphili Palazzo. Lots of rooms are let, but you can see part of the building, one of the few great Roman palaces with sumptuous apartments open. The private collection includes three paintings by Caravaggio and works by Giovanni Bellini, Filippo Lippi and Velasquez. Open Tuesday, Friday, Saturday, Sunday 10am-1pm, telephone 06/6794365, L2,000.

From here, go along via Sant' Ignazio to the piazza and church of Sant' Ignazio, a great Jesuit baroque church with a frescoed vault, and then to via del Seminario, on the left, and on to the Pantheon.

The Pantheon is the best preserved, most complete ancient Roman building in Rome, because it was consecrated later and used as a Christian church. The painter Raphael is buried here (he was only 37 when he died) and two Italian kings. It's a wonderful building designed by the Emperor Hadrian himself (who also designed his villa in Tivoli and built the great coast-to-coast wall in Britain). The huge dome, once tiled and gilded, is 43.3 metres (142ft) across, and the same height though larger than St Peter's. (St Paul's in London is 31 metres, 101ft.) The bronze-edged open eye (oculus) at the top is 9 metres ($29\frac{1}{2}$ft) across. It was largely built of concrete, not as modern a building material as some people think.

This amazing and atmospheric building, with its extraordinary engineering and design was an inspiration to Palladio, among other architects.

The piazza Rotonda outside, once a fish market, is packed with cafés and ice cream bars. Not far away, Giolitti, supposedly one of Rome's best, also serves snacks (closed Mondays). There are two reasonable hotels near here, the Abruzzi and the Mimosa.

In the 12th-century Church of Santa Maria Sopra Minerva, on the other side of the Pantheon, are frescoed chapels, the body of St Catherine of Siena and the tomb of Fra Angelico. The elephant carrying the obelisk in the square was designed by Bernini.

From piazza della Rotonda, take via della Rosetta, turn left along via Giustiniani to the Church of San Luigi dei Francesi to see Caravaggio's first great religious paintings in the St Matthew chapel.

Moneysaver

When the Italian Senate is in session, you can watch debates in the Palazzo Madama from a seat in the gallery.

Cross the corso Madama (Palazzo Madama, once a Medici palace, is now the seat of the Italian Senate) into piazza Navona. This square is a great meeting place too, and in the evenings it comes to life when all sorts of music makers and performance artists, students, tourists and Romans gather here. From Christmas to Epiphany (6 January) it is the scene of a huge toy fair. It's one of the most congenial piazzas in Rome, an interesting place to sit any time of day, watching children skateboard or grannies snooze beside Bernini's flamboyant Foun-

---

Local flavour

Rome is teaming with priests, and sometimes you may catch a glimpse of a bishop, his soutane piped in magenta, or a cardinal, piped in red, and usually red socks as well. The kindling of the Holy Fire on Saturday before Easter Sunday is a magnificent ceremony, especially in the old churches like Sant' Clemente and the great basilicas. On 5 August go to Mass in Santa Maria Maggiore to see the white flowers shower down from the dome to commemorate a miraculous snowfall in August.

Local Flavour

Caravaggio came to Rome in about 1589 when he was 16, and was patronised by a cardinal who took him to live in his palace and obtained the San Luigi commission for him. But Caravaggio was not an easy fellow. His pictures were too powerfully realistic for gentle taste. The priests of San Luigi wouldn't accept his first painting of *St Matthew and the Angel* because Caravaggio had painted the saint with dirty feet, and other realistic details upset other churches. Caravaggio was a wild character fighting and causing trouble with his gang of friends around Rome (police records tell us more about him than we can learn elsewhere), until finally he killed a man in a duel, fled Rome, and died four years later aged 40.

---

tain of the Rivers and in front of Borromini's Church of Sant' Agnese in Agone.

There are cafés and restaurants all round here. In nearby via dei Coronari at 233, **Da Gioacchino** is an unpretentious family establishment, with good reasonably priced food (closed Sundays). And north of here, on via dei Portoghesi, the popular Portoghesi hotel is good value.

At the end of this excursion into old Rome you must wander the old streets around here and go to campo dei Fiori, where before midday you'll find the market in full swing, or explore the near by streets with workshops. Go on to the piazza Farnese to see the Palazzo Farnese, begun in 1514 by Sangallo and continued by Michelangelo – the most perfectly proportioned and handsome 16th-century building in Rome (now it serves as

---

Moneysaver

A free show – the changing of the guard at the Quirinale Palace, home of the Italian president. At 4pm every day a military band plays and the guards change.

---

the splendid home of the French Embassy).

Local flavour

Street names in this old city area show what trades were carried on here: via dei *baullari*=trunk-makers (there's still one left); *cancelleria*=writing materials; *cappellari*=hat shops; *chiavari*=key-makers; *giubbonari*=jerkin-makers.

Turn right down vicolo dei Venti (high up on the wall of number 5 is a small Renaissance shrine), and continue into piazza della Quercia, where Palazzo Spada is all exuberance and decoration after the sobriety of Palazzo Farnese. There is a small collection of paintings here – family pictures among elegant aristocratic furniture in rooms once the scene of 17th-century *conversazione* and refined entertaining. It's very fine gallery includes portraits by Titian and Rubens and a Bruegel landscape. Open Monday to Saturday, 9am-2pm, Sunday 9am-1pm, L2,000, telephone 06/6861158.

From here retrace your steps along corso Vittorio Emanuele and head north-west towards the river, if there is time, to see the Castèl Sant' Ángelo. Hadrian originally built this as a family mausoleum; it later became a fortress and sanctuary for embattled popes, with a secret passage leading to the Vatican, Armoury and papal apartments. There is a terrace café on the ramparts. This is Rome's favourite day out. Open daily 9am-2pm. Sunday 9am-1pm, and Monday afternoon 2-6pm, L3,000.

Alternatively head down to the river towards piazza V Pallotti and cross the Ponte Sisto into Trastevere to visit the Villa Farnesina. Or you could wander eastwards into the old ghetto area (see another walk), towards the Palatine.

RIVER TIBER (TÉVERE)

For an unusual outing take a river bus ride under the bridges of Rome along the tawny Tiber, away from all the hassle on shore. The acquabus runs from May to September from Ponte Duca d' Aosta (in the north of the city, beyond the Villa Flaminia, buses 1, 48, 911) south along the river, stopping at Ponte Cavour, past the Castèl Sant' Ángelo to the Ísola Tiberina (L1,000). Four boats operate from 8am-8pm every day, leaving from both ends of the route every 20 minutes. Telephone 06/6869068.

Ponte Sublicio, over the Tiber, is where brave Horatio stood and defended the old wooden bridge against the Etruscans. Lars Porsena of Clusium was on the Trastevere side. Only the dauntless three (including Horatius) dared to face the ranks from Tuscany and protect Rome from ruin. (Read the *Lays of Ancient Rome* by Macaulay for the stirring tale.)

From the boat much of Rome is hidden behind recently built flood-prevention walls, and the road beside the river is more of a racetrack than ever since parts of Rome have prohibited cars. Most of the year it seems a wasted asset, but the river banks come to life briefly in June and July, and the island hosts a summer festival. However, it is a useful alternative route, and the Castèl Sant' Ángelo looks at its most impressive and monumental from water level.

To walk along the river bank, go to the Milvio Bridge (bus 911 from piazza Augusto Imperatore, or bus 1 from piazzale Flaminio), and walk along the left or right bank. The Ponte Milvio was first built in AD109.

OLD ROME TO PIAZZA DI SPAGNA

Take the acquabus from the Ísola Tiberina up river past Castèl Sant' Ángelo, get off at Ponte Cavour and look in at the Ara Pacis in piazza Augusto Imperatore. If you've ever read the book *I, Claudius* by Robert Graves or seen it on the telly, you may be interested to see portraits on the walls round the Ara Pacis depicting the amazingly wicked and devious court of the Emperor Claudius himself, Augustus' wife Livia, Tiberius etc. The altar was consecrated in BC13 to celebrate peace after wars in Gaul and Spain. South of here, if you are hungry, there are inexpensive eating places on via dell' Arancio.

Cross the Corso to window-shop along the streets that run parallel to each other, walking either along via della Croce (food shops), dei Condotti (jewellers) or Borgognona (clothes) to piazza di Spagna.

Moneysaver
In piazza Borghese, near Ponte Cavour, stands the Palazzo Borghese, still used by the Borghese family and not open to the public, but from the entrance on via Ripetta you may find the auction house which rents part of the palace open, so you can go in and look at the frescoed rooms. Napoleon's sister Pauline Borghese, who posed nude for Canova's statue of her (now in the Borghese Gallery) and scandalised Rome society, lived here with her husband Prince Camillo Borghese.

OLD ROME TO THE COLOSSEUM

Explore the area between campo dei Fiori and the Palatine, between the river and corso Vittorio Emanuele and via Plebiscito. Part of this was the old Jewish ghetto; it contains lovely little squares, such as piazza Campitelli and piazza Margana, piazza Mattei with its Fontana delle Tartarughe, and early Renaissance streets like via Portico d'Ottavia. These lead to the Theatre of Marcellus (completed by Augustus in AD13), and then on to the Ísola Tiberina, the island in the Tiber. Continue to Trastevere or take the boat up river.

Another route from piazza Margana brings you to piazza Aracoeli, where the old 14th-century steps will take you to the church of Aracoeli. There you will find the *Santo Bambino*, a little figure supposedly carved from an olive tree in the Garden of Gethsemane. He stands in a glass case except when he is carried to comfort someone sick in a Rome hospital, because he is thought to have miraculous healing powers. People write to him from all over the world, letters addressed to *Il Bambino*, Rome. There is also a chapel frescoed by the Umbrian painter Pintoricchio.

The wider steps will take you up to the Campidoglio and Michelangelo's wonderfully designed piazza, now unfortunately without the original statue of Marcus Aurelius on horseback which used to stand here. Behind it is the view down to the Forum.

Local Flavour
The six Vestal virgins, or priestesses, who guarded a sacred flame, keeping it always alight, were recruited aged six to 10. They were always dressed in long white robes, and lived a strange life, part austere, part privileged. If they broke their 30-year oath of virginity, the penalty was burying alive, but as long as they behaved properly, the state paid them well. Socially they were second only to the empress, drove round in carriages, had the best seats in theatres, and had great power. But the ritual that ordered their life took 10 years to learn.

Now is the time to go down towards the Forum itself (entrance along via della Salaria Vecchia) and to walk through the Foro Romano and explore the remains of the Vestal Temple, the brick façade of the Curia, home of the Senate of ancient Rome, and the many temples. Then, turning up the Palatine hill, among the pines and fir trees are the remains of the grey marble ancient Roman palaces, abandoned to grass and fennel, coloured with flowers in the spring. With a view back towards the great open space of the Circus Maximus, this is the place to picnic. When Domitian's vast palace up here was finished in AD96, he gave a huge banquet here for men only with everything, even meat and creamy puddings, eaten with the fingers, a sort of grand Imperial picnic. Raise a plastic mug to those old Imperial ghosts. From here go on to the Colosseum.

All the marble coating has been stripped from the Colosseum, and the pockmarks left show where the bronze pins that once bound it to the walls have been ripped out. It's the biggest ruin of Imperial Rome – ½km (⅓ mile) round, seating 45,000 spectators with standing room for 10,000. It was begun by Vespasian in AD72, finished by his son Titus in AD80 and launched with 100 days of celebration, when hunters slew 5,000 animals, young boys rode crocodile races, and criminals were thrown in among the beasts. Emperors watched from near today's wooden cross; women were segregated way up at the top. Sailors winched a slatted linen awning over sections of the audience to keep out the sun or rain. Below the arena are the animal pens from which lifts brought them up, and props for staging the hunts were kept here. There was a gladiators' school across the road. (In AD249, the 1,000th anniversary of the founding of Rome, 1,000 pairs of gladiators fought in the arena.)

It's a remarkable building, not only because it was built on drained marshy land; it was also designed to let at least 50,000 people enter and leave at the same time without harm through 80 exits. It used to look much more picturesque when the centre was just a grassy ruin, overgrown with as many as 420 species of plants, some exotic, which had sprung from seeds imported with animal food in ancient times. Despite once being such a scene of bloodshed, Roman newlyweds often come here to have their pictures taken.

Open daily 9am to one hour before sunset except Wednesday, 9am-1pm only.

THE FORUM AND ALONG THE RIVER

After exploring the Foro Romano, walk down via San Teodoro towards the river and the piazza Bocca di Verità. This Bocca (mouth) is a great open-mouthed face on the church of Santa Maria di Cosmedin. In the Middle Ages people, especially wives suspected of being unfaithful, were made to put their right hand into this mouth, and if they were lying the terrible stone jaw would clamp shut, cutting off their fingers. Look in at the church, built in the 6th century, with fine 12th-century mosaics.

Near by are two 2nd century BC temples, the rectangular Fortuna Virilis, and the pretty round Temple of Vesta (not really a Vestal temple, that's in the Forum).

From Santa Maria in Cosmedin, cross via della Greca and go down via di Santa Maria in Cosmedin, then take the steep path, Clivo di Rocca Savella, up to the Parco Savello (a small public garden filled with orange trees, and a view of St Peter's) and look in at the Church of San Sabina. Go on along via di San Sabina to the piazza dei Cavalieri di Malta, designed by the engraver Piranesi, with obelisks and cypresses, just like one of his drawings. There is a famous view looking through the keyhole of the door of the Knight's Priory on the right, to the Dome of St Peter's, framed by trees.

Further down along the river from here is the Testaccio area, once a drab, unnoticed

The Colosseum, where 55,000 spectators used to watch the gladiators fight

part of Rome, but now becoming full of inexpensive *trattorie* where you can eat real old Roman cooking. Going back down to the river, cross over the Ponte Sublicio to the old port area of the Trastevere district (where you will find the Sunday morning Porta Portese market).

Or continue on downhill on via di Porta Lavernale and via Marmorata to the Porta San Polo and the Protestant Cemetery beyond to pay respects at the grave of the poet Keats (whose tombstone reads, 'Here lies one whose name was writ in water'), and fellow poet Shelley.

Local flavour

The long Circo Massimo, ancient Rome's race track, stretching behind the Museo di Roma and Santa Maria in Cosmedin, held at least 30,000 people on race days in Roman times. There were 24 races a day, horse races ridden without stirrups filled in between with chariot races when 12 small chariots, or four large ones, hurtled round the track, urged on by the emperor and his family and all the best-dressed people in Rome. The 'Greens' were Rome's favourite chariot team. All races and games were free, though you needed a ticket and had to wear a toga. The ancient Romans were tremendous gamblers and all their spare cash was spent on betting.

If, when you reach the cemetery, you are hungry, try the Taverna Cestia, via Piramide Cestia 65 (closed Mondays); not too expensive, and with an outside terrace. Frequented by foreigners from the nearby FAO (Foudo Agricultural Organisation) office. From here you can take the metro from the Piramide stop back to the Colosseum or Termini.

Moneysaver

Children under 12 go free (accompanied by an adult) in all state museums.

PIAZZA DI SPAGNA TO THE VILLA BORGHESE

It is rather misleading, but the Villa Borghese means the huge park north of the Spanish Steps. Bus 110 goes there from the Termini train station. From the Spanish Steps area, walk down via Sistina to Piazza Barberini (on metro line A) where Bernini's Triton Fountain sends its water skywards, and on to the Palazzo Barberini, Rome's national gallery of art, a collection of paintings from the 13th to 18th centuries. Open daily 9am-2pm, L3,000.

From here, walk up the famed and notorious via Vittorio Veneto, where all the rich and famous used to gather. In the 50s and 60s many American films were shot in Rome, and stars like John Wayne, Stewart Granger and Elsa Martinelli would sit with Roman marquises and counts in the mirrored bars and restaurants on the via Veneto. At the Sans Souci they had to close the bars at 3.30am, or the stars (Sophia Loren, Anna Magnani, Claudia Cardinale) would have stayed all night. King Farouk sat around with his girlfriends – while the gossip columnists scribbled.

The Café de Paris is still there (and Harry's Bar), but after they made a film *La Dolce Vita* about it all, the celebrities moved away. Now, if you come and pay L8,000 for a coffee you will only see the tourists watching the tourists.

If you are planning to picnic in the park, buy food from *alimentari* or a *tavola calda* in side streets around here – there's nothing in the park itself.

Moneysaver

Under the Church of the Cappuccini on via Veneto are four subterranean chapels with walls hung with the skeletons and bones of 4,000 dead monks. Not as gruesome as it sounds, almost a work of art. Open daily 9am-12 and 2-6pm. Free. (You may give a small donation).

Pauline Borghese, Canova's white marble sculpture in the Borghese gallery

Turn right inside the park to visit the Borghese gallery. It's being restored and you never know what parts you'll be able to see, but it's definitely worth a visit anyway (and free during restoration). You'll probably see Canova's cool white sculpture of Napoleon's sister Pauline Bonaparte, downstairs. Pauline's husband kept this statue locked away, which the sculptor Canova found hard to bear. However, Canova was sometimes allowed to bring a few friends to see it, preferring to show it at night, palely gleaming by the light of a single candle. If the gallery is ever open late on summer evenings, ask the attendant to turn off the lights and see it by moonlight.

There are also paintings by Caravaggio, Rubens, Botticelli etc, open Tuesday to Saturday 9am-1.30pm. Sunday till 12.30pm.

There's a large grassy area (not very well kept) in the park, a stadium for show-jumping, the zoo (free for children), a children's playground with pedal cars etc, and a picturesque small lake and its own classical temple on an island. There are boats for hire on the lake and plenty of quiet shady space to walk and picnic in. This is one of the finest parks in Rome.

After lunch walk up the viale delle Magnolie from piazzale de Canestre to the Pincio, to see the view over Rome. Then visit the Villa Giulia in the north-west corner of the park, a beautiful building with a wonderful Etruscan collection, a garden and a restaurant, open in the afternoons till 7pm (closed Mondays).

The Villa Borghese itself and the Villa Giulia with all their gardens were never meant to be lived in. They were pleasure palaces for parties, just for a day and a night. The Villa Giulia was built by Pope Julius II. The Etruscan museum now in the villa was founded at the end of the 19th century, and holds sculptures from Veii, sarcophagi, tomb paintings, pottery (the black hard *bucchero* vases), terracotta figures and many other Etruscan items.

Ironically, it is the stick-like figures by Giacometti that most echo the thin Etruscan figurines. Museo Giulia, Piazzale di Villa Giulia 9, telephone 06/3601951. Open Tuesday to Saturday 9am-7pm, Sunday 9am-1pm, L4,000.

The only safe time to attempt a bicycle ride in Rome is Sunday morning. Pick up a bicycle near the piazza di Spagna on a Sunday morning (L3,000 per hour), and in about an hour and a half you can make a trip to the Colosseum, ride round by the Circus Maximus and back. If it isn't Sunday, you are perfectly safe to bicycle any day in the Villa Borghese.

CATACOMBS

Catacombs are underground galleries, excavated deep under the soil of Rome, where the Christians buried their dead during the years from the time of Nero to about AD310, when they were continually being persecuted. The pagans burned their dead, but the Christians didn't, and their hidden cemeteries remained intact because one of the most ancient Roman laws ruled that tombs of any kind were sacrosanct and not to be profaned. And by excavating their galleries, they made room for hundreds and thousands of bodies, laid out without coffins in *loculi*, shelved compartments covered in two shrouds between which was a layer of lime.

Several of these catacombs lie underground beside the old via Áppia. A 118 bus from the Colosseum will take you to the tombs of San Callisto, San Sebastian and Domitilla. The bus goes past all these catacombs and the huge round tomb of Cecilia Metella, and just past the Osteria Belvedere it turns off the old road, along the via Cecilia Metella to the Áppia Nuova. From this turning, if you want to walk on along the most picturesque part of the via Áppia Antica, beyond the fourth milestone, you must remember that you will have to return back along the road to catch the bus back. Both sides of the road are littered with fallen stones and shaded by cypresses.

San Callisto is the first catacomb, where many popes and Saint Cecilia were buried. (Closed Wednesdays.) Further along, the Catacomb of San Sebastiano (number 132) is closed Thursday. Both of these are much visited. There is also the Catacomb of Domitilla, at via delle Sette Chiese 132, closed Tuesday. All of these are open in the mornings till 12 noon, and then reopen at 2.30pm till 6pm, or 5pm in winter. Admission L3,000.

For a smaller, less frequented catacomb, visit Sant' Agnese fuori le Mura, inside Rome on via Nomentana 349, on bus routes 36, 60 and 62. Open 9am-12pm and 4-6pm, Monday to Saturday (get off the bus before the lights at via Santa Costanza), L3,000.

Other catacombs you may wish to see are the Catacomb of Priscilla in north-east Rome, via Salaria 430, shut Mondays, open 8.30am-12 noon and 2.30-5pm. Take bus 56 from piazza Barberini or 57 from Stazione Termini, L3,000.

VATICAN

Two of Rome's sights are particularly hard work; one is the Forum on a hot day, endless, shadeless and bewildering, and the other is the Vatican with its long dazzling galleries and hardly a seat to rest on. Only venture there if you seriously want to see the Etruscan museum or the Raphael rooms and the Sistine Chapel, and allow plenty of time. At Easter, and during July, August and September when the museums are open till 5pm, you can see St Peter's in the morning and get a snack lunch at the Vatican cafeteria while going round the museums there. The museums are open on Mondays when most other art galleries shut, but shut on Sundays, and cost L8,000. At other times of the year it is unwise to try and see St Peter's first in one morning. St Peter's is open all day from 7am-7pm.

Bus 64 from the Termini or piazza Venezia or largo di Torre Argentina (among other stops) takes you to its terminus, piazza della Città Leonina, on the right of the colonnade around St Peter's square. To get to the Vatican from here, walk along via di Porta Angelica, following the wall round to your left and then left again (it's quite a way) to the entrance on viale Vaticano. Alternatively, take the Vatican bus (every half hour from 9am-12.30pm) from the left-hand side of St Peter's square in front of the Vatican tourist office, which takes you through the gardens to the museums.

Moneysaver
Admission to the Vatican is free on the last Sunday of the month.

The Vatican Gardens have guided tours every day at 10am, March to October. Apply to Ufficio Informazioni Pellegrini e Turisti, Braccio Carlo Magno, piazza San Pietro, telephone 06/6984466.

Note: no one can enter St Peter's or the Vatican in shorts, and women must wear a skirt below the knees and cover their arms. Mass is said several times a day in St Peter's. There is a service of vespers on Sunday at 5pm.

St Peter's in the Vatican from where the Pope delivers his blessing

St Peter's is approached by Bernini's stupendous colonnade. The basilica was begun in 1506 and shaped by successive artists, Sangallo, Raphael, Michelangelo (who designed a large part of the main body of the church and the cupola), and finally Carlo Maderno who built the façade, obscuring part of Michelangelo's design. Inside, don't miss (on the right) Michelangelo's *Pietà*, behind glass because it was attacked and damaged in 1978 (the Madonna's left hand), his only signed work, done when he was 25, a strikingly young and sad *Madonna*; the *baldacchino* or great bronze canopy on its twisted columns by Bernini (not easy to miss); at the base of the last pillar on the right, a bronze statue of St Peter by Arnolfo di Cambio; on the left aisle a monument by Canova marks the spot where in the grottoes below, the three last members of the royal house of Stuart are buried (the Queen Mother paid for the tomb's restoration).

Many Popes lie buried in the crypt, including the most recent, John Paul I. In 1968, Pope Paul VI declared that the remains of St Peter himself had been identified there. To get to the dome, with its view over Rome, go to the right-hand side of the portico, facing St Peter's. There are 330 steps to the top; a lift saves 150. Access to the dome closes at 6pm, and may be shut when the Pope is in the cathedral, often on Wednesday mornings. Admission L2,000, lift L1,000.

On the other side of the square is an entrance to the necropolis below the grottoes where St Peter's tomb may be located. Small prearranged groups may visit – free. Apply to the Ufficio Scavi (excavation office) below the Arco della Campana. Open Monday to Saturday, 9am-12 noon and 1-5pm.

> **Local flavour**
> The Pope blesses the crowd from his study window, the second window from the right on the top floor of the Apostolic Palace, every Sunday at noon when he's in Rome. Just assemble in St Peter's square without a ticket.

VATICAN CITY

Founded in 1929, the Vatican is a state (population about 1,000) ruled by the Pope, with its own newspaper (*L'Osservatore Romano*), stamps, coins, train station, supermarket, department store, banks, radio station (Radio Vaticano transmits in 35 languages) and post office. It houses 10 museums and a famous garden. The Pope has the right to organise an army and move freely about Italy. The picturesque Swiss Guards (from the Catholic parts of Switzerland) in their blue, red and orange striped costumes, supposedly designed by Michelangelo, are mainly decorative. A Papal Guard, enlisted from the Italian aristocracy, guards the Pope's person. Nowadays the Pope has dispensed with much of the old pomp and ceremony, such as being carried aloft on a chair into St Peter's.

The Vatican post office is the most

efficient in Italy. Post your cards and letters there if you can. There's a post office branch near the entrance to the Vatican Museums.

To see the Pope, apply a few days in advance to the Prefect of the Ponteficial Household, through the bronze door at the end of the right-hand colonnade, for a Wednesday morning (about 11am) mass audience. (Office open Monday and Tuesday 9am-1pm, telephone 06/6982; also from 9am Wednesday, but all tickets may have gone by then.) In July and August the Pope may be at Castèl Gandolfo, with audiences there.

The Vatican Museums house the largest collection of antique art in the world: an Egyptian museum, an Etruscan museum, a history museum, and others, as well as what are probably the most appealing: the unique Sistine Chapel, the papal apartments decorated by Raphael, and the Pinacoteca (art gallery). Visitors have to go one-way round the museums; routes of various lengths are clearly marked.

If you are in a hurry, you can go straight to the Sistine Chapel from the entrance (despite the one-way system), climbing the circular ramps to the passage to the Atrio dei Quattro Cancelli (inner museum entrance), then up the Scala Simonetti to the second floor, following the series of galleries to the Sistine Chapel. However, once there, you can't go back to see the Raphael rooms. (Take tour A – then switch to C for the Raphael rooms.)

Pope Julius II commissioned Michelangelo (much against his will, he didn't consider himself a painter) to paint the Sistine Chapel, and Raphael to decorate his apartments.

Sistine Chapel Michelangelo started painting his only fresco, the eight scenes from Genesis, on the Sistine chapel ceiling in 1508, and finished it four years later. He covered 930 sq metres (10,000 sq ft) entirely alone (he sacked his seven assistants at the start), his advance payment running out long before he had finished. Afterwards, he could hardly bend his neck for months, and was obliged to read with his head tilted back.

The drama of the work was matched by the drama of the painting. While Michelangelo, paint in his eyes, lying flat on his back on the high scaffolding, candle strapped to his forehead, alone and behind locked doors, in considerable pain, tormented by lack of money and constantly pressured by Pope Julius to finish, was struggling to complete the work, a few rooms away his rival Raphael, with a host of helpers, was working on *his* frescoes.

Restoration (funded by a Japanese television company) began in 1980 to remove the accumulation of dirt, grime and soot, and also the animal glue past restorers had smeared over the surface as a varnish to brighten the colours. The cleaners work on 25cm (4in) squares, sponging the surface (not penetrating the pigment) with distilled water and a chemical mixture called AB-57. After three minutes they wash off the loosened glue and dirt, leave it for 24 hours, and then clean it again.

No colour has been added. Questions about the whole process remain: did Michelangelo paint in real fresco once only on wet plaster, or did he repaint on top, so that the cleaners are removing his over-painting and not that of past restorers? What is not in doubt is that the brilliant colours make the ceiling shine without lighting or varnish.

Michelangelo started the *Last Judgement* on the end wall 22 years later, and finished it after eight years when the Roman world had been shattered, Rome sacked, and Michelangelo himself a changed man.

In the *Last Judgement* note Michelangelo's self-portrait in the skin held by St Bartholomew (on the right of Christ); and in the bottom right-hand corner, the man with donkey's ears and a serpent round him is Biagio, a stupid papal official who thought the nude figures were indecent – 'More fit for a tavern', he said of them. Later, some had loincloths painted over them.

Another glory of this chapel are the panels on the side walls, painted by some of the best Tuscan and Umbrian painters of the time, including Pintoricchio, Botticelli, Signorelli, Perugino and Rosselli. At the time these panels were painted, the ceiling was plain blue with gold stars.

Local flavour
Don't miss an old iron stove against the wall at the end of the chapel. This is where voting papers, and damp or dry straw, depending whether black or white smoke is needed, is burned when the cardinals meet here to elect a new pope. The cardinals are incarcerated in this chapel, meals brought to them, until they reach a two-thirds majority, while all Rome (so it seems) gathers in St Peter's square to await the outcome. White smoke signals that a new pope has been elected.

Moneysaver
Children under 1 metre (3ft 3in) tall go free in the Vatican, students L5,000.

Before leaving the Vatican, it is well worth visiting the Pinacoteca, which also seems dwarfed by all the outstanding art around, but contains paintings by Fra Angelico (the story of St Nicholas at Bari), Giorgione, and the *St Jerome* by Leonardo da Vinci.

There is a toilet near the Sistine Chapel, by the way. The cafeteria is near the way out of the museums.

Vatican museums are open all year Monday to Saturday 9am-2pm. There are longer opening hours in Easter week, July, August and September – Monday to Friday 9am-5pm, last entrance 4pm, L8,000. Nearest metro stop is Ottaviano, which is served by bus 64.

The Vatican is closed 1 January, 6 January, 11 February, 19 March, 1 May, 29 June, 15 and 16 August, 1 November, 8 December, Christmas Day, Easter Monday, Ascension Day and Corpus Christi.

OUTINGS FROM ROME

TÍVOLI

There are three places to see here: Hadrian's Villa and the gardens of the Villa d' Este, with nearby Villa Gregoriana. You will need a whole day to see them all, so take a picnic, be prepared for walking and pick a fine day.

Tívoli is a hill town 35km (22 miles) east of Rome, where wealthy Romans built their villas and created spectacular gardens. If time is short, and you can only manage to see one of the three villas, the Villa d' Este is the most obviously spectacular and magical, with huge sparkling fountains, water falling and murmuring everywhere, running down staircases and from the breasts of sphynxes among tall trees and flowerbeds.

ACOTRAL buses leave every 20 minutes for Tívoli from 5.30am to midnight from via Gaeta, near via Volturno, across the piazza in front of the Termini train station, L3,400 return. Not all buses go by Hadrian's Villa, so be sure to ask for Villa Adriana if you want to get dropped there first. The journey takes about 1¼ hours. Orange CAT bus 4 runs between the villa and largo Garibaldi in Tívoli (L500 single).

The tourist office in Tívoli is in largo Garibaldi, telephone 0774/243522; the AAST office is at vicolo Missione 3, telephone 0774/21249. Sample an ice cream at the Orso Bianco number 106.

Villa d'Este in Tivoli on the lower slopes of the Sabine hills

The Villa d' Este was built in the 16th century, with gardens created by Cardinal Ippolito d' Este. (Entrance is just down the main square.) Open Tuesday to Sunday from 9am to about 1½ hours before sunset, L5,000.

The Villa Gregoriana, uphill towards Piazza Palatina from the Villa d' Este, is a less well kept park; its waterfalls have a 120-metre (393ft) drop. It is open the same times as Villa d' Este, L1,500.

Hadrian's Villa (Villa Adriana) is open daily 9am to 1½ hours before sunset (but check first if you intend to visit on Mondays). Telephone 0774/530203, L4,000. This is usually less crowded than the Villa d' Este. The Emperor Hadrian was passionate about architecture, and spent 12 out of his 21 imperial years travelling to Egypt and Greece and around his Roman world, returning to recreate the sights he'd seen. It took him 16 years to build the villa. (AD 118 to AD 134). He died four years later.

There's a scale model of the complex in the visitors' centre to help identification (also a café and bar). The Villa dell' Isola, or

Maritime Theatre, is where Hadrian was reputed to pull up his drawbridge and retreat to read his large library of books. After Hadrian's death, the villa fell into decline; Barbarians and Romans both ruined it and carted off the statues (some to the Villa d' Este). With its pines and cypresses, red earth and expanses of water, it remains a site of great peace and atmosphere.

Local Flavour

On the far left is the Valley of Canopus, a copy of an Egyptian canal which commemorates Hadrian's favourite, Antinous, who was drowned in the Nile in mysterious circumstances, to Hadrian's great grief.

FRASCATI

This is one of the hill-top towns called the Castelli Romani, famous for its white wine, south east of Rome and just east of Ciampino airport. To get there, take the ACOTRAL bus from the Anagnina stop on metro line A. Every half hour, L2,000 return. The tourist office is at piazza Marconi, telephone 06/9420331.

Many Roman noblemen built their villas out here among the Alban hills, with views to Rome and plains below. One is open – the Villa Aldobrandini just above the piazza, first begun in 1598 and famous for its views, 17th-century frescoes and fountains and grottoes (open Monday to Friday 9am-1pm). Ask at the tourist office for admission. There is also a 17th-century cathedral. For picnic supplies go to the market in piazza Porticella (from piazza Marconi take via Palestro and turn right at Villa Borghese).

A steep climb, 5km (3 miles) uphill behind Frascati, lies ancient Roman Tuscolo with a small theatre, ruins, wonderful views and wild flowers. If you walk in the opposite direction from Frascati, you come to Grottaferrata (3km, nearly 2 miles), with its Romanesque abbey of San Nilo which contains

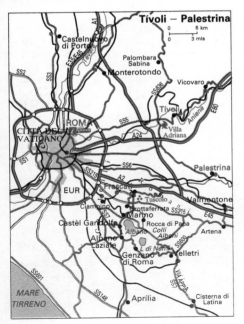

Tívoli – Palestrina

renowned mosaics and frescoes by Domenichino (open 9am-12 noon and 4-7.30pm, free, shut Mondays).

Instead of toiling back to Frascati, you can get a bus back to Rome from via A Santovetti, at the other end of the via del Popolo from the abbey, until 9pm (L1,000 single).

ÓSTIA ANTICA

Rome's old port, founded in the 4th century, was once a meeting place for foreigners, bringing their religions (the Persian god Mithras and the Egyptian Serapis) as well as their ships, their merchandise and workers with them. It was destroyed over the years by invading armies, the river silting up and the harbour drifting into disuse, until the mosquitoes and the wind-blown sand and tidal mud took over. No one built over it, and Óstia lay covered until the beginning of this century. Now excavations have revealed tombs, baths, theatres, warehouses, temples, small houses and shops in a green landscape. This makes a very good half-day trip, or bring a picnic and stay longer.

If you take the metro there are several morning and afternoon trains from Termini to Óstia Antica, 25 minutes. Trains go every half hour (20-minute journey) from the Ostiense train station near Porta San Paolo and the Piramide metro stop on line B, L700 single, L1,000 return. For information telephone ACOTRAL, 06/5915551.

The excavations are not far from the station and are well signposted. Tickets cost L4,000, over 60s and under 12s free. The site is open from 9am to 6pm (last tickets on sale

5pm, one hour earlier in winter). It takes at least three hours to visit the whole excavation area. There is also a museum (which may possibly be under renovation), open daily the same times. A snack bar is in the grounds. Bring the EPT leaflet with you, it has a full description and map.

Like Rome Óstia has its Forum and Curia or Senate House, and the Baths of Cisiarii and Neptune, both with mosaics; a Roman theatre where classical plays are put on in the summer; and in the south-west corner is a 1st-century synagogue, thought to be the oldest Western Jewish temple.

CERVÉTERI

This is one of the most interesting Etruscan sites. This ancient tribe spread over the Tuscan and Umbrian regions and down into Latium, flourishing in the 6th and 7th centuries, battling with Rome, and finally absorbed by her. Most of what we know about the Etruscans comes from their tombs,

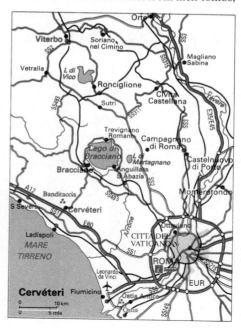

and Cervéteri is surrounded by a large necropolis, a city of the dead, called the Banditaccia. There are also remains of walls, temples, and a theatre, part of the old city of Caere which lies under modern Cervéteri, in its heyday it was one of the richest Etruscan cities.

The train doesn't go direct, so it is best to take an ACOTRAL bus, every half hour (40-minute ride). They go from outside the Lepanto station to Cervéteri, piazza Aldo Moro. The necropolis and museum are open all year, but closed Mondays. First stop at the 12th-century castle which houses the Museo Cerite; containing furnishings from the tombs, vases and sarcophagi. Objects from Cervéteri are in collections all over the world. Open May to September, Tuesday to Sunday 9am-2pm and 4-7pm; October to April only mornings, 9am-2pm.

From here it is almost a mile's walk to the necropolis, so take a special bus which runs to the site in spring and summer from the main square. All the tombs that can be seen are contained in this necropolis of the Banditaccia; not all are on show every day, they are opened in rotation to minimise damage. Open May to September, Tuesday to Sunday 9am-7pm; October to April, Tuesday to Sunday 9am-4pm, L4,000. The EPT leaflet gives a complete history and description of the tombs.

LAKE BRACCIANO

The cleanest lake in Italy, 25km (15½ miles) northwest and less than one hour's train ride from Rome, Lake Bracciano has plenty of beaches to swim from. Take the Viterbo line train from Termini. The town of Bracciano is above the lake, a picturesque old town with a massive castle, the Orsini Odescalchi, with great round towers, decorated with frescoes and filled with furniture of the 15th and 16th centuries. There is a wonderful view of the lake from the castle. Guided tours on Thursdays, Saturdays and holidays, 9am-12 noon and 3-6pm. Walk down the hill to find a beach. The tourist office is at via Claudia 72, telephone 06/9024451.

There is a camping site 3km (nearly 2 miles) west of Anguillara, on the southern side of the lake, with bus connections to Bracciano and Rome. Contact the Vigna di Valle camping site, telephone 06/9018645. L5,000 per person; tents and camping car L5,000-L5,500.

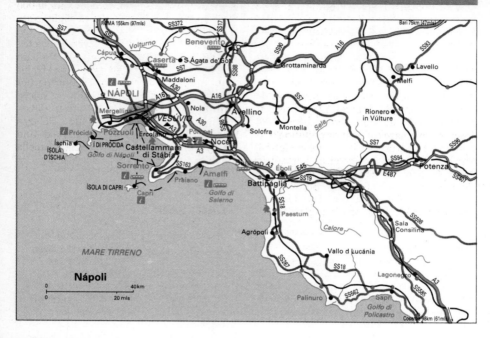

Nápoli

If you simply cannot stand the blaring of traffic, congestion, dirt, and the risk of bag-snatching, avoid Naples (Nápoli) and take a holiday at Sorrento or along the spectacular Amalfi coast. If you don't like any of those things, but would put up with them for the sake of seeing some wonderful mosaics (in the Archaeological Museum) and some famous paintings (at the National Gallery of Capodimonte) or the San Carlo theatre, then stay along the coast and visit Naples by day. But if you would like to explore the old town, walk along the bay, visit the Burning Fields and Pozzuoli, take a trip to the small island of Prócida, and generally immerse yourself in the city despite all its flaws, then spend some time in Naples (preferably out at Mergellina), and when you are sated and exhausted, move on down the coast.

If you have a car, it will not be an asset in Naples, which is a town strangled by cars. In 1907 Dan Fellows Platt, an American who was chauffeur-driven through Naples, said

Local flavour

Wherever you go in this region, the food will be delightful. Try, for instance, *frittura di triglia e calamare* (fried mullet and squid), *melanzane alla parmigiana* – a delicious dish found all over southern Italy and Sicily, sliced aubergines, fried, and baked with tomatoes, mozzarella and parmesan cheeses. *Sfogliatelle*, a Naples speciality of fine layers of flaky pastry (sometimes shell-shaped) filled with ricotta cream cheese, ham, etc and *maccheroni alla Napoletana* with tomato and cheese.

the people 'have made of this paradise a hell, in particular a motorist's hell'. But a car will mean that so many interesting parts of Campania, around Benevento and Cápua, south east of Salerno, and all the unfrequented but beautiful coastal towns in the

188

Gulf of Policastro which are rather remote for bus and train travellers will be accessible to you. (They *can* all be reached by public transport, but it takes more time.)

Naples has about 1¼ million inhabitants and is Italy's most important port after Genoa. It is set in a large and beautiful bay, with the volcano Vesuvius dramatically behind it. Not that you can always see the bay and the mountain; it often seems to be obscured in a haze (of heat or pollution?). It wouldn't be surprising if it were pollution, with all the traffic, the chemical works near Pozzuoli, and the new industrial building along the other side of the bay. But Neapolitans won't have it. Heat, they say. Sea mist. Come in winter, it's as sharp as glass then.

Moneysaver

Charter flights to Naples can vary tremendously throughout the year. In November or March, for instance, Thomson's *Airfare* catalogue lists flights at about two thirds of summer prices.

Whatever the present atmosphere, Naples comes trailing clouds of a glorious past. Founded by the Greeks, and once called Neapolis, the New City, it later became a cultural centre for the Romans. Virgil lived and wrote the *Georgics* and the *Aeneid* here. After the collapse of the Roman Empire, Naples was ruled by Byzantine dukes, Norman kings, Austrian, French and Spanish viceroys (Don Pedro de Toledo, 1532-54, was particularly outstanding). Then for some time, with minor interruptions (as when Joseph Bonaparte was crowned King of Naples), the Bourbons ruled, until in September 1860 Garibaldi entered Naples and Francis II retired to Gaeta.

From the 17th to the 19th centuries many English people came south to Naples and Campania, writers and wealthy aristocrats on the Grand Tour. The poet John Milton visited Posillipo in 1639 and probably saw the Solfatara, a model for his steaming hell in *Paradise Lost*. John Evelyn noted in his diary there were 3,000 churches and 30,000 'registered sinners' in Naples (a slight exaggeration?). From 1764 to the end of the century, the Grand Tourists were protected by the British Ambassador, Sir William Hamilton, who, after 1786, was joined by his beautiful wife-to-be, Emma. Evening parties at their home, the Palazzo Sessa, were spiced with Emma, thinly covered in a Greek costume, performing her 'attitudes'. Palazzo Sessa still stands today, unmarked and hardly known, in vico Santa Maria a Capella Vécchia among the workshops in Pizzofalcone.

Local flavour

Emma Hamilton (née Lyon, the blacksmith's daughter) came to Naples in 1786 on an exchange basis. Her lover, Charles Greville, swapped her with his uncle Sir William Hamilton (British Ambassador in Naples) for payment of debts. Emma was an immediate success with the court, and especially Queen Maria Carolina, who became a great friend, and through whom she gained very useful information for the British fleet. Admiral Nelson came back to Naples in 1798 after winning the battle of the Nile – only to lose his heart to Emma.

The Neapolitan court was extremely grand and sophisticated, with huge receptions at the palace at Caserta, luxurious balls, sparkling evenings at the San Carlo Opera. The French writer Stendhal wrote in 1817 that via Toledo was the 'most populous and gayest street in the world!' At least 400 families, or some said 3,000 Englishmen, lived in the city. But after Garibaldi came the social life ended, and with the glitter removed it was obvious that Naples, with the highest population density of any city in Europe, was basically a city of slums.

The city was badly bombed in the last war, and 100,000 Neapolitans still live in *bassi*, one-room dwellings. Most new building has been sub-standard and illegal. In 1975 a former mayor, among others, was indicted, and 22 buildings which had been illegally built where there should have been parks and schools, were demolished. And the recent earthquakes which destroyed towns in Campania also badly shook many buildings in Naples, making matters even worse.

After a cholera epidemic swept the city in 1884, fashionable literary and aristocratic society abandoned Naples and holidayed instead along the coast in Sorrento, and round the cape at Positano, Amalfi and Ravello.

It's interesting how the popular resorts have moved south over the centuries. The Greeks and Romans indulged themselves in luxurious villas at Cuma and Báia north of Naples, then Naples itself became the star, then Sorrento and the Amalfi coast, and now, because of the pollution in the Bay of Naples and the influx of tourists, the smart, select place for Neapolitans to spend time by the sea is the area between Palinuro and Sapri, further south again, where there are good beaches and clear water.

So where should the budget traveller stay today – Sorrento or Naples? It depends on the kind of holiday you want. No tour

Local flavour

It was on the coast around Sorrento that Odysseus is said to have escaped the deadly lure of the song of the sirens only by filling his sailors' ears with wax and lashing himself to the mast. What songs these mythical creatures, bird-body, woman-head, temptresses or soul-birds sang no one knows, or whether there were two or three, or if they were the daughters of Phorcys the sea god, or if they were ever here at all. But near Sorrento is the supposed site of their temple, and, myth or not, this is a siren coast.

operators (at time of writing) do cheap holidays in Naples itself, and there is little good cheap accommodation in Naples. On the other hand eating out is inexpensive, the food delicious and authentic, and you are on the spot to see the sights of the city. In Sorrento there is more budget accommodation, but eating out is more expensive and geared to tourists. Sorrento is closer to Capri, and about the same distance to Pompeii as Naples.

NAPLES

BUDGET FOR A DAY	
Morning coffee and cornetto	2,500
Visit market and buy leather shoes	10,000
Stand-up pizza for lunch	1,300
Spremuta (orange drink)	2,000
Circumvesuviana (train) - return ticket NAPLES to POMPEII	3,000
Lavatory	200
Good evening meal	22,000
plus accommodation	L41,000

Planes arrive at Capodichino airport, 4km (2½ miles) north of Naples. A frequent bus (number 14) goes to and from piazza Garibaldi in the centre, price L800. Taxi fare (double the price on the clock – you must pay for the return as well) is about L15,000. If

you are leaving the airport by bus, buy your tickets at the tobacconist in the airport departure lounge.

Buses and trains bring you to piazza Garibaldi, a vast confusing area of buses and traffic. At one end, the central train station houses not only main-line trains, but also the underground railway (the Metropolitana), as well as the Circumvesuviana line (one floor down), a suburban line which goes to Herculaneum, Pompeii and Sorrento. Trains and underground are both excellent. Buses can be incredibly crowded and held up by traffic.

Piazza Garibaldi and its environs are full of hotels which can be sleazy and unsafe. It is much better to stay slightly west of centre, in the Mergellina district. This part of Naples

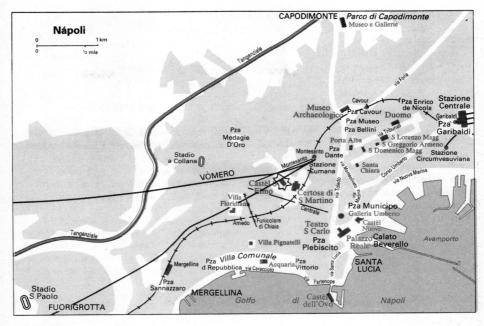

lies towards the western curve of the bay; Posíllipo is just beyond, with interesting walks, wonderful views of the bay and Vesuvius. It is quieter here, less hectic than the centre, with no problems about walking late at night, and it is served by the Metropolitana. Mergellina train station is a large and handsome place, with some trains leaving for Rome, a reminder that this area, climbing up the hill to the Vómero behind, is a fashionable suburb. It is also convenient for excursions to Pozzuoli.

There is one really inexpensive hotel in the Mergellina area, the Crispi, shabby and basic, but safe and reliable. Otherwise the hotels can be rather more pricy than the rock-bottom ones around piazza Garibaldi, but worth paying for. Naples has surprisingly few hotels – only about 130 altogether (compared with 300 churches). The Galles, Muller and Bella Nápoli, all in the piazza Sannazzaro region of Mergellina, are relatively inexpensive. As for restaurants, there are several around here. Seafood predomi-

Moneysaver

Fares on buses, trams, funicular and underground are L800 per journey. If you intend to travel about a lot buy a half-day ticket, L1,200, valid from 2pm to 11pm; or a full-day ticket for L2,000, valid for buses, trams, funicular, but not the Metropolitana. Buy tickets from tobacconists and validate them in the machine on the bus.

Local flavour

English newspapers are on sale at Mergellina station. A few standard handouts are all that's available from the information office there. Don't mention knees (*ginocchi* not *gnocchi!*) to the friendly but troubled lady at the desk – she suffers from them. *But*, interestingly, the state pays for people like her to take the thermal cures on the island of Íschia.

nates; you can have shellfish soups, roast bass and spaghetti with mussels, as well as many different pasta dishes. For good food and reasonable prices try a little place called Vini e Cucina, nearly opposite Mergellina station (11 little tables, choose the meat or fish you want from the display cabinet).

DISCOVERING NAPLES

MERGELLINA TO CASTÈL NUOVO

From Mergellina the 106 bus goes along the Riviera di Chiaia, past the gardens called the Villa Comunale, running along the waterfront. The aquarium in the gardens, with 200 different species, is famous for its local miniature sharks, and a giant turtle resident in tank 10 since 1928. (In the bad days of the last war, most of the tropical fish were cooked and eaten.) Open Tuesday to Saturday, 9am-5pm. Sunday 10am-7pm. Admission L1,000, under sixes L500.

The bus continues through the piazza Vittoria, a typical handsome Neapolitan square with statuary among palms, eucalyptus trees, pines, and flowering purple Judas trees. At 10A on via Partenope, overlooking Egg Castle (Castèl dell' Ovo), is the information office (English spoken), with lists of hotels, leaflets, maps and *Qui Nápoli* (the local guide). Continuing up via Santa Lucia (several good *pizzerias* in the street), turn left up via C Console to reach the piazza del Plebiscito and the Palazzo Reale, a dark red royal palace built in 1600, later a residence of the Bourbon and Savoy kings. Inside you can view the historical apartments and the 18th-century Court Theatre. This is a lovely little theatre where Alessandro Scarlatti performed several of his works; it was bombed in World War II, but has been completely restored and rebuilt (open Tuesday to Sunday, mornings only). If you don't want to go in, do look up at the grand staircase and the marble walls that look like the patterns of a Rorschach test (by Picchiatti, 1651).

Castèl Nuovo, built in 1282 and modelled on the castle at Angers

The triumphal arch of Alfonso, sandwiched between two towers of the old 13th-century Castèl Nuovo is a newly restored piece of Renaissance sculpture, first built in 1451. The San Carlo Theatre adjoins the Palazzo Reale, famous for its exuberantly decorated interior and the winter opera season. You may be allowed in to see it in the mornings, if they are not working on stage. The cheapest ticket is about L20,000 (up to L150,000), though prices vary for every performance. You are most likely to get a ticket for Sunday performances, others tend to be booked for the season (ask for the ticket office). Take your life in your hands, cross from here to the Galleria Umberto, a rather bleak shopping arcade, or go down to the Castèl Nuovo and the port (Molo Beverello), from where boats and hydrofoils cross to the islands of Capri, Ischia, Prócida and to Sorrento.

OLD NAPLES AND SPACCANÁPOLI

For an extraordinary contrast, walk from the wide spaces of the piazza del Plebiscito down the left side of the imposing San Francesco di Paolo church, a 19th-century copy of the Roman Pantheon, into the Pizzofalcone, a sliver of a street, with high tenements strung together with washing and, at ground level, stalls of green striped fish, little bream, mussels and all manner of seafood (*sarago, dorado, cozze, vongole*).

Local flavour
The composer Alessandro Scarlatti (father of Domenico), was Master of the Chapel to the Viceroy of Naples for many years (1684-1702 and again in 1708-17), composing a long series of operas. Although he lived and composed in Tuscany and Rome as well, it was in Naples that he died. He is buried in the church of Santa Maria di Montesanto (near the funicular station).

North from here, up via Medina and via Monteoliveto lies the heart of old Naples, narrow crowded streets lined with palazzo courtyards, churches, little workshops (hang on to your bag), a wonderful hive of activity. On the western edge of the area, the via Toledo and via Roma lead northwards to the Museo Nazionale and, further still, out to the art collections at the Capodimonte gallery. From east to west, it is split by a road called Spaccanápoli ('cutting Naples'), which has given its name to the whole area; the road is sometimes called via B Croce, changing to via San Biagio di Librai.

Conceal all valuables and try not to carry handbags and purses in this part of Naples.

To explore this part, begin at the piazza Gesù Nuovo, where the tourist office provides itineraries, continue along via B Croce and San Biagio dei Librai, turn left up via Duomo to the cathedral, and returning, turn right into via Tribunali, looking at piazza Bellini (very good pizzas here at the Pizzeria Bellini) and emerging into piazza Dante by way of the Pont' Alba. In piazza Dante is a well known *pizzeria*, the Dante e Beatrice (closed Wednesdays); also try the Antica Port' Alba, via Port' Alba 18.

Local flavour
On the via Gregorio Armeno, which runs up from via San Biagio (near the church of San Lorenzo Maggiore) to via dei Tribunali, you can wander into workshops making cribs, stables and grottoes out of clay and wood, and watch another artisan (Giuseppe Ferrigno) transforming buckets of damp clay into cows, sheep and baskets of fruit. Further up via Biagio, at number 81, don't miss the Ospedale delle Bambole, where Signor Grassi will smilingly let you poke about his hundreds of restored or damaged dolls, marionettes and masks of all ages.

There is a bewildering number of churches to see here. Don't miss the Santa Chiara, opposite the Gesù Nuovo, and its cloisters.

(Open 8.30am-12.30pm and 4-6pm.) The church was damaged in the recent earthquakes, but is restored, and the cloisters have astonishing pillars of majolica tiles and a garden full of cooing doves, irises and sweet-smelling stocks. You can sit on stone benches in the shade, but if you do, stray cats will want to join you.

Coming out of the cloisters, up via Santa Chiara, try the Tavola Calda there (no other name), just down the road from a remarkable (horrific, almost) leather mask shop.

Don't miss the church of San Domenico Maggiore, with its gilded ceiling and marble inlay (you come in by the altar). Just behind it is the Cappella di San Severo which is under restoration. If open, it houses an extraordinary veiled sculpture, the *Cristo Velato*.
The Museo Archeologico Nazionale The Museo Archeologico Nazionale, sometimes simply called the Museo Nazionale, at the end of via Pessina near the piazza Cavour, is one of the largest and most fascinating in the

world, worth a special visit to Naples to see. Principal glories are its Greek sculpture collection, the Farnese collections, and the mosaics, paintings, artefacts and sculptures from Pompeii and Herculaneum. The exhibits are sometimes only numbered, with very little description, so it's worth buying a catalogue (in English, L6,000). The liveliness, the brilliant colours, the minute detail, the expressions on the faces of the mosaics, are astounding. Especially interesting are numbers 10,015, 9978, 9084 – a Roman Brontë, 8732 – the Nile fauna.) The sense of movement in the 5th-century BC paintings, the swishing steps of the funeral chorus of women, the chalky sky blue, black, dark purple, browns and reds are all echoed in present-day Naples outside the window, with its rich red *palazzos* and bustling crowds. Open Tuesday to Saturday 9am-7pm, July to September; 9am-2pm, October to June; Sundays 9am-1pm. L4,000. Free for under 18s and over 60s.

Dog on a lead – mosaic in the Museo Archeologico Nazionale in Naples

Buses 24, 47, 49, 118 and 122 all go there. Number 24 also continues on to the Capodimonte Museum. Except for July to September both these museums are closed in the afternoon, and they are always shut on Mondays.

If you find yourself in Naples on a Monday hoping to see museums which are shut, don't forget that Herculaneum and Pompeii are both open, and it is a good idea to see them first, before the Archaeological Museum.

The Capodimonte Museum and Gallery houses the paintings which used to be in the Archaeological Museum, including two paintings by Caravaggio. (He came to stay in Naples in 1607). The palace's collection also includes, among others, paintings by Titian, Raphael and Breughel, a Massacio and a drawing by Michelangelo. Entrance hours and fee are the same as the National Museum. The first floor holds a lesser collection of 19th-century art. If time is short, go directly to the second floor. The royal apartments are elaborately decorated and also contain the Farnese armoury collection.

Local flavour

It is hard to get excited about Naples' own speciality, pizza, when it has circled the world for so many years. *Déjà vu, déjà* eaten! The English traveller Augustus Hare, wrote in 1883 about the 'horrible condiment called pizza (made of dough baked with garlic, rancid bacon and strong cheese) which is esteemed a feast'. What a great stand-up standby though, for a quick lunch. The best ones are thin, crisp when heated, and folded in a napkin. Ask for them hot (*calda*).

Local flavour

Tramezzini are what we would call sandwiches, made with flat slices of bread. A *sandwich* in Italian is made from a portion of a long crusty loaf.

VÓMERO

One more region to explore is the Vómero hill, with panoramic views of the bay, the Castèl Sant' Elmo, the Villa Floridiana and the beautiful Carthusian monastery of San Martino. Three cable cars (*funicolari*) go up there – the Funicolare di Chiaia (from via del parco Margherite) is the most convenient for the Villa Floridiana, also the Centrale, which goes from via Toledo near the Palazzo Reale. Nearest to Sant' Elmo, the Montesanto car, runs from piazza Montesanto, off via Tarsia, L800 return. Open 7am-10pm. The *funicolari* were originally built to take the workers up to till the fields on the Vómero hill.

Turn left out of the station (on via Morghen) and follow Eduardo Delbono street round the back of the castle grounds. On the corner of via Tito Angellini, before you turn right down the hill to the castle and San Martino, look in at the cameo shop of Sr Alfredo di Paola. Near by is Castèl Sant' Elmo, begun in 1349, and built like a six-pointed star, is open every morning except Monday, 9am-1pm, free admission.

The San Martino Museum and the dazzling white cloisters built by Cosimo Fanzago (1591-1678), Naples' most renowned architect, are open Tuesday to Saturday 9am-2pm, Sunday 9am-1pm. L3,000, free for under 18s and over 60s. The Villa Floridiana houses a famous ceramic and porcelain collection, open Tuesday to Saturday 9am-2pm, Sunday 9am-1pm.

Local flavour

The de Paola family have been cutting cameos (and engraving coral) here since 1928. Come into the shop and watch one member engraving – another six work upstairs. Mr de Paola may tell you about a cameo he sent to President Eisenhower. The shells they use come from Zanzibar and Florida. An ancient craft, students spend five years studying cameo-making at college.

POSÍLLIPO

When you tire of the noise and scramble in the centre of town, take a walk or bus ride along the west end of the bay from Mergellina to the Posíllipo district. The hills down to the sea along here are covered with elegant villas, and there are some bathing establishments near the shore. The view from the top road looking back across the bay is magical, especially at sunset. Walk along via Posíllipo or take a 140 bus from piazzetta Leone, near the piazza Sannazzaro, up to the end (not such a good view round the bay here, mostly of the chemical works), or stop off along the way and walk towards the edge, to Capo di Posíllipo for an outstanding viewpoint. Further along, at the Quadrivio, turn left (via Marechiaro) down the hill to Marechiaro, a little hamlet by the sea. Coming back down the via Posíllipo, take bus C21 up via Giovanni Boccaccio and ask for San Antonio. Look right across Naples from the viewpoint just under the church, and then wind down the Rampe Sant' Antonio back to piazza Sannazzaro.

ORIENTATION IN NAPLES

INFORMATION

TOURIST OFFICE
EPT *at the Central train station. Monday to Saturday 8.30am-8pm. Sunday 8.30am-2pm.*
Main office *via Partenope 10A.* ☎ *081/406289. Monday to Friday 8.30am-2.30pm and Saturday 8.30am-12 noon. (Buses 106, 122 and 150 pass near.) Be sure to get the* Qui Nápoli *booklet, with boats, trains, buses, opening times.* Nápoli-Top *lists entertainment.*
Information Office *piazza Gesù Nuovo.* ☎ *081/ 5523328. Monday to Saturday 9am-7pm, Sunday 9am-2pm. Specialises in information about the old centre, with routes, maps, etc. (Get to the piazza from via Roma and via Capitelli.)*
CIT *piazza Municipio 72.* ☎ *081/5525426. Travel agents, for plane, train and ferry reservations.*
CONSULATES
UK *via Francesco Crispi*
122, *near piazza Amedeo.* ☎ *081/663511. Monday to Friday 8.30am-1pm. Mid-September to June, Monday to Friday 9am-12.30pm and 3-5.30pm.*
US *piazza della Repubblica (at the west end of the Villa Comunale).* ☎ *081/7614303. Monday-Friday 8am-noon and 2-4pm.*
BANKS
To exchange money, try Banca Nazionale del Lavoro, piazza Garibaldi 6/ 8. ☎ *081/266833. Monday to Friday 10am-1.20pm. You can exchange in the train station, but not on such good terms. Open daily 7am-9pm.*
POST OFFICE
Piazza Matteotti, off via Armando Diaz. ☎ *081/ 5522019. Monday to Friday 8.30am-7.30pm. Saturday 8.30am-12 noon. Postal code 80100.*
TELEPHONE
ASST *at the central train station. Open 24 hours.*
SIP *at Galleria Umberto (opposite San Carlo theatre). Monday to Saturday, 8am-9.30pm. Also*
at via Depretis 40. Open 24 hours. Telephone code 081.
POLICE
English speakers available on ☎ *081/794111, or go to the Ufficio Stranieri (foreigners' office) at the Questura, via Medina 75, at via Daz. In case of emergency,* ☎ *113. The EPT have a special English-speaking complaints number 081/419888.*

TRANSPORT

TAXIS
Radio taxi – ☎ *081/364444 or 081/364340. Meter starts L2,300 plus L100 per 118 metres or 33 seconds. Supplements: Sundays and holidays, add L1,000; 10pm-7am, add L1,700; L400 per piece of luggage. Double tariff to the airport (ie about L15,000). Sample cost of central ride: from Mergellina to Pizzofalcone at 10.30pm, L7,000.*
TRAINS
Centrale *Piazza Garibaldi, the main station, with direct lines north and south, including Milan (seven*

hours, L46,000 single);
Rome (three hours, L12,800
single) and Sicily, and
connections with Bríndisi
and Lecce in Apulia.
Salerno is one hour south,
L3,500 single. For
information ☎ 081/5534188.
Information booths are open
in the station, 7.30am-10pm.
One floor below the main
station, the Ferrovia
Circumvesuviana serves
Herculaneum, Pompeii and
Sorrento (about every half
hour), ☎ 081/7792444.
Times of Rome and
Sorrento and Pompeii trains
are listed in Qui Nápoli.
Mergellina In west Naples,
off via Piedigrotta lies on
the Metropolitana line, and
is also a main line station
for some Rome trains.
Montesanto The Ferrovia
Cumana and Circumflegrea
lines both leave from piazza
Montesantò station, with
trains to the old Roman
towns of Báia and Cuma.
For Ferrovia Cumana
information,
☎ 081/5513328.
BUSES
Some useful routes:
15 Tribunali–Mergellina
**24 Piazza Vittoria–Ponti
Rossi**
**106 Mergellina–Piazza G B
Vico**
118 Via Diaz-Mergellina
**140 Piazza del
Gesù–Posíllipo**
152 Corso Novara–Pozzuoli
Tram No 1 Corso Garibaldi
– Aquarium – Mostra
d'Oltremare – San Paolo
Stadium
THE METROPOLITANA
In contrast to the buses

(very crowded) and the
streets (very dirty), the
Metropolitana (under-
ground railway) is just what
you don't expect –
comparatively uncrowded,
clean and cool. Trains are
not very frequent, though –
there is only one line.
From piazza Garibaldi
towards Pozzuli Solfatara,
these are the central
stations:
Piazza Cavour nearest stop
for the Museo Nazionale
and not too far from the
Duomo.
Montesanto for the cable
car station up to Castèl
Sant' Elmo and San
Martino. Also for the
Cumana trains out to Cuma
and Báia. Via Tarsia leads
from here to piazza Dante
and Spaccanápoli.
Piazza Amedeo for the cable
car up to the Villa
Floridiana. Restaurants and
good shops in this area.
Mergellina for hotels, port
and walks to Posíllipo. Sit
tight until you get to
Pozzuoli Solfatara – for the
camp site, Roman buildings
and volcanic crater.

ACCOMMODATION
AT MERGELLINA
Ausonia via Caracciolo 11.
☎ 081/682278. Bed and
breakfast, double with bath,
L85,000; without bath,
L65,000. Pleasant rooms,
small television room.
Bella Nápoli via Caracciolo
10. ☎ 081/663811. Double
L80,000 with frigobar,
television, shower, hair-
dryer. Recently refurbished.
No view, no noise. A capsule

for sleeping in. (Both the
Ausonia and Bella Nápoli
are at the piazza
Sannazzaro end of via
Caracciolo, near the
Marina.)
Hotel Crispi via Francesco
Giordani 2. ☎ 081/664804.
Up the hill from the
Mergellina station.
Inexpensive, basic, shabby
and safe. Doubles without
bath L45,000. Breakfast at
the bar down the road.
CENTRAL
Hotel Galles via Sannazzaro
5, on the corner of via
Caracciolo. ☎ 081/668344.
Double bed and breakfast
with bath L85,000. Garage,
television and tall, old-
fashioned rooms.
Hotel Muller piazza
Mergellina 7. ☎ 081/
669056. Doubles with bath
L60,000, breakfast
L15,000(!) Single, L35,000.
No credit cards or cheques.
Not very friendly.
Hotel Europa corso
Meridionale 15 (near train
station). ☎ 081/267511.
Telex: 720179, L55,000
without bath, L70,000 with
bath.
Hotel Torino via Depretis
123 (near the piazza
Municipio). ☎ 081/322410.

EATING OUT
Antica Port' Alba via Port'
Alba 18. ☎ 081/459713. A
pizzeria since 1830; try its
own four-part pizza
speciality. Open 9am-
midnight. Shut Wednesday.
Avellinese da Peppino via
Silvio Sparenta 31/35, off
piazza Garibaldi. ☎ 081/
283897. Honest, reasonably

Local flavour
Festivals Late afternoon processions in the cathedral, 19 September and 16 December, and in Santa Chiara on first Saturday in May, for the Liquefaction of the blood of San Januarius. Return of the pilgrims from Montevergine on Whit Monday down by the harbour, with costumes and flowers like an old-time Baccanalia. The *Struscio* (from the sound of silk dresses rustling) crowds parade in via Roma, Thursday and Friday before Easter. Festival of Piedigrotta, night of 7–8 September. On summer weekend nights there are many local festivals and fireworks. The Festival of Neapolitan Song is held in June.

Local flavour
Local wines: white Lacrima Cristi, a dry, scented wine from the slopes of Vesuvius – also red (Vesuvio Rosso). From the Phlegraean hills: Falerno, a full-bodied rich red wine which Horace, the ancient Roman poet, loved; try one from Azienda Moio di Mondragone.

Local flavour
For a special outing, delicious sea food and a wonderful view of the island of Íschia, try the *spaghetti alle vongole* on the terrace at A Fenestella, via Marechiaro 23, in Posíllipo.

priced. *Try 'rigattoni alla Bellavista'. Good seafood. Open 11.30am-midnight. Shut Saturday.*
La Continella *via Cuma 42.* ☎ *081/404884.*
Da Ciro *via Santa Brigida 71 (off the bottom of via Toledo).* ☎ *081/5524072. A well-known spot for classic Neapolitan food. Moderately priced. Shut Sunday and all of August.*
Dante e Beatrice *piazza Dante 44.* ☎ *081/349905. Very popular (but lots of*

room). Try zuppa di cozze *(mussel soup). Shut Wednesday.*
Osteria della Mattonella *via Nicotera 13, right in the middle of the old city off via Chiaria.* ☎ *081/416541. First-rate Neapolitan food in a small restaurant lined with majolica tiles. Finish with a small glass of Frangelico, a liqueur made from hazelnuts, not easy to find elsewhere. Very good value. Open 12.30-4pm and 7-11.30pm. Shut Monday.*

La Pappardella *via Cilea 253.* ☎ *081/643820.*
Ristorante Pizzeria da Marino *via Santa Lucia.* ☎ *081/416280. Reasonably priced. Popular with locals; pizzas and fish.*
Tavola Calda *via Santa Chiara, beside the church. Simple, inexpensive local cooking. Shut Sundays.*
Vine e Cucina *corso Vittorio Emanuele 762, opposite the Mergellina station.* ☎ *081/660302. Excellent unpretentious cooking.*

Moneysaver
Certain museums are free for those under 18 and over 60 – the Museo Archeologico Nazionale, the Capodimonte Gallery, the apartments in the Palazzo Reale, the Villa Pignatelli, ceramics in the Villa Floridiana. Museo Nazionale Ferroviario. Admission is free to the transport museum in Corso San Giovanni a Teduccio, telephone 081/472003. Monday to Saturday 9am-12 noon.

Local flavour
Stop by one of the stalls with bags of lemons and oranges hanging round for a *spremuta*, the juice of at least four oranges freshly squeezed into your glass. Orange or lemon – *arrancia* or *limone*. Lemon is incredibly sour. *Mozzarella in carrozza* is a bar snack – fried mozzarella (buffalo cheese) sandwich. *Calzone*, rather stodgy dough filled with *prosciutto* (ham) and mozzarella.

SHOPPING

Inland from the piazza Vittoria, the via dei Mille and the via Chiaia are fashionable areas for clothes shops. The smart place to have a coffee on the via Chiaia is the Gran Café Gambrinus. The piazza Martiri near by, and surrounding streets, are packed with antique dealers.

In ironmongers, such as at via Antonio Ranieri 63 (near Forcella market) look for the special Neapolitan coffee pots, which you invert, and the coffee filters down.

Don't buy cassettes of Neapolitan songs from the street stalls, they are cheap but of very inferior quality. **Colonnese bookshop** via San Pietro a Maiella 33, near the Port'Alba, off piazza Dante has second-hand books and old views of Naples.

Baracca e burattini piazza Museo 2, just by the entrance to the Museo Nazionale, makes dolls, masks, marionettes. **Keramike** piazza Bellini 64, and **La soffitta** via Benedetto Croce 12, for ceramics. Also **Lisa Weber's workshop** via Paladino 4, off via San Biagio.

Ospedale delle bambole via San Biagio dei librari 81. Dolls, marionettes.

ENTERTAINMENT

Consult Nápoli-Top, the 'what's on' guide to Naples night life and Qui Nápoli for times of theatres etc. The San Paolo football stadium (capacity 80,000), home to the Nápoli club, is at Fuorigrotta, beyond Mergellina, ☎ 081/615623. Edenlandia, the amusement park, is on viale Kennedy in an area called the Mostra d'Oltremare, ☎ 081/619711. Night clubs and discos are listed in Qui Nápoli. San Carlo Theatre, via San Carlo, ☎ 081/7972111.

Moneysaver
Take advantage of cheap markets in the morning at piazza Nazionale (north of the train station) and piazza degli Artisti, to the west on the Vómero hill. A very cheap market fills the streets around the Church of San Pietro ad Aram, off the Corso Umberto, near via Forcella – it looks like an outpost of North Africa. New leather shoes, L10,000, cheap leather bags (could have fallen off the back of a vespa?). Worth looking at, anyway.

Local flavour
The ice cream is exceptionally good but so many varieties can be confusing: *limone* (lemon), *caffè* (coffee), *banana*, *pistachio*, *coco* (coconut); *tiramisu* (made of chocolate, coffee and vanilla); *nocciola* (nuts); *zuppa inglese* (cream, vanilla, candied fruit); *fragola* (strawberry); *ananas* (pineapple); *stracciatella* (cream and chocolate); *cioccolato* (chocolate). They will give you a large cone, unless you ask for a small one (*piccolo*).

OUTINGS FROM NAPLES

CASERTA

Caserta is 25km (16 miles) from Naples, about 45 minutes by train, leaving the Central station about every half hour (first train 7.15am, L5,000 return). You may travel in a double-decker train. Buses leave every 20 minutes, for an hour's journey, from piazza Porta Capuana.

Considering that the Palazzo Reale (also called the Reggia) at Caserta is known as the Versailles of Italy, it seems a great shame that to get to it from the train station you must cross a revolting wasteland of tussocky grass, plastic bags and bottles. And the first part of the famous gardens inside are unkempt, the grass uncut; the formality of the design, depending for effect on contrasts of grass, trees and statuary (no flowers) is undermined by the raggedness and lack of care.

The palace, built between 1752 and 1774 for the Bourbon King Charles III, is huge, with magnificent apartments (often used for historical films). The park, laid out by the same architect, Luigi Vanvitelli, is a long, 4km (2½-mile) avenue interspersed with statuary and fountains, leading to a cascade of water and up a wooded hill to an English garden with shrubs and temples. It's a long walk on a hot day – but a minibus goes up round most of the garden every half hour, L2,000. There is a restaurant in the station, one near the entrance to the English Garden (the Mulini Reali), and one near the palace itself (called the Antica Locanda Massa, 1848).

The palace is open Monday to Saturday 9am-1.30pm, Sunday 9am-1pm, L3,000. Gardens open 9am to sunset, L2,000. There are plenty of places to have a picnic here, but at weekends there will be thousands of Neapolitans too. Caserta Vécchia, a hand-some old town, is 10km (6¼ miles) north east by bus from here, and Benevento, east of Caserta, can be visited by bus (1½ hours) leaving from Piazza Garibaldi in Naples.

PRÓCIDA

Prócida is the smallest, nearest, least visited, and most off-the-beaten-track of the bay's three islands. While not as spectacular as Capri or Íschia, it is unspoilt, with bays and beaches, and small villages of flat-topped houses with a Greek feel to them. For an interesting day's trip, you could also go on to Íschia from here, or return via Pozzuoli. Or take a few days or a week off in the quiet of the bay. There are a few hotels and some self-catering flats to rent, as well as camp sites.

Fishing, vine-growing, and cultivation of oranges and lemons (some reputedly almost 900 gm, about 2 lbs in weight) are the island's main occupations. It is joined by a bridge to its own small satellite island, Vivara, a haven for 180 different species of birds.

Hydrofoils and ferries leave from the Molo Beverello, Mergellina, and Pozzuoli. A ferry, leaving Molo Beverello 9.20am arrives Prócida 10.20am, costing L9,800 return (coffee and cornetto on the boat L2,000). Or take a single, and leave yourself the option of going on to Íschia by hydrofoil, or returning to Pozzuoli.

Sea traditions continue on the island of Prócida off the coast of Naples

From the port, walk over the hill to Coricella, a fishing port, or take the bus to the other end of the island, to Chiaiolella. There are beaches at spiaggia Chiaia, Chiaio-cella, and Ciraccio. Take the road up from the port to Prócida town to the ETP offices, via Principe Umberto 1, telephone 081/8969067. This is a very helpful office, with maps, hand-outs and lists of hotels and flats which they rent. They have rooms on the waterfront at Coricella (watch the fishermen put little crabs into baskets to catch octopuses).

There are several restaurants near the port; many are shut on Wednesdays.

The ETP office will organise boat trips with fishermen round the island.

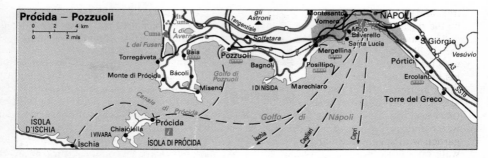

Prócida — Pozzuoli

ORIENTATION IN PRÓCIDA

ACCOMMODATION
ETP Residence via Principe Umberto 1. ☎ 081/8969067. Flats to rent around the island. Prices till end of May, and from October to December are about L100,000 per person per week, but rise to double that in July and August.
Hotel Riviera via Giovanni da Prócida 36. ☎ 081/ 8967197. April to June and September L50,000. July and August L60,000. Double room with bath only.
Pensione Savoia via Lavadera 32. ☎ 081/ 8967616. L45,000 (no private baths).

There are several camp sites on the island.
POSTAL CODE
80079.

EATING OUT
Cantinone di Zio Luigi near the port by church. Good local food, shut Wednesday. **Pizzeria DA 36** by the port.

HERCULANEUM

Herculaneum (Ercolano), once a town of elegant villas, small shops, and fishermen's houses, was destroyed with Pompeii in the Vesuvius eruptions of AD79. But unlike Pompeii, Herculaneum was preserved, rather than burnt, by layers of mud, sand and ashes, so that upper stories and woodwork, frescoes, mosaics and household objects still remain. Herculaneum is about one-third the size of Pompeii, and in a few hours you can get a real feeling of its life and times.

Take the Circumvesuviana train from Central station towards Sorrento, and get off at Ercolano. (15 minutes, L1,200 return). Walk downhill for about 500 metres (550 yards) to the entrance. Open daily 9am to one hour before sunset, L5,000.

VESUVIUS

Vesuvius is the only active volcano on the mainland of Europe, but not very active now, despite its name which means 'the unextinguished'. Neapolitans call it *la buona-nima* (the good soul) to placate it, should the beast want to cause trouble again. The most recent eruption was in 1944.

A blue SITA bus goes four times a day only from the Ercolano station (the first one departs at 8am, last one back at 6.30pm), L1,200 return part of the way up to the top. The chair lift doesn't work any more. The west route takes a round trip of three to four hours, easy walking. From the toll road to the south there is a steep climb. You will have to pay at the top for a compulsory guide (L3,000) even if there isn't one! Be careful round the rim of the crater. There's a sheer drop 3,000 metres (1,000ft) down the mountain. Charles Dickens described a visit he made with a certain Mr Pickle of Portici (related perhaps to Mr Pickwick?) who suddenly fell head first into the crater 'skimming over the surface of the white ice like a cannonball'. He was all right, luckily.

On the lower slopes vines grow, and the plump, egg-shaped *marzano* tomatoes.

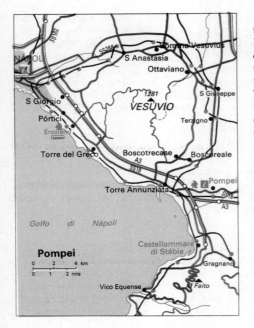

Pompei
0   2   4 km
0   1   2 mls

POMPEII

There are several routes (including a main-line train) to get to Pompeii, but the easiest and most frequently served is the Circumve-suviana line, direction Sorrento (past Erco-lano). It leaves about every 40 minutes and takes about half an hour, L3,000 return, with stops at Pompeii Scavi and Villa dei Misteri. Turn right out of the station to the tourist office and entrance. Buy a good map of the ruins (several guides have indecipherable maps, so look carefully before you buy). The excavations are huge, and you could waste time missing the best sights.

Local flavour

About the eruption of Vesuvius, Goethe wrote: 'Many a calamity has happened in the world, but never one that caused so much entertainment to posterity as this one.'

There are no trees to give shade, though there is a restaurant in the centre near the Forum for food, drinks, guidebooks and a decent lavatory (L200). The ground is uneven and often gravelly, so wear comfor-table flat shoes, but not open-toed sandals. To do the whole place justice would probably take about four hours, but of course you can do a shorter circuit. Some of the sights definitely not to miss are the Basilica on your right (a court of law), and the temple of Apollo on your left as you walk towards the Forum. (Note the little diamond-shaped tufa bricks in the long wall on your right.) From the Forum, turning down via dell' Abbon-danza past the house of the Wild Boar, take the second right, via dei Teatri, towards the Triangular Forum and the Large Theatre. From here you look across to the Gladiators' Barracks – good place to picnic.

In July, August and September, classical concerts are held here, usually on Friday, Saturday, Sunday at 9pm, tickets L10,000 to L30,000. From the little theatre beside it cross the via Stabiana going east for two blocks, to the House of Menander and the House of Lovers. Turn north to meet the via dell' Abbondanza again.

This street, part of the New Excavations, is lined with little shops and leads down to the huge Amphitheatre. For a shorter route, turn left up towards the via Stabiana to the Stabian baths. A little road right, via dei Lupanare, off the via dell' Abbondanza brings you to the Lupanare, a little bordello. Going left from here up via degli Augustini, you will eventually find yourself back at the other end of the Forum. And you've only seen about a tenth of the site!

Courage! Near by is the cafeteria. And not far away, don't miss the House of the Tragic Poet, the House of the Great Fountain, the House of the Vettii (wonderful frescoes), and the House of the Faun, all north of the Forum.

The other villa to see if you have time (and it is some way away on its own, north west along the via Consolare beyond the Porta Ercolano) is the Villa dei Misteri, with a whole series of remarkable frescoes.

Pompeii was a large commercial city before AD79 when, in a very short time, on 24 August, Vesuvius erupted and 2,000 inhabitants were killed and the entire town covered with pumice and ash. Pliny the Younger wrote that 'darkness overspread us, not like that of a cloudy night, or when there is no moon, but of a room when it is shut up, and all the light extinguished'. They thought the end of the world had come, and for many it had.

Although some paintings and artefacts, especially the frescoes, survived and remain in place, many originals have been removed to safe keeping in the Archaeological Museum in Naples. (The faun in the House of the Faun, for instance, is a copy.)

Local flavour

The big slabs in the roads were placed there for pedestrians to cross without getting their feet muddy. There are more toga cleaning shops (and bakers) than any other kind in Pompeii.

POZZUOLI

To the west of Naples, beyond Mergellina and Posíllipo is an area known as the Phlegrean (Burning) Fields, where the volcanic seething and bubbling of the not-so-far-underneath underworld breaks to the surface in hissing steam. Low extinct craters fill the area between Naples and Cuma where the Greeks and Romans, undeterred, but with ears cocked for the mythical sounds of Hell beneath them, built innumerable villas. All their fine building has crumbled now, but you can visit the temple and amphitheatre at Pozzuoli, and the Solfatara, a huge elliptical crater, 752 metres (827yds) across, where steam and sulphurous smoke spurt into the air.

The easiest route to the Solfatara is to take the Metropolitana (L800) to its terminus at Pozzuoli Solfatara, which takes about 30 minutes from piazza Garibaldi. (Do *not* get off at the Campi Flegrei.) Turn right, then left up the hill along via Solfatara. Either take a 152 Sepsa bus, or walk the 500 metres (550 yards). Open 9am to sunset, L3,000. Walk within the guidelines; the ground is very hot in parts, and hollow-sounding. From the Bocca Grande (big mouth), behind the small pavilion, steam emerges at 162 degrees Celsius.

The camp site right next to it, called Vulcano Solfatara, telephone 081/8673413, open April to mid-October, is good and well-run.

Down the hill from the Metropolitana station is the Roman Amphitheatre, open daily, L2,000

Local flavour

The amphitheatre is the third largest in Italy and scene of vicious gladiator fights. The Emperor Nero was said to have amazed people with his exploits, once killing a bull with one blow in this arena.

The Ferrovia Cumana line (from Montesanto or from Mergellina) will take you down into the centre of Pozzuoli, by the sea, just by a Roman market called the Serapeum. (Climb up from here to the amphitheatre). A 20-minute Sepsa bus ride, L800, will take you to Báia.

Local flavour

Báia was the Roman's fashionable bathing resort. This is where Caligula built a bridge of boats, and Nero, alas, murdered his mother, Agrippina. It was a place of debauchery and exotic living.

North of here is Lake Averno, a strange unearthly place that Homer and Virgil thought was the entrance to Hades. To go on to Cuma, to see the temples and caves of that early Greek colony (founded in the 8th century BC), take the Ferrovia Cumana to the Cuma stop.

PROVINCE OF CAMPANIA

If your budget stretches to private transport, there are some fascinating places to go in this region.

While visiting Caserta, make a small circular tour to the north including Santa Maria Cápua Vétere, site of a very ancient pre-Etruscan city, and Sant' Angelo in Formis where there is a Basilica up on the hillside with antique columns and second-century frescoes. Caserta Vécchia itself should not be missed. South east of Caserta, at Maddaloni, turn northwards towards Limarola. A spectacular aqueduct crosses the road and the whole valley. It was built in the 18th century to supply water for the fountains and waterfalls in the palace gardens at Caserta. After 11km (7 miles) along this road, turn right for a 7km (4½-mile) run to Sant' Ágata de' Goti. Like the other Sant' Ágata, near Sorrento, this is a stunning site, built on the edge of an abyss, an interesting little town with picturesque small cafés.

A couple of interesting detours off the Naples–Sorrento motorway: for the first one leave the motorway at the Pórtici exit, and on L Apa, on your right, you will find the Donadio coral factory, where you are welcome to go in and look around. For the second one, make a detour towards Castellammare di Stábia (Al Capone was born here). Take the road up into the hills, towards Monte Faito, with splendid views towards the bay with lay-bys to stop at, eventually ending down on the coast at Vico Equense. The road is very winding, and the road surface sometimes unpredictable.

From Salerno southwards, take the SS18 (48km, 30 miles) to Paestum, to see the Greek temples. After Paestum turn right on to the SS267 to Agrópoli (7km, 4¼ miles) then on the SS447 down to Palinuro. (The Saline hotel on this road has rooms and a swimming pool.) There are a couple of restaurants down on the harbour at Agrópoli. This is a scenic coastal route through unspoilt towns. Continue round the cape of Palinuro by way

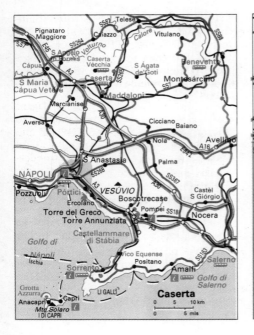

Caserta

Paestum

of Camerota (a long sandy beach) to the little seaside town of Scário and on to Sapri. From Sapri you can get back on the motorway again and return via Éboli to Salerno.

You can make a detour from this route, leaving the motorway at the Polla exit, to the Pertusa grottoes (70km, 43 miles from Salerno).

SORRENTO

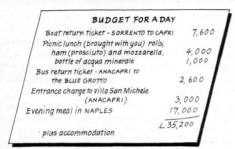

BUDGET FOR A DAY

Boat return ticket - SORRENTO TO CAPRI	7,600
Picnic lunch (brought with you) rolls, ham (prosciuto) and mozzarella,	4,000
bottle of acqua minerale	1,000
Bus return ticket - ANACAPRI to the BLUE GROTTO	2,600
Entrance charge to Villa San Michele (ANACAPRI)	3,000
Evening meal in NAPLES	17,000
	L 35,200
· plus accommodation	

Sorrento, 50km (31 miles) from Naples across the bay, has been a resort town since the Romans Agrippa and Augustus had their villas here. It flourished again in the 18th and 19th centuries when the Bourbon princes built houses here, and aristocratic and artistic people from all over Europe came for the mild winters and beautiful setting.

Ibsen, the Norwegian dramatist, finished writing *Peer Gynt* here. The German composer Wagner and the philosopher Nietzsche stayed here and had a famous quarrel. Siren voices drew them here, as they tried to tempt Ulysses and his crew hundreds of years before. Torquato Tasso, the Italian poet, was born here in 1544.

Moneysaver

From mid-November to mid-March, the Sorrento tourist office organises free entertainment, including a coach tour up into the hills, concerts, dances and local singing. Hotels give special one-week and weekend rates during this period. Ask the Azienda Autonoma di Soggiorno di Sorrento, via L de Maio 35. Telephone 081/8782104 for details of Sorrento Inverno.

Now the centre still retains its elegant buildings, but there are too many tourists (80 per cent British), too many snack bars and too many hotels. However, it is still a useful base for trips to Capri and along the wonderful Amalfi coast – even to Naples itself, Herculaneum and Pompeii. If you only want to visit the Archaeological Museum and spend a day in Naples, or visit Herculaneum and Pompeii, then it is easy to take the Circumvesuviana train from here. The atmosphere is totally different from Naples. You will exchange the vibrant, working, dirty, hectic metropolis for a tourist mecca.

Sorrento does have charm, though, and it also has reasonable hotels. Its role as package resort can be turned to the budget traveller's advantage. As it is not primarily a bathing resort – none of the towns around here are, the beaches are too small and the bays rocky – it is a year-round town. Many hotels stay open through the winter, there is entertainment out of season, with some tour operators offering very good deals.

> **Local flavour**
>
> Sorrento is famous for intarsia – inlaid wood – work. You can watch demonstrations of the craft at Ferdinando Corciano's shop on via San Francisco.

> **Moneysaver**
>
> Thomson holidays offer a week in Sorrento, half-board for under £200, flight included, during the winter months. An independent traveller could hardly better these terms, and could perhaps afford to spend a night away on Capri or along the Amalfi coast, using local transport, to counteract the 'packaged' feeling.

From Naples airport, Curreri run a coach direct from the airport to Sorrento at 12.30pm and 5.30pm. Otherwise take the bus outside the airport to piazza Garibaldi in Naples, then the Circumvesuviana line, one floor down in the Central station. Sorrento is the last stop on the line. L2,900 single, about an hour. Trains leave every 40 minutes.

There's not a lot to do in Sorrento. The Circolo dei Forestieri on via de Maio is a bar with live music in the evenings (open all year). Villa Pompeiana, behind the Bellevue Syrene Hotel, has a bar with music in the summer season. The Villa Rosa, corso Italia 14/20, is an underground nightspot with dancing, open daily 8pm-4am.

Apart from public transport, the roads can be explored by scooter, and there are a number of footpaths. A few suggestions follow:

To Capo di Sorrento To walk out to the point at Capo di Sorrento for a swim and a wonderful view, take the corso Italia which runs into the via del Capo. Continue, as it turns into a footpath, past Maxim Gorki's villa, turn right down to the sea and ruins of the Roman Villa di Pollio, known as the Baths of Queen Giovanna. Or take a bus to Capo di Sorrento and walk on for about 15 minutes.

To Sant' Ágata sui Due Golfi Take the SITA bus to Sant' Ágata sui Due Golfi, which is, just as the name says, a headland with views towards the two gulfs of Naples and Salerno. The little church has a fine altar. Opposite is the Bar Orlando, run by Alfredo Cliento. From here walk up the hill to an area called the Derserto, with an even better view.

> **Local flavour**
>
> Signor Cliento once owned an extraordinary cat called Jolly, and wrote a book about him: *Jolly the Cat that Smoked: the history of a cat prodigy* (in Italian). He could even, apparently, smoke while flying through the air. What did he die of – flying or smoking! Signor Cliento may tell you.

To Massa Lubrense Walk to Massa Lubrense. Set off on the road to Capo, and instead of going down to the Villa di Pollio, keep left through Villazzano, until you reach the little village of Massa Lubrense. Follow the via Palma, via Roma, and the via Marina past the Church of the Madonna della Lobra (near the supposed site of the legendary temple of the Sirens); this will take you down to the shore. A long trek will take you on to Termini, and a further 4km (2½ miles) up the hill to Sant' Ágata.

There are two camp sites at Massa Lubrense, two more around the headland, near Nerano, and another near Croce, just south of Sant' Ágata. The tourist office lists two two-star hotels in Sant' Ágata: La Pergoletta, telephone 081/878145 and O Sole Mio, telephone 081/8780005. At Massa Lubrense, in Marina della Lobra, is the Villa

Fiorella, telephone 081/8789242. All three have restaurants and are open all year.

Vespa and car hire can be a good way to explore the peninsula, but the roads round the coast and up into the hills are very winding and full of traffic in the summer – suitable only for good and confident drivers.

Never ride a scooter with luggage on your back; it is easy to overbalance backwards when climbing up the steep hills.

ORIENTATION IN SORRENTO

INFORMATION
TOURIST OFFICE
Via L de Maio 35, off piazza Antonino towards the sea. ☎ 081/8781115. Very helpful. Maps, hotels, and the Sorrentum, an Italian/ English monthly tourist magazine with train and boat times. The Quest leaflet has bus times, Monday to Saturday, 8.30am-2.30pm and 4.30pm-8pm. Closes at 7pm October to June.
POST OFFICE
Corso Italia 210, near piazza A Lauro. Open Monday to Saturday 8.15am-7.30pm. Postal code: 80067.
TELEPHONES
SIP, piazza Tasso, near via Correale. Open daily 9am-1pm and 4-9.30pm. Telephone code: 081.

TRANSPORT
BUSES
SITA buses run from the station and from piazza Tasso all along the coast to Salerno.
BOATS AND HYDROFOILS
to Capri, Íschia and Naples leave from the port, down the steps from piazza Tasso. Caremar and Gruson traghetti. First boats to Capri leave at 6.55am, 7.50am, 9am, 10am, then a gap till 1.45pm. Return L7,600. Hydrofoil (aliscafi) go about five times a day to Capri (L5,500 single, 15 minutes), Naples (30 minutes) and Íschia (one hour).
CAR AND SCOOTER HIRE
Ciro's via degli Aranci 93B. Near the station. ☎ 081/ 8782522. Cars, L75,000 per day plus 19 per cent tax and insurance. Mopeds, L23,000 (over 13); Scooters, L34,000 (over 17), prices excluding tax and insurance. Open daily 8am-9pm.
Antares corso Italia 287. ☎ 081/8772983. Mopeds L21,000; scooters L32,000 (over 18).

ACCOMMODATION
Del Mare via del Mare 30. ☎ 081/8783310. Two-star, small, overlooking the sea. Open all year. Restaurant.
Loreley et Londres via Califano 2. ☎ 081/8781508. Two-star, near cliffs, old hotel with garden and restaurant. Open March to November. L55,000 out of season. Full board only July and August, L60,000.
Il Nido via Nastro Verde 62. ☎ 081/8782766. English spoken. Up the hill, with views. One-star, open all year.
Savoia via Fuorimura 48, near piazza Tasso. ☎ 081/ 8782511. English spoken. Double bed and breakfast L56,500. Closed December-January. Reduced terms other winter months.
HOTELS WITH POOLS
Floriana Park corso Italia 298. ☎ 081/8781804. One-star. Open mid-March to mid-October.
Gardenia corso Italia 258. ☎ 081/8772365. Two-star, open March-October.
Girasole corso Italia 302. ☎ 081/8781371. Three-star, open March-November. (Pool being built 1990).
Villa Igea via Capo 96. ☎ 081/8781007. Open March-October, one-star.
Sant' Agnello A few kilometres from Sorrento (but actually now joined to it) the stop before Sorrento along the Circumvesuviana line, has some inexpensive hotels with swimming pools:
Florida vico L Rota. ☎ 081/8783844.
La Pace via Tordara 60. ☎ 081/8781460.

EATING OUT
CENTRAL
Antica Trattoria via Reginaldo Giuliani 33, off corso Italia. ☎ 081/8071082. Canneloni alla Sorrentina L4,500. Open daily 10am-3pm and 7pm-1am.
Kursaal via Fuorimura. ☎ 081/8781216. Reasonably priced. Famous for its huge spread of antipasti.
O'Parrucchiano corso Italia. ☎ 081/8781321. Good local

traditional food.
OUT OF TOWN
Taverna del Curato *via
Casarlano 10b, a half-hour
walk uphill from piazza
Tasso by way of via
Fuorimura and via*

Atigliana. ☎ *081/8771628.
Homemade fettucine del
Curato and their own wine.
Closed Wednesdays October
to May, otherwise open
daily midday to midnight.*
Mastu Rocco *corso Italia*

*97, in Sant' Agnello, one
stop on the Circumvesuviana.*
☎ *081/8782442. Family-run
trattoria. Open for lunch
midday to 4pm. Shut
Mondays September
to June.*

OUTINGS FROM SORRENTO

CAPRI

This is an island which is very romantic, very desirable – and very expensive, so the trick is to be as self-sufficient as possible on a trip to Capri. Bring a picnic and walk a lot, evading sharks and crowds. Crossings from Sorrento are about every hour. L7,600 return on the ferry; hydrofoils cost about double. It's best to buy a single ticket, so that you can return by another company if their times suit you better. Fares from Naples, Molo Beverello, a much longer distance, are about twice the price.

The Grotta Azzurra (Blue Grotto) is a tourist trap, very pricy, and you have very little time to see anything. One boat takes you there, another whisks you in and out of the grotto – the total cost is about L13,000. Boats leave from the Marina Grande for the 2km (1¼ mile) trip from 9am until two hours before sunset. It takes 1½ hours altogether.

A walk up on via Tiberio leads to Villa Jovis, the Roman Emperor Tiberius' old palace, from where he threw his enemies on to the rocks below. Open 9am until one hour before sunset, L2,000. On the way down, go by way of the Arco Naturale for a view as far as Paestum on a clear day. Also up here, La Cantina del Marchese, via Tibero 7, serves good local food at a reasonable price (a Capri rarity); shuts Wednesdays from October to June.

On the southern side of Capri town, the Certosa, a 14th-century monastery, is open Tuesday to Sunday, 8am-2pm. Both this and the nearby Giardini di Augusto, with wonderful views, are free.

In Anacapri, across the island, a 20-minute chairlift ride up from piazza Vittoria (L5,500 return) takes you to the top of Mont Solaro. Also in Anacapri, the Villa San Michele, the home of the Swedish writer Axel Munthe, is full of classical sculptures. Open daily 9am until one hour before sunset, L3,000. The Church of San Michele has a splendid tiled floor depicting paradise.

The *funicolare* runs from the Marina Grande to Capri town every 15 minutes, 6.35am-9.15pm, L1,300. All local buses cost L1,300 a ride. Buses also go about every 15 minutes from the centre of Capri (via Roma) to Anacapri and Marina Piccola (the best place for swimming). If you have rented a scooter in Sorrento, it would be useful to bring it over on the ferry with you.

The tourist office is near the dock at Marina Grande. Also in piazza Umberto L in Capri town. Anacapri, at via G Orlandi, off the main piazza.

AMALFI COAST –
POSITANO

The remaining excursion destinations in this chapter can form one scenically spectacular tour, depending upon your time – and your budget!

Take a SITA bus (pay on the bus) from piazza Tasso for a wonderful hour's drive to Positano (L1,200). Take a seat near the window on the right-hand side, so that you look along the coast and straight down to the blue-green sea below, as the bus clings around the sheer cliffs. (Trust the drivers!)

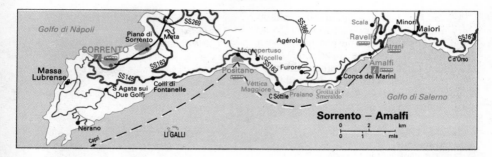

From Sorrento to Amalfi, by little coves and villages strung between heaven and the deep emerald sea, the houses perch and lean from the rocks, while little islands (Li Galli) and minute boats trail the water. It is really beautiful and absolutely not to be missed. The houses (no blocks, no screaming hotel names) enhance the view, sometimes white, pink, in clusters, seemingly built by steeple-jacks. How do you train to be a builder on this coast – on a tightrope?

If you get off the bus at the top of the hill in Positano and walk down, along via Pasitea, you will pass boutiques full of embroidered and encrusted skirts and blouses, with women in the shops ironing flounces and lace. Don't buy the first one you see, for the whole road, the whole town is full of dress-makers making different, and yet the same, exuberant stitching, in purples, oranges, browns, strung with gold baubles, a very particular Italian kind of finery (and if you look carefully, because of so much competition it is not all wildly expensive).

Positano is full of colour. The many-coloured houses spill down the hill. The church cupola is covered with green and yellow tiles, overlooking the grey sand, the bright boats, the black-dressed women. If you want an inexpensive bed for the night, try the Pensione Villa Verde, on via Pasitea, just down the road from the bus stop. Telephone 089/875506, open from April. L27,000 per person bed and breakfast. Further on is Il Gabbiano, viale Pasitea. Telephone 089/875801. L65,000 bed and breakfast, open from Easter till end of May, L80,000 in August. Near the centre is La Bougainville, via C Colombo 25, telephone 089/875047, L60,000. (Decent lavatory by the car park behind the beach.)

Local flavour
Positano used to be a prosperous trading port, bringing silks and spices in from the Middle East, until the coming of steam in the 19th century sent the boats elsewhere. At that time about three quarters of its inhabitants emigrated to America, most of them to New York.

Positano: houses cover the slopes and spill down to the sea

Moneysaver
Save some money by taking a bus from Anacapri to the cliff above the grotto (every 10 minutes, L1,300). Or for the same cost as the Blue Grotto trip, take a two-hour boat trip all round the island from the Marina Grande.

A local bus makes a circuit of Positano every half hour, otherwise you must go up and down the stairs and narrow alleys. Visit the church to see the Byzantine Black Madonna. Look across at Franco Zeffirelli's villa (it's pink). The second Sunday in August the *Sbarco dei Saraceni*, a mock sea battle, lights up the bay with fireworks.

Local flavour

The little islets out in the bay, called Li Galli, once belonged to the Russian ballet director Diaghilev, who left them to the dancer Leonid Massine. They now belong to the dancer Rudolf Nureyev and can't be visited.

Detour to Montepertuso   For a trip well off the beaten track, take the yellow bus into the hills from the bus stop by the Positano sign (coming into town from Amalfi) up to Montepertuso. Buses leave at 8.30am, 1.30pm and 7.30pm out of season, but about every hour in the summer. From Montepertuso, 350 metres (385yds) up, a path dips and curves round the mountain, leading you after about half an hour to the hamlet of Nocelle, famous for its walnut trees (*noci*). It's a wonderful walk, scented with broom and rosemary, with views down to Positano and across to the little Li Galli islands. From Nocelle, having rested on the stone terrace in front of Santa Croce, you can go back down to the coast by way of a stepped footpath to Punta San Pietro near Laurito. The Pensione Luisa in Montepertuso serves good food.

AMALFI COAST – PRAIANO

Véttica Maggiore and Praiano, on the next headland along the bus route, have spectacular views and are the less touristy resorts that Italians recommend. Down the hillside from the bus stop near the church, the Hotel Le Sirene is open from the end of March to October.

Local flavour

Up at Montepertuso there is a large hole in the rock (you can see it from down on the coast) which was formed, so legend says, by the Virgin Mary. The Devil issued a challenge to the Madonna – that whichever of them could pierce the rock could claim the village. The Devil tried first, but could hardly chip the limestone, while the Virgin Mary walked through the rock effortlessly, leaving an opening as a sign of her passing. Spectacular fireworks on 2 July every year mark the victory.

The Hotel Bellavista, telephone 089/874054, open April-October, offers half-board for L46,000 per person, L52,000 July and August. Postal address: 84010 Praiano (Salerno).

Near Praiano, perched on a hill, is the only camp site along here, at La Tranquillità. Bungalows are also available with terrace and bath. Telephone 089/874084. Above La Tranquillità, try the Ristorante Continental for open-air eating. Open daily. Rooms, restaurant and camp site are open March to November.

Further along the coast, past the little coves of Marina di Praia (sandy beach), don't miss looking down at the gorge of the Vallone di Furore before arriving at the Grotta di Smeraldo (Emerald Grotto) in the bay of Conca dei Marini. The grotto is worth a visit, with underwater stalagtites and stalagmites, just as brilliantly clear as the emerald green water at the Capri grotto. Open June to September 8am-6pm. (L4,000 for lift down and boat into the grotto.)

Local flavour

Wagner and Ibsen both stayed at the Hotel Luna on the southern tip of the bay in 1894. (The same family still run it). Walk up the steps just past the hotel for a seat and a view of the next little town, Atrani, safely out of the way of the traffic.

AMALFI COAST – AMALFI

For only L1,200 (pay on the bus) the SITA bus will bring you round the Lattari mountains to Amalfi. In the Middle Ages this was an important maritime republic, rival of Venice and Genoa; now it is mostly a tourist centre. With a much wider sea front than Positano, it is beautiful in a different way, the front a blue sea of buses in the daytime, but at night the buildings perched all above the crags are lit up, and with twinkling lights along the coast it is magical, and it doesn't matter too much about all the other people. Amalfi is a good base for trips along the coast (to the grotto, and Atrani), and up to Ravello. In Amalfi itself don't miss the bronze doors (made in Constantinople in 1066) on the astonishing Duomo and the elegantly white-arched cloisters (13th-century Moorish in style), especially when lit in early spring evenings. The Cloisters of Paradise are open 9am-1.30am and 3-8pm, L1,000). Concerts are given here from July to September, tickets L5,000.

Local flavour

Amalfi was famous in the Middle Ages for its water-driven paper mills, and exported paper all over Europe. Only a couple of the ancient mills survive. Walk up via Fiume, straight up the valley from the town centre to find, tucked into the hill, Antonio Cavaliere's old mill and shop (founded 1500). For L3,000 a sheet, buy thick, beautifully watermarked watercolour paper. (Mill open Monday to Saturday 10am-7.30pm.)

There are good walks from Amalfi. Try going to Pogerola, or up the Valle dei Mulini, pausing at the Lemon Garden (open June to September) for an inexpensive lunch, and on to Pontone and Ravello, through Scala (the long route). Alternatively cut across the hill from Pontone to the Atrani valley and up to Ravello. Along the coast, Atrani is a pretty town with a small beach, just a short walk from Amalfi.

Moneysaver

For real bargain accommodation: the Hotel Le Sirene offers low-season (not July and August) bed and breakfast for two L42,000. Half-board, L35,000 per person. There is a verandah with a good view and a small beach below (which has a lot of steps). It is run by a young Anglophile couple. 15 rooms, 84010 Véttica de Praiano. Telephone 089/874013.

A fountain on the seafront in Amalfi

ORIENTATION IN AMALFI

INFORMATION
TOURIST OFFICE
corso delle Repubbliche Marinare 19/21, in the courtyard of the Biblioteca, a handsome large yellow building on the seafront.

☎ 089/871107. Open Monday to Saturday, 8am-2pm all year. June to September also 4.30-7pm. The nearby toletta *(L300) is for 'ladyes and man'.*

TRANSPORT
BUSES
Terminus and list of times, on piazza Flavio Gioia on the seafront. Very inexpensive buses go along the coast (Sorrento L2,400; Positano L1,200; Salerno L1,800; and up to Ravello L600).

BOATS
Boats go daily to Capri, mid-March to mid-October

(L9,000 single) eg leave 9am, return from Capri 4.30pm, and to Íschia (L12,500 single). Boats to the Grotta dello Smeraldo (4km, 2½ miles, away) L6,000.

ACCOMMODATION
Hotel Amalfi *via dei Pastai.* ☎ *089/872440. Open all year. No meals November-February. Central. Double bed and breakfast L50,000-L55,000 with bath. View to hills. Garden with orange trees. Two garden rooms. Top-floor restaurant. 40 rooms. Quiet. Third person in room, L15,000.*
Centrale *Opposite the Duomo.* ☎ *089/871243.*

Double bed and breakfast with bath L70,000-L85,000. Majolica-tiled floors. Upstairs restaurant (three flights, no lift) with view to Duomo and sea.
Hotel Lidomare *via Piccolomini 9.* ☎ *089/ 871332. Double bed and breakfast, L65,000-L85,000 with bath. All with verandah and view to sea (and buses). Sitting-room with grand piano. Used to be private house of present owners. (They also own the Parsifal in Ravello). Large, nicely furnished, 13 rooms.*
Pensione Sole *84011 Amalfi.* ☎ *089/871147. Clean, pleasant, modern, but no sea view. Open all year. English spoken. Double bed and*

breakfast L50,000-L60,000 (with bath). Reductions for children. 15 rooms.

EATING OUT
Lo Smeraldino *at the north end of the harbour.* ☎ *089/ 871070. Popular local pizza restaurant.*
Taverna degli Apostoli *Largo Augustariccio.* ☎ *089/ 872991. Right by the cathedral, it used to be the town prison.*
Trattoria da Baracca *piazza Ferrari, overlooking the small square.* ☎ *089/871285. Excellent* bruschetta con alici *(toast with tomatoes and anchovies) L2,000.* zuppa di pesce *(fish soup) L13,000. Very filling, almost a meal.*

Local flavour
On the first Sunday in June, every four years; Amalfi is host to a historic regatta of the four ancient Sea Republics: Genoa, Pisa, Venice and Amalfi. Amalfi's next turn is in 1993. The 25th, 26th, 27th of June and the 30th of November are festival days for St Andrew the Apostle (Sant' Andrea) whose remains (except his head) lie in the cathedral crypt.

Local flavour
Amalfi has two unusual fountains – one in the cathedral square spouts drinking water from a nymph's nipples and a frog's bottom – one on the seafront is a charmer, a little couple crouched under an umbrella.

Local flavour
Ravello is famous for its wine, especially Sammarco, Gran Caruso, and Episcopio. The Sammarco vineyard's warehouse is at Casa Venicola Ettore Sammarco, via Civita 9. It is near a bus stop 3½km (2 miles) from Amalfi on the road to Ravello. L2,500 a bottle.
(Open Monday to Saturday 8am-1pm, 3pm-7pm; Sunday 8am-1pm).

AMALFI COAST – RAVELLO

From Amalfi and Atrani, take the bus up to Ravello (every hour, L600), a small, quiet town full of flowery gardens, perched on the mountain high above the crowds: beautiful even when the sea mists roll up the valley in early spring. Visit the cathedral and ask the custodian if you can see the bronze doors (made in 1179 by Brasano of Trani). Walk across piazza Vescovado and under the medieval tower into the Palazzo Rufolo, wonder at its Saraçen cloister, wander round its garden and formal flowerbeds, and look at the great views far below and beyond the curving mountains and the sea. (Open 9.30am-1pm and 3-7pm. October to May 2-5pm. L1,000). Charles II of Anjou, Robert the Wise, King of Naples, Pope Hadrian IV, perhaps Boccaccio, and definitely Wagner (who came up by mule) have all lived here. (Ravello was a very prosperous independent city in the 13th century, with a population said to have been 36,000.)

Walk right to the end of the ridge to see the Villa Cimbrone and its magnificent garden (open 9am-4pm), and see en route the enormous wisteria over the Il Giordano hotel car park. The best place to eat, and not expensive, is Cumpa Cosimo, via Roma, packed out for Sunday lunch. Netta, the owner, ever smiling, and with great efficiency, serves (among other things) delicious *crespolini* (a savoury pancake), and tasty, tender chicken with little peas. Closed Monday November-March, telephone 089/957156.

A stay in Ravello is for contemplative people and walkers, or those who just like to look at scenery. (Greta Garbo once stayed for a month at the Villa Cimbrone). Walk the pathway inland up to Mount Brusale (641 metres, 705yds), past Lacco. Or follow the road round the head of the valley, to Scala. (The buses up and down from Amalfi stop here.) Walk about one kilometre (five-eighths of a mile) up towards the Campidoglio area for a meal at the Ristorante-Pizzeria Belvedere, via V D'Amata, open daily for lunch and dinner, July to September, shut Wednesdays, April to June, and only open Saturday and Sunday from October to March. Past the Villa Cimbrone, the track takes you down to Castiglione.

From behind the cathedral square, walk down the valley to Torello and Minori on the coast. The bus will take you back to Atrani or Amalfi. The 1:35,000 scale map of the *Peninsola Sorrentina and Costiera Amalfitana* marks all the footpaths and tracks.

Local flavour

Minori has a little first century AD Roman villa with ceramics on view, (free, open 9am to sunset) and an open-air theatre; there are concerts, etc from July to mid-September. For information contact the Pro Loco, piazza Umberto, Minori. Telephone 089/877607.

Local flavour

Ravello hosts a classical music festival, first week of July. Concerts in the garden of the Villa Rufolo, June, July, August. They build out scaffolding over the edge of the hill and cover it with a blue carpet, so the musicians look as if they are floating on the sea. L12,000 for numbered seats. L6,000 unnumbered.

ORIENTATION IN RAVELLO

ACCOMMODATION
Try the Villa Amore, a long walk from the bus stop towards the Villa Cimbrone, but moderate in price, comfortable (antimacassars on the sitting room chairs), every room with bath, balcony and view.
Villa Amore ☎ 089/857135. Double bed and breakfast L70,000, full board L60,000 per person. Open all year. 16 rooms.
Hotel Toro piazza Vescovado. ☎ 089/871520. Open March-October. Central, with garden. No sea view.
Hotel Parsifal piazza Fontana. ☎ 089/857144, fax 89/857972. A converted convent, with sea views and terraces. Open March-October. High season bed and breakfast, double L95,000 (less off-season). Also inexpensive out of season:
Villa Maria ☎ 089/857170. **Bonadies** ☎ 089/857137, is a small, inexpensive pensione. **GISAF** via dell Marra 5, 84010 Ravello (SA). ☎ 089/857344 has apartments for rent. One, sleeps four, with view and small garden, and costs L500,000 per week to end of June.

APULIA, THE 'HEEL' OF ITALY

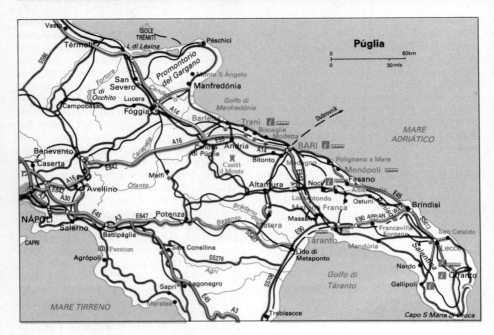

To hear a northern Italian talking, even today, you might think that the south was a wild and barren country, full of bandits and the very poor, and far from civilisation.

It's true that to most tourists Apulia (Púglia), Cálabria and Basilicata are unknown lands, which means that, for instance, you can stand on a sparkling April day (Saturday, 1pm) in the enormous piazza in front of the cathedral in Trani and be the *only person there*. The Tranese are all at home or in the restaurants and the hordes of sightseers have not yet arrived.

Now is the time to visit Apulia. It may not yet be geared up to tourists, with only a few hotels, but eager hotel-keepers are fast upgrading their accommodation, putting in showers, repainting the peeling plaster, even making the hot water hot (but still forgetting the plug occasionally), so that inevitably the prices will rise. They have already bounded up in the last couple of years.

Of the three southernmost regions of

Local flavour

One very good reason to visit Apulia – for the delicious food: *spaghetti alle vongole* (clams) or with a mixed fish sauce (*ciambotto*), mullet, *dentixes* or lamb spit-roasted over oak twigs, *melanzane alla campagnola* (grilled aubergine in oil, garlic, basil and parsley) or *orecchiette*, a small round pasta with a hollow pressed out with the thumb, looking like little ears.

Italy, Cálabria, with its mountains and tiny remote villages and steep-sided seaside towns, is most suited to touring with a car. Basilicata, the poorest region suffered very much from the recent earthquakes. Matera, with cave houses called *i sassi* on its eastern border, and on its western edge, one of the best seaside resorts, Maratea. But Apulia is in many ways the most accessible, the most varied, and the easiest region to travel

214

around in, whether by car, train, or bus. It is also the tamest and the most populated.

The Gargano peninsula in the north, the 'spur' of the high heel, as it were, is the only really hilly part of Apulia. It's a wild headland of rocky seaside villages, grottoes along the coast and, to the north, a little group of islands, the Trémiti, which you can visit by boat. This part *has* been discovered by tourists, but is still beautiful. There are many camp sites, and it gets crowded in July and August. You really need a car to travel about here.

Local flavour

Northern Apulia produces some first-rate DOC wines. Try the deep ruby red Cacc'e mitte di Lucera, and the red, white or rosé from Castèl del Monte. San Severo is another delicious wine. Rosso di Barletta is a dry red, sometimes aged in wood (labelled *invecchiato*). Rosso di Cervignola is a Fóggia wine, full-bodied, red, and a bit tart.

The rest of Apulia is flattish but not totally without hills; down its centre runs the *murge* (pronounced 'moorjay'), three central plateaux of chalky rock, steep on the side facing the Adriatic (with wonderful views along the coast), sloping down to the Gulf of Táranto to the west. The Adriatic coast is studded with little fishing ports with sandy or shingly beaches, until it comes down to Ótranto and along the southernmost tip of Santa Maria du Léuca, where the cliffs are rugged and higher, and the grottoes hide among the rocks.

Apulian architecture has developed here in a unique way. You will not find settlements of little cone-shaped dry stone houses (called *trulli*, pronounced 'truly') anywhere else; the Norman cathedrals (known as Apulian Romanesque) are unlike any others, and in Lecce the churches look more like theatres and are decorated in a unique style known as *barocco Leccese*. A *trullo* (singular) is a cone-shaped building made of flat stones,

overlapping so that they span a vault and meet at the top, built without mortar. You will find them on the *murge*, the plateaux between Noci, Alberobello, Cisternino, and Martina Franca, called the valley d'Itria. Similar stone-built shelters and houses are seen on the coastal strip up from Bari, and in the Salentine Peninsula, south of Lecce; they look like gnome houses.

They were probably originally shelters for workers and animals, easily built because the limestone just below the surface of the plateau was easy to dig out and simple to split into layers. The actual construction is not unique, but the way they developed into groups and villages, and their decoration is special. The *trullo* is the rare bird of Apulia.

In the 16th century the Count of Conversano began colonising the territory around Alberobello, moving in outlying farmers to make a dense settlement. Then under later rulers in the 17th century, people were offered special concessions to build their farms and live on their own plots of land, so that a densely populated countryside would not afford hiding places for bandits. That is why this part of the countryside is thickly dotted with peasant buildings. The single *trullo* was joined to others, so that as many as 17 little cones may cluster together to make one homestead.

Local flavour

Duke Gian Grolamo II,'the One-eyed of Apulia', encouraged the building of *trulli* because the Spanish king who ruled the whole area at the time decreed that all new houses were to be taxed. Duke Gian, a somewhat unwilling taxpayer, cunningly devised to have the houses built without mortar so that they could, at a word that a Spanish inspector was arriving, be dismantled and transformed into piles of stones or little stone walls.

Trulli continued to be built until this century, but new ones are now rare. They are, however, protected, and many have been rebuilt and extended. The largest known space spanned by a single *trullo*, a wine room in Alberobello, is 6 metres (20ft) square. The roofs, covered with their limestone shingles, are used for drying figs, tomatoes and beans, and many have a wooden attic floor, making a storage space for grain and flour. The walls are very very thick and get cold and damp in winter, so you will see the inhabitants sitting out in front for light and warmth when the weather is fine.

The top of the cone is usually covered in brilliant white lime plaster, with a little geometric or symbolic shape on top. The stone slopes are decorated with whitewashed symbolic signs, some Christian, some pagan and magical, sometimes just initials of the family inside. All these variations, the way the *trulli* are grouped and decorated, makes *trulli*-spotting an addictive pastime. You may see an unusual curve in a new oblong building, or a cone appearing among flat roofs, and know that a *trullo* is concealed there.

Other similar kinds of buildings were the *specchie*, watch towers, ancient and now ruined large stone structures, some up to 15 metres (50ft) high. You can see some, for instance, in the area around Francavilla Fontana.

A little history to make sense of, and indicate, some things to look for as you travel around: First and earliest are the dolmens and menhirs (standing stones), dating back at least to 1000BC. Look for dolmens and caves near Bischéglie and Molfetta, up the coast from Bari, and the famous 'monk'-shaped menhir near Modugno, also further south in the Salentine Peninsula. Then the Greeks came and colonised the region. Egnázia, on the Adriatic coast south of Monópoli has Greek remains. Táranto was also a Greek colony.

There are remnants of the early native tribes, called the Messapians (meaning dwellers between two seas), at Céglie Messápico and Mandúria particularly. See their remarkable pottery in the Provincial Museum at Lecce. The Romans came next, building the Appian Way to Bríndisi, from where the Roman Empire traded with the East. A column stands at the end of the road.

When the Roman Empire fell, the Lombards battled here, and also the Byzantines. Bari fell to the Saracens in 843. Then, in the 11th century, the Normans came. The brothers Robert and Roger Hauteville conquered Apulia and Sicily and became lords and dukes of Apulia. They were violent, cruel, wealthy and exotic, fighting the Saracens, and building castles and cathedrals. Robert's second wife, Sichelgaita was as remarkable as himself, an expert amateur poisoner who liked to wear men's clothing and had her own custom-made suit of armour.

From Apulia the Crusaders sailed to the East, and trade followed. This was Apulia's heyday, until the end of the 13th century and the end of the reign of Emperor Frederick II, known as the Wonder of the World.

Frederick II built this octagonal hunting lodge in the 13th century

Absent rulers, especially the Spanish, who only cared for revenue, reduced Apulia to the poverty people still associate with it. But in recent years, government money, better communications, more trade, improved agriculture, the elimination of malaria, and a great aqueduct bringing water to this dry area has transformed Apulia. Buildings and ancient monuments are being restored; unfortunately the *in restauro* sign hangs over many buildings – particularly in Lecce.

To answer those northern sceptics who scorn Apulia, it is easy to over-react and oversell the region. Lecce has been called the 'Florence of the South', and though it is an elegant, refined and quiet city with some extraordinary buildings, it is small and easily seen in a couple of days – not at all like Florence. A week is too short, and a fortnight would not be long enough to see the whole region from spur to heel.

Based in Bari or Trani go by train and bus to King Frederick's castle at Castèl del Monte, the huge dazzling white cathedrals and seaports and beaches up the coast to Barletta, and down the coast to Monópoli. Inland, frequent trains go to Alberobello and Martina Franca and the *trulli* country. Based in Alberobello, you can visit nearby towns such as Locorotondo or Cisternino with their white-walled old centres, almost Greek in appearance. The sea coast is within reach from here as well. (The beaches between Polignano and Monópoli are especially recommended by locals.) A reasonably fast train will take you from Bari down to Lecce.

From Lecce, public transport serves the seaside at San Cataldo, or the walled city of Acáia, and down to the romantic seaport of Ótranto and its nearby grottoes.

In early spring, the countryside in the *murge* is coloured orange with little wild marigolds, pink with almond blossom, and if you walk along the small country roads and step over the verge, you can release an overpowering scent of sweet rocket, a herb much used in Apulian cookery.

Local flavour

The Apulians say that sweet rocket has aphrodisiac powers; try it and see. It has a powerful, pungent smell. Here are two local recipes.

Recchie ai tre colori This is *orecchiette*, the pasta shaped like little ears, cooked with the herb, drained, and then dressed with a fresh tomato sauce, topped with grated pecorino cheese. The three colours of the name are the white cheese, the green rocket and the red tomatoes.

Recchie a ruchetta e patate Recchie cooked with the sweet rocket and baked in layers, with sliced potatoes, garlic, olive oil, and garnished with lightly browned hot peppers.

The centres of these Apulian towns are neat, trim and clean. These parts are not at all the bleak and wicked south of the myth. The unpleasant side of Apulia (and not only for the visitors) is the bag-snatching that goes on in Bari and Barletta. Young lads on mopeds and on foot (*sciappatori*), darting about the narrow streets of the old parts of the town are a hazard to be reckoned with. Put your camera in a tatty string or plastic bag, money in a belt, passport and other precious things out of sight. (All this can be a fattening experience for a woman, but worth it for peace of mind!) Don't miss Bari because of this, though. You can see all the best sights without venturing into the narrow streets of the old city. And in general Apulian people are really friendly and welcoming.

To get to Apulia, Alitalia and British Airways do direct scheduled flights to Bari and Bríndisi from Heathrow and Manchester throughout the year. There is also a flight via Naples. From the beginning of April to the end of October two direct flights fly out of Gatwick to Bari. From May to November, Italy Sky Shuttle run a charter flight on Wednesdays to Bríndisi from Luton.

Cheap flights to Naples are much more frequent throughout the year. Italy Sky Shuttle and Thomson all do flights there from Luton and Gatwick. You could make a two region holiday by spending, say, one week around Naples or down the coast, and then move on to Apulia for another week or so, flying back from Naples. Italy Sky Shuttle's 'open jaw' scheme means you could fly to Naples and then return from Bríndisi.

Coaches leave for Fóggia from the piazza Garibaldi in Naples and there are also good train connections with Fóggia, Bari and Bríndisi. There are main roads which cross Campagna and Basilicata via Potenza and Altamura to Bari. The motorway, A16, cuts right across from Naples to Canosa, from where you can branch north to Fóggia, for the Gargano Peninsula, or south to Bari and Táranto.

Travelling by train to Bari from London's Victoria station will take you about a day and a half, with Lecce about two hours further on. The price will be about the same as the air fare – a little more if you book seats and couchettes all the way there and back.

Apulian specialities   Every town has its local variations, or particular dish, but here are some of the commonest specialities.

Lampasciuni are little wild onions either boiled and used in salads, or often as a dish on their own with other antipasti dishes, charcoal broiled and sometimes in a sweet-sour sauce.

Tiella di funghi A *tiella* is a baked casserole dish (from the Spanish). This is made with sliced potatoes, onions, mushrooms in layers, with oil, garlic and parsley.

Taralli These are little hard but crumbly biscuits, often in a knot shape. They are cooked in boiling water for a second before being baked. They are usually savoury, flavoured with fennel and pepper.

Sgombri all'aceto Cold mackerel which can be preserved in oil in a glass jar. The mackerel is filleted, wrapped in canvas, simmered in salted water 'just long enough to recite the Lord's Prayer'. Then it is drained, covered with vinegar for an hour, and dressed with oil, crushed mint and minced garlic.

Breads The typical large loaf of Apulian bread, weighing $5\frac{1}{2}$ kilograms (12lbs), is called *scanata* in the north. It is made of yeast, hard grain flour, water, salt and boiled potatoes.

Focaccia are flat round buns.

Puddica is made of the same dough, with the surface pitted with little indentations filled with slivers of tomatoes and garlic. Before baking, they are sprinkled with olive oil, salt and oregano.

Focaccio barese is a sort of pizza filled with fried onions, olives, anchovies and ricotta.

Gnemeridde Chitterlings of lamb and kid, sometimes with ham stuffed into entrails, and grilled or stewed in oil, onion, tomatoes and *pecorino*.

Polpette Meat balls, usually baked in tomato sauce, not to be confused with *polipi* or *polipetti* (octopus).

FARM HOLIDAYS IN APULIA

Two state agencies, Agriturismo and Vacanze Verdi (Green Holidays) list reasonably priced rooms and apartments. Their head office is at via G Petroni 23, 70124 Bari, telephone 099/21233. All provide locally grown food and wine and an insight into local life. Most require people to stay for seven nights. Prices vary, average L20,000 per person per night, self-catering. Some examples:

Local cooking classes on a farm, 7km (4¼ miles) from the sea at Salento. English spoken. May to October, 15 day periods. Write to Giovanni De Bene, Loc Cocumola, Minervino de Legge (LE). Telephone 0836/95307. Five camping spaces available.

The Villa Cenci, near Cisternino, is partly a hotel, partly a group of old *trulli*. Apartments and rooms, board and half-board, bicycles, swimming pool. Up to L30,000 per night. April to September. Write to Pietro Bianco, via Verdi 1A, 772015 Fasano (BR). Telephone 080/13668.

On an olive farm, near Galatone, south west of Lecce, 8km (5 miles) from the sea. A country estate with six apartments, 16 camping spaces, and full or half-board. Bicycles, tennis. Write to Maria Grazia Castriota, Masseria 'Lo Prieno', Loc Orelle, 73044 Galatone (LE). Telephone 0833/865443.

Learn about making olive oil near Ostuni. Tennis, riding near by. Seven apartments, nine rooms, six camping spaces. Board and half-board. Stay 10 nights. English spoken. Write to Pasquale Gargasole, Corso Roma 34, 72100 Brindisi. Telephone 0831/222579.

BARI

BUDGET FOR A DAY	
Cappuccino and cornetto	1,800
Visit San Nicola - free	
Buy present of postcard of Apulian scene by local artist	4,000
Lunch	8,000
Return train ticket - BARI to BITONTO	1,700
Lemon tea	700
Dinner in BARI at O.K. Bar	18,000
	L 34,200
plus accommodation	

An active seaport with a fascinating harbour, Bari has an old town of confusing, narrow, higgledy-piggledy streets and a newer area of wide streets laid out on a grid. A walk up tree-lined corso Cavour to the Molo San Nicola on a Sunday morning will take you from 20th-century sophistication to the timeless trade of the coastal fishermen.

The urge to upgrade hotels is particularly strong in Bari, pushed on by the Mondiali (World Cup) in 1990, and an increasing number of business visitors. The Fiera del Levante on the outskirts of town, is a permanent exhibition centre, and something is now going on there every month of the year. Bari is anyway a big city of about

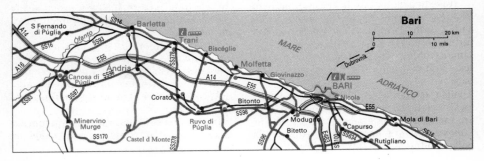

Local flavour

The best baby octopuses – *polipetti* – are caught in the waters off Bari. The Adriatic is very deep here, and apparently very salty, so that the octopuses have a better flavour. First of all they are beaten with a wooden flail. If you go down to the Molo Sant'Agostino on a Sunday morning, you will see the men and boys doing this, as they do all over the Mediterranean. Here in Bari they also dip them over and over again in the sea water, spuming it up through the octopus until the water is foaming and milky. Then they transfer the octopuses to wicker baskets, and the fishermen stand by the stalls endlessly shaking the baskets, and dipping them in water. If you ask them why they do it they may cut a bit off for you to taste. The shaking makes the octopuses curl and probably tenderises them. In any case, raw octopus is very tasty, and not tough and rubbery as it can be when cooked. It is often served as an *antipasto* in an oil and vinegar dressing, or chopped and served with other shellfish, also raw. Is it safe to eat? The writer speaks for herself when she says she has eaten lots of raw octopus and shell fish in Bari, and never come to harm.

Moneysaver

Take a double room at the Pensione Giulia for L45,000 without private bath. Have breakfast at the Café Gran Mokador across the other side of the piazza Umberto, a *cappuccino* and *cornetto*, L1,800, evening meal at the OK Bar round the corner from the via Crisanzio for L10,000. With a walk round the old port, a visit to San Nicola, a free viewing of the Pinacoteca (the Provincial Picture Gallery) and a snack lunch, this could be a fascinating and very inexpensive day. Also treat yourself to a really good ice cream on the corso Cavour and join the evening walk about 6.30pm.

The 12th-century church of San Nicola in Bari – plain but with some ornate carvings

400,000, the capital of Apulia, the principal port for boats to Yugoslavia, and only incidentally a tourist city.

Despite its size, all the sights, the cathedrals, churches, harbour, shops and the train station are within walking distance (not with baggage – but it is on the level). For a pleasant, inexpensive hotel near the station, try the Pensione Giulia, and there are also two more hotels (Hotel Romeo and Hotel Costa) at number 12 via Crisanzio, and the Albergo Serena is at 69 via Imbriani.

To get to number 12 via Crisanzio from the train station, walk up the left hand side of the piazza Moro and turn left when you come to the piazza Umberto (only about 100 metres, 110yds).

Principal sight in Bari is the San Nicola church just inside the old city walls, inland from the Lungomare Augusto. The ancient, flat-roofed buildings around it are topped by a forest of emaciated television aerials. The church itself, built in 1089, severe, basically plain, has lions with curling hair, bulls, birds with hatted human heads and all manner of curious little decorative bits.

The two incongruous towers either side of the façade are later additions. Inside, behind the altar, with its ciborium – altar covering – sheltering it (the oldest in Apulia), is a very special thing – a throne, not very big, supported by little anguished figures desperately trying to hold it up. This is Bishop Elia's throne, carved at the end of the 11th century and a renowned example of Apulian art.

Downstairs in the crypt are the bones of St Nicholas. Also, just down the steps on the right is a red and white column which people touch for luck. Apparently St Nicholas and two angels delivered it in 1089, just in the nick of time when Bishop Elia needed one more column. All the columns down here are different. There's one on the left as you stand facing the altar that has strangely modern-looking semi-abstract carvings – birds in the corner and faces in the middle. Don't miss the mosiac floor, or the marble panels in front of the windows, the light illuminating their patterning.

Back upstairs again, ask to see the Treasury at the beginning of the right aisle – there are many treasures, though the so-called coronation crown of King Roger the Norman was in fact made later.

St Nicholas is the patron saint of Russia, protector of children, scholars, merchants and sailors, and his help is called on by travellers beset by robbers. So it's ironic that his relics should have been stolen by Bari sailors and brought from Asia Minor to Apulia in 1087.

From 7-10 May there are festivities around the port and the church in honour of St Nicholas, with a procession of boats out to sea from the Molo San Nicola.

The Duomo is not far away, but probably more easily approached from the other side of the old city, just up the road from the castle. Don't miss the frieze at the very top, running along the side wall, and a little-pierced stone window on the north side. Underneath the rose window on the south side, some very strange animals jut out of the wall. Inside there is a rose design marble floor, and underneath a recently discovered 9th-century basilica.

The Pinacoteca Provinciale is on the third floor of a grey-and-white towered institutional-looking building on the lungo N Sauro, on the non-harbour side of the Rotonda. Enter round the side, or get to it from the middle of town, along the via Carulli. The Pinacoteca is free, has the best view in Bari of the harbour and bay (left of room 5), and is open on Sunday morning, so you can combine a visit with a walk along the *lungomare* with all the other people in their Sunday best. Things to look out for:

Room 1 – the panel showing St Nicholas' amazing life; a 14th-century Madonna and child in painted wood; 11th-century plaques of winged and smiling lions. In room 3 – St Peter the Martyr (by Giovanni Bellini) standing with a book in one hand and a palm in the other, his head on one side, his look thoughtful as if thinking 'what does the future hold?' The answer could be 'not a lot,' as he also has a knife through the top of his head and another in his heart. There are several rooms of Venetian paintings, including Tintoretto and Veronese, and a display of clothed clay figures from Naples. Finally, there is a special collection of 20th-century Italian paintings, including Morandi, De Chirico, Morvelli, Lega, Campigli and Fattori.

Don't miss a huge 17th-century woodcut (about $2\frac{1}{2}$ metres by $3\frac{1}{4}$ metres, 8ft by 11ft) on cloth by Petrus Wouthers of Arsena. This is an amazing work, a copy of Poussin's *Last Supper*, printed by 30 workers on three presses with 40 different woodcuts. The cloth seems to be in six strips. Not surprisingly the description says, *una scarsissima richiesta causando un rapido fallimento dell' impresa*, which means that this job was so colossal it bankrupted the firm. So perhaps this may be the only one that was made.

Moneysaver

Ask at the desk of the Pinacoteca if they still have the collection of postcards of Apulian scenes by the local artist Michele de Giosa for sale. At L4,000 they are good value, useful for little presents.

The place to walk when shops are open is the via Sporano, a traffic-free street which goes from the centre of the piazza Umberto up to corso Vittorio Emanuele; all the smartest shops, noticeably expensive furs, and fabrics by the metre. Smart young things gather here on Sunday morning in the middle of the street. Look in at the elegant Mincuzzi clothes shop – on a corner, left hand side going up. Also walk up the wide corso Cavour, three blocks away. It's the place for an ice ceam or a drink about 6 or 7pm. Have a look at the Teatro Petrizzelli, the opera house, and at the end of the street there's the Pasticceria Motta for snacks, sweets, *piadine* and more ice creams. English style is all the rage – even in the shoe shops, where you can buy an Italian pair of 'Doc Martin's' (misnamed 'Dock Master's').

There are several restaurants in the area between the piazza Eroi de Mare and corso Cavour. One is the *Pizzorante degli Artisti*, a little *trattoria* upstairs with red chairs, white covers, pictures of Charlie Chaplin, and a large, voluble owner. Very good cold baked peppers and *spaghetti alle vongole*.

Local flavour

Apulia has been a productive wine-growing area since Roman times. There are 13 DOC, controlled *apellation* wines, the *mejri* or first quality:

Aleatico di Púglia There are two reds under this name, both naturally sweet. If aged at least three years the wine will be labelled *Riserva*. Full mellow taste.

Copertino Comes from Lecce province. A red and a rosé. The red is full-bodied, for serving with roast and grilled meat.

Locorotondo A white wine from the *murge*, best after a year. Served with fish dishes.

Matino A dry red and rosé wine from Lecce province. Served with meat and pasta.

Moscato di Trani There are two dessert wines, both naturally sweet, produced in Bari province, from Bitonto and Biscéglie northwards.

Ostuni White Ostuni and red Ottavianella both come from the Ostuni region.

Primitivo di Mandúria A strong red, slightly sweetish wine, produced inland from Táranto.

Local flavour

Apulian cheeses are made from sheep's, goat's and cow's milk, and even still some buffalo's milk from around Fóggia. *Mozzarella* is made from buffalo milk, *mercia* from sheep's milk, *scarmorza* from cow's milk.

Sheep's cheeses are fresh *ricotta* – salted ricotta which is hard, often grated on pasta and called *cacioricotta* – and strong ricotta which is called *scant* in dialect. *Scant* is a hot-tasting cheese used for spreading on bread and pizzas, made by stirring fresh ricotta every day for a month with a wooden spatula, adding a little salt and powdered hot peppers.

Caciocavallo, provola and *provolone* are made from cow's milk, wrapped in a casing shaped like watermelons, or smaller round shapes. *Provolone* has a higher pecentage of fat than *caciocavallo*. The little cheeses are useful to buy for picnics, as they keep moist but don't spread or smell; the taste is very mild.

Burrate are buffalo's milk versions of *caciocavello*.

Pecorino is a hard sheep's cheese which tastes particularly good when it comes from the *murge* meadows, where the lentisk tree grows and gives a peppery taste to the cheese.

There are two inexpensive restaurants in the largo Adua, inland from the *lungomare*. The Poldo, at number 25 is recommended by the Barese (shut Sunday). The Taverna Adua is just along the road at number 18. On the edge of the old city, just opposite the castle, a good fish restaurant with an informal atmosphere is trattoria Al Pescatore. There is an outside grill and shellfish display. Try *insalata di mare* – raw octopus, mussels, clams, squid. Or an *orata*, charcoal grilled. Cover costs L1,500 with complimentary *bruschette* (tomato-covered toast) and olives. Good *torta di noce* (walnut gateau) and *mimosa*, a creamy cake. Shut Mondays. Main dishes are about L13,000.

Around Bari – cathedrals and castles

Apulian Romanesque churches are typically austere, built of dazzling white limestone, with majestic façades. The front is usually divided into three sections, with pilasters, elaborately carved porches to the doors, small, thin rounded windows, usually with a rose window at the apex. The plain surface gains its contrast of light and shade from friezes, blind arcades, arches protruding just a brick or two, carvings, occasionally small sections of mosaic, corbels, all manner of curious animals, birds with human faces, lions and elephants supporting pillars. The outside always repays a very careful walk round, looking high and low. Inside there are usually carved pulpits and bishops' thrones, also crypts with beautifully carved pillars and mosaic floors. The symbols and carvings are an intriguing mixture of Byzantine, Saracen and French.

Even if you easily tire of churches, there are three you should not miss – San Nicola in Bari, for its amazing throne; Trani, for its imposing beauty and situation on the harbour; and Bitonto, because of its elegance and its carvings. Both Trani and Bitonto are easily reached by train from Bari. Also up the coast, on the same rail line as Trani, are Barletta, Biscéglie, Molfetta – probably the next most handsome – and Giovinazzo. All these towns are ports, and as well as the cathedrals, they have great solid Norman castles.

To make a longer tour, if you have a car, drive up the coast from Bari, visiting the ports just mentioned, and at Barletta turn inland to Canosa, which has the oldest bishop's throne in Apulia, and then via Minervino, where there is a panoramic view of Apulia, to Castèl del Monte. Here is the octagonal hunting lodge built for Frederick II, a massive and unique castle. Open 8.30am-7pm. Sundays and holidays 9am-1pm. Nearby is a large restaurant with a few rooms. Ostello de Federico. Closed Mondays. Telephone 0883/83043. Reasonably priced.

A night here would give you time to see the remaining places at leisure. From Castèl del Monte either go to Ándria, a large city with a much restored Gothic cathedral, or straight on to Ruvo di Púglia. Arrive here in good time, because the Museo Jatta, at via Bovio 53, which has a large collection of 5th and 3rd-century BC terracotta vases, is only open from 9am-2pm, shut on Sunday. The cathedral is very fine. From here you reach the last town on the tour (saving one of the best till last), which is Bitonto. And if you arrive in the afternoon, you will find the Museum of Popular Art, the Museo delle Tradizioni Popolari, via Regina Corte 29, is open from 5pm to 8pm every day. Bitonto Cathedral has recently been restored.

ORIENTATION IN BARI

INFORMATION

TOURIST OFFICE
Local Office *piazza Aldo Moro 33A, on the right of the square in front of the railway station. Open Monday-Friday 8.30am-1pm and 4-7pm, Saturday 9-11am. They provide a good map of Apulia with roads and rail, and other maps showing castles, camp sites, grottoes, etc, but rather imprecise.*
Regional Office *corso Italia 15.*
Independent Tourism Office *corso Vittorio Emanuele 68.*
CIT *OFFICE*
Via A Gimma 159 (not much help).
ALBERGO DIURNO
In the piazza Roma, by the train station.
POST OFFICE
Piazza Battisti. Open Monday to Friday 8.30am-8.30pm. Saturday 8.30am-1pm. Postal code 70100.
TELEPHONE
SIP, via Oriani, near the castle. Open daily 8am-9pm. ASST, outside the station on right. Open daily 7am-10pm. Code 080. Many local numbers have recently had a 5 prefixed to them. If you have trouble obtaining a local number, try adding a 5.

TRANSPORT

AIRPORT
Bari-Palese airport is 9km (5½ miles) north. A bus brings passengers into the town centre. The Alitalia air terminal is at via Calefati 37/41.
TRAINS
Piazza Aldo Moro. Bari-Nord, north side of piazza Aldo Moro beside the main station.

ACCOMMODATION

Albergo Serena *via Imbriani 69.* ☎ *080/540263. Going from the direction of the train station towards the old town, turn right halfway up the corso Cavour. Double rooms con bagno, by which they do not necessarily mean a private bath, or even shower, but a basin and bidet, L50,000. Breakfast coffee available.*
Hotel Costa *via Crisanzio 12, 70122 Bari.* ☎ *080/5210006. On the third floor. Bar and small sitting room; good decoration in entrance, not so great in the charmless bedrooms. All rooms have shower, lavatory and hot water (next door's plumbing works well too, by the sound of it). Double room and coffee and chocolate bun for two L86,000, single L45,000 (credit cards accepted, no restaurant).*
Hotel Romeo *via Crisanzio 12, 70122 Bari.* ☎ *080/5216380. Second floor but with an office on the ground floor, charges about the same as the Giulia with no breakfast available, ordinary rooms and unfriendly proprietor. (No credit cards accepted.)*
Pensione Giulia *via Crisanzio 12, 70122 Bari.* ☎ *080/5216630. A room (with three beds) and* shower, lavatory, bidet, basin (all working), with hot water (only one bedside lamp) costs L56,000. The rooms are huge, with vaulted ceilings, some painted plain, some with murals. Full breakfast served in the bedroom is L6,000. There are some curious large spaces for sitting, one with television and two huge long pictures of dogs. The management is friendly and the place clean, but there is no restaurant. Credit cards accepted. Room without bath for two L45,000, single L33,000.

EATING OUT

Pasticceria Motta *corso Cavour, snacks, sweets, ice creams.*
Pizzorante degli Artisti *via G Bozzi 79/81. Open for lunch till 2.30pm then 7.30pm to midnight. Closed Wednesdays.*
Ristorante Il Mulino *via de Giosa 7.*
Ristorante Poldo *largo Adua 25. Shut Sunday.*
Taverna Adua *largo Adua 18.*
Trattoria Al Pescatore *via Federico II di Svevia 10. Shut Mondays.*

ENTERTAINMENT

Pick up a copy of BariSera to see what's on. Bari is a great cultural centre, with several theatres and many cinemas.
Casa di Pulcinella *via G Petroni 16/5, has occasional puppet plays.* ☎ *080/5219974.*
La Dolce Vita *has late-night*

cabaret ('*Roberto Negri, alis Roberto Negri in a performance of comic pantomaim. The new comics come to Sweet Life'* [sic]). Shows start at 9 or 10pm. ☎ *080/226285.*
Teatro Petruzzelli corso Cavour (worth a visit just to see inside) has opera in

January, February, then mixed shows, concerts, ballet, etc. ☎ *080/5241761.*

MUSEUMS
Archaeological Museums
Palazzo Anteneo, part of Bari University in the piazza Umberto. Tuesday-Saturday 9am-2pm. Closed Monday.

Free.
Castle Monday-Saturday 9am-1.30pm and 3.30-7.30pm. Sunday 9am-1pm. L2,000.
Pinacoteca Provinciale via Spalato 19. Tuesday-Saturday. 9.30am-1pm. and 4-7pm. Sunday 9am-1pm. Closed Mondays. Free.

BITONTO

Bitonto is easily reached from Bari, by train from the Bari-Nord station on the north side of piazza Moro, beside the main railway station. Trains leave frequently, the 3.15pm, for instance, will give you time to see the town, returning at 5.23pm, 6.26pm or 7.23pm in time for dinner in Bari. Return ticket L1,700.

Local flavour
At the cathedral look up at the pierced stone windows on the top storey. And just above eye level, on the side, note the little figures like mermaids holding up their divided tails, carved in stone in the windows. Near by, to the right, a stone archbishop seems to be levitating up the wall. The main door has a complete tympanum, unlike San Nicola in Bari. Inside there are elaborately carved capitals, an ambo (pulpit) on the south side, and a handsome crypt.

There is a rather boring 1km ($\frac{5}{8}$ mile) walk from the station to the *centro storico*. Take the main road, via Matteotti in front of the station, walk up to a large crossroads, with an ilex tree-lined square with benches on your left. (All the old men of the town congregate here in the early evening.) Turn right past the ancient arch with a clock, and go straight on, looking at the little old courtyard on your left, and then the doorway of the Biblioteca-Museo. Turn right to the cathedral.

Round behind the cathedral is a little *pizzeria* 'Alla Cattedrale'. From here wander round the narrow streets of the old town. Look for the piazzetta Don Giuseppe Morosin where the end building has a veranda supported on stone heads, opposite the church of San Francesco d'Assisi. There's a decorated arch in the via Maggiore, opposite a convent. But there are lots of interesting things to see. You might pass an old man crocheting a rug from multicoloured wools outside his house, and don't be surprised if an old lady mending a shirt at her front door answers, 'Ciao' to your, 'Buona sera', and holding you with strong hands says 'We are all the same,' and kisses you.

Local flavour
A lemon tea, *té limone*, L700 will refresh you for the walk back to the station.

TRANI

Trains for Trani leave Bari from platforms 2-4 Ovest, along to the end of platform 1 on your right. They are frequent till about 9am, then a gap to midday and 1.27pm, and at roughly hourly intervals thereafter. L5,000 return. (The first workers' train leaves Trani for Bari at 4.49am. No wonder there's a long midday siesta.) An AMET bus goes to Trani from the piazza Eroi del Mare in Bari.

Trani is the prettiest fishing port of this entire stretch. From the station, walk down the via Cavour to the piazza della Repubblica – a tree-arcaded square (with a tourist office). Go straight on and you will reach piazza Plebiscito, then into the public gardens. From both ends of these gardens you will get great views – one southwards towards the Benedictine Abbey of Santa Maria di Colonna.

Local flavour

Just by the entrance to the gardens is the ground-level clock, in green gravel and white pebbles, with the day's date written out. The hands move, it works, with all working parts underground.

From here, walk round the port until you reach the cathedral on the far side, and coming round you will find yourself in a great bare square. If you stand with your back to the sea in the empty square, at midday, looking across the square with the cathedral on your left, the lines and shadows are extraordinary, as if you were in the margin of a De Chirico painting.

Trani's port was built by Venetians in the 14th century, but for centuries before that it was an important seaport – the Crusaders sailed east from here. Among the pilgrims was a young Greek carrying a heavy cross, who only ever uttered two words 'kyrie eleison'. Simple or holy (perhaps both), he was canonised soon after his death in 1094 as San Nicola Pellegrino (the pilgrim), when the people of Trani adopted him as their patron saint and began building a cathedral. (San Nicola Pellegrino has no connection with Bari's San Nicola.)

The cathedral has famous bronze doors, made by the same Barisano who cast the doors at Ravello and Monreale. The cathedral is exceptionally restrained and beautiful both inside and outside. Underneath it there is a Byzantine crypt, and below that a Roman catacomb. The cathedral is open 7am-12 noon and 3-7pm. There's a picture of St George and the Dragon in the crypt.

Near the cathedral, around the via Ognissanti, is the old town, several more churches, the castle and vestiges of a medieval Jewish community.

In a big, handsome grey and white stone Palazzo Quercia (1755), facing the harbour, is the trattoria La Darsena, offering pasta in cuttle-fish ink sauce and pesce alla griglia (grilled fish). Full meal and wine L40,000; shut Monday.

Trani is very short of hotels in the centre of town. New ones are now being built, but mostly on the edge. The Royal is a three-star hotel not far from the train station. The tourist office lists two other three-star hotels, the Capirro and the Riviera.

Moneysaver

For inexpensive accommodation which could be a useful base for a short touring holiday, especially with children, try the Pensione Lucy. It is opposite the Villa Comunale, down near the port. Signora Lucia has 13 rooms, all with cooking facilities. The rooms are large and clean, with bath. Prices vary from L65,000 for couples, L80,000 for four, up to one costing L120,000 for six people. This is virtually an apartment on the top floor with access out on the roof and views across the bay to the cathedral (floodlit at night). Open all year. Regulars book from year to year, so enquire early, though out of season should not be a problem.

There is no restaurant at the Pensione Lucy, but the Trattoria Emanuela near the port, with its distinctive yellow and white parrots outside, serves good local food (shut Wednesday). Signora Lucia speaks no English herself, but her daughter does, and she can cope with letters in English. It's possible to reach the Gargano Peninsula from here, but you would have to stay the night.

On 3 May, the Festa della Santa Croce, there is a procession of boats out to sea. The first Sunday in August is the feast day of San Nicolas the Pilgrim.

Local flavour
The fishing boats come in and out about 6pm in the evening and around 7-8am in the morning. There is a beach near by.

ORIENTATION IN TRANI

INFORMATION
TOURIST OFFICE
Piazza della Repubblica,
☎ 0883/43295. Also at via Cavour 83, Trani 70059,
☎ 0883/41126.

ACCOMMODATION
Capirro ☎ 0883/46912.

Pensione Lucy piazza Plebiscito 11.
☎ 0883/41022.
Riviera ☎ 0883/43222.
Royal not far from the train station. ☎ 0883/588010.

EATING OUT
Trattoria La Darsena via Statuti Marittimi 98.
☎ 0883/47333. Shut Monday.

Trattoria Emanuela near the port.

SHOPPING
Market Day Tuesday, but there are regular fish and vegetable markets on weekday mornings at the end of via Ognissanti. There are shows of local handicrafts in August, particularly woodwork.

CENTRAL APULIA

BUDGET FOR A DAY

Return train ticket - BARI to ALBEROBELLA (1 hour 10 minutes)	4,700
See trulli houses and have lunch	20,000
Look at locally made knotted shawls (prices vary so shop around)	
Snack supper in BARI	7,000
	L 31,700
plus accommodation	

The following are some suggested outings to the grottoes at Castellana, to Alberobello and the trulli area.

By train, from the last track of the central station at Bari, on the Ferrovia del Sud-Est line trains go to Castellana Grotte, Alberobello (1 hour 10 minutes), Locorotondo, Martina Franca ($1\frac{1}{2}$ hours, L4,700) and on to Táranto. Trains leave every two to three hours between 7.15am and 9.30pm.

By bus, Sud-Est pullman coaches leave via Caldarola in Bari for Conversano, Castellana, Alberobello. The firm of Viaggi Bocuzzi, via Sparano 143, Bari (telephone 080/219033) run coach tours, but they are expensive – L30,000 for a day tour of Castellana and Alberobello. But there is about a $3\frac{1}{4}$km (2 mile) walk from the station at Castellana to the grotto, so you might think it worthwhile. They also do a trip down to Lecce and the Zinzulusa grotto – L60,000.

It would be cheaper for a group of four to hire a car for a few days to potter around the region, giving yourself the freedom to make longer trips, including the pottery town of Grottáglie, the troglodyte dwellings at Massafra, Castellaneta and Matera to see the sassi, buildings cut into the rocks.

Local flavour
Rudolph Valentino, the silent-movie star, was born in Castellanata in 1895. Apulians are very proud of him. There's a Bar Rudy, and a barber's shop called Basette di Valentino, meaning Valentino's side-whiskers.

They have a statue of him, naturally.

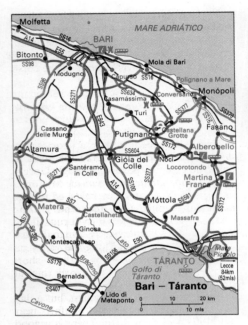

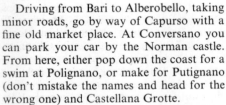

Bari – Táranto

The caverns of the Castellana grottoes

Leaving the grotto, on the road towards Alberobello before the car park, there's a cheese-making dairy on your right, where you can see them making *provolone*.

The prettiest road from here is cross-country, not via Putignano. The road meanders through fields of almond and cherry trees.

ALBEROBELLO

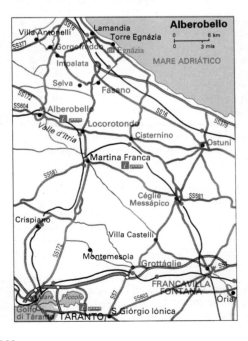

Driving from Bari to Alberobello, taking minor roads, go by way of Capurso with a fine old market place. At Conversano you can park your car by the Norman castle. From here, either pop down the coast for a swim at Polignano, or make for Putignano (don't mistake the names and head for the wrong one) and Castellana Grotte.

The Castellana grottoes are a whole series of remarkable underground caverns (110 steps and a lift up). There are gold and yellow stalactites and stalagmites, like long twisting curtains of orange alabaster. The caves are well lit, but not cheap; an hour's trip costs L10,000; children from six to 14, L8,000. A longer trip is about 3km (2 miles) and takes two hours, ending up at the small but delicate White Grotto. L20,000, children L18,000. (It's always 15 degrees Celsius underground.) Short trips start at 8.30am, and then every hour till 7pm. The long trip (to the Grotta Bianca) goes on the hour from 9am-12 noon and 3-6pm. From August 1-31, a special nightly tour leaves at 9pm, but they sometimes change times.

Centre of the *trulli* country, trains and buses link Alberobello with Bari, the Valle d'Itria, Martina Franca, Lecce and Táranto.

There are thousands of the little cone-shaped *trulli* in Alberobello, especially on the encampment covering the whole of one hillside, the Rione Monti. It's a tourist centre hosting bus loads of trippers. But up in the town if you walk about or stay a night or two you'll discover a quiet, almost vespa-free zone, where *trulli* are mixed up with new buildings.

Cone-shaped trulli houses in Alberobella

Local flavour
Until 1797, when the citizens finally got their freedom, no one in Alberobello was allowed to build a house with mortar, only dry stone on stone. After that, the *trulli* were such a reminder of their feudal poverty, that by 1875 laws forbade anyone building a house without mortar! Now the *trulli* are a national monument, and new buildings have to be in keeping.

A good place to stay is the Lanzillotta, right in the centre, on piazza del Popolo. (Entrance is round the corner). Simple, pleasant rooms, with balconies looking over the town, a lift; everything works, including the heating. The tourist office is in this piazza, and, just off it going down the hill is a restaurant with rooms above, Da Miniello Ideal Riposo – a small place with a big name. Some rooms have a shower, verandah and view across to the Rione Monti.

Explore the old houses in the Rione Monti area, and on the town side, the Aia Piccola area. The Sovrano is a two-storeyed *trullo*, up behind the big church (SS Meddici Cosima e Damiano) at the end of the corso Vittorio Emanuele.

In the countryside, the uplands behind the Rione Monti are worth exploring on foot. Cross over the main A14 road which goes to Noci, and follow the small roads.

Around Alberobello   For a short scenic drive from Alberobello, take the road to Selva di Fasano, passing through Gorgo-freddo, Impalata (even a roadside Madonna in a *trullo* here), though fields of orange marigolds, lupins, oak trees and grazing cattle. After Torterella the road runs along the rim of the hill with views down to the sea. At Fasanno turn back along the valley on SS172d to Locorotondo or make a short detour to the coast, to see the Greek ruins at Egnázia.

Not exactly typically Apulian, but a day out for the children, the Zoosafari, near Fasano is well signposted. There is a good variety of animals and amusements, and a restaurant. Open every day, 31 March to 30 September (October to December, closed Tuesday) 9.30am (varies slightly) till sunset. Car plus two people L15,000; extra passenger L5,000; children under four free.

Locorotondo is a hilltop town (accessible by train) with wonderful views from the Villa Comunale over the Itria valley, with its little gnome-domed *trulli*, across to Martina Franca. Wander about the immaculate white-washed streets, bedecked with flowers; don't miss the little Chiesa Greca.

A short train ride will take you to Martina Franca, an elegant 18th-century town, well worth a visit. In the triangular piazza Roma is a ducal palace designed by Bernini. Follow the via Vittorio Emanuele past graceful townhouses to the rococo church, a curved colonnade, and also La Tavernetta at number 30, for reasonably priced local food. The old men sit out in the evening in the central piazza XX Settembre (park your car here). Shops are closed on Thursday evening.

The tourist office is in piazza Roma.

Lean over the terrace in the via Pergolesi, outside the town walls for a marvellous view.

The Festival of the Itrian Valley here, at the end of July, hosts international opera, concerts and recitals.

You can make a round trip by car via Locorotondo to Cisternino, a little white-washed hill town with a rather Greek feel, and on to another hill town, Ostuni if you have time. Otherwise turn south via Céglie Messápico to Francavilla Fontana. Park by the castle and walk round to the cathedral square. From Francavilla turn west for about 12km (7½ miles) to Grottáglie, strongly recommended for anyone interested in ceramics.

Grottáglie is the ceramic centre of Apulia. A dozen or more ceramic workshops are tucked into grottoes in the hill near the castle, freely open for visitors to wander.

A 3ft painted majolica wine container from Grottáglie's ceramic workshops

Return by Martina Franca, and instead of going through Locorotondo again, take the country road west through peaceful countryside.

Moneysaver
Have a good look round first, then buy little hand-painted dishes straight from the artist (L5,000). Or buy from source storage pots and dishes which are dispatched from here (from the Gaetano Fasano workshops especially) to Liberty, Harrods and other fashionable London shops.

Moneysaver
And weightsaver . . . it is quite in order, if you are eating another course, to ask for half portions of the pasta. This is quite normal. *La metà = half. Mezza porzione*= half-portion.

Local flavour
The shop at via Pasubio 1 sells olive oil from insecticide-free olives. They also rent *trulli* in the country. Write to C da Lama Colonna 5, 1-70011 Alberobello. Telephone 080/725762. L40,000 for two per night. English spoken.

Local flavour
Capocollo, a kind of salami from Martina Franca, is renowned. The meat is pickled for ten days, washed in wine, spiced with peppercorns, dried and smoked over burning oak twigs.

Another tasty delicacy is *spiedo martinese*, pieces of lamb, baby goat, chunks of veal and slices of sausage spit roasted together over an oak or holm oak fire.

The local white wine Martina Franca or Martina is good. A DOC wine.

Local flavour
Traditional designs: extraordinary 1 to 1⅓-metre (3 to 4ft) high painted majolica figures, men with brigand-moustaches, women with large bare breasts and dangling earrings, exuberantly painted in yellow, greens and blues. Legless(!), they are wine containers, traditionally given as wedding presents. Also find 1⅔ metre (5ft) high brown pots (*capasumi*) typical fighting cock designs and little whistles shaped like cats and cockerels.

ORIENTATION IN ALBEROBELLO

INFORMATION
PRO LOCO
Piazza del Popolo. ☎ 080/
721916. For hotels, etc.
COUNCIL OFFICE
Next door, upstairs, for
leaflets and advice.
☎ 080/721008.
POST OFFICE
Piazza XXVII Maggio.
Postal code 70011.
PUBLIC TELEPHONE
Central Bar, piazza Di
Vagno 8. Telephone code
080.
PUBLIC LAVATORIES
Alberobello must have the
most fragrant lavatory in
southern Italy – in a small
house surrounded by flowers
in the largo Martellotta,
facing the Rione Monti.
L200.

TRANSPORT
BUSES
Sud-Est buses go to Bari
and Táranto. Autolinee
Lentini services go to the sea
at Monópoli (25km, 15½
miles) from the piazza del
Popolo. Laneve buses go
from here too; Lucarella go
from the piazza XXVII
Maggio, near by.

ACCOMMODATION
Pensione Lanzillotta piazza
Ferdinando IV 31. ☎ 080/
721511. Double bed and
breakfast L60,000. Dinner
L16.000. Genuine local food.
Pensione Miniello via
Balenzano 14. ☎ 080/
721188. L40,000 double.
Tourist menu in restaurant.
CAMPING
At Bosco Selva, signposted.
South of the Rione Monti.

EATING OUT
L'Agora piazza Curri 3.
Apulian food, including
home-made pasta. Meal
about L22,000.
Il Guercio di Puglia largo
Martellotta. ☎ 080/721816.
Terrace. Good cooking but
not cheap, about L18,000-
L20,000. Closed Wednesday
in winter.

SHOPPING
Almost every house in Rione
Monti seems to sell
something. The knotted
shawls, made on a wooden
frame, are unique to
Alberobello. Prices vary.

LECCE

Trains go about every hour to Lecce from
Bari, trundling through fields lined with dry
stone walls, containing olive trees, artichokes, peas, beans, tomatoes, interspersed
with vineyards and dotted with almond trees.
The fortunata terra di Púglia, the lucky land
of Apulia, the poet Dante called it.

Prosperous in Roman times, a powerful
city under the Normans, Lecce went into
decline until the Spanish rule in the 17th
century, when its architects and builders
blossomed. They built churches and palaces
in exuberant style, with twisting pillars, little
cherubs (putti), flowers, fruit and figures in
profusion. The golden limestone the sculp-
tors carved was so soft, that as you pass some
of the town walls you can pick shells out of
the crumbling stone – one reason why so
many buildings in Lecce are always under
repair. Just when Sir Christopher Wren was
building in England, Guiseppe Zimbalo
(nicknamed Zingarello, the gipsy), was going
a little crazy in Lecce, designing some of the
most extravagant and flamboyantly decorated churches in town.

Lecce is a very civilised university city with
a strange absence (after Bari) of lurking
youths and screaming vespas. You can walk
the streets with ease; the mobile street cleaner
is everywhere, with his four bins and his long
and short besoms. All the interesting old part
of town is within easy walking distance.

Local flavour
Sample Gran liquore San Domenico, an
ancient recipe liqueur made by friars at
the San Domenico convent. Flavoured
with angelica, calamus, coriander,
cardamom, mint, it's strong stuff. Also try
the aperitif, Amaro San Domenico. Padre
Peppe is another stiff and godly brew, an
elixir of walnuts.

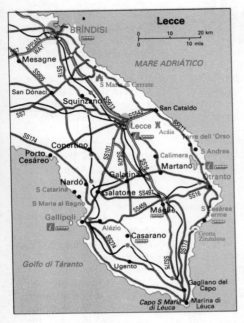

babies the other) with a great spread of *antipasti*. Up the end of this road is the castle, built in 1539 round an old Norman centre, and skirting round it to the left you will arrive at the centre of town, the piazza Sant' Oronzo.

This is the most mixed-up square in southern Italy. Below lies a Roman amphitheatre; the column next to it once marked the end of the Appian Way in Bríndisi. There is a Baroque chapel, a palazzo, a former town hall called the Sedile (16th-century) which houses the tourist office, and, bringing it all up to date, a mammoth National Insurance Building and rooftop Coca-Cola sign.

Detail of the exuberant façade of Lecce's famous church, Santa Croce

From the train station walk up viale Oronzo Quatra, and on your right you will soon pass the Grand Hotel, highly recommended, even though it is a bit of a walk into the town centre. This is good value, with style, spacious rooms and a courtyard restaurant. Continuing on, turn right at the lights into viale Gallípoli, which will bring you to the Museo Provinciale on your left, a beautifully laid out museum which belies its provincial location. What look at first sight like Greek vases were made in Apulia in the 5th century (known as Gnathian, from the Greek colony at Egnázia). The remarkable collection includes bronze buckets, fish plates, unique high-handled jugs (Messapian).

Turn left at the crossroads, up the wide viale Francesco Lo Re (take the opportunity to peer through gateways on the left at some exotic Moorish villas), and when you reach the ancient archway (Porta San Biagio) on your left, turn into the old city. Two turnings further go right into the via Marine Brancaccio past the Gambero Rosso, a popular local *trattoria* (television one end, wives and

Turn down the via Templari, past the Bar della Borsa, and there on your right is the most famous church in Lecce – the Santa Croce, decorated with what looks like royal icing. Built between 1548 and 1646, it is a riot of fruit and figures and little fat cupids. Restoration was completed in March 1990. Next to it, look at the Palazzo Governo, once a monastery, and the 16th-century Convento dei Celestini. Note the capitals.

Moneysaver
Next to the church of Santa Maria buy *pizzo* and *puccia* – black olive bread and pizza-bread with tomato, a local speciality, tasty and filling. In the Bar della Borsa try hot chocolate, so solid you must eat it with a spoon.

Behind here, the public gardens are open till 9.30pm, with bands and open-air concerts in the summer. Further north, on the via Manfredi, the Chiesa Sant' Anna is worth seeing for its wooden ceiling, paintings, and papier mâché Madonna.

From in front of the Santa Croce, walk towards the Hotel Patria (good, reasonable restaurant here, double room with bath L75,000) turn left into the piazza and then straight ahead and left again into via Rubichi. A permanent exhibition of local crafts is open here 10am-1pm and 4.30-8pm, closed Sunday. Rather pricey, but it shows the scope of Lecce's specialities: papier mâché figures (*cartapesta*), wrought iron, baskets, copper and pottery.

Stroll down via Emanuele (west of piazza Sant' Oronzo) in the evening to mingle with the smart people and window-shop at the elegant stores. After Chiesa Sant' Irene on your right, there's a great food shop, Panetteria Valentina, on the corner of via Archiv Petronelli. Local delicacies include quince cheese (*cotognata*), figs and almonds covered in chocolate and, at Easter, lambs made of almond paste.

The piazza Duomo, to the left, is a square with only one opening, (which is something of a rarity). The Palazzo del Vescovo, the Bishop's Palace, next to the cathedral, is a wonderful building but may be under scaffolding. In the Palazzo del Seminario, on your right, is a Baroque well set in a courtyard of orange and lemon trees, don't miss it, (open 7am-1pm, and 4-7.30pm).

At the end, towards Porta Rudiae, the old city gate, is the church of San Rosario, Zimbalo's last work. It should be restored by now; at the time of writing it was full of scaffolding; pigeons cooing and sitting on angels' heads, flying about the twisting encrusted columns and riding on winged lions. Through the gate turn left, and left again, and you are back in viale Gallípoli, full circle.

Around Lecce   Ótranto is a fishing town and port, once the capital of Byzantine territory in Apulia. It is an hour by train from Lecce, L5,000 return, change trains at Máglie. It has beaches near by, up and down the coast at Sant' Andrea and Torre dell' Orso. The tourist office, on largo Cavour, helps with rooms and Agritourist lodgings, and there is another tourist office at via Basilica 8, near the duomo.

Hotels to try are:

Albania   via San Francesco di Paola 10, telephone 0836/81183. Small, new, with parking.

Il Gabbiano   telephone 0836/81251, L50,000 with bath.

Albergo Ester   via Giovanni XXIII 19. Telephone 0836/84169.

Santa Cesárea Terme is a seaside resort with spectacular coastline; two buses a day go from via Adua in Lecce. Just along the coast is the Zinzulusa grotto – a sea cave with stalagmites.

Gallípoli is an old port, with nearby beaches on the west side of the peninsula (Santa Maria al Bagno and Santa Catarina). From Lecce go by train (every half hour) or bus, both journeys take about an hour and cost L3,200.

The tourist office, corso Roma 225, next to piazza Fontana Greca, is open Monday to Friday.

If you have a car, north east of Lecce 14km (8¾ miles) lies Santa Maria di Cerrate, with an intriguing museum housed in old buildings showing oil-mills, restoration techniques and local traditions. Open 9.30am-

1pm, 3.30-7pm (5.30pm in winter), closed Monday. From here drive down the coast, past many beaches, to Ótranto, and continue round the coast to visit the grottoes at Romanelli and Zinzulusa.

Local flavour

An alternative route inland between Lecce and Ótranto goes via Martano. At Calimera there is a first-aid centre for animals (part of the Natural History Museum). All kinds of animals are looked after here, and children might enjoy this. The old deserted and ruined castle of Acáia is in this area.

Archaeology buffs should stop off at Alézio, a few kilometres due east, inland from Gallípoli, to see the museum and archaeological park devoted to the mysterious early settlers, the Messapians. Open 8am-12 noon and 4.30-6.30pm, 1 May to 30 September. Other months it opens 8am-12 noon and 2-4pm. Near by at Monte d'Elia is a necropolis (6th to 2nd century BC).

Local flavour

Festivals

May 2-6 Festival of S Irene and della Croce.

May 19-21 Flower festival.

June 8-10 Bread festival.

July 25 SS Giacomo and Fillippo.

August 6-13 Chess tournament.

August 24-26 Feasts in honour of SS Oronzo, Giusto and Fortunato.

September Wild chicory festival.

November 5 Bread festival, te lu paniere.

December 13 feast of S Lucia.

ORIENTATION IN LECCE	

INFORMATION

TOURIST OFFICE

In the Sedile, piazza Sant'

Oronzo. Open Monday to Friday, 9am-1pm and 5.30-7.30pm. Saturday, 9am-1pm. ☎ 0832/46458. Staff here are very conscientious, and they have a good town

map showing the churches and palazzos.

POST OFFICE

Via F Cavallotti 4. Postal code 73100.

PUBLIC TELEPHONES

SIP, at corner of via San Nicola and via degli Studenti, outside the Porta Nápoli. Open daily 8.15am-8.30pm. Telephone code 0832.

TRANSPORT

If you only want to visit this Southern part of Apulia, Bríndisi is the nearest airport with direct charter and scheduled flights from the UK. Main-line trains connect with Bari and Fóggia to the north, Francavilla Fontana, Grottáglie and Táranto to the west, and Lecce to the south.

TRAINS
Piazza stazione, at the end of viale Oronzo Quarta. FS mainline trains go north; Ferrovie del Sud-Est go around the peninsula.

BUSES
On via Adua, parallel to via Táranto, just outside the west walls, for Casarano, Gallípoli, Máglie, Ótranto.

On viale U Foscolo, 41/c for Bari, Bríndisi, Fóggia, Táranto.

CAR HIRE
The tourist office recommend Antonio

Miraglia, Corte dei Guarini 12, ☎ 0832/26167. Also, Maggiore, via Táranto 76, ☎ 0832/20184.

ACCOMMODATION

Grand Hotel *viale O Quarta 28, near the train station. ☎ 0832/29405. Double L75,000 with bath. L52,000 without. L5,000 breakfast per person, or about L2,000 coffee and cornetto at the bar. Dinner L18,000.*
Hotel Patria Touring *piazza G Riccardi 13. ☎ 0832/29431. Double L75,000 with bath. L64,000 with WC. L7,500 breakfast per person.*
Hotel Capello *via Montenegrappa 4, to left of station. ☎ 0832/28881. Double L50,000, single L33,000. Breakfast at bar downstairs. Decent but basic.*
Soggiorno Faggiano *via Cavour 4, near the post office. ☎ 0832/42854. Reputed to be cheap and ramshackle.*

EATING OUT

Gambero Rosso *via M Brancaccio 16. ☎ 0832/41569. Inexpensive.*
Gambrino *piazza G Riccardi*

13, opposite the Santa Croce. The restaurant of the Hotel Patria. ☎ 0832/29481. Reasonably priced. Shut Sunday.
Snak Bar *via Salvatore Trinchese, off the piazza Sant' Oronzo. Inexpensive sit-down and take-away food.*
Trattoria Lu Turcinieddhu *via Duca degli Abruzzi, off the via Cairoli, a continuation (across the via Gallípoli) of the via O Quarta. ☎ 0832/20513. Good value, pasta and pizza. Closed Thursday.*

ENTERTAINMENT

Lecce has several theatres, with plays, opera seasons in February and March and a choice of cinemas with recent US and British films (dubbed). The cheapest ticket for the opera is about L8,000. Consult the tourist office about shows, films, music and spectacles they put on in July and August, the Estate Musicale Leccese. The first week-end in July, the Liros Society sponsors dance and drama in the beautiful floodlit piazza Duomo (☎ 0832/27007).

Local flavour
Far from being out on a limb, Lecce is so up to date that they recently put on (in Italian translation) a new play by the British dramatist Michael Frayn, a month *before* its premiere in London!

Local flavour
Apulian appetisers:
Fave frite Broad beans fried in hot oil.
Bruschette Toasted bread brushed with garlic, salt and olive oil.
Fricio Short strips of pastry.

GARGANO PENINSULA

Promontorio del Gargano

Local flavour

Feasts and festivals around the Gargano area:

February 14 Vico Gargánico. St Valentine's day, orange festival.

Good Friday Celebrations all over, but especially torch processions at San Marco in Lamis and singing at Vico Gargánico.

April 23 St George's Day. Oxen races at Peschici. Tournaments, bands, fireworks on the Scialara beach at Vieste.

May 7-10 Processions from Vieste to the sanctuary at Merino. Fireworks etc.

May 8 Pilgrimage to the sanctuary at Monte Sant' Ángelo.

June 24 Feast of San Giovanni at San Giovanni Rotondo.

July 20 Feast of Our Lady of the Light at Mattinata.

September 16 Nightwatch and procession at Monte Sant' Ángelo.

The Gargano Peninsula is a promontory of hills, shady forests (the Foresta Umbra), unspoilt countryside, but above all, of wonderful coast and beaches. To explore it, especially the interior, you need a car. But the fishing villages and sandy shores to the north are accessible by train and bus. Don't come in August if you can avoid it, but during other months the Gargano is ideal to camp, bathe, lie in the sun and visit the Trémiti islands to the north.

To visit the north coast, take the train from San Severo (on the main line north west of Bari) up to Rodi Gargánico, and then the bus to Péschici and Vieste. For the south take the train from Fóggia to Manfredónia and then buses to Monte Sant' Ángelo.

Manfredónia is an unattractive place, but from here you should unmake the bus trip (half an hour, L2,600 return) up to the ancient town of Monte Sant' Ángelo. This holds the Santuario di San Michele, a famous pilgri-

mage site, where, according to tradition, St Michael the Archangel left his red cloak after appearing to the shepherds. (Open daily 8am-12 noon and 3-8pm). Don't wear shorts to visit, or you'll be turned away.

Northwards from here by car, drive into the Foresta Umbra, a wonderfully peaceful place except on Sunday, when almost the whole of Fóggia seems to come here to picnic.

Ferries go round the coast from Manfredónia to Vieste and Rodi Gargánico, and from there to the islands, but the easiest way to the islands is to go by train from San Severo and stay at Rodi Gargánico or Péschici for day trips out to the two main islands, San Dómino and San Nicola. Ferries run from 1 June to 15 September daily from Péschici (11.10am, L18,000), Rodi Gargánico (11.55am, L14,000) and twice daily from Vieste (9am and 10.05am, L27,000). Both islands have sandy coves and little inlets with clear green water. Take a picnic with you, since restaurants and food shops are expensive.

If you are touring by car, you will be able to visit the quieter coast south of Vieste. Vieste itself, though popular in high summer, is still a picturesque whitewashed village. Round the coast, dip down into small craggy bays such as Cala di San Felice and Cala Sanguinára, until you reach Mattinata, a little Greek-looking town piling up the hillside.

From here turn inland to Monte Sant' Ángelo. West again on route SS272, about 19km (11¾ miles) farther, is San Giovanni Rotondo, another sacred place of pilgrimage for Apulians. Padre Pio, who bore the

stigmata of Christ, lived and died here.

Apulia's fish, vegetables and fruit are part of a healthy diet. All over Italy though, pasta forms the base of many dishes – there are some 200 shapes with maybe 600 different names

ACCOMMODATION

FÓGGIA
Hotel Asi via Monfalcone 1. ☎ 0881/23327.
PÉSCHICI
Morcavello via Marina 6. ☎ 0884/94005.
Péschici via S Martino 31. ☎ 0884/94195.
La Pineta via Libetta 77. ☎ 0884/94126.
Pensione Graziella corso

Garibaldi 17. ☎ 0884/94033.
RODI GARGÁNICO
Albano via Scalo Marittimo. ☎ 0884/95138.
Delle Fave via Trieste. ☎ 0884/95185.
MANFREDÓNIA
Albergo San Michele via degli Orti 10. ☎ 0884/21953.
VIESTE
Albergo Lido via Silvia Pellico 17. ☎ 0884/76709.
Hotel Merinum lungo Mare Enrico Mattei. ☎ 0884/76721.
Outside the town on road

SS89 towards Fóggia
Posta del Falco Hotel and restaurant. ☎ 0884/33634.
CAMPING
There are literally hundreds of camp sites round the coast, and you should have no difficulty in finding space. There are at least 80 around Vieste alone, on pine-covered headlands. You are not *allowed* to pitch a tent on the islands.
Remember, an International Camping Carnet may be required.

SICILY AND THE AEOLIAN ISLANDS

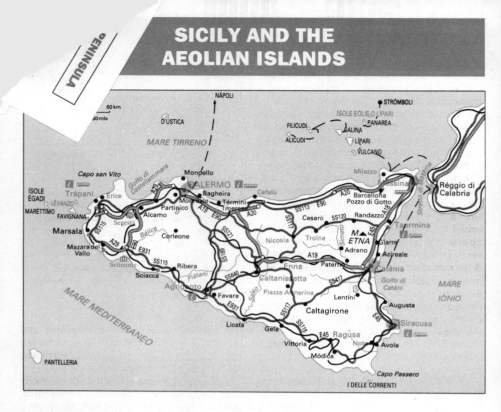

Sicily is the largest region of Italy, 25,708sq km (9,926sq miles), five million inhabitants, and there is much to see. Don't expect to 'do' it all in a week or even a fortnight. The places which escape you this time will give a good excuse to come again and explore a different corner.

Sicily is an awkward shape for the visitor – the plum sights are many, and spread out all around the island. There is an embarrassment of riches for the sightseer, (but also of poverty among the populace). A tour of just the classical sites, for example, would take you from Taormina in the north east (spectacular Greek theatre), south to Syracuse (Siracusa) (once a Greek colony, rival to Athens), north west to Piazza Armerina (floor after floor of lively Roman mosaics), south to Agrigento (acres of Greek temples), up the south west coast to Selinunte (another Greek site, still being excavated), and on to Segesta (one remarkable temple and amphitheatre). And that is only one aspect of Sicily.

The principal towns are connected by frequent and comfortable buses (buses here cost about the same as trains). Trains go round the coast, but are slower and less reliable towards the interior. Special coach trips, of which there are many, including round-the-island tours, are much more expensive. Based at Palermo, or Taormina or Catánia, it is quite possible to take a coach trip to the other side of the island in one day, but it would mean a very early start. It would perhaps be better either to hire a car, or divide your holiday between centres, exploring the vicinity by local buses.

Motorways cross the centre of the island, linking Catánia with Palermo and Cefalù and Trápani. These are free and a pleasure to drive on, with wonderful views. The eastern stretch (toll) from Catánia up to Messina and round to Milazzo goes through more built-up country, but has some spectacular coastal views (takes about one hour, tolls L4,500). Both motorways stop short of, and do not bypass, Palermo or Catánia, leaving the driver in the thick of city traffic. The rest of the projected linking motorways are still only dotted lines on the map, and in reality are stretches of long-abandoned concrete overgrown with weeds – not a promising sight. Driving in Palermo is hair-raising.

Local flavour
Lorries piled high with lemons, decorated three-wheeler trucks loaded with white garlic, prickly pears (*fico d'india*, Indian figs, the Sicilians call them), smoking chemical works, Serpotta's white sculptures, Palermo's black *palazzi*, purple bougainvillaea, clear blue seas are typical sights of Sicily.

Important: be sure to lock your car in Palermo, and don't leave anything you value visible. Also hide money, bags and cameras. Although other towns (notably Taormina) do not demand the same vigilance, never tempt fate or a thief.

Sicily has been colonised and fought over for thousands of years by the Greeks, the Romans, the Normans, the Arabs, the Spanish and the French right up to the second World War, when it was bombed and fought over again. Palermo and Trápani in particular suffered badly, and have still not been rebuilt. Mount Etna has added its own brand

Local flavour
Sicily has difficulty keeping the alcohol percentage of its wines low enough because of the intense sun! Good wines to try include:
Duca del Castèlmonte – white and rosé, slightly sparkling
Toree Salsa – smooth mellow red
Rapitala – red, white, rosé
Settesoli – also **Feudo dei fiori, Bonera** and **Settesoli Faustus** – typical red and white
Nube Tonda – rich ruby red
Regaleali – slightly sparkling white
Corvoa, Duca di Salaparuta – red and white
Donnafegata – white

of upheaval, with volcanic eruptions and earthquakes. The people are poor, and it is a shocking place. So be prepared for surprises, both pleasant and unpleasant.

Except for an area around Catánia, Sicily is a mountainous country. It's all hills, giddying winding roads and sudden startling views. On the whole the interior is sparcely cultivated, long deforested, with bare rocks, remote tiny peasants' huts and occasional hill-towns hideously defaced with half-finished concrete buildings straggling up the hillsides. These are the ready-made modern ruins of Sicily, courtesy of the Mafia: the result of government money for rebuilding mysteriously disappearing before the walls managed to cover the skeletal rooms. Everything is rough, craggy, old, dusty, peeling. The centres of the old towns are claustrophobic, twisting, narrow, decaying. It gets very hot in summer, and the fields parch, and the old town streets cluster for shade. Come in spring, if you can, when the countryside is astonishingly covered with wild flowers – a mosaic of purple vetches, orange marigolds, yellow and white daisies and orchids.

However, some of the countryside is quite different – around the lower slopes of Etna, where the volcanic soil makes orange and lemon groves grow in profusion, everything

239

seems to grow luxuriantly. Between Palermo and Trápani there are green fields and trees and many crops. Up in the hills, behind Palermo and Cefalù, agriculture flourishes with vines and cattle. While down south, around Agrigento, the landscape is the barest, most remote of all.

The best beaches and the clearest waters are around the Aeolian Islands (Ísole Eólie) to the north, and at Capo san Vito on the western tip. Sicily is not renowned for its beaches, but Cefalù has good sand, the little island of Lévanzo, in the Egadean Islands (Ísole Égadi) has lovely small bays, and there are resorts within striking distance of Palermo and Taormina.

An ideal grand tour of Sicily would include Palermo, the Gulf of Castellammare, Segesta, Érice, Selinunte, Agrigento, Piazza Armerina, Ragusa, Noto, Syracuse, Catánia, Taormina, Etna, the Aeolian Islands, Cefalù, with excursions, time permitting, to Lévanzo in the Egadean Islands, and round Etna. All of these can be reached by public transport. But cutting across the island, for instance from Selinunte to Taormina, could take nine hours by train and bus. Sicily has nine provinces, and most transport goes to their capitals: Syracuse, Catánia, Ragusa, Trápani, Agrigento, Enna, Caltanissetta, Messina and Palermo. Catánia and Palermo are principal focuses for buses and trains.

> **Moneysaver**
> Buy the ACI (Automobile Club d'Italia) map of Sicily. On one side is an excellent map of the island, while on the back are town maps, maps of the smaller islands, routes and sights – almost a guidebook in itself.

The two main tours here are centred on Palermo and Taormina, one a hectic metropolis, the other a sort of Sicilian Shangri-la, with Trápani or Érice and the Aeolian Islands as other options. To get here you could try using Italy Sky shuttle charters, fly into Palermo and out of Catánia or vice

versa. Or, arriving by boat from Naples at Palermo harbour (the only way to see that entire beautiful mountain-framed bay, the Conca d'Oro), you could then return by coach or train via Messina, and back up the mainland to Naples or Rome. Many combinations are possible.

> **Local flavour**
> Wherever you go, revel in Sicilian cooking. Try grilled swordfish, *pescespada alla griglia*, or tuna, *tonno*; *spaghetti alla Norma*, named after Bellini's opera – a sauce of tomatoes, aubergines, basil and ricotta cheese; *pasta con sarde*, pasta with a sauce of sardines, parsley and pine nuts; *involtini*, rolls of stuffed fish or meat; *schiacciate*, layers of pasta stuffed with cheese and anchovies.

Train There are several ways of getting to Sicily. From the Italian mainland, an express train leaves Rome at 8.50am, or Naples at 11.07am, arriving at Messina at 5.45pm, Cefalù 8.36pm, and Palermo at 9.25pm. A connecting train from Messina, leaving 6.02pm arrives at Taormina at 6.26pm, Catánia 7.24pm, and Syracuse 8.50pm. (Price: Rome-Taormina, first-class L72,000, second-class L42,000). Long-distance trains get very full on Sundays, so book a seat. There are also Rapido and night trains.

The newspaper, *Giornale di Sicilia* (L500) has a useful list of main-line train times and some ferry crossings on page 2.

Boat The Tirrenia Line operates boats from Naples to Palermo. There is one crossing a day, at 8.30pm, which takes 10½ hours. Deck seats L49,500, *poltrona* (inside seats) L61,100. The service to Catánia leaves Thursdays at 8.30am and takes 15 hours, return service Wednesdays.

Siremar do crossings from Naples via the Aeolian Islands to Milazzo, leaving at 9pm Wednesday and Saturday from 1 October to 31 March. The service operates Thursday and Saturday from 1 April to 31 May;

Tuesday, Thursday, Saturday 1-15 June and 16-30 September; and Monday, Tuesday, Thursday, Friday, Saturday from 16 June to 15 September. (About L60,000 to Milazzo, arriving 11.20am. L48,600 to Strómboli, the nearest island to Naples, arriving 5am.)

Grandi Traghetti lines run the cheapest boats from Genoa to Palermo, with most distance covered for least cost. Boats leave Genoa Monday 6pm, Wednesday 12 midnight, Saturday 11am; returning from Palermo Tuesday 9pm, Friday 7.30am, Sunday 3pm. Journey time: 22 hours. Cost L49,000 single.

Grandi Traghetti via M Stabile 53, Palermo, telephone 091/587832. Sunday-Friday 8.30am-5pm. London office: c/o Associated Oceanic Agencies, Eagle House, 109-190 Jermyn Street, London SW1, telephone 071-930 5683.

Siremar via Principe di Belmonte 1c, Palermo, telephone 091/582688. Via dei Mille 28, Milazzo, telephone 090/9286381.

Tirrenia via Roma 385, Palermo, telephone 091/333300. Open 8.30am-1pm and 3-5pm. London office: c/o Serena Holidays, 40-42 Kenway Road, London SW5, telephone 071-373 6548/9.

Car ferry   There are two car ferry routes to the island:

Villa San Giovanni – Messina About 25 crossings daily in each direction on the State Railways, 35 minutes.

Independent ferries run every 20 minutes day and night. Fares about the same in both – cars from L15,000, depending on length. L700 per person.

Réggio di Calábria – Messina About ten crossings a day in each direction, 50 minutes. From Messina, first departure 5.05am, last departure 8.50pm. From Réggio di Calábria, first 6.55am, last 9.55pm. Cars from L12,700 according to length. L700 per person.

Coach   SAIS run a fast coach, the Dionisio, leaving Rome 7.30am, arriving Messina 5pm, Catánia 6.30pm, Syracuse 8pm. A connecting bus at Messina takes travellers to Taormina. Cost L70,000 Rome-Syracuse, including lunch. The return bus leaves Syracuse 8.30am, Catánia 9.30am (Taormina

8.50 to connect at Messina), Messina 11.15am, arriving Rome 8.45pm. Book and pay at the bus station at least one day prior to travelling.

Connecting coaches leave Palermo 7am, Agrigento 6.45am, Ragusa 6am, Enna 8.15am for Catánia.

SAIS offices are in:

Rome Piazza della Repubblica 62, telephone 06/465924 and 06/4742801

Palermo Via Paolo Balsamo 16, telephone 091/6166028

Catánia Via d'Amico 181, telephone 095/536168

Messina Piazza della Repubblica 6, telephone 090/771914

Agrigento Via Ragazzi del 99, telephone 0922/5952260

Enna Bus Terminal, telephone 0935/21902

Taormina Bus Terminal, telephone 0942/23916

Travel firm, **Costanza Viaggi** via San Pancrazio, telephone 0942/23494

Air   From Britain there are direct charter and scheduled flights to Palermo and Catánia. Or fly the more frequent flights to Naples and Rome in off-season, and continue by bus or train.

Transport in Sicily   SAIS Etna buses leave Catánia airport for Catánia and Taormina 7.50am, 8.15am, 10am, 12.30pm, 1.15pm, 4pm, 7.30pm. On Sundays and holidays, only the 10am, 12.30am and 7.30pm run.

From Taormina there is a weekday service to Catánia airport, 6.10am, 7.15am, 7.45am, 10.15am, 1pm, 5.30pm and 7pm. Sundays and holidays, only the 7.45am, 10.15am and 5.30pm buses run. Journey time 1¼ hours, cost, L5,000.

From Palermo airport at Punta Ráisi, 31km (19 miles) west of the city, buses go about every hour into the centre of Palermo, behind the Teatro Politeama, starting at 6.30am. The last one leaves 10.30pm, but usually waits for the last flight in. Buses to the airport leave from 5.40am. Last bus 10.20pm. L4,000.

The tourist office is just across the piazza Castelnuovo from here.

FARM HOLIDAYS IN SICILY

Agriturist, the government agency which organises these holidays, has an office at via Alessio di Giovanni 14, 90144 Palermo, telephone 091/346046.

Giarre One apartment, five rooms and three caravan places between Taormina and Catánia 2km (1¼ miles) from the sea. Contact Giovanni Russo, corso Italia 80, 95018 Riposto (CT). Telephone 095/931259. Minimum stay three days.

Mascali Two apartments. Not far from Taormina and Giardini Naxos, 250 metres (830ft) up. Contact Marcello Iacona, via Simeto 29/C, 95030 Gravina di Catánia (CT). Telephone 095/422401. Minimum stay three days.

Between Milazzo and Cefalù on the north coast. Five apartments, five villas. Riding, bicycles, tennis and swimming pool near by. Contact Gaetano Milio, Loc San Gregorio, 89071 Cap d' Orlando (ME). Telephone 0941/955008. Minimum stay seven days.

Salina (Aeolian Islands) Seven apartments on a caper-growing farm. Tennis and swimming pool (3km, 2 miles). Contact Luciano Sangilio, via Nilo 2, 98050 Malfa (ME). The farm is 'Il Gelso', Loc Malfa. Minimum stay seven nights.

Balestrate 1km (⅝ mile) from sea. One apartment available May to September. Contact Caterina Caselli, via dei Nebrodi 55, 90146 Palermo. Telephone 091/523378. Minimum stay eight days.

Cefalú In the Madonie mountains, behind the town, 700 metres (2,330ft) up. Thirteen rooms. Board and half-board available. 15km (9½ miles) from the sea. Riding school, art courses, natural foods, trekking, archery. Contact Angela Lanza, C da Pianetti, 90010 Gibilmanna (PA). Telephone 0921/21890.

Piana d'Albanesi Near the town in the hills behind Palermo. 700 metres (2,330ft) up. Ten rooms with board and half-board available. Riding. The address is Az agr Poggetto, Loc Pianetto, 90030 Santa Christina Gela (PA),

but for booking contact Transporti Rapidi, via Sardegna 76, 90144 Palermo. Telephone 091/502929. Open April to October. English is spoken.

Local flavour
Feasts and festivals in Sicily

February 3-10 Almond blossom festival at Agrigento

February 3-5 Sant'Ágata, patroness of Catánia. Carnival at Acireale

Thursday before Easter Foot-washing ceremonies in cathedrals around the island. Heavy crosses carried in Caltanissetta

Good Friday Sicilian death cult day. Most famous procession is at Trápani, others at Enna and Acireale

Corpus Christi (first Thursday after Trinity Sunday) Floral processions

May 1-4 Folklore festival, Agrigento

May 5-12 Monreale week

First Sunday in May Festival of the Patrocinio di Santa Lucia at Syracuse

May 9 and 10 Sant'Alfio at Trecastagni, with painted carts, etc

May 29-31 Folklore festival, Taormina

June 29 SS Peter and Paul. Major fiesta everywhere

July 11-15 Santa Rosalia. Procession up Monte Pellegrino, Palermo

September 8 Birth of the Virgin Mary

September 27 Fishermen's festival at Palermo

November 1 Ognissanti – present-giving for children

December 31 Traditionally a day for gambling – to test next year's luck!

Local flavour
Average maximum temperatures:

May/June	23.6-27.0 (° Celsius)
Jul/Aug	29.7-30.0 (° Celsius)
Sep/Oct	28.2-25.0 (° Celsius)

TAORMINA

BUDGET FOR A DAY

Coffee and brioche	2,000
Return bus ticket TAORMINA to MOUNT ETNA	24,000
Picnic lunch	5,000
Buy almond cakes from Mamma Mia shop in Taormina	7,000
Espresso coffee	800
Send off postcard to U.K.	600
Telephone U.K. - 3 mins	5,000
Dinner	9,000
	L 53,400
plus accommodation	

Taormina – Etna
0   10 km
0   5 mls

Taormina is built on and between several mountain crags which rise up from the coast quite close to Etna. You need a head for heights in Taormina, it is perched high, with sheer drops. Far below is the sweep of the bay and the little island, Ísola Bella; far above is the snow-capped summit of Etna, pink in early light, sometimes shrouded in cloud, sometimes with just a wisp of smoke or cloud above it.

It is the prettiest, and one of the most spectacular towns in Sicily to stay in. Because it has been a tourist town for so long, the usual Sicilian bleakness, poverty and decay haven't lodged here. Except for the cars and buses toiling and hooting up the hill, it is quiet. The main street, corso Umberto, is traffic free. Early this century, wealthy English and Americans built villas here, planted gardens, and came for the mild winters.

Although the weather can be treacherous and changeable, April and May are the prettiest months here, with red and purple bougainvillaea leaning all over the walls. Most hotels stay open all year, some closing briefly at the end of November and reopening for Christmas. In the past, when the English aristocracy came here for their winter health, the town shut down in the heat of summer, but now the coaches come with packaged holidaymakers. January can be a good month. The air is clearer, the views more defined, and you can wander the town freely. (The Jolly Hotel hosts free concerts at Christmas and Easter, and Taormina has a spectacular carnival.) But it is hard to be precise about weather. Residents say summer starts later now and lasts longer.

Local flavour

Florence Trevelyan, who lived in the Villa Paradiso (now a hotel), created a wonderful garden which is now open to the public, full of rare and scented plants, green shade and birdsong, eccentric pagodas for bird-watching, with a superb view to the bay and the mountain.

Get to Taormina by plane to Catánia or down the coast from mainland Italy (see page 240). From here it is easy to get to the Aeolian Islands, inland to Randazzo, to the summit of Mount Etna, down the coast to Catánia and on to Syracuse. West from

243

Syracuse are the 18th-century towns of Ragusa and Noto. This side of the island provides wonderful contrasts of islands, mountains, coast and classical sites. From Taormina it is also possible to take a coach to Piazza Armerina, Agrigento and Palermo. From Catánia, take the bus (or drive) to Enna and Piazza Armerina and directly on to Palermo, or make a detour to Cefalù. (This brings you to your second base, Palermo.)

If you are visiting for a day by car, it would be wise to make for Mazzarò, on the coast, park, and take the *funivia* (cable car) up to the town. The railway station (called Taormina Giardini) is down on the coast, some way from the town, but a bus plies regularly up the hill. There are good coach connections and bus excursions from Taormina up and down the coast, as well as to Etna, to the interior, and up to the Aeolian Islands. The coast road is narrow and can get very snarled up, and with the train trundling along by the sea as well, it can seem less than idyllic down by the coast.

Local flavour

The Greek Theatre, Taormina's most famous monument, was probably built by the Greeks in the mid 3rd century BC, then enlarged by the Romans (it could hold 5,400 spectators). It was used first for plays, then for gladiatorial fights, and now it is used for summer plays and festivals. At other times pay L2,000 entrance as cover charge and take your seat at the most dramatic picnic spot in Europe, with the sea and Etna beyond and little green lizards around your feet. Don't miss the views from the top in the other direction as well.

There are many hotels in Taormina with a wide range of prices, and despite its being such a tourist attraction, you can find reasonable rooms here. (Interior decoration is often shabby, but the rooms are clean.) Just up the road from the bus station, on via Pirandello on your right, is an excellent

inexpensive *pensione*, the Svizzera; Signora Vinciguerra speaks perfect English. There are some large family rooms, with views to the hills and sea.

Next door is the English church (service 11am Sunday). The resident vicar has a lending library of local history, and English paperbacks for sale (L5,000 for three).

Local flavour

D H Lawrence lived for a while up the hill here, in the via Fontana Vecchia.

Turning left in the main street, corso Umberto, you will pass the Palazzo Corvaia on your right which houses the tourist office. The road on your left leads up to the Greek Theatre. Further along the corso, up the Salita Dente, is the Hotel Residence, a larger hotel with a shady garden, bar and sitting-room, and pleasant and spacious rooms, all with bath. There are sea views from the top floor only.

Further along the Corso are two inexpensive little hotels. Off the pretty piazza del Carmine is the Villa Gaia. It is small, shabby, clean, basic, no lift, but the bedrooms have tiny terraces with views to the mountain, and there is a little garden with hibiscus, tangerine, and a yellow climbing plant, *zampa di gatto* (cat's paw) climbing up a pine tree. The owner, Signora Zuccharo, loves flowers and speaks a little English. Further along there's the Cuscona, another (not so charming)

Taormina, one of Sicily's most spectacular towns, with Mount Etna in the background

inexpensive *pensione*. Basically furnished, a lift takes you up to the sunny upstairs sitting and breakfast-room with views of Etna. There is free parking near by.

From the end of the Corso, past the piazza Duomo, turn down towards via Roma and another reasonable *pensione*, the Villa Shuler, which comes highly recommended. Walking along the via Roma, you go past the San Domenico, the most expensive hotel in Taormina, which was once a monastery (wonderful viewpoint here). Coming round the hill, you reach the Villa Paradiso and the public garden.

Farther along the Bagnoli Croce, right opposite the gates to the Public Garden, and hardly noticeable, is the little Villa Pompeii, with only five double rooms and one single. There is no sitting-room, but your breakfast is served on a large terrace looking over the gardens and Etna. Two charming sisters keep it open all year. You must book.

One more hotel to try for perhaps a longer stay, or in the out-of-season months, is the Villa Carlotta, where the Bagnoli Croce meets via Pirandello. With a shady orange-grove garden (table-tennis under the trees), it is comfortable and roomy. English is spoken.

To get to the beaches, the cable car will take you up and down to the seaside. Cross the main road for beaches at Mazzarò and a little further south at Ísola Bella. This island is state-owned and has a small free beach (pebbly, clear water). For L6,000 from about the end of March (depending on the weather) and L10,000 from June to September, you can hire an umbrella, two chairs, changing room and shower. There are pedalos and two-man canoes, L10,000 per hour. Farther north are more beaches, Spisone, Mazzeo, Caravella and Letoianni. To the south is Giardini Naxos.

Walks   The town map shows where the stepped paths are:
To the beach From the Belvedere Guardiola on via Pirandello, down the steps and cross the road to Ísola Bella. There is a bar (The Venus) halfway down, *and,* more important, half-way up!
To the Lido La Caravella Take the steps down from behind the cemetery.
To the station Take the steps down from via Roma, near the Hotel Monte Tauro or Villa Shuler down towards Villagonia (no cable-car up this side).
To the Santuario Madonna del Rocca and the Castle A stiff walk leads up from the Circonvallazione road, but a wonderful view and a little chapel carved out of the rock await you. From here walk up to the castle, where there

is a restaurant and the best view of the Greek theatre set against the sea.
Castelmola There's a long walk up to this town above Taormina, or take the bus up and walk down. In the bar San Giorgio famous names are written – Rockefeller, Churchill, Strauss, Ford. It is also renowned for its almond wine.
Taormina is principally a town for wandering in, but there are some architectural sights: the Greek/Roman theatre, of course; the remains of a *gymnasium*, now called the Naumachiae; the Odeon, or 'small theatre'; the Arabian-looking Palazzo Corvaja; the Palazzo Duca di San Stefano; the Badia Vecchia (the old abbey); the Palazzo Ciampoli, which now houses the Palazzo Vecchio hotel, a handsome building outside, but a grim hotel inside.

Local flavour
A curiosity is a Byzantine painting known as the 'non hand-made Madonna', now in the cathedral. Found in an old well, it was thought to have been left there by the angels, untouched by human hands.

Local flavour
You will find that the stepped paths around the town are old mule-tracks. That's why the steps seem long and awkward for human feet.

ORIENTATION IN TAORMINA

INFORMATION
TOURIST OFFICE
At the side of the Palazzo Corvaia, piazza Santa Caterina. ☎ *0942/23243. Open daily 10am-1pm and 5-8pm. The ticket office here sells tickets for summer concerts, etc. English is spoken. Ask for the town map showing paths, hotels, sights. It gives information on all bus excursions, train times, etc.*
POST OFFICE
Piazza San Antonio, at the end of corso Umberto, towards the hospital. Open Monday to Saturday 8am-

6.30pm. Postal code 98039.
TELEPHONES
SIP via San Pancrazio 6, in the Avis office. Open Monday to Saturday 8am-12.30pm and 4.30-8pm. Sundays 9am-12.30pm. Telephone code 0942.

TRANSPORT
TRAINS
Railway station at Taormina Giardini, down on the coast. Buses about every 30 minutes to and from town.
BUS STATION
Via Pirandello. ☎ *0942/ 625301 and 23916.*
TAXIS
at the bus station.
FUNIVIA

Cable car near the top of via Pirandello. Open all year. Sundays 9am-8.30pm. Weekdays 8am-8.30pm. Stays open later from July to 20 September. L1,000. Tickets from the machine (no change given). It takes L50, 100, 200, 500 coins and L1,000, 5,000 and 10,000 notes. Operates every 15 minutes.
PARKING
Free car park by the Duomo. Otherwise cars park at the sides of streets.

ACCOMMODATION
Cuscona corso Umberto 238. ☎ *0942/23270. Double bed and breakfast with shower L50,000. Closed*

November to March.
Hotel Residence *Salita Dente 4.* ☎ *0942/23463. Closed end of November till Christmas. Double bed and breakfast L84,000, L45,000 single (with shower).*
Villa Carlotta *via L Pirandello 81.* ☎ *0942/ 23732. Closed November. Rooms L64,700 double, L35,200 single. Breakfast L13,000 per person.*
Villa Gaia *via Fazzello 34.* ☎ *0942/23185. Open all year. Double bed and breakfast with shower L51,000.*
Villa Pompeii *via Bagnoli Croce 88.* ☎ *0942/23812. Double bed and breakfast L44,000.*
Villa Schuler *piazzetta Bastione 16. Closed November to the end of February.* ☎ *0942/23481. Double bed and breakfast L66,400, L44,000 single. Open Christmas and New Year, otherwise closed mid-November to mid-March.*
Pensione Svizzera *via L Pirandello 26.* ☎ *0942/ 23790. Closed from the end of November until Christmas. Double bed and breakfast L50,000, single*

L30,000. L22,000 per person in a three-bedded room, L20,000 in a four-bedded room. All with shower.
CAMPING
S Leo, via Nazionale, at the foot of the hill, just by the turning up to town. ☎ *0942/24658.*

EATING OUT
L'Angolo piazza del Duomo (on a corner near the cathedral). Evenings only. Pizzas baked in a wood-burning oven.
U Bossu via Bagnoli Croce 50. Good grilled swordfish and melanza alla parmigiana.
Grotta Azzurra *via Bagnoli Croce 2. Closed Tuesday. A bit touristy, but the sea food is good.* Trenette *(noodles) alla pescatora, L7,000. Sarde a beccafico (stuffed sardines) L10,000.*
Il Giardino just by the public gardens, sit outside.
Trattoria Piccolo Mondo *piazza San Pancrazio 18. Pizzas L4,500-L7,500 and other dishes.*

SHOPPING
MARKET

Wednesday.

ENTERTAINMENT
Many concerts and shows are performed in the summer months in the Greek theatre and the Palazzo Corvaia. An international arts festival, and ballet and film festivals take place between May and September.
Greek Theatre *Open 9am-7pm every day. L2,000. Concerts are held here in summer.*
Water Ski Club *via Nazionale.* ☎ *0942/52283.*
The town has several discos and night spots.
Tout Va *is an open-air disco at via Pirandello 70, overlooking the bay. 10pm-3.30am.* ☎ *0942/23824. Cover and first drink L12,000.*
The Ombrello *just off the piazza Duomo, is a disco for the 40s age group. Mainly South American music. Open 9.30am-3am every day. Each drink L7,000.*
Otherwise the main entertainment is eating out in the evening, with many places to choose from. It's not cheap, so try to picnic at midday and indulge at night.

RANDAZZO AND ALCÁNTARA

If your budget stretches to car hire, there is a superb half-day's drive out into the country-side around Etna – a round trip to Randazzo, Bronte and the Alcántara Gorges.

Take the SS114 south through Naxos and

turn right at Diana, up the mountains to Linguaglossa, a handsome town. Keep on to Randazzo, through open hills to your right, Etna on your left. Great cascades of black clinker lava almost cross the road at one point. In spring the hills are covered in flowers. Randazzo has an enormous market on Sunday morning. Fork left on the SS284 to Bronte, and here turn right towards Cesarò. When you meet the SS120, turn right, and then shortly left towards Maniace, or Nelson's Castle. You will find it sign-posted right from Bronte. This so-called castle was given to Lord Nelson, but was once an abbey. Now being restored, it lies near a rocky river with cypresses and a beautiful garden and atmosphere.

Return along the SS120 to Randazzo. Turn left to Móio Alcántara and keep on to Francavilla di Sicilia and to Gola di Alcántara. Here strangely shaped gorges bring icy, clear blue-green water down from Etna. You pay L2,000 for a lift down, and (for the intrepid) L5,000 for hire of high rubber boots to wade through the narrow chasm. Closes 7pm. There's a café here. Drive back to Taormina via Gaggi and Giardini.

SAIS buses make a special Sunday morning trip, leaving 8am, to Randazzo via Alcántara, returning from Randazzo at 12 noon (1½ hour trip there) without guide or reservations. Pay on the bus. They also do a trip to the Alcántara gorges and on to Calatabiano for a guided 'gluttonous visit' to a sweet factory. Monday and Thursday afternoon, L18,000 (lift cost included).

If you are touring by car, and continue on to the central hill towns of Nicosia and Troina, or simply want to take your time in these regions, you can spend a comfortable night at the Villa Miraglia. About 18km (11 miles) north of Cesarò on the SS289 road to San Fratello. Bed and breakfast L60,000. Telephone 095/696585.

Moneysaver

Restaurants and food can be expensive in Taormina. Try the Standa supermarket, via Arcageta. Open 8.30am-1pm, 4.30-8.30pm. Shut Sunday. Sample the orange-coloured piquant sausage *calabrese*. Etna Rosso is a decent wine. Even the screw-topped ones can be quite good. Try Porto Palo. Cartons of apricot (*albicocca*), pear (*pera*), and peach (*pesca*) juice are delicious.

Local flavour

Some special Sicilian sweets (*dolci*)
Granita – lemon sorbet.
Cannoli – cooked almond paste, filled with sweetened ricotta cheese and pistachio, covered with candied peel.
Cassata Siciliana – the basis is *pan di spagna*, a sort of sponge cake spiced with cinnamon, vanilla and pistachio, filled with ricotta, and covered in icing and almond paste.
Pasta reale – a light almond paste shaped into various forms, usually fruit.
Our word marzipan comes from *pasta de martorana*, an almond paste made in Palermo.

MOUNT ETNA

Mount Etna dominates the north-eastern corner of Sicily even when it disappears into a cloud. About 3,000 metres (10,000ft) high, Europe's largest volcano is still active – very active as recently as 1983, when it erupted for seven weeks, and lava flowed down to Catánia. It is an unpredictable beast, and it is best not put your hand too close to the cage. Guided tours will take you up as near to the summit as they judge best. It is not cheap, and you may not see much activity, but the view can be marvellous. Wear stout shoes and warm clothing for the windy heights. From Catánia an AST bus leaves the railway station at 8am for the Rifugio Sapienza, at 1,900 metres (6,250ft) (accessible via Zafferana). The bus returns about 4pm, fare L3,800. From there a SITAS minibus, costing about L30,000, will take you to within 30 minutes of the crater. SAIS excursion buses go from Taormina on Tuesday, Thursday, Saturday at 8am to Sapienza; return fare L24,000, supplement L31,000 for alpine guide and jeep to the crater. They also do a trip at night up the north side, leaving at 3pm and returning at midnight, costing a hefty L55,000 (Mondays).

The lower eastern slopes of Etna are

crowded with orange and lemon groves; the northern and western sides are thick with wild flowers in the spring. The hoopoe, horned owl, red woodpecker, cotumix, and wild cats and porcupines are said to live on the mountain.

THE AEOLIAN ISLANDS (ÍSOLE EÓLIE O LÍPARI)

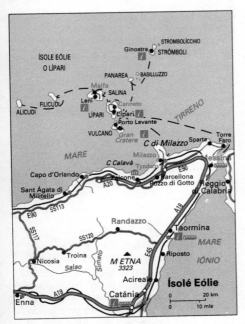

Ísolé Eólie

There are seven islands, all different, in this archipelago. Some are extinct volcanoes, some still active, all are surrounded by clear waters, flying fish and porpoises. These islands haven't been spoiled by too many visitors. There are good beaches – bring your goggles. You could see two of the nearest islands in a day (just) – Vulcano and Lípari or Salina, using the hydrofoils. Alternatively, spend a night on Lípari and do some island-hopping from there.

The easiest, most frequent and cheapest access is from Milazzo. Milazzo is a fairly ugly place, but arriving by road, it improves once you get past the oil refineries. Surprisingly, the water in the harbour is so clear that from the harbour's edge you can see shoals of quite large fish, motionless in the sunlit water. Giunta buses run here frequently from Messina. By train it is an hour from Messina (L4,200), four hours from Palermo (L11,300). By car from Taormina, via the motorway round Messina, the drive takes about 1¼ hours (toll L4,500), a beautiful drive along the craggy coast. Park your car along the front (but not where there are restricted zone signs) if you are going on the hydrofoil. Or you can take the car ferry to Lípari (L30,700 for a car up to 4 metres, 4½yds, long).

Traghetto = ferry boat, car-carrying, takes twice the time of the hydrofoil, costs half as much.

Aliscafo = hydrofoil. These run much more frequently than the ferries.

To go directly to the further islands for a day trip from Milazzo means an early start (7.05am) in the high season (1 June to 30 September), or a midday hydrofoil at 12.20pm (1.10pm in other months). This would just give you a couple of hours on Strómboli before the hydrofoil back at 5.30pm.

If you are driving between Milazzo and Cefalù, make a detour (exit 'Falcone', then in the direction of 'Chiese della Madonna' off the motorway) to the almost unknown headland of Tindari. Breathtaking views; Greco-Roman theatre.

Moneysaver

Children aged one to four go half-price on the hydrofoils, but aged four to 12 are half-price on the ferries. So a return trip to Lípari, for example, would cost a family of two adults and two children over four (in the summer season only) L45,600 by ferry and more than double that on the hydrofoil. However, between islands, trips are short and the hydrofoil can be easier, and not too expensive to use.

THE AEOLIANS – LÍPARI

A fascinating island for historians, because it shows all the different layers of civilisation in the Mediterranean from Neolithic to the present. There's a renowned archaeology museum and volcano museum here. But it is chiefly a pretty island, the most frequented, with several hotels, camping site, scuba diving schools, water-skiing and sailing classes. Visit the southern end of the island (called the Quattrocchi) for its view of four headlands. There are thermal baths at San Calogero on the west side, once used by the Romans – water temperature is 55 degrees Celsius.

A round-the-island bus leaves from behind the Esso station at the end of corso Vittorio Emanuele in Lípari town. Times tend to vary quite a lot. Ask the bus driver, or at the office near by. A bus should, for example, leave for Canneto (where there's a camping site and good beaches) at 3pm, and it should return at 3.40, 5 and 5.50pm. The round trip takes an hour. From the centre of Canneto, walk on round the coast northwards to find white beaches. You can rent bikes and mopeds; but the hire of a vespa for a day (L25,000) is not so much less than the cost of bringing a car on the ferry.

Lípari is 50 minutes by hydrofoil from Milazzo, two hours 50 minutes by ferry. Last hydrofoil back leaves at 6pm (1 June to 30 September, 7.45pm). That's too early – it's just when the hot day cools and the harbour is looking its most picturesque. If you come in May, you will have the beaches almost to yourself, but the water is cool.

The island of Lípari, fascinating for historians, and a pretty island on which to stay

Visit the Aeolian Archaeology Museum in the Palazzo Vescovile, open Monday to Saturday 9am-2pm, Sundays 9am-1pm. The volcano museum is next door; also visit the castle and the cathedral, built by the ubiquitous Roger II of Normandy.

Local flavour
Pumice is mined here, such a light stone that it floats in water. Don't be alarmed if you see lumps floating in the sea.

ORIENTATION IN LÍPARI

INFORMATION
TOURIST OFFICE
Corso Vittorio Emanuele 202. ☎ *090/988095. Telex 980133 Eólie 1.*
They have lists of apartments, rooms and restaurants as well as hotels. Open Monday to Thursday 8am-2.30pm and 4.30-7.30pm. Friday and Saturday 8am-2.30pm.

BANK
This is the only Aeolian island with a bank.
TELEPHONE
Code for the islands: 090.
POSTAL CODES
Lípari – 98055. Canneto, Lípari – 98052. Other islands – 98050.
BICYCLE, MOPED AND VESPA HIRE
Roberto Foti, via F Crispi 31. ☎ *090/9812352. Open Easter to October 15 every day, 8.30am-7.30pm.*

Bicycles L12,000, mopeds L22,000, vespas L25,000 per day.

ACCOMMODATION
Oriente via Marconi 35. ☎ *9811493. Bed and breakfast L54,000, July and August L75,000. Open all year.*
Poseidon via Ausonia. ☎ *090/9812876. Bed and breakfast L75,000, July and August L85,000. Open all year, sea views.*

CAMPING
Available at Canneto, right
by the beach. Baia Unci.
☎ 090/9811909. Some
shade, hot water, showers.

L7,000 per tent. Open April
to October.

EATING OUT
Trattoria d'Oro via

Umberto, just off the corso
V Emanuele. Good local
cooking, open daily
11.30am-3.30pm and 7pm-
midnight. Menu L17,000.

THE AEOLIANS – SALINA

Made up of six extinct volcanoes. Famous
for sweetish, amber-coloured wine (Malm-
sey), Malvasia, named after the town of
Malfa. A very fertile island with cliffs, creeks
and accessible beaches. They grow a big fat
tasty caper here, also a good red wine.

The tourist office in Santa Maria Salina is
on via Notar Giuffre, telephone 090/
9843003. Saline has several villages with
hotels. There are two in Santa Marina
Salina: the Punta Barone, Lungo Mare
Giuffre, telephone 090/9843172; and the
Pensione Mamma Santina, via Santina 26,
telephone 090/9843054 (also, in summer,
telephone 090/9843190).

For farm holidays here, see the beginning
of this chapter.

THE AEOLIANS – PANAREA

Smaller and further out, towards Strómboli,
this is one of the prettiest islands, surrounded
by little islets. Take a boat trip round the
island to see the natural rock statues on the
islet of Basiluzzo, renowned for its clear
waters and scuba diving. There are fumar-
oles, springs, olives, capers and cactus growing. Despite its small size, the island has
several hotels in San Pietro, but they can get
very full in August. Try the Tesoriero,
telephone 090/983098, open April to

October, or the cheaper Locanda Roda,
telephone 090/983006, open all year. The
Cincotta, telephone 090/983014, and La
Piazza, telephone 090/983003 both provide
food but are pricier.

THE AEOLIANS – VULCANO

Nearest to the mainland, Vulcano stinks;
sulphur fumes hang everywhere. If you look
up as the boat comes in, to where the
mountain is puffing white smoke, you can see
the greeny-yellowy sulphur crumbling out of
the hillside. It's a lunar-looking island in
parts. An hour-long trek goes up to the crater
– prepare yourself for tough going.

The Gran Cratere is 386 metres (1,053ft)
high. Thucydides mentioned it exploding in
the 5th century BC, and they expect another
eruption within the next 20 years. Bathe in
mudbaths – free – at the Laghetto di Fanghi.
It's known as 'taking the lava'. Clean yourself off afterwards in the bubbling water of
the Aguacalda.

Other sights are the isthmus of Vulcanello,
the Grotta dell' Allume and the Cavallo
caves. The isthmus has such strange shapes,
it's called the Valley of the Monsters.

Local flavour
Rossellini filmed his movie *Vulcano* here.

ORIENTATION
IN VULCANO

Quite a few tours come here
– you can get a day trip on
the SAIS coach from
Taormina (costing L46,000,
leaves at 6.30am on

Wednesdays). The hydrofoil
fare from Milazzo, return, is
L26,000 (35 minutes), or by
ferry, L14,000 (one hour 20
minutes).

INFORMATION
TOURIST OFFICE

Porto Ponente.
☎ 090/9852070.

ACCOMMODATION
At Porto Ponente:
The Conti ☎ 090/9852012,
and Orsa Maggiore
☎ 090/9852018.

THE AEOLIANS – STRÓMBOLI

Ever since the film *Strómboli* with Ingrid Bergman, this is probably the best known Aeolian island. The volcano on Strómboli still spits furiously night and day. You can take an escorted hike, lasting about three hours, to the summit, 927 metres (3,060ft) up. You need tough, comfortable shoes, torch, warm clothes, thick socks, lots of liquid to drink and unlimited energy. Trips, in groups of 10, leave from Ficogrande at the stairs of via Nunziante, escorted by experts (Nino, Prospero and Antonio). Telephone 090/986093 or 986175 to book, the tours do fill up. The climb is at night, to see the sparks flying and the lava running; return about 1am. April to October, L15,000.

You'll need a hotel for a night and a day to recover.

ORIENTATION IN STRÓMBOLI

INFORMATION
TOURIST OFFICE
Ficogrande. ☎ 090/98623.

TRANSPORT

From Milazzo to Strómboli takes about two hours by hydrofoil. L24,600 single, six hours by ferry, L13,400 single. From Lipari the cost and times are a third less.

ACCOMMODATION

Villaggio Strómboli via Regina Elena, ☎ 090/986018. Open all year.
Miramare via Nunciante 3. ☎ 090/986047. Open March to September.
Pensione Scari Località Scari. ☎ 090/986006.

CATÁNIA

The second biggest city in Sicily, and the devil to drive in and out of, Catánia is not very attractive, though it has an imposing central square. It has been through difficult times. In 1669 Etna erupted, and a torrent of lava flowed over the 60ft-high (18 metres) city walls. Then in 1693 Catánia was swallowed up in an earthquake, only 2,000 of its 24,000 inhabitants surviving.

The piazza del Duomo has a renowned – and strange – Fontana dell' Elefante, elephant fountain, made of black volcanic rock. In the piazza Bellini is Bellini's birthplace with a museum, open 9am-1.30pm. There are the remains of a Roman amphitheatre, coated in black lava, half-way down the via Etna in the piazza Stesicro the public gardens, Giardino Bellini, are very elegant.

The motorway, coach or train will take you quickly from Taormina to Catánia. If you have a car, you could drive the slower route, SS114. There is an even smaller road which winds between the orange groves and the sea, via Riposto, and meets the main road just before Acireale. Riposto is a handsome town, Acireale is a fairly large resort. From here on, there are little bays and towns, rather ruined by the road, but with views of the Cyclops rocks. Aci Trezza has the best view.

Local flavour

Legend of the Riviera dei Ciclopi: Bizarre black conical rocks, known as the Cyclops' Islands, sprout in the sea just by the small town of Aci Trezza. The story goes that after Odysseus had blinded the one-eyed Polyphemus (the Cyclops) and escaped from his cave, Polyphemus in a desperate blind rage hurled the rocks after his ship, where they remain to this day. The name Aci (unromantically pronounced Archie) refers to Acis, a handsome shepherd boy, son of Pan, who loved the water nymph Galatea. Unfortunately Polyphemus loved her too, and finding them together, overcome with jealousy, crushed Acis to death with a rock. Afterwards Galatea transformed Acis' flowing blood into a river.

From Catánia to Syracuse, avert your eyes from the coast for about half the way, where the view is of tall striped refinery towers, and fix them on the best sight, the roadside flowers. There is tremendous industrial development all along this coast, centred around Augusta. Unbelievably, there ·are beaches and camping villages near here. Yet Augusta has recently been reported and condemned for its pollution – this is not a place to linger.

ORIENTATION IN CATÁNIA

INFORMATION
TOURIST OFFICE
Information from via Etna 83. ☎ *095/313993. Also at the railway station and the airport office.*
TELEPHONE CODE 095.

TRANSPORT
BUSES
Bus station Piazza Teatro Massimo, off via Vittorio Emanuele.
SAIS office via Vittorio at 41. ☎ *095/316942.*
AST buses also go from here. Office at number 10. ☎ *095/348083. Open 5am-8.30pm.*

Catánia is a bus junction for many trips. The journey to Taormina takes 1½ hours, L3,700; to Syracuse (15 a day) 1½ hours, L4,500; Enna (seven a day) 1¼ hours L7,000; Palermo (four a day) 3 hours, L14,500; Agrigento (four a day) 3 hours, L13,600.

TRAINS
Railway station piazza Papa Giovanni XXII. ☎ *095/ 531625. Trains go every hour to Syracuse and Messina. Trains also go to Enna, Agrigento and Palermo costing the same as the bus, and not so reliable in timing.*

ACCOMMODATION
Hotel Moderno (two-star) via Alessi 9. ☎ *095/326250. A converted 18th-century palace.*
Hotel Savona (one-star) via Vittorio Emanuele 210. ☎ *095/326982. Large rooms, central location.*
EATING OUT
Gastronomy C Conte, via Etnea 185. For snack food, tavola calda, and take-aways, and well worth trying. Open Monday to Saturday 11.30am-9pm.

SYRACUSE

In the 5th and 4th centuries BC Syracuse was a mighty city with a population of half a million. Founded by the Carthagenians, the Greek colony became a rival to Athens itself. But the Romans conquered it, and even Archimedes who lived here could not succeed in despatching them, though he tried with ingenious devices such as mirrors and magnifying glasses to dazzle them. Then the Saracens came in AD878 and destroyed Syracuse once again.

Now there are three cities – the old island of Ortygia, the middle new, boring, bustling city, and just north of that the archeological park called Neapolis (open 9am-6pm) entirely surrounded by new buildings.

Neapolis, which is not far from the train station, has the largest Greek theatre in Europe, cut out of rock. Aeschylus first performed his play, *The Persians*, here.

The Paradise Quarry near by contains a weird man-made cave, called Dionysius' Ear because of its shape. Some say it was a prison. It has an extraordinary echo. It is possible Dionysius, tyrant of Syracuse, could have put his ear to a hole above ground and listened to his prisoners' secrets? It's all a mystery.

Local flavour
The story (or one of them, there are variations) goes that Arethusa, a river nymph who lived in Greece, was loved by the river-god Alphaeus who changed her into a spring which flowed underground and emerged in Ortygia, mingling with the waters of the river Alphaeus. (Coleridge wrote about where 'Alph the sacred river ran through caverns measureless to man, down to a sunless sea'.)

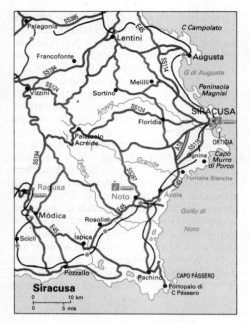

Siracusa

0   10 km

0   5 mls

An old man at Syracuse market, who makes baskets from olive prunings

Also there is a huge Roman amphitheatre with a water trench in the middle for mock sea battles perhaps, or crocodiles.

A walk down to the via Teocrito leads to cool catacombs and the National Archaeological Museum (open Tuesday to Sunday 9.30am-2.30pm and 3.30-5pm). One of the best archaeological museums in Italy, it is great for children too, with buttons to press and working models.

The buses come and go at piazzale Marconi near the baronial post office at the end of corso Umberto, across the bridge in Ortygia. Ortygia is a rather bleak and discarded, but fascinating area. Walk to the piazza Pancali, and then down the corso Matteotti to the piazza Archimede. Turn left down via Maestranza for the tourist office at number 33. If they are shut downstairs, walk upstairs in the courtyard. They have good maps, lists of hotels, and a sheet of bus times. Come back up the street and turn left into via Roma and left again along via Minerva. This will bring you alongside the cathedral and into piazza Duomo which is full of wonderful buildings.

The cathedral is the history of Sicily in one, as it is partly a Greek temple, with bits added on over the centuries. Look inside the Palazzo Beneventano. There are several restaurants around here to try, the Minerva in the square, and the Trattoria La Foglia in via Capodieci near a papyrus shop. Walk down to the harbour where the Syracusans walk along the Foro Italico. Here is the Arethusa fountain, *not* attractive, with ducks huddling round and papyrus fronds growing.

Around Syracuse   Local buses will take you to nearby beaches south of the city (not next to chemical plants). Further down the coast are the seaside villages of Fontane Bianche and Lido di Ávola with good sandy

---

Local flavour

Saturday morning market in Syracuse, just over the bridge on Ortygia island, is typical of all Sicilian markets: huge bloody chunks of tuna, whole swordfish, piles of very white flat onions and vegetables galore. See little pink fish, big clams (*fasolani*), piles of little white, brown-lined snails (*lumache*) quietly moving, all alive. And up at the end, back to the sea, there's an old man with baskets made of olive prunings – some huge and vase-shaped; his hands, all torn and bleeding. Two hours later there's nothing of the market left, only a great space big enough to park a hundred cars.

254

beaches. The reefs of Plemmirio and Ognina have very clear water for scuba divers.

Within bus-reach are two remarkable towns, Ragusa and Noto, both rebuilt after the earthquake of 1693 in honey-coloured limestone and Baroque style. AST buses to Ragusa go at 8.30am, 11.15am, 1.30pm and 2.30pm, returning in the afternoon at 2.15pm, 5pm and 7.20pm weekdays. On Sundays only the 8.30am goes there, and the 2.30pm returns. Buses to Noto are more frequent, about every hour, with three coming back in the afternoon to Syracuse on Sundays (45 minutes, L5,200 return).

Noto has a dense centre, packed with interesting churches and houses. Look through gateways. Don't miss the horses, maidens and grimacing faces supporting the balconies on the Palazzo Nicolaci in the via Corrado Nicolaci. This street is carpeted with flowers on the third Sunday in March, the 'Infiorata – saluto alla primavera'. The Duomo is in the piazza Municipio, just off this road.

There is a folklore festival here during the second week in August. The tourist office in Noto is in the piazza XVI Maggio.

Another trip, if you have a car, is to take the mountain route via Caltagirone (ceramic centre) to Piazza Armerina and Enna.

Continuing the large tour, and en route to Palermo from Catánia along the motorway, make for Piazza Armerina. Take the exit for Mulinello. After the wide sparse valleys, thinly growing barley, with scarce herds of brown-faced sheep, the drive to Piazza Armerina seems verdant. The landscape changes to green fields, poplars and eucalyptus. The town itself is well worth seeing, especially round the cathedral. The square is paved with dark grey and white shell pattern stones, and the cathedral is really orange in colour, with lovely curved brick patterns high up. The steps up to the main door are very ancient. The whole city is open, with trees, a pleasure to visit. The tourist office is in piazza Garibaldi 1, open Monday to Saturday, 8.30am-1.30pm; Tuesday to Friday it is open 5.30-7.30pm as well.

For hotels in Piazza Armerina, try the Park Hotel Paradiso, telephone 0931/85700, or the Selene, telephone 0931/80254.

To get to the mosaics at the Roman Palace of Casale, a few kilometres outside, follow the signs saying 'Mosaici', and don't miss an acute-angled road turning off to your right before you get out of town. Otherwise you will find yourself on the main SS192 road again, with no exit to the villa. Drive as far as you can, down to the restaurant. There is parking behind. The Villa Roma di Casale

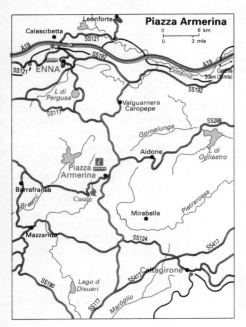

At Villa Roma, Piazza Armerina, are some of the largest and most complete Roman mosaics

lies in a romantic setting of flowers (pinks) and nut-trees.

The villa was built about 300BC, probably as a hunting lodge. Covered by a landslide in the 12th century, it lay undiscovered until 1916. Excavations began in 1950. It has the largest and most intact Roman mosaics existing. Not as refined as those at Pompeii, they are on a grand scale, with hunting scenes, animals, fish and strange bikini-clad girls. Unfortunately it has very narrow viewing platforms which get clogged with people. It is less crowded around 2pm, but it could be hot then in high summer because the mosaics are enclosed in glass buildings. Nevertheless it is well worth going to see – open daily 9am to one hour before sunset (L2,000).

Enna, near by, just off the motorway, is a somewhat grim city with a great medieval castle, hideously built up one side of the hill, but perched 931 metres (350ft) high with an astonishing view. You can see from one side of Sicily to the other from Torre di Frederico II in the public gardens.

Local flavour

Papyrus only grows in two places: along the Nile and up the little river Ciane, near Syracuse. The Egyptians used it for making boats, sails, sandals, writing paper and even ate it, raw and cooked. The Romans imported the raw material to make their paper. Since the 16th century it has been established here.

Visit the Fabbrica del Papiro, 35/37 via Capodieci, or the shops down via Padova (towards the harbour from the piazza del Duomo) to see them making papyrus paper (free entry). Papyrus pictures are for sale. A few shaggy papyrus plants grow in the Arethusa fountain.

ORIENTATION IN SYRACUSE

INFORMATION
TOURIST OFFICE
Via Maestranza 33.
Telephone 0931/66932.
Monday to Saturday 8am-1pm and 4.30-7.30pm.
TELEPHONE CODE
0931.
POSTAL CODE
96100.

TRANSPORT
TRAINS
To Catánia (1¼ hours, L5,300), to Taormina (2 hours, L8,200).
BUSES
SAIS and AST in piazza della Poste.

ACCOMMODATION
ON ORTYGIA
Gran Bretagne via Savoia 21. Bed and breakfast L55,000. Three rooms with shower. A homely, pokey, higgledy-piggledy place. Room 8 has its own verandah. One room for five with painted ceiling. Restaurant downstairs, special menu price L14,000.
Grand Hotel viale Mazzini 12. ☎ 0931/65101. L56,000 double, L34,000 single. Breakfast L6,000 per person. Open all year. Rather large and gloomy, but with harbour views.
Villa Politi via M Politi 2. ☎ 0931/32100. A three-star dilapidated hotel with a swimming pool, northeast towards the sea from the Archeological Museum. L77,500 double, L51,000 single.
NEAR THE STATION
Archimede via F Crispi 67. ☎ 0931/64236, and **Aretusa** via F Crispi 75. ☎ 0931/65020. Both have doubles for about L50,000 (with bath and breakfast).
CAMPING
Agriturist have a camp 4km (2½ miles) away, not on the beach. ☎ 0931/721224. Take buses 34 or 35 from Foro Siracusano on corso Umberto. The same bus, no 34, will take you to the camp site at Fontane Bianche. ☎ 0931/790333.

PALERMO

BUDGET FOR A DAY

Visit National Gallery of Sicily	2,000
Buy presents - coloured cards of Sicilian prints (L500 each)	1,000
Return train fare PALERMO to CEFALU for swim	7,800
Lunch of seafood from waterfront stall	5,000
Fruit juice at bar	1,300
Visit the Chiesa di San Giovanni degli Eremiti in Palermo	Free
Dinner	15,000
	L 32,100
plus accommodation	

At first sight, Palermo is an overwhelming confusion of streets, markets, decaying palazzos, cars, noise, and mayhem. But patience, and long walks, reveal the many sights, churches, catacombs, marionettes, markets, as well as the shady parks and squares. Get the local tourist map, which clearly marks all the churches, museums and theatres. What it doesn't show is how to get to the more outlying places; so some bus instructions and favourite spots are mentioned later in the chapter. Buses in Palermo's clogged traffic seem engaged in a slow transport race with pedestrians (buses get there last). But you may just want to rest your feet and look about.

Palermo has the usual confused history of southern Italy and Sicily; founded by Carthaginians, ruled by the Arabs whose influence remains strong, then dominated by the Normans (Roger II of Hauteville), allowed to decay by the Spaniards, and once again dominated and allowed to decay by another tyranny, the Mafia. So Norman castles and Baroque churches, paupers' and princes' houses exist side by side.

Get to Palermo by air (Punta Ráisi airport), by sea from Naples or Genoa, or via Messina from mainland Italy.

Palermo itself needs several days to explore. From here make excursions to Cefalù, Monreale, Mondello, Trápani, Érice. You can reach Agrigento in a day trip from here. An off-the-beaten-track trip by car goes round the Golfo di Castellammare

to the clear beaches of Capo san Vito.

A stay in Trápani (or Érice) gives you time to visit the little island of Lévanzo, the beaches and nature reserve at Capo san Vito, the medieval hill-town of Érice, the Greek temple and amphitheatre at Segesta, and the less well-known, but remarkable classical site of Selinunte.

Coming from the airport, buses arrive on via J La Lumia, behind the Politeama Garibaldi Theatre. Next to that is the Gallery of Modern Art facing on to piazza Ruggero Settimo. On the other side of the street is yet another large square, piazza Castelnuovo, at the far end of which is the tourist office.

From here go up the via Ruggero Settimo and via Maqueda to a crossroads which is a good reference point. Called the Quattro Canti, it's where via Maqueda and the corso V Emanuele cross. Buses 1, 3, 4, 7, and 38 go along via della Libertà to the Quattro Canti.

A short walk from the railway station up the via Maqueda will bring you to the same point. A few steps from here you will find the piazza Pretoria with an enormous 16th-century fountain full of rather silly looking figures, and the Palazzo del Municipio. Across the street, in via Maqueda, you should look at the church of San Guiseppe dei Teatini, exotic baroque. Just down the street from here is San Cataldo with its rose-red Arab domes, and the Martorana church next to it, with 12th-century mosaics inside.

257

You can either return to the Quattro Canti from here, to go down the Vittorio Emanuele, or launch yourself into the little side streets packed with stalls and people. There's a market in the piazza Ballaro near by, but the whole area is one big market: pale green zucchini like metre-long snakes, round bright purple melanzane, tunny fish from Favignana with huge heads, little wild strawberries L3,000 a box. You may lose your way here, or you may find yourself near the Church del Gesù. Make your way back to the via Vittorio Emanuele and walk south till you find the cathedral on your right.

The cathedral (open 7am-12 noon and 3.30-7.30pm) is an amazing sight outside, with mosaic decorations on the rounded apse, curved crenellations and little majolica domes. The inside is gloomy but houses six royal tombs, including King Roger II of Hauteville and King Frederick II of Swabia, the 'Wonder of the World'.

Walk across the piazza della Vittoria under the huge palm trees. At the end is the Palazzo Reale, a Norman palace built on by the Arabs, added to by the Spaniards, and now used by the Sicilian government (a typical Sicilian building!). Open Monday to Saturday 9am-1pm and 3-5pm. You can see King Roger's room, and his chapel, the Cappella Palatina. Persuade the curator to put the light (*luce*) on, so you can see the carved roof and the mosaic walls properly.

The red saracen domes of the Norman Chiesa di S Giovanni degli Eremiti

From here walk back towards the gardens, and cross the road into the via dei Benedettini. At number 3, the Chiesa di San Giovanni degli Eremiti, with its little Norman church crowned by red Saracen domes, an overgrown garden and a little cloister, and a very special atmosphere. Don't miss it. Open May to July 9am-10pm; March to April, 9am-1pm; August to December 9am-1pm and 4-6pm; December to March 9am-1pm. Free. (The curator dissolved into laughter while trying to remember these times.)

The number 24 bus will take you near the Villa Malfitano, once owned by the English Marsala merchant, Joseph Whitaker. His valet now lives there and will show you round. Telephone the Whitaker Foundation, 091/560522. Ballroom, smoking-rooms, Louis XVI furniture, surrounded by 17 acres of garden, it is another glimpse of Palermo's past, when English kings visited and the Prince of Lampedusa dined there.

From the Quattro Canti down via Vittorio Emanuele going towards the harbour (buses 3 and 24 go this way), you will reach piazza Marina, departure point for many buses. (Don't miss the banyan tree with roots stretching down from the branches, desperately searching for earth in the air.) Not far from here are the Villa Giulia and the Botanical Gardens, also the exceptionally good National Gallery on via Alloro.

Proceeding down to the piazza Santo Spirito and turning right, will bring you to the Marionette Museum, at number 1 via Butera. Ring the bell and go upstairs. There's a marvellous, beautifully displayed collection of traditional Sicilian puppets, Saladins, knights and Saracens, but also puppets from all over the world – mermaids, blue-skinned wild men, figures of cane and feathers, old wooden jointed lions. There used to be a show here on Saturdays, but not enough people came, so now they only function to order for groups of 20 or so. Monday to Saturday 9am-1pm and 4-7pm, shut in August, L2,000, children half-price.

Local flavour
Sicilian puppets are usually about a metre (3ft) tall, and they tell heroic stories of the days of Charlemagne, and of battles with the Moors and Saracen warriors. Orlando and Rinaldo are the heroes. The fair Angelica (with a high-pitched man's voice) is the heroine. There are magicians and monsters, but mostly battles: beating of feet and clashing swords, heads and arms cut off and bodies ripped from top to toe.

If you want to see a show, ring the museum, telephone 091/328060, and see when they have one planned. Or else ring Signor Cuticchio on 091/6169086, or try his theatre on vicolo Nicolo Raguso 6, telephone 091/329194.

From the piazza Santo Spirito, the number 24 bus will take you up via Vittorio Emanuele and along via Roma. Just off this street is another market, the Vucciria, with a restaurant, the Shanghai, poised above it.

Further down the road, and in another world, is the Grand Hotel des Palmes, via Roma 396. Wagner wrote parts of his opera *Parsifal* here (his piano stool is under glass in the bar). It's rather expensive to stay here, but fun to have a drink. At the piazza San

Local flavour
To visit the Catacombs, a somewhat ghoulish but interesting sight, on via dei Cipressi, take the 27 bus from piazza Castelnuovo. There are 8,000 mummified corpses, many dressed. Open daily 9am-12pm and 3-5pm, L1,000. The Prince of Palagonia is buried in the little church.

Moneysaver
The Shanghai, vicolo dei Mazzani 34, telephone 091/589702, is an exciting, ramshackle restaurant above the market, run by Benedetto Basile. The fish is hoisted up in wicker baskets from the market below. It's rough and ready and cheap, and the swordfish is very good.

Domenico, behind the church, is the Oratorio del Rosario. Ring the bell of 16 via Bambini to be shown a famous Van Dyck altarpiece. Usually open 9am-1pm. (Van Dyck lived in Palermo.)

Other sights include the Palazzo Cinese and the Ethnographic Museum 'G Pitre' out in the Parco della Favorita. All the buses to Mondello pass here (numbers 14, 15, or 77). The villa was built for Queen Maria Carolina in 1799 and is all decayed charm and imitation Chinese decoration. The museum has a collection of folk art including painted carts and carriages. Usually open 8am-3pm. The National Gallery of Sicily is in the Palazzo Abbatelli, via Alloro, beyond the piazza Marina. Closed Monday, other days open 9am-1.30pm, Sunday till 12.30pm. Tuesday and Thursday it opens in the afternoon 3-4.30pm. L2,000.

Local flavour

On special occasions ordinary farmers' carts with two wheels and long shafts are fitted with high decorated sides, exuberantly painted all over. The scenes show Garibaldi landing on the island, or a well known saint, or Charlemagne's knights fighting the Moors. The horses are festooned in plumes and pennants. The Museum of the Sicilian Cart is in the Palazzo Daumale on the seafront at Terrasini. Telephone (before visiting) 091/8882767. The tradition probably dates from when Garibaldi liberated the island in 1860. On today's hearses the wreaths are piled up on each side, like the sides of the carts. Also many modern three-wheeler trucks and some lorries have hand-painted decorated panels.

Local flavour

If by any chance your glasses break, the opticians, Ottica Galeazzo, via E Amari 127, down behind the Politeama theatre, are very helpful.

Local flavour

In the Vucciria market (*vucciria* is a dialect word meaning voices or hubbub) stalls sell all kinds of take-away food. Try *panelle*, fritters made of chick-pea flour, or *calzone*, pizza dough wrapped round meat or cheese and deep-fried. A Palermo speciality is *guasteddi*, rolls filled with calf's spleen, ricotta cheese and hot sauce. *Buon appetito!*

Around Palermo   The tourist leaflet listing the month's events also includes walks and excursions organised by the WWF (telephone 091/322169), the CAS (Club Alpino Siciliano) (telephone 091/581323), and the CAI (Club Alpino Italiano) (telephone 091/6254352), all organisations concerned with wildlife. The WWF organises a tour into the Madonie mountains up behind Palermo and Cefalù, leaving the via E Amari at 8.30am on a Sunday, but check. Most of the excursions run on Sunday.

Also at the tourist office in piazza Castelnuovo, ask for the leaflet about *Turismonatura*. It is in Italian but has maps and pictures and shows routes up into the hills. There's also a calendar of trekking, bird watching, and other trips throughout the year. There are falcons and eagles and many migratory birds in the mountains. It also gives details of riding establishments. Prices vary, but a day's trekking could cost about L60,000.

Moneysaver

On a summer evening out at Mondello, or after a swim, try the seafood at the waterfront stalls – all kinds of inexpensive snacks. A complete meal here could come to only L7,000.

Eleven km (7 miles) north west of Palermo is Mondello, a fashionable seaside resort with good beaches. Take buses 14, 15 or 77, or the express bus 6. L6,000. For other beaches take the 28 bus from via della

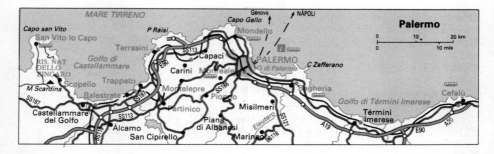

Libertà to Sferracavallo, which offers more space, but is rockier than Mondello. Or take the number 3 out to Addaura.

An AST bus from the piazza Lolli will take you (every 30 minutes) to Bagheria, 15km (9½ miles) east. The nobles of Palermo built their villas here in the 17th and 18th centuries. Visit the Villa Valguarnera, off corso Umberto, and the Villa Butera with its wax figures. Don't miss the Villa Palagonia (entrance in piazza Garibaldi) with its surrounding walls studded with weird statues. They say the Prince of Palagonia, mad with jealousy of his young wife, locked her in this villa and gave the bizarre, misshapen statues the faces of her supposed lovers. Walk up the crumbling staircase and see, before the whole villa crumbles to dust, the extraordinary marble ballroom with glassy ceiling. Open 9am-12.30pm and 4-6pm.

A worthwhile excursion is a visit to Mount Pellegrino. Take bus 12 and walk up the hill.

Bus 8/9 or 9 leaves every 20 minutes for Monreale, 10km (6¼ miles) south west. High on a hill overlooking Palermo and the Conca d'Oro, set against a background of mountains, stands a wonderful Norman cathedral built by William the Good (1173-86), filled with golden mosaics. Also be sure to look at the west end of the church and go into the cloisters to look at the carved capitals and mosaic columns. The church is open 8am-12.15pm and 3.30-6.30pm. Take L100 coins for the light machine. Cloisters L2,000.

Cloisters at Monreale with mosaic columns and carved capitals

Cefalù was originally a fishing village, but is now quite a large seaside resort with a long sandy beach. The centre is brooded over by a high promontory, and set against the hill is a magnificent twin-towered Norman cathed-ral. It's possible to make a day trip here from Palermo and have a swim, either by train (one hour, L7,800 return) or by a SAIS bus, which also takes an hour and costs L8,200 return.

ORIENTATION IN PALERMO

INFORMATION

TOURIST OFFICE
Piazza Castelnuovo 34.
☎ 091/583847. At the furthest (west) end, away from the main street. From the station, take bus 7 red or 46, or walk up via Maqueda past the via Cavour to the big double square of Ruggero Settimo and Castelnuovo.

Ask for maps, what's on, and Agriturist information. Open Monday to Friday 8am-8pm, Saturday 8am-2pm.

Another office at piazza San Sepolcro, off via Maqueda near the Quattro Canti, is open Monday to Saturday 8am-2pm.

Offices at the railway station and airport are open Monday to Saturday 8am-8pm.

POST OFFICE
Via Roma, just by the Museo Archaeologico Regionale. Open Monday to Friday 8am-7.30pm. Saturday 8.30am-1.30pm. Postal code 90100.

TELEPHONES
ASST, via Lincoln, opposite the station. Open 24 hours. SIP, via Belmonte, turning before the square, right off via Ruggero Settimo. Open daily 8am-8pm. Telephone code 091.

TRANSPORT

BUSES
Local buses AMAT, L700 fare. Bus station in front of railway station. ☎ 091/222398.

Filli Camilleri-Argento. ☎ (0922)39084. To Agrigento, 2¼ hours, three per day, L15,000 return. From via Balsamo (near train station).

Autoservizi Segesta buses (also from via Balsamo) go 19 times a day direct to Trápani (1¾ hours, L17,000). Office at via Balsamo 26. ☎ 091/286039.

SAIS, via Balsamo 16, ☎ 091/6166028, go to Cefalù, Monday to Saturday, six per day, 1 hour, L10,000 return); Catánia, 16 per day, 2¼ hours, L23,500 single; and Syracuse, Monday to Saturday, five per day, 4 hours, L18,000 single.

TRAINS
Station in piazza Giulio Cesare. ☎ 091/6161806. To Milan (22 hours, L50,000 single), to Rome (15 hours, L48,800 single), to Naples (13 hours, L42,200).

ACCOMMODATION

Bristol via Maqueda 437, near the Martorana Church. ☎ 091/589247. L45,000 double. Two-star.
Centrale corso V Emanuele 327, central location. ☎ 091/588409. L68,000 double, plus L8,000 per person for breakfast. Three-star. Ask for rooms at the side or back. English spoken. Restaurant. A bit shabby. Parking.
Hotel Elite via M Stabile 136, in the same block as the Hotel Touring. ☎ 091/329318. L53,000 double, L33,000 single. L3,500 breakfast per person. Two-star.
Hotel Joli via Michele Amara 11, on the corner by piazza I Florio. ☎ 091/6111766. Newly refurbished, pleasant large rooms. Rooms L53,000 double, L32,000 single. Breakfast about L3,000 at the bar.
Hotel Touring via M Stabile 136. ☎ 091/584444. L68,000 double, L45,000 single. Two-star.
Orientale via Maqueda 26. ☎ 091/6165717. L32,000 double without bath, L37,000 with bath (one only), L18,500 single. No breakfast. Ancient, not very comfortable but atmospheric. One-star.

SHOPPING
Along the via Maqueda, buy pottery and chandelier drops from the little shops Lampadario – chandelier.

Don't miss the flea market (mercato delle pulci), open daily in piazza Peranni, near the via Papireto. To reach it take the via Amedeo, across the corso Vittorio Emanuele from the Porta Nuova.

ENTERTAINMENT

Palermo tends to shut down in the evening around 9pm, apart from the restaurants. Most people go out to Mondello, the beach resort along the coast. Take buses 14, 15, or 77 from behind the Teatro Politeama in the piazza Sturzo; express bus number 6, in summer, from the train station along via della Libertà. Take bus 28 from the via della Libertà out to the Villa Boscogrande, the palazzo where Visconti filmed The Leopard. There's a bar and disco there.

Consult Un Mese a Palermo and l'Ora for the classical music programme in the Politeama Garibaldi theatre in piazza Ruggero Settimo, opera and plays at the Teatro Dante in piazza Lolli, and films, art shows and other cultural events all over town.

OUTINGS FROM PALERMO

GOLFO DI CASTELLAMMARE

If you have a car, you can visit the Golfo di Castellammare, it is well worth a detour. This is a beautiful bay with several good beaches and resorts. Terrasini, nearest to the airport is popular, and so is Castellammare del Golfo, both of which are large towns. But either side of Castellammare are several small towns along the coastal road SS187. Trappeto is a small fishing village, completely unspoiled, with only one hotel. Just along the coast is Balestrate, and between these two is a long stretch of sandy beach. Further along the coast, beyond Castellammare, is Scopello, a more popular town, with a pebble beach and high cliffs. The coastal road stops here, and between here and the point of San Vito is a nature reserve, the Zingaro. There are walks from Scopello which link with the road further on, and the reserve can be approached from Capo San Vito as well.

To reach Trappeto take the road to Monreale, SS186, west along the via Vittorio Emanuele out of Palermo. Turn right at Partinico until you reach the SS197, turn left. If you wish to continue on to Segesta, Trápani and Érice on the motorway, you can join it at Balestrate, Álcamo or Castellammare.

Accommodation in Trappeto: La Sirenella, via XXIV Giugno. Telephone 091/8788356. Ten rooms, five with sea view and balcony. The beach immediately below is seaweedy – but there is a clear beach about 500 metres (550yds) along. Restaurant: speciality kuskus di pesce. Double bed and breakfast L50,000 in May and June, L45,000 before May, and L60,000 July and August (children half-price).

San Vito lo Capo is the name of the seaside town on the cape called Capo San Vito (confusing). For inexpensive lodgings here try the Sabbia d'Oro, via Santuario 49, telephone 0923/972508. (Postal code 91010). San Vito is renowned for its clean, clear water.

Local flavour

The Zingaro Nature Reserve extends for about 7km (4¼ miles) on the peninsula of Capo san Vito from Torre dell' Impiso to Scopello. There are three walks. The coast route is 6km (3¾ miles) long and only goes up to 80 metres (267ft) around bays and rocks and promontories. The middle route is 13km (8 miles) long, at a height of about 400 metres (1,330ft). The mountain path goes from Scopello up to Mount Scardina, or, from the other side up from Cosenza. After 5km (3 miles) it reaches a height of 800 metres (2,665ft). The peak, inhabited by birds of prey, is called Aquila, Eagle Peak.

Coming from Palermo, if you are in no hurry and would like to see some very remote parts of Sicily, turn right towards Montelepre, after passing Monreale and Pioppo. This will take you on a wild and winding road round the mountain and eventually back towards Partinico.

Partinico was where the notorious bandit Giuliano was born, and Montelepre was his headquarters. It certainly feels like a mountain fortress. (Giuliano was shot in the 1950s. A book, *God Protect Me From My Friends*, by Gavin Maxwell tells his story.) Also at Partinico, about the same time, the social reformer Danilo Dolci endeavoured to lead the local unemployed in useful schemes like dam-building.

spoil or drown the tinkling of the sheep bells and the bird chatter. There is a discreetly sited bar and a shop, and from there a 20-minute walk up the hill will take you to a Greek amphitheatre cut into the hill, with views down the Gulf of Castellammare.

The town (now destroyed), theatre and temple were built by the Elymians, who also occupied Érice and Trápani and claimed to be Trojans. Virgil says Aeneas ploughed a furrow here. Carthage was the town's ally at one time, but also besieged it. Finally the Arabs destroyed it in the 10th century AD. The temple – never finished, the columns never fluted – is in Doric style and was built towards the end of the 5th century BC.

Doric temple at Segesta, standing amidst the sound of sheep bells and bird song

> **Moneysaver**
> A collective in Partinico has been organising alternative holidays for the past 13 years, designed to show people how Sicilians live. Stay with a local family for about L26,000 a day, full board. Or you can rent a villa, probably home of a migrant worker living in West Germany. The co-operative will arrange tours, get a cook, and find drivers and guides. You will need a good phrase book – no English is spoken here except by Ignazio, who founded the cooperative and is an English teacher. For further information, write to Cooperativa Turistica Vacanze Alternativa, Centro Cultura Populare UNLA, via dell' Avvenire 9, 1-90047 Partinico, (PA) Sicily.

The theatre is open from 9am to one hour before sunset, L1,500. No charge for the temple, see it any time. Buses go from the bus station in Trápani at 8am, 10am, and 2pm, returning at 1pm, 4.15pm and 6pm, L3,500 return.

There is no good way of getting from Palermo to Segesta by public transport.

SEGESTA

If you can only spare the time for one excursion from Palermo, then go to Segesta. Even if you don't like old Greek ruins, you must see the temple at Segesta; just off the motorway (A29) between Palermo and Trápani you suddenly come upon it. Turn up to the car park, and the temple is right above you. Even the sound of foreign guides can't

> **Local flavour**
> In odd-numbered years, mid-July to the first week in August, classical plays are put on in the theatre. Special buses leave from Palermo and Trápani for the performances. Check with the tourist office.

There is a deserted god- and train-forsaken station about a mile from the temple, and one train (at the time of writing) from Palermo (via Milo), leaving 10.20am, arriving Segesta 11.57am. But trains back to Palermo from Trápani leave Segesta at 10.21am and 1.18pm. However, there may be more now – check locally.

TRÁPANI

Not a very inviting city and port, surrounded by salt flats, Trápani was badly bombed in the last war. Closest port to North Africa, Tunisian immigrants come through here, and the African influence is strong – *kus-kus* the favourite dish. It's a useful base; boats leave from here for the Égadi Islands. Buses go to Érice, up the hill behind Trápani, about every hour (L2,300), and about seven times a day up the coast to San Vito lo Capo (1¾ hours, L3,800). The bus station, right behind the railway station, is unpleasant, but the bar is surprisingly salubrious, with good snack meals.

Trápani has three majolica-domed churches, and viewed from the coast, they make a romantic profile. There are some rough hotels in the centre – avoid the Moderno.

Local flavour

The writers Samuel Butler and Robert Graves both believed that the *Odyssey* was written here by a princess.

ORIENTATION IN TRÁPANI

INFORMATION

TOURIST OFFICE
Piazza Saturno, at the end of corso Italia, open Monday to Saturday 9am-1pm and 3-7pm, Sunday 9am-12pm.

As Trápani is a provincial capital, they have leaflets about San Vito lo Capo, Érice and Selinunte and a map of the area.

ACCOMMODATION

Cavallino Bianco
Lungomare D Aligheri. Some way along the seafront (car or taxi needed). ☎ *0923/21549. Open all year. A modern, hideous block right on its own, but ask for a room with view of the bay – even Trápani looks good from here. Restaurant. Double with shower L51,000. Breakfast L7,000 per person.*

Nuovo Russo via Tintori 4. In the centre of the town, near the port. Double L64,500 with bath, L50,100 without. L4,500 breakfast. Charmless but decent.
Vittoria via F Crispi 4. ☎ *0923/27244. L64,000 double with shower, L42,000 single. Breakfast is a coffee and cornetto at the bar (L2,000). A business hotel near the station, newly decorated with views to the open square.*

ÉRICE

Érice is a closed and secret city, very ancient and unmarred, perched up on top of a high hill behind Trápani. Fields of flowers creep up the mountain to this very dense town, and at first it is rather daunting walking up the cobbled streets, set in squares, worn to a polish. Here there are castles, a temple to Venus, a cathedral with a fine interior and carved stone rose window, towers, museums, (exceptional pastries and cakes), and an astounding view down to the sea. It has a theatre with an elegant pillared interior, and an 'English' public garden.

Érice was founded by a mythical Eryx, or Érice, son of Venus, who became king of the Elimi who also founded Segesta. The Phoenicians dedicated a temple to Astarte here, the Greeks to Aphrodite, even Aeneas is supposed to have been here among other worshippers of Venus (including sailors, whom the priestesses looked after very well, apparently). The Arabs captured the town, and called it Mohammed's Mountain, and the Normans came later and built a castle

265

here. Since medieval times it has survived virtually unchanged.

> ### Local flavour
> The views are so far-reaching that they say that a sharp look out from the heights of Érice (over 700 metres, 2,330ft) could, on a clear day, count the ships that set sail from Tunis.

Other sights include old Phoenician walls with mysterious incisions, the Agro-Forestale museum (there is a research centre here), and down the hill is the Museo Cordici, with a display of local ceramics.

> ### Local flavour
> Érice is famous for both ceramics and rag-rugs, typically in arrow designs.

ORIENTATION IN ÉRICE

INFORMATION
TOURIST OFFICE
Via Conti Agostino Pepoli 56. ☎ *0923/869388.*
POSTAL CODE
91016.
TELEPHONE CODE
0923.

ACCOMMODATION
There are only three hotels in Érice. The Emilio has been recently modernised, with great attention to detail and really pretty bedrooms. The Moderno is pleasant,

about the same price. The Edelweiss is not so elegant but has six rooms with a view down to Capo san Vito. All have restaurants. Eating out can be expensive, but there's quite a choice of trattorias and pizzarias.
***Edelweiss** vicolo San Domenico.* ☎ *0923/869159. Room only L51,000 double, L30,900 single. Breakfast L8,000. Extra bed in room L17,000. Evening meal L30,000.*
***Emilio** via V Emanuele 67.* ☎ *0923/869377. Double bed and breakfast L94,600, room only L74,000. Evening*

meal L45,000.
***Moderno** via V Emanuele 63.* ☎ *0923/869300. Double bed and breakfast L90,000-100,000 according to season. Evening meal L35,400.*
The tourist office has a list of rooms.

ENTERTAINMENT
***Blu Notte** disco and bar, via San Rocco. Open 10pm. Closed Monday.*
***Al Ciclope** via N Nasi, and the **Boccaccio** via dei Misteri are also discos.*
***Della Vittoria** via San Rocco. This cinema is being converted into a theatre.*

THE ÉGADI ISLANDS

Three islands make up this group, Lévanzo, Favignana and Maréttimo; they are bleaker and less captivating than the Aeolian

Islands. Favignana has a port with handsome dockside buildings, a few beaches, and lots of camp sites. L12,800 return from Palermo by hydrofoil. The island is famous for the *mattanza*, the centuries-old annual

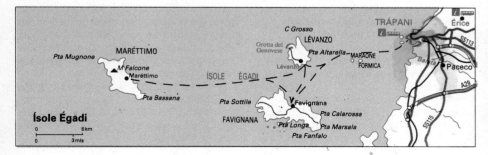

Ísole Égadi
0 — 6km
0 — 3mls

Tuna fishing off Favignana: the mattenze *(hauling the catch)*

spring tuna fishing. A square of nets is anchored in the bay, fishermen form their long shallow boats round, and the tuna are speared up with long black-flagged harpoons. It still occurs, but the catch has been drastically reduced by big boats overfishing further out.

A good way to explore the island is by boat, or hire a bicycle for L4,000 a day.

Lévanzo is the most attractive for a day's outing, with tiny coves for bathing and a bar with a wonderful view. Also, up in the cliffs, a mule-hike or hill-walk away from the harbour, is the Grotta del Genovese, with prehistoric cave drawings (including a tuna fish).

SELINUNTE

From Trápani, take the motorboat down to Castelvetrano and on to Selinunte, to one of the least known, but most spectacular ancient Greek temple sites. The people of Selinunte battled against Segesta, who asked the Carthagenians for help. They came and killed 16,000 inhabitants of Selinunte, and later on the people destroyed what was left of their city to prevent it falling into Roman hands. For centuries Selinunte remained undiscovered, and much excavation is still going on here. Meanwhile a part of the site, the Collina Orientale, is freely open to the public. There is a beach at Selinunte, so a visit here could be combined with time by the sea.

ORIENTATION IN SELINUNTE

ACCOMMODATION
Alceste via Alesto 23.

☎ *0924/46184.*
Giani via A Pigafetta 2.
☎ *0924/46222. Double L54,000. Double bed and breakfast L70,000.*

Lido Azzurro via M Polo 98, right on the seafront.
☎ *0924/46057. L35,000 double room, breakfast L7,000 per person.*

Local flavour

Something unusual, to be found just by the Castelvetrano motorway exit, on the south side next to the Vanico Sports Centre, is the only cork factory in Sicily, belonging to Vito Bua and Sons. They will be glad to show visitors round. There used to be many cork trees in this region and around Etna and Caltagirone. However, they were all cut down by direction of the government to make way for vines, and the result was that the cork had to be imported.

Now, the government is talking of uprooting the vines – to make room for cork trees!

MARSALA

Marsala wine was originally produced by an Englishman, John Woodhouse in the late 18th century, as competition for port and sherry. He set up a laboratory at Cannizzo near Marsala. It is often a sweet dessert wine, but when made by the solera method it can also be a dry, fruity aperitif called Marsala vergine. Names to look for are Marsala Pellegrino, Montalto, or Florio. De Bartoli is the best, but hard to find.

You can see the wine being made at the Florio plant (owned by Martini) at Marsala. Closed Friday. Visit the wine museum, signposted on the road between Selinunte and Castelvetrano.

AGRIGENTO

Trápani – Agrigento

```
0       15      30 km
0          15 mls
```

Ancient Agrigento, then called Akragas, was founded in 583BC as a Greek colony. Pindar called it 'Man's finest city'. Of that fine Greek city more than 20 temples still remain in the Valley of the Temples, covering a huge, shadeless area. They are floodlit at night until 11.30pm (10.30pm from October to April). If you come on a day trip bring your picnic and lots to drink with you, the snack bars on the site are very overpriced.

Take bus 8, 9 or 10 from the station, and ask for San Leone. A short walk will bring you to the Museo Nazionale Archaeologico (closed Monday). It is a good idea to look in here before embarking on the temples, to get some idea of what used to be in them. The first temple in the archaeological park is the Temple of Heracles, the oldest, built about 520BC (eight tapering columns). The Temple of Concord is the best preserved of any Greek temple in the world except for the Thesion in Athens. Oddly enough, it was a

Christian church for 1,200 years, and newly-weds often come to be photographed here. The next temple is the Temple of Juno, with a sacrificial altar on the eastern side.

Local flavour

Near by in the hamlet of Caos is the house where the playwright and author Luigi Pirandello lived. Take bus 11 from the snack bar and get off at Villaseta, or bus 8 if you are in Agrigento. There is no entrance fee, and the custodian is usually there to let you in. Be sure to go in the morning. There are fascinating photographs to see, and Pirandello's ashes are buried behind the house under a pine tree.

Across the road from the snack bar is the Temple of Jupiter, the biggest Greek temple ever built, and now the biggest ruin. Inside you will see a copy of one of the giants (called Telamones) which used to support the structure. Also see the Oratory of Phalarais and the square Tomb of Terone, the Temple of Castor and Pollux, and the temples at the rock sanctuary of Demeter.

Local flavour

The Settimana Pirandelliana, from end of July to early August is a week's festival of open-air plays, operas and ballets at Caos. Admission L10,000. Telephone 0922/23561 for information.

There are cultural events in the Valley of the Temples in July. And on the first Sunday in February the Almond Blossom Festival (and international folk festival) takes place there.

There are trains to Agrigento from Palermo and Catánia, but enquire about how long they will take, because there has been work on the line for years. A bus goes from via Lincoln, Palermo (2¼ hours, L15,000 return), and piazza Bellini, Catánia

($2\frac{3}{4}$ hours, L25,000 return).

Down the coast from Selinunte is not so easy. There is a 8.20am and 12.25pm bus to Sciacca (45 minutes, L2,000) and then walk to Villa Comune to take the bus on to Agrigento ($1\frac{1}{2}$ hours, L5,000).

ORIENTATION IN AGRIGENTO

INFORMATION

TOURIST OFFICE
APT, viale della Vittoria 225, just off piazza Moro. ☎ 0922/26922. Monday to Friday 8am-2pm and 4.30-7.30pm, and Saturday 8am-2pm.
   Also AAST, piazza Moro 5, in the Banco di Sicilia building up from the train station. ☎ 0922/20454. English spoken. Monday to Saturday 8.30am-2pm and 5.30-7.30pm.
TELEPHONE CODE
0922.

POSTAL CODE
92100.

ACCOMMODATION

Bella Nápoli piazza Lena 6. ☎ 0922/20435.
Hotel Belvedere via S Vito 20. ☎ 0922/20051.
Hotel Colleverde via dei Templi. ☎ 0922/29555.

BIBLIOGRAPHY

FOR ADDITIONAL INFORMATION ABOUT THE HISTORY, ART AND ARCHITECTURE OF ITALY THE FOLLOWING BOOKS ARE RECOMMENDED:

THE COMPANION GUIDE TO VENICE, HUGH HONOUR (COLLINS)

ESSENTIAL VENICE, TOM POCOCK (THE AUTOMOBILE ASSOCIATION)

THE VILLAS OF TUSCANY, HAROLD ACTON (THAMES AND HUDSON)

THE COMPANION GUIDE TO ROME, GEORGINA MASSON (COLLINS)

ESSENTIAL ROME, CAROLE CHESTER (THE AUTOMOBILE ASSOCIATION)

A TRAVELLER IN THE SOUTH, JOHN JULIUS NORWICH (LONGMAN)

FOR AN AMUSING VIEW OF A TUSCAN HOLIDAY: *SUMMER'S LEASE*, JOHN MORTIMER (PENGUIN)

ACKNOWLEDGEMENTS

THE AUTOMOBILE ASSOCIATION WOULD LIKE TO THANK THE FOLLOWING ORGANISATIONS FOR THEIR HELP IN THE COMPILATION OF THIS BOOK: THOMSON HOLIDAYS LTD. GREATER LONDON HOUSE, HAMPSTEAD ROAD NW1 7SD ITALY SKY SHUTTLE, 227 SHEPHERDS BUSH ROAD, LONDON W6 7AS

AUTHOR'S ACKNOWLEDGEMENTS
I WOULD LIKE TO THANK MY INDEFATIGABLE TRAVELLING COMPANIONS - ANDREW CUNNINGHAM, JOANNA KELLY, DERYN O'CONNOR AND ANNE O'RORKE. ALSO MANY THANKS TO ANNAMARIA ARRUFOLI FOR INFORMATION AND HOSPITALITY, AND TO ARABELLA BOXER (TUSCAN RESTAURANTS), CHRIS ROBERTS, DR LORENZA SANTO, EVANDRO PAPINI, DR MARY HOLLINGSWORTH, DR VITTORIO CIPOLLA, NICOLETTA LUPERINI AND SUSANNA ROBINSON

FINALLY MY SPECIAL THANKS TO ILSE BARKER FOR HER INVALUABLE HELP IN TYPING AND CORRECTING MY MANUSCRIPT.

READER'S REPORT
BUDGET GUIDE ITALY

Please use this form to record your comments on any aspect of your visit to Italy which is covered in our book. Whether it is additional information, an exciting discovery, a criticism of any hotel or restaurant, or a change of opening time we would like to hear from you.

Please write to:
The Editor, *Budget Guide Italy*
Editorial Department
Automobile Association
Fanum House
Basingstoke
Hants RG21 2EA

YOUR COMMENTS REGARDING:

YOUR COMMENTS REGARDING:

YOUR NAME (BLOCK CAPITALS)

YOUR ADDRESS (BLOCK CAPITALS)

AA MEMBERSHIP NUMBER

READER'S REPORT
BUDGET GUIDE ITALY

Please use this form to record your comments on any aspect of your visit to Italy which is covered in our book. Whether it is additional information, an exciting discovery, a criticism of any hotel or restaurant, or a change of opening time we would like to hear from you.

Please write to:
The Editor, *Budget Guide Italy*
Editorial Department
Automobile Association
Fanum House
Basingstoke
Hants RG21 2EA

YOUR COMMENTS REGARDING:

YOUR COMMENTS REGARDING:

YOUR NAME (BLOCK CAPITALS)

YOUR ADDRESS (BLOCK CAPITALS)

AA MEMBERSHIP NUMBER

INDEX OF PLACES

W

Z

BUDGET GUIDE
FRANCE

From the Channel ports of
Normandy in the north to the
sun-bathed hills of Provence,
Budget Guide France reveals
unusual places to visit as well
as familiar tourist attractions
such as the splendid châteaux
of the Loire and the mountain
scenery of Chamonix

Available at good bookshops and AA centres

BUDGET GUIDE
BRITAIN

From the Scottish Highlands in
the north to the Cornish
peninsula in the south west,
Budget Guide Britain reveals
unusual places to visit as well
as familiar tourist attractions
such as the Shakespeare
country of the Midlands and the
Georgian elegance of Bath

Available at good bookshops and AA centres